The barbarian temperament

The barbarian temperament

Toward a postmodern critical theory

Stjepan G. Meštrović

London and New York

First published 1993
by Routledge
11 New Fetter Lane, London EC4P 4EE

Simultaneously published in the USA and Canada
by Routledge
29 West 35th Street, New York, NY 10001

© 1993 Stjepan G. Meštrović

Typeset in Baskerville by
Ponting–Green Publishing Services, Chesham, Bucks
Printed and bound in Great Britain by
Biddles Ltd, Guildford and King's Lynn

British Library Cataloguing in Publication Data
A catalogue record for this book is available from the British Library.

Library of Congress Cataloging-in-Publication Data

Meštrović, Stjepan Gabriel.
  The barbarian temperament: toward a postmodern critical theory/
Stjepan Meštrović.
  p. cm.
Includes bibliographical references and index.
  1. Postmodernism–Social aspects.   2. Civilization, Modern–1950-
3. Regression (Civilization)   I. Title.
HM73.M479   1993
303.4–dc20   92-45836
                                                                  CIP

ISBN 0–415–08572–1 (hbk)

ISBN 0–415–10241–3 (pbk)

To my daughter, Ivy Elizabeth,
her daddy's own Yellow Rose of Texas,
"she's the sweetest little lady a fellow ever knew,
her eyes are bright as diamonds,
they sparkle like the dew."

Contents

Preface

How can one make sense of the so-called civilized world at the present juncture of our *fin de siècle* with the *fin de millennium*? Are we living at the height of civilization, or just through a latter-day barbarism? These are the central concerns of the present study. I start the present analysis where I left off in my *Coming Fin de Siècle* (1991), with the theory and philosophical nuances that lie beneath the term *fin de siècle*. It was invented a century ago to connote so much more than the straightforward meaning, "end of the century." It implied the corrupt, sickly, decadent, and degenerate aspects of modernity. These same traits can be found easily in our *fin de siècle* culture: One often hears the word "decay" with reference to the state of modern cities, race relations, the family, relations between the sexes, religion, and the general state of morals. As for sickliness, one thinks immediately of AIDS as well as the postmodern AIDS of culture and the sickly state of the economy. Corruption? Polls indicate that most Americans regard politicians and government officials in general as being routinely corrupt. Degeneration is now so routine that Western pre-school children are taught how to avoid the dangers of cocaine and other drug use, AIDS, sexual molestation from adults who care for them, and other dangers that children in previous generations hardly imagined. In the United States, many children must pass through metal detectors to go to school, lest they carry weapons that they might use on each other or their teachers. Can we even speak meaningfully of childhood innocence anymore?

But *la maladie de fin de siècle* implied more than straightforward disgust at the barbaric perversions of modernity. It conjured up images of perfumed corruption, prestigious sickliness, and a dressed-up decadence. Concern with this malady that afflicted modernity was hardly confined to French intellectuals of a century ago. The American *fin de siècle* sociologist, Thorstein Veblen (1857–1929), argued in his 1899 classic, *The Theory of the Leisure Class,* that American culture symbolized the latter-day barbarism that would eventually engulf the entire Western world. Although Veblen is ranked among the most famous American classical founders of sociology, and although one finds vestiges of Veblen's influence on C. Wright Mills, David Riesman, and Jean Baudrillard, it is safe to say that he was never admitted into mainstream sociological theory. Talcott Parsons ignored him and the Frankfurt School failed to make use of his insights. Leading contemporary sociologists such as Anthony Giddens and Jürgen Habermas write as if Veblen never existed. I take Veblen seriously.

Thus, in Chapter 1, I begin with an analysis of what Baudrillard takes from Veblen, and what he discards. Both thinkers use America as a vehicle for discussing the future of the modern world. America replaces France as a symbol for the phenomena that concern and ought to concern sociologists. To be sure, this is a controversial move, yet I follow their lead for the sake of a concise discussion. Also, America is used as a vehicle for discussion because it involves so many thinkers and themes that are relevant: Freud hated America; Tocqueville explored American habits of the heart, which became habits of the mind for Veblen, and which Baudrillard rejects; Bellah returned to Tocqueville's America in his *Habits of the Heart,* Durkheim and Weber treated America by implication as the seat of anomie and the Protestant ethic, respectively, and Veblen's treatment of America in his *Theory of the Leisure Class* reemerges again in David Riesman's *Lonely Crowd.*

The new theoretical position that I construct is a sort of critical theory which assumes that the human animal cannot be tamed by civilization. This raises the question of how one should teach virtue or achieve the good society, a seemingly insoluble problem that can be traced back to Plato. The purpose of the book is not to arrive at an answer, but to pose the problem of barbarism in a new light.

Despite the controversial nature of the argument being put forth here, one has only to glance at the broad outlines of the twentieth century, or watch CNN regularly, to take it seriously.

This has been a century saturated in the blood of victims who were sacrificed for the sake of lofty, "rational" goals espoused by both sides of the political spectrum, from Nazism to Communism and so-called Democracy. From the Final Solution to the Gulag to Hiroshima to the Gulf War, and now the cruel war in former Yugoslavia – how long can social scientists pretend that humanity is becoming less barbaric? Perhaps a sober analysis of the cruel malice that the human animal is capable of will finally lead to searching questions and long-lasting solutions.

In Chapters 2 through 7, I lay the groundwork and attempt to construct the basis for a new, postmodern critical theory by finding neglected affinities among Veblen, Baudrillard, Max Horkheimer, Pitirim Sorokin, Emile Durkheim, Georg Simmel, and Sigmund Freud. To be sure, some of these thinkers are emphasized more than others. At first blush, these seem to be strange, or at least unfamiliar bedfellows. I shall explain briefly my rationale, but let me state from the outset that my use of the phrase "critical theory" is not meant to revivify the efforts of Horkheimer, Theodor Adorno and the other members of the Frankfurt School, nor to offer anything like a positivistically useful theory. (In Chapter 2 I use Veblen and Durkheim to criticize modernist conceptions of science). Instead, my aims are to point to anti-Enlightenment sentiments in the works of these seemingly diverse thinkers; complete a neglected trajectory in Horkheimer's thinking, namely, his affection for Arthur Schopenhauer's philosophy; supply a "depth" sociology as well as psychology that are lacking in Baudrillard; and subvert Durkheim and Freud from existing, reified images of them as the *status quo* functionalist and the sexually obsessed doctor of the mind, respectively.

Before going further, I should relate my experience in using Veblen's *Theory of the Leisure Class* as one of several required texts in a university sociology class that I taught last year. Various students began to complain almost immediately that I was too demanding to ask them to read non-textbooks, and to require a term paper as well. They demanded the more typical requirements: to read a textbook, and to take multiple-choice tests. Two weeks into the semester, the class offered great resistance to Veblen's poignant illustrations of modern barbarism. One night, I was awakened by the sound of broken glass that came from the baby's room. Someone had thrown a jar filled with urine through the window – luckily, our newborn baby was unhurt in her crib. Outside, someone had spray-painted my car with the word "dick."

The culprit or culprits were never found. I am aware that the incident may not have been related to my requiring the class to read Veblen and hand in a term paper. Yet the initial hostility in the class was so palpable, intuition tells me that this barbaric incident was related to my using Veblen in class to sensitize students to the hidden barbarism in modern societies. Eventually, the class got to appreciate Veblen's insights, and I still get cards and letters from former students who thank me for having worked with them on their writing. If they are to be believed, it seems that most of their other professors do not require them to write papers, which is an interesting insight into contemporary higher education. In any event, the lesson I learned from this painful experience is that Veblen is hard to take. He strikes hard at the West's high image of itself. Modernists believe that they are superior to the barbarians who live in some imaginary fourth world invented by Baudrillard. I still use Veblen, but I now take up a lot of class time to prepare the students for the shock they will experience when they read him, especially the shock of realizing that barbarism lies at the core of modernity.

This is the same reason that I am taking up several pages to prepare the reader for what will follow. If the reader is offended or angered by the thesis that modernity is only a latter-day barbarism, he or she should realize that it is not an original argument attributable to me. Veblen had already made it – and angered many people a century ago. There is no substitute for reading Veblen's *Theory of the Leisure Class* prior to reading my book. If the reader is now properly angry at Veblen, he or she should try to find illustrations of Veblen's points in contemporary society. I predict that like my students, the reader will find many points of contact between reality and Veblen's accusations: One has only to think of present-day crime rates, drug abuse, sexism, white-collar crime and government corruption, environmental abuse, and horrendous waste among the many other topics that Veblen addresses. Conspicuous consumption and leisure, as well as the never-ending striving for prestige, are integral aspects of modern living. I try to supply many such concrete examples in Chapter 1 and throughout the book to help the reader in this regard. If one lets down one's defense mechanisms, and considers the daily diet of inhumanity that comes in through the information media, one can at least grant Veblen the benefit of the doubt – modern humanity might be more barbaric than most people care to admit. And if the reader grants Veblen and me this benefit of the doubt, he or she should keep in mind that Veblen offers an antidote. He does not just call modernists barbaric, and leave it at that – and neither do I.

Some readers might wonder why I do not consider Marx. Let me state that I regard Marx's (1983) writings on alienation as first-rate, and that I admire his skills as a qualitative sociologist as well as his apparent compassion, expressed in *Capital* ([1858] 1977), for suffering workers. Yet even here, it is evident that his compassion was saturated with contempt for the vampire-like bourgeoisie, as he called them. Moreover, I cannot abide by Marx's utopianism nor his faith in social engineering. Nietzsche had already warned us to beware of great systematizers, because the will to impose systems eventually leads to the hangman and the gallows. Veblen was concerned with the social injustices that worried Marx, but unlike Marx, Veblen never promised the reader a rose garden. And Veblen did not explain injustice with reference to class struggle, but the persistence of barbaric cultural habits that seem to never go away. Moreover, I tend to agree with Sorokin (1959) that stratification will never be eliminated: the best that one can hope for is a somewhat just distribution of wealth, talent, and prestige. I cite many reasons throughout my book for regarding Veblen as superior to Marx.

I do not intend to enter the controversy on whether communism was fair to Marx's intentions. Nevertheless, it is true that one of the reasons I do not rely on Marx is that communism has finally fallen in some – albeit, not all – regions of the world since 1989. And I agree with Zygmunt Bauman (1992) that Marxism and communism are both modernist doctrines. I would make the more obvious point that Marx had his day in the sun: Marx probably influenced more people, directly or indirectly, than any other sociologist. The same cannot be said of Veblen and the other intellectuals I take up, who remain peripheral to mainstream thought. Despite all the debates for and against Marx, and all the efforts to determine what he "really" meant, I believe that he as well as Hegel were simply wrong to think that they could predict or hasten the end of history. Veblen and the other thinkers I take up teach us that even modernists cannot escape the heavy weight of history.

Although I begin with Veblen, I move on to Horkheimer and other anti-Enlightenment thinkers, especially Freud and Durkheim. My intent is to show that Veblen was not just an iconoclast, and beyond that, to explore his affinities with other intellectuals who were seeking a nonrationalist basis for social order. Without Durkheim, any attempt at a postmodern critical theory will fail to account for the socio-cultural basis for individualism, and will fail to distinguish adequately between healthy individualism versus the narcissism that characterizes life in mass society. Without Freud, postmodern critical theory is at a loss to explain the nonrational bases for the many proto-fascist and cruel aspects of modern life. For example, for all his merits as a social critic, Baudrillard cannot do better than conclude that sadism is just another fiction in a social world made up of images rather than realities. And it is high time to overcome the artificial barrier between psychology and sociology enshrined in the absurd reification of Freud as a psychologist and Durkheim as a sociologist, respectively. A workable postmodern critical theory must be able to account for individual and society simultaneously. In these regards, I am bound to be met with considerable skepticism, prejudice, and hostility. Let me explain my motives.

First, it is true that I seek to offer an alternative to Habermas's own efforts to complete the Enlightenment project. I would not dream of questioning Habermas's position as the acknowledged heir to the Frankfurt School, and I take up Habermas only because he serves as a convenient foil. My intention is to argue that the modernist faith in the ability of rationality to contain barbarism has been severely shaken in recent years. Whereas Habermas seeks the basis of society in rationality, I argue that the fundamental basis of society is nonrational. The impotence of the modern West to contain or prevent genocide in the war in Bosnia-Herzegovina in 1992 through negotiation and other rational means is a convenient, albeit tragic illustration of the failure of rationality to contain barbarism. After the Holocaust, one heard the refrain, "Never again!" Alas, the fall of communism in this century has been accompanied by steady increments of various forms of fascism throughout the world. I am fully aware that my argument is controversial, and complex. I ask only that the reader not personalize my disagreement with Habermas. I take issue only with his argument, and other arguments like it, nothing more.

Second, the alternative to rationality that I offer is compassion. If rationality is insufficient to hold societies together, I argue, social order might be dependent upon the stronger forces of empathy and other derivatives of compassion. By compassion, I do not mean pity, charity, socialism, nor any vulgar imitation of the ability of humans to identify with the suffering of others – literally, to co-suffer. I point to Schopenhauer's ([1841] 1965) treatise on compassion as the most succinct statement of what I intend. Moreover, I document Max Horkheimer's admiration for Schopenhauer in precisely this regard, as well as the concerns with "love" and its derivatives, including empathy, found in the works of Simmel, Sorokin, George Herbert Mead, Veblen, Durkheim, and Freud. The reader has every right to disagree with me. I ask only that he or she acknowledge that I document my argument, and that I be judged on the basis of the philosophical meanings of the concepts I employ.

Third, the reader would be wrong to depict me as merely some sort of earnest disciple of Arthur Schopenhauer's philosophy. Several reviewers of other books I have written have again personalized what should be an impartial argument, and have managed to miss completely the fact that Schopenhauer is far more important for what he can teach sociologists rather than philosophers. My reason for emphasizing Schopenhauer is straightforward: According to numerous historical sources, including Georg Simmel (1902, [1907] 1986), Schopenhauer was the philosophical superstar of the previous *fin de siècle*. Schopenhauer has to be taken seriously for the simple reason that sociology was born in the very time-period and cultural milieu that made him famous. Contrary to some misplaced criticisms of my position, I do *not* argue for any sort of direct, cause and effect relationship between his philosophy and the works of any of the founding fathers of sociology. My true position is much simpler, and far easier to defend: Schopenhauer is important because he rebelled against Kant and Hegel, and was Nietzsche's self-acknowledged master.

Fourth, and perhaps most important for the distinctive aspect of the present work, I make much of the intellectual connection between Schopenhauer and Horkheimer. Consider the following brief but pregnant remark by Arthur Hübscher:

> Several lectures, which Horkheimer has held before the Schopenhauer-Gesellschaft and later has made available in published form in his books, are without exception documents of a profound, original relationship to Schopenhauer's world of ideas. They are certainly also documents of a decisive clarification and further development of beginnings which may be found in his early publications. As far as the "wicked optimism" is concerned, with which Schopenhauer reproached "Hegel and his gang," there are not traces of this even with the young Horkheimer . . . Horkheimer's late works are marked by the sober unmasking of a reality which it is impossible to seize either with utopian hopes in progress nor with an escape into impotent traditions. One of Schopenhauer's fundamental insights is confirmed and developed in its multiple problematic aspect: all attainable happiness stands in an irreversible, reciprocal relationship with suffering; the removal of all wants and suffering always leads to others; and this primary constitution of the state of the world can never and nowhere be repealed. What can be done and achieved is this: that in a wretched and hopeless world, to the extent that this is possible, one tries to struggle for a meaning of the human condition, strengthens the self-assurance of the individual against the collective forces, and consequently also keeps alive "the longing for that other," in which a residue of human solidarity is manifest. Doing, acting is not rejected; it is being affirmed in its narrowly delimited possibilities.
>
> (1989: 272–3)

Hübscher claims that Horkheimer's contempt for mass society is derived from Schopenhauer's philosophy. This is because Schopenhauer "does not address society, the large mass; he fits poorly into the conceptual framework of modern sociologists; [and] he addresses the single individual" (ibid.: i). Rather than accept this assessment as a given, I regard it as a point of departure for a much-needed analysis of individualism and society. Many chapters are devoted to this problem, so I will

only summarize my argument here: Critical theory's concept of
mass society is currently passé because it cannot account for the
simultaneous existence of individualism as well as mass conformity in modern societies. Thus, some postmodernists hope
that the overthrow of oppressive narratives will liberate the
individual and lead to tolerance. This is wishful thinking that
fails completely to account for the hatred and sadism sometimes exhibited by unrestrained individuals. On the other
hand, writers like Robert N. Bellah, Christopher Lasch, and
Allan Bloom depict individual freedom as mainly narcissistic
and harmful. Their solution is some conservative return to
tradition which is out of sync with modernity. My resolution of
this problem stems from a new reading of the trajectory from
Schopenhauer through Veblen and Freud to Durkheim and
other sociologists from the previous *fin de siècle*, namely: individualism is itself a tradition rooted in cultural habits, and
comes in at least two varieties, egoistic narcissism versus the
"higher" individualism that is essential to peaceful coexistence
with others. Chapters 6, 8, and 10, especially, are devoted to
this discussion.

I need to address what might prove to be another major
stumbling block for the reader, the topic of suicide, broadly
defined. I had to touch on this topic for straightforward reasons:
Suicide is Durkheim's best-known work; self-destruction is one
of Freud's keenest insights; and the problem of the meaning of
life is an integral aspect of the implicit existentialism exhibited
by Veblen, Sorokin, Schopenhauer, Horkheimer, and the other
thinkers I consider. When confronted by the concept of barbarism, the smug Westerner who is protected by his or her
superiority complex thinks automatically of murder, crime,
genocide or some other act committed by one human agent
against another – and usually in some fictitious, remote, fourth
world. The thinkers that I consider challenge this unfounded
complacency by pointing to the implosion of aggression in the
heart of modern societies whose results range from stress to
bona fide suicide. In Chapter 9 especially, I consider the psychic
wounds, subtle sadism, and vicarious cruelty that are part and
parcel of modern living. I disavow completely any and all
positivistic aspects and approaches to the problem of suicide
that have dominated social research since Durkheim and Freud.
Indeed, I contend that the bulk of this research has missed

completely the existential and humanistic aspects found in the works of sociology's founders, all of whom were concerned in some way with the question, "What is the purpose of life?"

For example, when Veblen charges that the quest for prestige is ultimately useless, because it does not benefit humankind, he is being existential – and expressing a moral concern. Many contemporary sociologists consider such concerns unscientific. But the always cynical Veblen makes one question the purpose of science if it only helps some individuals in their careers, yet fails to benefit humanity. Here I have arrived at one of the many issues raised in this book, and a convenient point for ending the preface.

The present work is offered in the spirit of seeking dialogue and promoting useful discussion (in Veblen's sense). In writing this book, I have benefited from discussions with the following colleagues, none of whom are responsible for any errors that the reader may attribute to me: David Cartwright, Barry Glassner, Susan Greenwood, Michael Kaern, Richard Koffler, David Riesman, Chris Rojek, and Barry Smart. I am very grateful to them. Finally, I would like to express my deepest gratitude to my wife, Amber, who is my most important source of intellectual as well as moral inspiration.

Chapter 1

How to comprehend barbarism in the midst of enlightenment

Who reads Veblen anymore? Jean Baudrillard (1981) does, and uses portions of Veblen's thought to depict a postmodern culture that is dominated by simulations, violence, objects, and discourses that have no firm origin, referent, ground, or foundation (Rojek 1990). It has become common for intellectuals who are engaged in the problematic postmodern discourse to hark back to the previous *fin de siècle* for referents even as they deny referents. Thus, Veblen's famous notion of "conspicuous consumption" becomes the centerpiece for Baudrillard's pathetic vision of the postmodern human, lost in a sea of circulating fictions, for whom consumption – which is not just passive, but an active mode of relating – is the only referent that is left from the grand narratives of modernity. According to Baudrillard, "Consumption is the virtual totality of all objects and messages presently constituted in a more-or-less coherent discourse" (1988: 22). Besides consumption, there is only violence in postmodern America, such that "you feel anything could blow up at any moment" (Baudrillard 1986: 60).

Both Veblen and Baudrillard use America as a symbol for the future, as a vehicle for discussing the fantastic possibility that barbarism can coexist with civilization. "The Americans are barbarians," according to Baudrillard (1986: 67), but adds: "The Americans are not wrong in their idyllic conviction that they are at the center of the world, the supreme power, the absolute model for everyone" (ibid.: 77). Similarly, and according to David Riesman, "Veblen plainly regarded American capitalists as latter-day barbarians" (1964: 395). Consider that in *America* (1986) and *The Theory of the Leisure Class* (1899), Baudrillard and Veblen respectively wrote about the "same" culture, and regarded it as the prototype of a new sort of modern barbarism – but how differently they approached their subject matter! Like Tocqueville ([1845] 1945) before him, Veblen searched for American habits, customs, mores, and other aspects of culture. In contrast to Tocqueville, Baudrillard (1986: 3) went "in search of *astral* America, not social and cultural America, but the America of the empty, absolute freedom of the freeways, not the deep America of mores and mentalities, but the America of desert speed, of motels and mineral surfaces."

Veblen locates barbarism in the persistence of habits and other cultural phenomena whereas Baudrillard depicts postmodern violence as rootless and existing without culture: "Everything is charged with a somnambulic violence and you must avoid contact to escape its potential discharge" (Baudrillard 1986: 60). Baudrillard denies that the America of the 1980s is the same as Veblen's version of the America of the 1890s for the simple, Kantian reason that with the passage of time, the *fictions* that made up Veblen's America have changed. Veblen clung to the old-fashioned, anti-Kantian notion that habits defy time, space, and causality – that habits can and do serve as the roots, ground, and referent for culture. By contrast, Baudrillard depicts America as the "ideal type of the end of our culture" (1986: 98), and as a cultural desert: "For the desert is simply that: an ecstatic critique of culture, and ecstatic form of disappearance" (ibid.: 5). America represents "the zero degree of culture, the power of unculture" (ibid.: 78). Veblen stands for the cultural narratives that Baudrillard and the postmodernists abhor, so Baudrillard guts his theory, takes what he needs, and discards the rest. To confuse matters further, Baudrillard denies that he is a postmodernist (Gane 1991). But despite this disavowal, he is regarded as the foremost spokesperson for postmodernism, and we shall treat him as such (Kellner 1988, 1989a, 1989b, 1990; Rojek 1990; Smart 1992). The theoretical gulf between the traditional, cultural sociology of Veblen and the postmodern, anti-cultural sociology of Baudrillard haunts all contemporary efforts to understand the persistence of barbarism within modernity and civilization.

Baudrillard and the postmodernists find Veblen's world-view – and especially the notion of culture – too constraining, view, or the freedom in Veblen's typically *fin de siècle* vision. For in both the Enlightenment narratives that Veblen criticized and the postmodern anti-narrative narratives represented by Baudrillard, reality is nothing but a fragmented heap of appearances and contingencies. The main difference is that the Kantians tried to connect and make limited sense of the fragments (within the parameters of space, time, and causality, but without venturing into essences), whereas Baudrillard and the postmodernists delight in discarding even the limits to contingency found in Kantianism. The ground or referent for both the modern and postmodern discourses is remarkably similar: an intellectual aversion to discourses that posit any sort of permanence, including the will, character, essence, habits, customs, culture, the soul, and all the other things that were used to describe human motivation for finding truth at least since Plato.

To appreciate the rest of Veblen's relevance for understanding contemporary barbarism, one must seek the ground or referent for the *fin de siècle* spirit that nurtured his thought and writings, and compare it with our postmodern *fin de siècle*.[1] This is something that most postmodernists, following Baudrillard (1981) and Lyotard (1984), are unprepared to do, because postmodernism purports to rebel at all narratives – and the idea of culture is regarded as one such mythical and oppressive narrative. Lyotard (1984: xxiv) defines postmodernism as "incredulity toward metanarratives." Postmodernism has thereby become a rigid, self-devouring, anti-narrative narrative. America, as the prototype of the postmodern future, is "the land of non-history, of the non-event, but at the same time the site of the constant swirl, the uninterrupted rhythm of fashion, that is to say, the site of tremors going nowhere" (Baudrillard 1986: 102).

Yet quite a few authors seem oblivious to the debate between traditionalists and postmodernists, and have innocently found striking parallels between our *fin de siècle* and the previous *fin de siècle*, especially in America.[2] America has been and continues to be the focal point of sociological analyses of culture, modernity, and postmodernity. Freud loathed America, Tocqueville was fascinated by it, Hegel dismissed it from his considerations of the end of history, Riesman documented the end of its innocence, and Baudrillard (1986: 23) sees in it "something of the dawning of the Universe" – albeit, "it is the world center of the inauthentic" (ibid.: 104). For Baudrillard, "the whole of America is a desert" such that "culture exists there in a wild state" (ibid.: 99). Yet against Baudrillard, some American cultural traits that are discussed by these and other authors seem not to have changed appreciably for over a century, and America continues to be used by many authors as the vehicle for a discussion that takes on cosmic proportions. This may be the secret reason why postmodernists smuggle bits and pieces of Veblen, Hegel, Nietzsche, Freud, Tocqueville, and other *fin de siècle* thinkers and commentators on America into their discourses. Affinities, points of connection, and continuities are found by postmodernists almost despite themselves.

VEBLEN FOR THE 1990s

For the sake of argument, or just perversity and fun – two motives that postmodernists allow – let us try to take in more of Veblen as he relates to our times. The overall aim is to suggest that, contrary to Baudrillard and the postmodernists, cultural continuities do exist and persist, and offer a more substantial explanation of barbarism than postmodern theories. For instance, it is astonishing how well Veblen's description of America in the 1890s applies to the America of the 1990s: The accumulation of wealth at the upper end of the pecuniary scale implies privation at the lower end of the scale. The institutionalization of the leisure class hinders cultural development by its inertia and resistance to change, through its prescriptive example of conspicuous consumption, waste, and conservatism, and through maintaining a system of unequal distribution of wealth that benefits itself. The habits of the leisure class – especially its quest for status, prestige, and useless ostentation – eventually permeate the middle and lower classes. These days, the *right* brand of tennis shoes, perfume, automobile, clothing, and other material possessions are deemed to be essential for "making a statement," and ultimately, it is believed, for power and success. For example, contemporary shampoo advertisements convey the message to women that silky, glossy hair – presumably due to their products – will give women *power*.

To amuse itself, the leisure class whips up enthusiasm for war (recall the Gulf War of 1991 and all that talk about a New World Order), and establishes a predatory temper in general for the rest of the population to follow. Hence the incessant declarations of war against crime, AIDS, poverty, potholes, drugs, and the recession, among many other targets. Government becomes a predatory occupation, marked by scandals, conspicuous waste, and militarism. Addiction to sports becomes a substitute for and an extension of this warlike tendency, even as the leisure class engages in ostentatious moralism to compensate for its own immorality. Religious devotion takes on the character of fetish worship, no different from the reverence for economic activity. But genuine morality, the habits of self-abnegation and love of neighbor, diminish in intensity. As illustration, one has only to refer to the "Me" generation and its almost complete lack of guilt or moral conscience regarding the damage caused to the environment and the so-called Third World by its voracious and conspicuous consumption. The leisure class retards cultural development and conserves what is obsolescent. The conservative attitude of the wealthy class comes to be regarded as a mark of respectability. To be conservative is to be reputable, to hold honorific values, and to adhere to points of view that are understood to be a matter of course.

In our *fin de siècle*, the front pages of English newspapers display Prince Charles at polo games while the front pages of American newspapers show President Bush waging war from a fishing boat off the coast of Maine. Meanwhile, the poor have become poorer, and the rich have become richer, while the media refer to "compassion fatigue" in order to explain why hardly anyone really cares about starvation and other suffering in the world. Baudrillard cuts us off from history, whereas Veblen shows us that history repeats itself. Yet both agree that barbarism thrives within modernity.

Veblen taught that barbaric *habits* coexist with civilized habits, and are even exacerbated by modernity, which is ideally supposed to foster the fruits of the "instinct for workmanship": Efficiency, rationality, organization, and above all – civilization. The first and major stumbling block here is the concept, *habit*, which denotes something semi-permanent that is able to transmit social traits across generations without recourse to heredity or even the mind, but through the medium of culture (Bellah 1959; Camic 1986; Guala 1973; James [1890] 1950). It proved impossible for orthodox economics or sociology to absorb Veblen's emphasis on habits, because the rationality assumption that informs these disciplines precludes the possibility of nonreflective behavior (Waller 1988). And habits seem to be relatively independent of the Kantian categories. More on that later. For now, let us focus on Veblen's insight that habits act as the ground or referent for the transmission of barbarism, as well as all other aspects of culture, including its benign and peaceable aspects.

Veblen uses this once-common but now foreign-sounding starting-point to arrive at the incredible, seemingly paradoxical conclusion that barbarism coexists with its opposite, civilization. In the words of David Riesman, Veblen's main contribution to sociology was the daring, satirical claim that "modern society was, in its essential tone, only a latter-day barbarism" (1964: 391). Riesman adds:

> To view modern civilization as still barbaric at its core seems less funny today than to those who laughed in 1899 (at the end of the "splendid little war" with Spain) at *The Theory of the Leisure Class*. It is a measure of Veblen's strength as a social critic that *no rounded judgment of his work can be made that is not also a judgment of American society, now as well as then*.
>
> (Ibid.: 391–94, emphasis added)[3]

The notion of barbaric habits seems to be an oxymoron: One has become used to thinking of barbarism as something pre-civilized that defies all rules, patterns, and habits. The traditional meanings of *barbarian* signify a foreigner, one whose language and customs differ from the civilized speaker's language. Veblen mixes up this comfortable understanding of language games. In Western history, barbarians were all those who were non-Greek, non-Latin, and non-Christian. Over many centuries, barbaric acts came to denote rude, wild, and uncivilized character (in modern terms, behavior). A barbarian *is*, in the very core of his or her being, brutal, savagely cruel, inhuman, and merciless – the complete antithesis of civilized. Veblen does not bother with trying to explain this paradox. He just goes ahead and spins his narrative. It is extremely important to note that Veblen does not describe action, behavior, or fictions – terms recognizable to modernists and postmodernists – but habits, social character, cultural customs, and a sort of ethic – terms that are hardly ever used by contemporary social scientists except with derision.

Thus, in *The Theory of the Leisure Class*, Veblen ([1899] 1967) found many of the following barbaric *habits* operating in his *fin de siècle* America, and by extension, our *fin de siècle* America as well as Western, modern, and postmodern cultures: the love of liquor and intoxicants, the love of war or what he calls "habits of the fight," along with hunting, gambling, sports, and religion. Menial labor is looked down upon. One has to give the appearance that one does not have to work for a living, or at least, that one does not have to get dirty to make a living. Hence, all the postmodern detergents that get clothing "cleaner than clean," brilliantly white, "super-white," and so on. To be reputable, postmodern malls, clothing, automobiles and other objects must be *perfectly* clean, *absolutely* unblemished, and *completely* spotless. In reputable grocery stores, one will not find a single bruised apple, or blemished peach, or wilted head of lettuce. These less-than-perfect fruits and vegetables are not given to the poor, but thrown away.

Members of the opposite sex are depicted as trophies in advertisements, films, and comedy routines. Sexual prowess is regarded highly. Postmodern barbarians love the archaic and the obsolete, and are highly susceptible to nostalgia – cable television has even invented the nostalgia channel. Veblen also discusses modern superstition, astrology, cap-and-gown ceremonies, the popularity of trivia (one thinks immediately of the game "Trivial Pursuit"), and the admiration for swindlers, among many other phenomena, as instances of the persistence of barbaric habits.

All of these habits depend upon a certain degree of ceremonial pomp and circumstance, conspicuously displayed as an integral part of pursuing these habits, in order to highlight one's high status. Veblen's civilized barbarian owns dogs and other "useless" pets, regards horse racing as a cultured sport, cultivates his or her lawn (as a throwback to feudal pastures) at a tremendous cost, and in general, *pursues conspicuous waste as a sign of prestige.*

Even the most ardent supporter of the modernity project has to concede that many, if not most, of Veblen's observations still ring true – despite the fact that modernists refuse to concede that Veblen follows any method other than satire – and that Veblen's book still seems fresh. In fact, many of the traits and habits that Veblen uncovered are much more developed in our *fin de siècle* compared to his. For example, the Western world is drowning in waste; toxic, nuclear, or otherwise harmful to continued life on this planet. College sports have become a multi-billion dollar industry, complete with gambling on the games, and on the side. Las Vegas (referred to as the "great whore" by Baudrillard 1986: 3) has become a gambler's shrine, as have cruise ships on international waters. When Michael Milken was convicted of insider trading, the *Wall Street Journal* published letters from his defenders who complained that putting him in jail would be like punishing Michelangelo. The predatory mind-set that Veblen criticized has become the staple of "games" that our economists use to predict economic behavior. The term "corporate piracy" has become so common that its barbaric meanings are hardly noticed. Useless "junk bonds" and the predatory take-over of ailing companies for the sport of it fueled the economic "growth" of the Reagan era, and were also responsible for the subsequent crash of 1987, and the recession of the 1990s.

Narcotics have not only become bigger business than Veblen could have imagined, alcohol and tobacco lost the sinful taint they had in his time. For example, Virginia Slims sells its cigarettes by wrapping them up in feminism with its famous line for denoting prestige, "You've come a long way, baby." Anhauser-Busch broadcast advertisements that link their beers to American Civil Religion:[4] George Washington required beer as a staple for his troops at Valley Forge, and beer is part of "The American Way of Life." The mighty Phillip Morris Company discounts medical reasons against smoking by shrouding itself in the United States Constitution in its advertisements. More than ever, athletic and sexual prowess are associated with intoxicating beverages and narcotics: one's favorite sports and sex idols try to sell one these poisons as a sign of "making it."

Postmodern hunters and anglers have access to killing equipment, camouflaged clothing, even "game farms," that enable them to kill more efficiently than ever, and that have taken away the chance element that used to be a part of "sport." The timid animal rights movement targets the scientific professions and some aspects of the fur industry, but has not challenged the right to hunt for the "sport" of it. Even the wearing of furs continues: "fake" furs are worn for those whose consciences are bothered by the useless slaughter of exotic animals, or who notice that real furs are simply out of fashion. But the underlying principle is the same: wearing furs is a sign of prowess and prestige, just as it was for our barbarian ancestors. The affiliated selling of weapons to ordinary citizens is likewise a multi-billion-dollar industry that frequently invokes the United States Constitution for prestige.

Contemporary humans continue to revel in habits of the fight. Gratuitous sex, fraud, and violence have become the essential ingredients of our *fin de siècle* cinematic "style." The more gruesome, graphic, and frequent the violence, the better the ratings. Arnold Schwarzenegger – whose first major break in the film industry occurred with his portrayal of *Conan the Barbarian* – played the villain in *Terminator* and the hero in *Terminator 2*, but his switching allegiance to good or evil did not matter to audiences, for in both films, the barbarism that was displayed ensured that the films would be "block-buster hits." The cinema lobbies are filled with video games that again feature barbaric violence. In addition to "real" wars – described by Baudrillard as "unreal" simply because they involve television imagery – Western humanity has declared metaphorical wars on just about everything, from cancer to drunk drivers. From Veblen's perspective, it is significant that President Bush always seems to be on vacation when he is waging a war or discussing one, from the 1991 Gulf War to the 1991 war in Yugoslavia. His aides explain that by waging war from a fishing boat in the waters of Maine or the back of a golf cart, he is sending a "message" that he is relaxed (as if reading a book would not convey a similar message). But according to Veblen, the President is engaging in the conspicuous display of habits pertaining to sports that are closely related to the barbaric habits of the fight enshrined by war. And the crucial point, from Veblen's perspective, is that the display of these barbaric habits is not offensive to most of the population, but is taken for granted, even admired.

Superstition reached as far as the White House during the Reagan years, with the revelation that the Reagans consulted astrologers. Of course, the White House has befriended Billy Graham for many years now, and displays this fact conspicuously during wars. Far from losing strength as predicted by the positivists, religious devotion is as strong as ever, and Sunday School is still the arena where civic leaders "network" for more power and prestige. Magic and the crudest superstitions are found in all walks of contemporary life, from the lucky charms worn by sports heroes to New Age books that are the best-selling sections in shopping mall bookstores (see O'Keefe 1982).[5]

Consider Veblen's sociological analysis of "the lawn, or the close-cropped yard or park, which appeals so unaffectedly to the taste of the Western peoples" ([1899] 1967: 133). Veblen continues:

> The lawn unquestionably has an element of sensuous beauty, simply as an object of apperception, and as such no doubt it appeals pretty directly to the eye of nearly all races and all classes; but it is, perhaps, more unquestionably beautiful to the eye of the dolicho-blond than to most other varieties of men . . . This racial element has once been for a long time a pastoral people inhabiting a region with a humid climate. The close-cropped lawn is beautiful in the eyes of a people whose inherited bent it is to readily find pleasure in contemplating a well-preserved pasture or grazing land.
>
> (Ibid.: 133)

Thorstein Veblen would hardly believe just how right he was if he were alive today, and took a Sunday drive through any American suburb – which is, typically, populated more by whites than minorities. The maintenance of lawns as an *unconscious*[6] throwback to feudal pastures is a cardinal rule in suburbia. Ordinances make sure that citizens may not park their vehicles on their lawns (so as not to damage them), may not grow "weeds" in their front lawns, and must keep their lawns mowed. Americans are obsessed with keeping their lawns trimmed, weed-free, and looking green. Billions upon billions of dollars are spent on fertilizers, insecticides, and other poisons that eventually spill into the water supply. "Public parks of course fall in the same category with the lawn; they too, at their best, are imitations of the pasture," according to Veblen ([1899] 1967: 135). The surest way to destroy a beautiful natural landscape is to declare it a national park. But Americans in particular and Westerners in general now imitate the pasture with "astroturf," an expensive and dangerous counterfeit that lends prestige to sporting events even as it cripples many athletes.

Consider Veblen's remarks on the dog in the light of postmodern habits pertaining to canines:

> The dog has advantages in the way of uselessness as well as in special gifts of temperament. He is often spoken of, in an eminent sense, as the friend of man, and his intelligence and fidelity are praised. The meaning of this is that the dog is man's servant and that he has the gift of an unquestioning subservience and a slave's quickness in guessing his master's mood . . . He is the filthiest of the domestic animals in his person and the nastiest in his habits. For this he makes up in a servile, fawning attitude towards his master, and a readiness to inflict damage and discomfort on all else. The dog, then, commends himself to our favor by affording play to our propensity for mastery, and as he is also an item of expense, and commonly serves no industrial purpose, he holds a well-assured place in men's regard as a thing of good repute. The dog is at the same time associated in our imagination with the chase – a meritorious employment and an expression of the honorable predatory impulse.[7]

(Ibid.: 141)

The standard photograph of a middle-class family still highlights a dog or two to convey respectability. The First Family's dog or dogs are routinely displayed and discussed in the media. It was reported by the news media in 1992 that Barbara Bush, the wife of President George Bush, made much more money by writing and selling a book about their pet dog than President Bush's salary. Advertisements frequently feature dogs in seemingly irrelevant ways – to sell photocopiers, for example – until one remembers Veblen's discovery that the useless dog conveys status. Dog food and dog care products now take up a full aisle in grocery stores, and pet cemeteries are becoming increasingly common.

As for reviving archaic styles as signs of distinction, postmodern humans have revived the Victorian era in their decor, fashion, and advertisements. Nostalgia is also big business, remaking and selling films, stories, songs, and novels from the 1950s and earlier times. Gothic script has come back. Prior to Hitler's rise to power, Veblen (1917) warned that the Gothic revival was one of several signs that the barbaric habits were becoming stronger.[8]

One of Veblen's favorite targets is fashion. As with other prestigious cultural objects, "in order to be reputable," fashion "must be wasteful" and useless ([1899] 1967: 96). Hence the prestige of the "high heel [which] obviously makes any, even the simplest and most necessary manual work extremely difficult" (ibid.: 171). Something similar is true for the skirt:

> It is expensive and it hampers the wearer at every turn and incapacitates her for all useful exertion. The like is true of the feminine custom of wearing the hair excessively long.
>
> (Ibid.: 171)

"Dress must not only be conspicuously expensive and inconvenient; it must at the same time be up to date" according to Veblen (ibid.: 173). The more frivolous and useless the adornment – for example, the ostrich feather added to the hat, or the frills added to the underwear – the more honorific it becomes. Veblen concludes:

> When seen in the perspective of half-a-dozen years or more, the best of our fashions strike us as grotesque, if not unsightly. Our transient attachment to whatever happens to be the latest rests on other than aesthetic grounds, and lasts only until our abiding aesthetic sense has had time to assert itself and reject this latest indigestible contrivance. The process of developing an aesthetic nausea takes more or less time.
>
> (Ibid.: 178)

In general, Veblen regards as prestigious and barbaric anything that is "wasteful." He explains that "it is here called 'waste' because this expenditure does not serve human life or human well-being on the whole, not because it is waste or misdirection of effort or expenditure as viewed from the standpoint of the individual consumer who chooses it" (ibid.: 97). By Veblen's standards, a good deal, if not most, of postmodern culture does not serve human life or human well-being on the whole, and is therefore barbaric.

The reader is no doubt able to supply his or her own

contemporary observations to substantiate the relevance of Veblen's observations for our times. And the disturbing conclusion drawn by Veblen is that the totality of these habits betrays our barbaric temperament, despite our seemingly sincere belief that we are enlightened, modern, and civilized. But here we have returned to the problem of trying to make sense of our contemporary era, which is decidedly split between the postmodernists who preach the end of culture, and the positivists who find Veblen's study so unscientific that it is beneath their dignity to address it. This epistemological problem – how do we know the world? – is at the heart of current debates that flow from postmodern discourse, and requires further discussion.

WHAT HAPPENED TO SOCIAL CHARACTER?

Veblen received a cool reception from his contemporaries, although his *Theory of the Leisure Class* came to be regarded eventually as a sociological classic. Nevertheless, in our time, it is again being dismissed as nothing but a satire[9] (except for Baudrillard, who is often similarly dismissed by more conventional scholars). This reaction has been rationalized by noting that, like Simmel, Veblen does not cite his sources, and does not make his theoretical scaffolding clear. But this is a cop-out with regard to Veblen, as well as Simmel, who is finally being assimilated into sociology (see Frisby 1984, 1986). Both Veblen and Simmel work from a coherent theoretical ground that is evident for those who care to seek it out (Riesman 1953). In fact, both sociologists rely primarily on a similar German philosophical scaffolding to construct their social theory that was used later as the referent for critical theory and some postmodern theory.[10] Veblen has been neglected, or used in a fragmented way, first, because his message is a direct affront to the *status quo,* and second, because he based his analyses on the notion of *cultural habits,* not observable events. He was not alone in either regard: from Tocqueville to Tönnies, Durkheim, and Freud, Veblen's method was the rule, not the exception.

The concept of "habit" was used routinely by intellectuals from the previous *fin de siècle.* Its usage can be traced all the way back to Plato and Aristotle to refer to general and permanent

traits in human intercourse (Lalande [1926] 1980: 392–8).
After the 1920s, the concept of habit was dropped suddenly
from the social scientific vocabulary (Camic 1986). Twentieth-
century positivists and behaviorists began studying behavior
and events, not habits, and at the end of the twentieth century,
postmodernists began studying fictions. Why? Habits refer to
settled dispositions or tendencies to act in certain ways that are
partly unconscious or otherwise involuntary (Waller 1988).
Habits are second nature, all the things that are done as a
matter of course and routinely, stereotypes that are fixed and
rooted in one's social and individual *character*.[11] To act habitually is to act on the basis of the heart, not the mind, to be ruled
by the will, not "rational social action." Habits are like the
essences that neo-Kantians despise. They flow from the
"shadow" that Carl Gustav Jung (1959) claimed is part of the
collective and private unconscious.[12] They imply a depth that
Baudrillard (1986) mocks in his quest to convince us that
society is like a TV screen or a desert. Habits are permanent,
anti-intellectual, and act as the ground for motives. In a word,
habits are non-modern.

In order to satisfy their assumption that the mind can rule
the passions, modernists had to drop the concept of habit, and
did their best to assimilate *fin de siècle* thinkers into modern
paradigms. This is essentially what Parsons (1937) achieved in
his *Structure of Social Action*: Sociology's founding fathers were
forced by Parsons into the modern mold of utilitarian social
theory, the very utilitarianism that most of them criticized
vehemently. This worked for a while, except that it played to a
very limited audience. As our century draws to a close, the
postmodernists are challenging the seriousness of Parsons and
the modernists, but not their philosophical assumptions. Consider, for example, Baudrillard's (1986: 55) flippant claim:
"Drive ten thousand miles across America and you will know
more about the country than all the institutes of sociology and
political science put together." It must be emphasized that
both Parsons and Baudrillard, the modernists and the postmodernists, do not take seriously Veblen and his *fin de siècle*
contemporaries, among them, Durkheim, Freud, Jung, Simmel,
and James.

The modernist dream is erected on the assumption that
liberation from traditional habits and traditional culture is a

beneficial process overall. Marxism is just one such modernist doctrine among many, and they all come complete with an esoteric, jargon-filled vocabulary. However, the general population cannot understand postmodernists any more than it understands mainstream sociologists. It has become cynical, and is returning to the traditional vocabulary of habits to explain everyday life (Bloom 1987; Kanter and Mirvis 1989). For example, Americans in the present *fin de siècle* have turned decisively conservative: Over three-quarters of them favor the death penalty, putting away society's "bad guys" into prison for life, and "throwing away the key." Disenchanted by the promises made by the medical profession, Americans turned to the fitness craze as a last resort to reviving puritanism: Barry Glassner (1988: 247) concludes that "Americans now accept the notion that a person becomes ill not because of natural physical processes but because of immoral action." Pretty, trim people are good,[13] and audiences hate to see pretty people die in films. In countless other ways, Americans are vindicating Veblen by betraying the persistence of habits and social character that he uncovered almost a century ago: a healthy body, trimmed lawn, prestigious car, extravagant house, and obedient dog (among other barbaric habits) indicate prestige, and therefore good character. On the other hand, Americans are quick to render a negative judgment on the character of someone who possesses an overweight body, unkempt lawn, an economical car that otherwise conveys that it is "cheap," a small house, and other signs of struggling to make a living, and therefore, low status. And this, despite decades of modern consciousness-raising about equality and the benefits of modern living for all.

One might want to object that we are over-generalizing. But how else can one explain all the billions of dollars that are wasted – from Veblen's perspective – on diet programs, fertilizers, that extra racing stripe on an automobile that will never be in a race, a huge house with closets the size that rooms used to be in former days in order to accommodate objects that stem from constant consumption, athletic shoes and athletic suits for a generation that is less physically fit than previous generations – among the countless other wasteful, useless, and extravagant habits of this postmodern generation? And consider postmodern advertisements: They attempt to sell the prestige and power that their products will supposedly convey upon the consumer much more than workmanship or even rational reasons for regarding their products as beneficial. Veblen would claim that these are all examples of the persistence of barbaric habits.

Baudrillard paints a similar portrait of the barbaric post-modern American, only he does so without any recourse to the notion of habits or culture. In Baudrillard's words:

> The generation that has come from the sixties and seventies, but has rid itself of all nostalgia for, all bad conscience about, and even any subconscious memory of those wild years. The very last traces of marginality excised as if by plastic surgery: new faces, new fingernails, glossy brain-cells, the whole topped with a tousle of software . . . "*Clean and perfect.*" The Yuppies . . . But this easy life knows no pity. Its logic is a pitiless one. If utopia has already been achieved, then unhappiness does not exist, the poor are no longer credible . . . The have-nots will be condemned to oblivion, to abandonment, to disappearance pure and simple. This is "must exit" logic: "poor people must exit". The ultimatum issued in the name of wealth and efficiency wipes them off the map. And rightly so, since they show such *bad taste* as to deviate from the general consensus.
>
> (1986: 110–11; emphasis added)

One can find plenty of illustrations of Baudrillard's claims. But Baudrillard fails to explain how and why the "must exit" logic is generalized across a population if culture as such does not exist. In what sense does this, or any other, logic exist, if not culturally? Baudrillard never bothers to address this issue. By contrast, thinkers from the previous *fin de siècle* other than Veblen sought equivalents for cultural habits in their vocabulary: customs, mores, folkways, collective representations. In all these cases, they were following a program that is anathema to modernists: human behavior is grounded in centripetal forces that lead to and flow from the past, mother, nation, and community even as humanity is pulled by centrifugal forces that lead to progress and that constitute Habermas's (1987) modernity project. Except for the Frankfurt School, David Riesman (1950), and Bellah *et al.* (1985), very few twentieth-century sociologists followed the lead established in the previous *fin de siècle*. But those who did, struck deep chords in the popular mind.

It is striking in this regard that in his *America*, Baudrillard agrees with the trajectory from Veblen to Riesman that somehow, America represents modernity (and by extension, postmodernity). But he refuses to go along with Veblen's (and Tocqueville's) conclusion that there exist two Americas, one based on democratic habits, and the other based on the barbaric habits that led to slavery and the extermination of the Indians. According to Baudrillard (1986: 88), it is

> as if good and evil had developed separately. Is it possible that one can, while keenly feeling both these aspects, pass over the relation between them? Certainly it is, and the same paradox faces us today: *we shall never resolve the enigma of the relation between the negative foundations of greatness and that greatness itself.* America is powerful and original; America is violent and abominable. We should not seek to deny either of these aspects, nor reconcile them. But what has become of this paradoxical grandeur, the New World's original situation as described by Tocqueville?

Baudrillard is aware that "Tocqueville's central idea is that the spirit of America is to be found in its mode of life, in the revolution of mores, the moral revolution" (ibid.: 91). But he refuses to use Tocqueville's original phrase, "habits of the heart," to describe the hypocrisy, racism, violence, sense of egalitarianism, individualism, and other "bad" as well as "good" aspects of modernity and America uncovered by Tocqueville. Instead, Baudrillard calls on us to reverse our traditional value-judgments:

> It is Disneyland that is authentic here! The cinema and TV are America's reality! The freeways, the Safeways, the skylines, speed, and deserts – these are America, not the galleries, churches, and culture. Let us grant this country the admiration it deserves and open our eyes to the absurdity of some of our own customs.
>
> (Ibid.: 104)

Clearly, neither the postmodernists nor the positivists take seriously the concepts of habit and culture that were crucial to Tocqueville, Veblen, and the other founding fathers of socio-

logy. It does not seem to occur to Baudrillard that the cinema
and TV and the freeways might mirror, embody, or otherwise
refract America's cultural habits. Had he penetrated beneath
the surface, he might have noticed that the cinema and TV are
almost exclusively white, and that Tocqueville's chilling conclusion seems to be coming true, that whites and blacks will
never live in harmony in America. And the highways of America
that Baudrillard found so enchanting are crumbling, because
the middle class refuses to pay more taxes to keep them up –
Tocqueville discussed this tragic aspect of shortsightedness on
the part of the electorate as well.

The positivists also miss the power of the cultural explanations illustrated by Tocqueville and Veblen. For example, were
they to take Tocqueville or Veblen seriously, contemporary
positivists would fault them for their unscientific sampling. The
same charges have been levelled at Theodor Adorno, other
critical theorists, Riesman, and Bellah. By what right do these
popular writers (another strike against them) draw general-
izations based on their "flimsy" evidence? They didn't use
random samples, surveys, hypotheses, or any of the other
standard positivistic techniques. They merely interviewed some
individuals in a seemingly haphazard manner, and proceeded
to generalize that their observations applied to everyone. One
should not miss the implicit message in positivist dogma that
their version of the scientific method carries prestige, while the
student of culture who tries to make sense of cultural habits is
supposedly engaging in a low-status undertaking. (But Veblen's
retort might be that positivism carries prestige precisely because
it is frightfully expensive with regard to huge research grants,
yet ultimately useless to the well-being of general humanity.)

Actually, the method used by Tocqueville, Veblen and their
successors is complex, and is based on defensible philosophical
assumptions. Habits cannot be "observed" by positivistic
methods, because the moment that they are made self-conscious
by paper and pencil, they cease to be habits and turn into
rationalizations. One has to sneak up on habits, find them
operating unconsciously, in their original milieux. And by
virtue of being habits, they are general, so that one has every
right to conclude that most suburban Americans – who are
overwhelmingly white, and have left the minorities to suffer in
the inner cities – value the appearance of their lawns, even if

one has not surveyed their opinions on lawns. Such a survey would not be useful, because white Americans regard the care of their lawns as something akin to brushing their teeth (another seemingly automatic habit that is not universal), and could not give a rational account of either habit. The actor who is asked to explain his or her habits would react incredulously.

Another reason why habits cannot be operationalized, tested, and otherwise assimilated into the positivistic program is that habits are not universal laws that rule the natural world, as positivistic truths are supposed to be, but reflect one's particularism. An analysis of habits would distinguish Americans from, let us say, Germans or Croatians, and that is a threatening thing to do in a culture that subscribes, at least officially, to the doctrine that all persons are part of the same global world. Postmodernists also challenge the universality of positivistic "truths," and this is another reason why they habitually turn to *fin de siècle* thinkers in their attacks on the modernity project. But even postmodernists do not embrace the concept of habit, because it implies a cultural ground or referent for discourse, and postmodernists work from the same fragmented, abstract universe devoid of culture that modernists believe in. Moreover, habits are invisible dispositions that are assumed to operate even if they contradict observable behavior. For example, a racist heart can hide itself, and convince positivists that it is not prejudiced, with complete sincerity, yet remain. racist. This may explain why National Opinion Research Center opinion polls find that Americans are less prejudiced than they were a generation ago even as American society is being ripped apart by racism. Just because white Americans are now more likely *to say* that they would not mind a black person moving into their neighborhoods is not a good reason to believe them, when everyone knows, and demographers have shown, that "white flight" away from ethnic city centers into suburbs has occurred on a massive scale. Thinkers from the previous *fin de siècle* assumed that secret dispositions do not parade openly for positivists to observe them. This is why the hallmark of their thought involved the cynical unmasking of surface phenomena in order to find dark secrets. Veblen was a master at exposing hypocrisies, but many of his *fin de siècle* colleagues were engaged in similar cynical projects, from Durkheim to Pareto and Freud.

For example, consider that following the Los Angeles riots of

1992 – the worst in American history – there did not occur a long-lasting and collective soul-searching of the racism that might be lurking in the American collective consciousness (after Durkheim). Instead, President Bush blamed former President Lyndon Johnson's "Great Society" program and welfare. The Los Angeles Chief of Police explained that the riots were mostly the work of gangs and criminals, who would be prosecuted. For all the rationalizations that were offered, nobody came close to taking up Veblen's or Tocqueville's arguments that perhaps racist cultural habits had persisted and continue to persist secretly beneath the appearance of modern egalitarianism. Yet Tocqueville's words seem to still ring true: "Slavery recedes, but the prejudice to which it has given birth is immovable" ([1845] 1945: 373).[14]

Not just President Bush and the modernists, but also Baudrillard and the postmodernists will have nothing to do with Tocqueville's and Veblen's typically *fin de siècle* suspiciousness. Baudrillard (1986: 81) reproaches the Europeans for seeking out heresies or other forms of dissidence, for searching out superstitions, for always being on guard. Baudrillard prefers the naive Americans, for whom

> a face does not deceive, behaviour does not deceive, a scientific process does not deceive, nothing deceives, nothing is ambivalent (and at bottom this is true: nothing deceives, there are no lies, *there is only simulation*, which is precisely the facticity of facts).
>
> (Ibid.: 85)

He adds that "the Americans are a true utopian society, in their religion of the *fait accompli*, in the naivety of their deductions, in their ignorance of the evil genius of things." But again, Baudrillard regards naiveté as more than an American or modern habit: It is the prototype of the postmodern attitude that he espouses and that he believes is taking over the world. In this regard, too, the postmodernists join forces with the positivists, both of whom regard as absurd the notion that a hidden reality might lurk beneath a facade of appearances.

By contrast, Riesman (1950, 1953) – an uncommonly suspicious American – digs beneath the facades presented even by Tocqueville and Veblen in their search for essences. Riesman finds in Veblen's thought signs of Marx, Bellamy, and German *fin de siècle* Romanticism. These Romantic influences also reached Tocqueville, and include Kant, Hegel, Schopenhauer, Bachofen, and the founders of *Völkerpsychologie*, Lazarus and Steinthal. For example, a complete reading of Veblen (1899) reveals that he held to Bachofen's (1861) "myth" (for what is real these days?) that prior to the onset of barbarism, humanity lived in peace under matriarchal influence. This is the supposed source of the peaceable habits that offset the barbaric habits for Veblen.[15] Tocqueville, too, was aware of the "noble savage" myth found in French Romanticism, from Rousseau to Chateaubriand and Lamartine. It is as difficult to prove as it is to disprove this matriarchal "myth," but there is no doubt that some versions of this myth influenced Marx, Engels, Morgan, Henry Adams, Jung, Freud, Durkheim, Frazer, and a host of other *fin de siècle* luminaries who regarded society as a manifestation of the primitive Great Mother archetype.[16] To pick one example out of many, Durkheim ([1925] 1961: 92) wrote that "society is the benevolent and protecting power, the nourishing mother from which we gain the whole of our moral and intellectual substance and toward whom our wills turn in a spirit of love and gratitude." Like Durkheim, who was concerned with moral regeneration in the face of degeneration caused by modernity, Veblen ([1910] 1943) sought to establish a modified version of Christian morals as an extension of these matriarchal habits to offset the barbaric habits of mind (see Leathers 1986). And even Baudrillard (1986: 88) concedes that Tocqueville sought to nurture the "good" America while realizing that the "bad" America would always remain.

Let us be clear as to what is at stake here. For Veblen, as for many of his contemporaries, the drama of social life is to be explained on the basis of the interplay between peaceable versus barbaric cultural habits. So-called Western civilization is not merely an example of unlimited and unbridled progress toward liberal democracy or other benign traits, as claimed by thinkers from Hegel ([1899] 1965) to Francis Fukuyama (1992). Veblen believes that Western civilization is fundamentally peaceable *as well as* barbaric, and that this dualism will never be resolved completely. Postmodernists, modernists, and positivists cannot digest Veblen's, Tocqueville's, Durkheim's, or many other intellectuals' efforts from the previous *fin de siècle* to posit a dualism of human nature or *homo duplex*. Hence, there arise among modernists efforts to obfuscate barbarism in modern cultures, and among postmodernists efforts to deny the very existence of culture, much less "good" versus "bad" culture. Much is at stake here.

BARBARISM AS MORE THAN A TV IMAGE

Yet, there is more to Veblen and his *fin de siècle* contemporaries. Veblen hits hard with this *fin de siècle* arsenal of concepts. He regards the Aryan "race" as the most likely to revert to and maintain barbaric habits ([1899] 1967: 197):

> It seems probable that the dolicho-blond type of European man is possessed of a greater facility for such reversion to barbarism than the other ethnic elements with which that type is associated in the Western culture . . . Except for the fear of offending that chauvinistic patriotism which is so characteristic a feature of the predatory culture, and the presence of which is frequently the most striking mark of reversion in modern communities, the case of the American colonies might be cited as an example of such a reversion on an unusually large scale.

Riesman (1953) notes that in *Imperial Germany and the Industrial Revolution*, Veblen ([1915] 1964) correctly predicted the rise of German fascism that led to World War II based on his analysis of these Aryan habits, and that he was highly critical of American chauvinism and imperialism in the beginning of the twentieth century. Even if Veblen ought to be dismissed according to positivistic standards, it is intriguing that he seems to have been a better prognosticator compared to the positivists who were predicting that rational social order was just around the corner. Veblen ([1915] 1964, 1917) singled out imperial Germany and Japan as two cultures that grafted industrialism onto a barbaric set of cultural habits at the beginning of the twentieth century, with disastrous consequences for the rest of the world. He never meant that Germany or Japan were permanently or essentially barbaric, only that barbaric values dominated over peaceable traits in the first half of this century. Veblen's traditional thinking predicted correctly the cause of widespread slaughter in this century.

But there is more. Veblen felt that among the Aryans, there

were groups who possessed more of the peaceable character traits, and these typically became farmers, whereas the nomadic herders of sheep, cattle, and horses – the famous cowboys – were more barbarian and power-hungry. The cowboys were more likely to possess these "habits of the fight," and turn to crime or run for political office than the peaceable types. It is interesting that the American West and South, which were settled more by herders and adventurers than farmers, as noted even by Tocqueville ([1845] 1945: 411), *still* exhibit higher rates of homicide, some other crimes, and other pugnacious traits compared with the rest of the USA.[17] Can Veblen be dismissed simply because he subscribed to the notion of social character, which is offensive to modernist sentiments? Many years after Veblen, Dinko Tomasic (1948, 1953) also argued that in the USSR and Eastern Europe, the Bolsheviks as well as latter-day communists were more likely to come from groups that made a living from herding than from farming. He isolated the Ural and Dinaric Alps as two important sources of the brutal values that informed communism in practice, much like Tocqueville pointed to the South for the source of aristocracy and cruelty in America. For the purposes of our discussion, it is significant that the cowboy image is still powerful in the USA – he is the Marlboro man, and has given rise to the "urban cowboy." Moreover, ex-communists in the former USSR and Eastern Europe are being elected in droves after they "converted" to democratic ideals. If Veblen is correct about the persistence of cultural habits, the future seems frightening in a world that is claiming to seek a peaceable New World Order on the flimsy basis of surface transformations to modernist, egalitarian ideals without investigating into underlying and persistent character traits. One thinks of the famous song in the hit musical *Oklahoma* – can the farmer and the cowboy be friends?

The questions which beg answers, from Veblen's perspective, are: have the habits of the fight that he exposed in America in particular and the modern West in general diminished or persisted into the present *fin de siècle*; how can one make sense out of one's reply to this question, and what can be done about it?

The first obstacle concerns reconciling Veblen with the dominant, contemporary belief that we are more civilized than our ancestors, and that civilization is a benign thing overall.

Nowhere is that belief expressed more strongly than in the writings of Norbert Elias (1982) and his enthusiastic followers. Elias is praised by conventional scholars, because he examined etiquette books in a systematic and empirical manner to conclude, conveniently, that the civilizing process is alive and well. In *The Civilizing Process*, Elias examines etiquette books since the Middle Ages to conclude that as it has become civilized, humanity has imposed increased self-constraints on brutality and offensive sights, smells, and bodily functions of all sorts. Postmodern humans no longer conduct business in bed, and are careful to conceal and restrain their urges to belch, pass gass, cough, spit, and pick their noses, among other disgusting habits. Bryan Turner (1985) regards "Elias's historical sociology as a massive vindication of Weberian sociology," without noting the vast controversy that surrounds the question how Weber's emphasis on increasing rationality should be interpreted (see Käsler 1988; Sica 1988). Elias has been stamped with the modernist Good Housekeeping Stamp of Approval.[18] One is supposed to accept that postmodern humans are more courteous and polite, and hence less barbaric, than our ancestors.

Veblen would say that all our efforts to display conspicuous manners – and that is a key point, that it is alright to engage in disgusting habits in private, but not in public – testify to the persistence of the barbaric temperament. The barbarian, at least for Veblen, loves to engage in ceremonial behavior, especially if its essential aim is fraud: that is how the predator habitually stalks his or her prey, and practicing the habit is gratifying even if actual prey is not always involved. Modernists pretend to be civilized. Despite all their courteous *external* behavior, it is not certain that the *inner* character is no longer barbaric. For example, Elias is correct that civilized humans have imposed more rules on how sports are conducted, ostensibly in order to minimize bloodshed and naked violence. But he does not address the fact that spectators are often disappointed when no one is hurt or injured at a sporting event, and that a common expression uttered by "civilized" sports fans during the heat of the battle is, "Kill the son of a bitch!" The results of sporting events are routinely presented by the news media by using the vocabulary of war, that such and such a team was mauled, demolished, terminated, and so on by the opposing team. Even the most cursory examination of how sports fans behave at a match – the profanity, aggression in the stands, the trash that is left behind, the liquor that is consumed – suggests that Veblen's barbaric habits operate despite the civilized constraints and rules that are supposedly imposed on the contest. Even the pre-game cheerleading and exercises in civil religion and other devotional observances testify to the barbaric temperament, if one examines these events from Veblen's perspective.

It is necessary to drive this point home, to expose how Elias and his followers draw an incorrect conclusion based on a pristine but narrow examination of evidence. Veblen would have us examine the entire sporting event, not just the rules of etiquette. Let me review some observations from a football game between the Texas Aggies and the University of Texas Longhorns that Veblen would probably have noticed as well. The night before the game, a pile of logs five stories high was lit and students danced around it consuming alcoholic beverages and intoxicants. This primitive ritual is referred to as "Bonfire," and is refracted in countless "tailgate" parties across America in localities that are not as willing or are not as able as Aggies to destroy trees. Prior to the opening of the game – which is signalled by a cannon blast – the team mascot is paraded. The Aggie mascot is a collie named Reveille. Reveille is treated as a sacred object, a focal point of veneration, like some Hindu sacred cow: if she decides to sleep on a student's bed, the student must move to make room for her. She will be buried in a sacred burial ground reserved for her predecessors and successors, surrounded by sacred grass on which one must not walk.[19] She watches over the game, as if she could lend magical power to the Aggies. As the fans anticipate a touchdown or goal, the male cheerleaders stand beneath the goalposts clutching their genitals in some masochistic ritual that is performed in full view of the middle-class spectators. Every score is marked by cannon fire, followed by the cheerleaders getting on their knees and bowing to Reveille. The half-time entertainment usually consists of a military marching band or civilians who engage in military maneuvers. Now I ask any unbiased reader: how are all these rituals really different from the barbaric rites documented by Malinowski and other anthropologists? The collective representations that surround Bonfire, the aura attached to dog, cannon, sexuality, and masochism all point to

Veblen's analysis of primitive throwbacks to barbaric mentality.

As another example, consider how the 1991 Gulf War was presented by the media essentially as a sporting event. It was touted as "the showdown in the Gulf." The bombing crews were sent off by their ground crews using cheers that one finds at football games, and these were repeated upon their return. On my campus, students began wearing T-shirts that displayed the words "Gig 'em Troops" as a variation on the football motto, "Gig 'em Aggies." True to Elias's (1982) claims, the display of actual carnage was not shown on television, and the number of enemy casualties was never revealed by the Pentagon. For this reason, Baudrillard referred to the Gulf War as unreal, because TV presented a simulation of reality.[20] But the actual killing was done using incendiary bombs that were eventually condemned even in the Vietnam War, and the destruction of humans and the environment was as merciless and savage as that exhibited in the bombings of Hiroshima, Nagasaki, Dresden, and Vietnam (see Riesman 1954, 1976, 1977). The mere fact that the actual sight of mutilated bodies was covered up does not mean that savage cruelty was not inflicted and dressed up in habits of sport.

Is Elias correct that humanity is becoming more civilized because it restricts direct perception of and participation in violence,[21] or is Baudrillard correct that the restrictions serve only to make the violence seem less real, and therefore more palatable? Or is it Veblen who is correct, that sports are a throwback to barbaric habits of the fight, and therefore postmodern wars are fought as if they were a sporting match?

These questions touch on the central issue that concerns us here, how one should explain barbarism in relation to the modernity project. Yet one cannot make headway in arriving at a satisfactory explanation so long as one is restrained by modernist methodological and philosophical assumptions. Indicting modernity using modernist tools is like having an all-white jury sit in judgment on a case that involves the brutalization of a black victim. To repeat, both postmodernists and positivists remain trapped in the neo-Kantian prison of discussing phenomena that are not connected to any ground or referent, and that deny the notion of culture. Therefore, we cannot expect a verdict in favor of Veblen's cultural explanation. But this does not necessarily mean that Veblen was wrong.

It does mean, however, that modernist methodological and philosophical assumptions need to be analyzed closely from the perspective of the problem that concerns us here: does the barbaric temperament lie at the heart of modern methodology and the philosophy of never-ending progress?

Chapter 2

Methodological and empirical issues in perceiving modern barbarism

For the sociologist as for the historian, social facts vary with the social system of which they form a part; they cannot be understood when detached from it.

(Durkheim [1912] 1965: 113)

We have already quoted David Riesman's (1964: 391) summary of Veblen's major contribution to sociology as the perplexing idea that modern culture is essentially only a latter-day barbarism. Almost anyone who has read Veblen's *Theory of the Leisure Class*, and especially the rest of his books, will probably be inclined to agree readily with Riesman that this is what Veblen intended. But what does it mean? The positivists and the empirically minded academic social scientists will demand empirical verification, proof, or at least documentation of whatever it might mean. The required proof is generally quantitative and statistical, which is a sharp departure from Veblen's more qualitative and philosophical analyses. The positivists will invoke the Kantian categories of space, time, and causality, whereas Veblen wrote in terms of timeless archaic habits. To satisfy contemporary canons of empirical research, one should demonstrate some of the following: that barbarism – defined and operationalized perhaps as wars, homicides, victims of violence or some other variable – either correlates with periods of general enlightenment, perhaps even *the* Enlightenment, or increases with the development of history or modernity in general. The empiricist will want evidence to support the claim that modern barbarism is the same as or worse than the barbarism in, let us say, early Greek civilization. Of course, the empirical aim will be to *disprove* that barbarism correlates with modernity or civilization, because strict positivists claim that nothing can be proven true, even though hypotheses may be proven false.

In moving from Veblen's formulation of the problem of barbarism as coexisting with the spirit of civilization regardless of time, space, and causality to the empirical formulation of the problem as an issue of statistical correlation, it is no longer certain that one is talking about the same problem. For example, a modernist reaction to Veblen's provocative thesis might be that modern instances of barbarism, such as the Holocaust or the Gulags, pale in comparison with the campaigns of the Roman Empire or Genghis Khan. Or they might point to the brutalities exhibited in the war fought in Bosnia-Herzegovina in 1992 as instances of primitive tribalism that no longer afflict the civilized West. Veblen's reply might be that even if most of the civilized West did not participate directly in the Holocaust, the Gulags, or more recently, the genocide in Bosnia-Herzegovina, it participated vicariously in these barbaric events. Despite its collectively expressed outrage at the inhumanity in these and other instances of twentieth-century barbarism, the civilized West took its time to respond. For example, in the case of the genocide in Bosnia in 1992, Western audiences were exposed to televised depictions of grisly horror – in color, no less – but rebuffed for many months the pleas of the Bosnian government to help stop the carnage. Veblen would condemn such cool contemplation of someone else's suffering as an instance of quasi-barbarism, in line with his other analyses of vicarious consumption and vicarious leisure. Yet such considerations of vicarious barbarism do not enter into modernist discussions.

The modernists refuse to admit that modernity itself is a peculiar blend of cultural traits and philosophical assumptions that constitutes a world-view. Instead, modernists want to claim that their view of the world is universally valid, and thereby betray a paradoxical provincialism. When confronted with instances of savagery, modernists resort to the we–they distinction: "we" are civilized, and "they" are barbaric. Modern empiricists cannot assimilate Schopenhauer's anti-Kantian claim that the human animal is and always will be barbaric, notwithstanding so-called progress and enlightenment. Veblen and his *fin de siècle* colleagues drew off this Schopenhauerian

philosophical base to offer a cultural interpretation of history
that is not amenable to contemporary scientific analyses. This
does not mean that they were unscientific, but that their
understanding of science is not the same as the contemporary
versions of science.

Moreover, Veblen reserved some of his sharpest barbs, not
for the state of knowledge in developing countries, but for
modern, academic science and for Western institutions of
higher learning. He was one of the earliest proponents of the
idea that the scientific establishment itself is a *cultural* product
of the leisure class. For Veblen, academia was the pinnacle of
the wasteful, useless, ostentatious, and barbaric habits that he
criticized generally. In a sense, to hand Veblen's hard-won
insights to the academic establishment that shunned him is to
turn him over to the enemy. One cannot expect a fair verdict.
Veblen will be dismissed, as he has been in the past, as an
iconoclast, satirist, and cynic.

Because it is expected that a sociologist in the present *fin de
siècle* will address these issues in the conventional way, I shall
review previous efforts by Pitirim Sorokin, Emile Durkheim,
and Francis Fukuyama, among others, with regard to empirical
conclusions regarding barbarism and civilization. But because
the primary aim in this book is to try to resolve the mystery of
the connection between barbarism and modernity, I shall not
assume automatically that modern empiricism is capable of
offering such a resolution. On the contrary, I shall give Veblen's
case a fair hearing. This chapter shall be leading to Veblen's
and Durkheim's alternative conceptualizations of science and
educational institutions as *cultural* activities, not the privileged,
non-cultural position that most scholars seem to ascribe to
science. And far from concluding that science can help tame
barbarism, Veblen and Durkheim followed the philosophical
trajectory of the previous *fin de siècle* which led to the disturbing
conclusion that science and enlightenment in general can
coexist with barbarism – perhaps even exacerbate it.

MODERN SCIENCE AS A CULTURAL ASPECT OF THE BARBARIC LEISURE CLASS

The gist of Veblen's view of modern science is that it arose with
industry as a useless, honorific activity of the leisure class. The

reader should be reminded of Veblen's definition of "useless" as that which does not serve human well-being "on the whole," no matter how useful it is to some specific individuals or strata of society ([1899] 1967: 97). We have seen in Chapter 1 that the useless is prestigious in general life. Veblen transfers this insight to academic institutions, which shape the taste of the novice "by inspiring an habitual aversion to what is merely useful, as contrasted with what is merely honorific in learning" and "by consuming the learner's time and effort in acquiring knowledge which is of no use, except in so far as this learning has by convention become incorporated into the sum learning required of the scholar, and has thereby affected the terminology and diction employed in the useful branches of knowledge" (ibid.: 394).

Science carries prestige, and this connection testifies to the fact, according to Veblen, that science, as an institution, arose from "its parent stock of magic ritual and shamanistic fraud" (ibid.: 365).[1] The point of departure for all institutionalized learning consists of the devotional practices of the priestly classes (p. 364):

> Learning, then, set out with being in some sense a by-product of the priestly vicarious leisure class; and, at least until a recent date, the higher learning has since remained in some sense a by-product or by-occupation of the priestly classes.
>
> (Ibid.: 367)

Of course, Veblen does not mean that academics are really priests, but that culturally speaking, they exhibit the habits of priests: "The learned class in all primitive communities are great sticklers for form, precedent, gradations of rank, ritual, ceremonial vestments, and learned paraphernalia generally" (ibid.: 367).

It cannot be denied that these ritualistic paraphernalia are just as strong in the present *fin de siècle* university setting: the cap and gown, matriculation, and graduation ceremonies, as well as the conferring of scholastic degrees, dignities, and prerogatives. Scholars argue among themselves very much along the lines of theologians debating the precise meaning of lines in sacred texts. Prestige is a vital component of academic advancement: One must graduate from the *right* universities, publish in the *right* journals, and circulate in the *right* academic circles. Academics are still notorious sticklers for form, and take up many pages in scholarly journals seemingly arguing about form much more than substance. Above all, academics are still involved in initiating their students into this world of forms, ceremonies, and ticklish paraphernalia. Woe to the student who writes a brilliant essay without citing sources in the approved format! Ditto to the student who achieves an empirical demonstration that does not use the latest statistical techniques. Even when academicians review each other's work, they typically harp on a picayune error.

Veblen regarded the content of academic learning as being useless overall. In his day, this involved the learning of dead languages – specifically, Latin and Greek – which conferred status upon the student who could master them, but little if any useful knowledge. In our day, universities demand more computer science and obsolete computer languages (like FORTRAN) than ever before, and many of my students complain that they will never use this knowledge again. Veblen depicts "higher learning in its best development, as the perfect flower of scholasticism and classicism, [and] a by-product of the priestly office and the life of leisure" (ibid.: 387).

However, Veblen believed that because the conservative attitude is generally considered honorific in modern societies, all innovation is regarded as vulgar. The institutions of higher learning *retard* the growth of knowledge much more than they promote it, at least according to Veblen:

> It has generally held true that the accredited learned class and the seminaries of the higher learning have looked askance at all innovation. New views, new departures in scientific theory, especially new departures which touch the theory of human relations at any point, have found a place in the scheme of the university tardily and by a reluctant tolerance, rather than by a cordial welcome; and the men who have occupied themselves with such efforts to widen the scope of human knowledge have not commonly been well received by their learned contemporaries.
>
> (Ibid.: 380)

Riesman (1953) has documented the many ways that Veblen acted in accordance with his criticisms of academic institutions. Veblen exhibited this hostility toward academia even in his writings, in which he does *not* cite sources or otherwise follow academic format. Riesman has also followed the spirit of Veblen's formulations to depict higher learning in America in unflattering terms as wasteful, geared toward consumerism, and egocentric.[2] The academic's first temptation is to dismiss Veblen's and Riesman's criticisms as satirical and overstated, and perhaps that is true to some extent. Contrary to Veblen, it is certain that *some* useful knowledge has emerged from the universities through the use of the scientific method. However, it is just as true that Veblen seems remarkably relevant to the contemporary crisis of higher education that concerns the general population and the intelligentsia alike. In recent years especially, the American public has been demanding accountability for the vast sums of public monies that have been spent on research. It is forcing university professors to justify why they enjoy high salaries and prestige while teaching only six hours per week in many cases.[3]

Veblen's cynicism regarding academic researchers resonates also with some recent scandals in academia, as well as a general sense of confusion regarding the scientific establishment. For example, consider the ongoing debate, and resulting scandal, between the National Institute of Health in the United States of America and the Pasteur Institute in France regarding the patent for discovering the AIDS virus. Much more than mere knowledge and the well-being of humankind are at stake. Prestige and vast sums of money – including royalty payments payable each and every time a blood sample is screened for the AIDS virus – are at the center of the controversy.

Or consider the impotence of scientists in trying to settle definitively a burning issue in American politics and popular culture: who really killed John F. Kennedy? In line with Baudrillard's claim that the video dictates reality, the American public was far more swayed by Oliver Stone's 1991 film *JFK* than the prestigious scientific commentary and conclusions reached by the Warren Commission and subsequent official investigations and commissions. It often seems true that Hollywood and Madison Avenue have taken over the domain that used to be ruled by science.

The postmodern public is confused by scientific claims that are contradicted by other scientific claims. It is told that DDT is safe, and then that it is not. Saccharin is safe, and then it causes cancer. The chemicals that are sprayed on fruits and vegetables cause and do not cause cancer, depending upon which team of scientists is believed. Ditto for the effects of smoking, alcohol, sugar, fats, paints, lead used in pipes, asbestos, and a host of other substances that the average person encounters in daily life. Is the ozone layer really being depleted? Scientists disagree on the answer. Are carbon emissions in the United States really harming the world's environment, or is that a ploy by the environmental lobbies? Are the rainforests in Brazil really the world's lungs? Are genetically engineered tomatoes really safe? The postmodernists give the advice that one should learn to be comfortable in the absence of certainty (Rosenau 1992). But this is much easier said than done, and is a cop-out in any case. For example, the students at my university are openly cynical concerning the once-sacrosanct claims of science. They tell me that they "go along" with our teaching so that they can get a good grade and fulfill their course requirements. They are fully aware of the ceremonial and prestigious functions of the university, and are not the slightest bit embarrassed to say so. In general, and in line with Veblen's predictions, postmodern students have become cynical credentials hustlers; the curriculum has become a wasteland of trivia and pseudo-scientific pretense; and professors have become entrepreneurs who sell their wares on the open market (Scott 1986).

Finally, the failure of the scientific establishment to deliver on some of the fantastic promises it has made in this century has contributed to a growing sentiment among the public that can be described as being anti-science. For example, from the invention of gunpowder to Reagan's "Star Wars" research, every major technological innovation in weapons was supposed to make further wars practically impossible.[4] But wars continue to be waged, and millions of people die from them. The birth control pill was supposed to solve the problem of overpopulation, but it clearly has not. The Green Revolution has not put a halt to world-wide deaths in the millions from malnutrition. Scientific breakthroughs cannot solve automatically the world's pressing social problems for the simple yet powerful reason that these are problems that involve human cultures. So long as the cultural backdrop and cultural reasons for war, overpopulation, nutrition and other phenomena are neglected, it is unlikely that pure science will save the world. Science retards action much more than it promotes it, because it leaves open the possibility that each and every finding can be superseded. To be effective in contributing to a humane world order, science must be made to fit in with other cultural endeavors. Some of the other reasons why the so-called empirical and scientific approaches are problematic have already been covered by C. Wright Mills (1959). Mills argued that the bureaucratic ethos has penetrated into the scientific domain such that the practice of science requires being associated with a research institution and large sums of money. But this means that modern scientists must now take on some of the functions of public relations executives, administrators, and businessmen. Research itself becomes a career. When this occurs, vitae must be padded, superiors must be placated, reputations must be maintained, and cliques are formed to continue the flow of money. Short-term research of limited, easily solved problems will be preferred to long-term research of intricate problems, because bureaucracies thrive on short-term results that lead to prestige. In the end, Mills concludes, vast sums of money will be spent on research that is relatively useless to humanity.[5] Veblen would depict such uselessness as a manifestation of barbarism in the civilized West.

A standard limitation to empirical methodology is cited by various philosophers of science as follows: facts cannot speak for themselves but require theory to lend meaning to the facts under discussion (Flew 1985; Gellner 1992; Trigg 1985). This means that from start to finish, *interpretation* of the facts and how they are manipulated statistically is crucial. For instance, with regard to the problem that concerns us, it is vitally important to determine whether there exists *one*, linear Western history that leads from primitive to modern societies, or several linear Western as well as non-Western histories (Spengler [1926] 1961, [1928] 1961), or several cyclical histories (Sorokin 1957), or perhaps some other alternative (Park and Burgess 1921; Schopenhauer [1813] 1899). But these are theoretical, philosophical, and ultimately cultural, not empirical issues.

The neo-Kantian assumptions of modern science prohibit the researcher from making any essentialist connection between two correlated variables. The relationship between the variables might be accidental or otherwise spurious. But no matter how refined the statistical techniques that are used to tease out the spurious factors, the end result is that ultimate causes may not be inferred. In general, Barry Smart (1992) is right to point out that an important aspect of the postmodern revolution is that the faith in science that used to be axiomatic has been shaken. Far from being neutral, twentieth-century science has been dominated by military needs, assumptions, and agendas; it has not lived up to its promises; it has thrived while basic literacy has declined; and it coexists with fundamentalist religious beliefs. For example, a 1991 Gallup Poll found that 48 per cent of Americans believe in the devil; 47 per cent agree that "God created man pretty much in his present form at one time within the last 10,000 years"; and 40 per cent agree that "man has developed over millions of years from less advanced forms of life, but God guided this process, including man's creation" (*New York Times*, 26 July 1992: E5). Similarly, an informal poll in my university classes suggests that most of my students believe in the biblical version of the origins of the universe over the scientific version.

I would add the following final doubt regarding the high status ascribed to so-called detached and objective scientific methodology. Detachment is compatible with sadism, so that the emotional coldness and neutrality that are essential to scientific work may actually be detrimental to humanity as a whole in the long run. Because modern science has been severed from culture since Descartes and Francis Bacon (Gellner 1992), the task of making scientific achievements genuinely useful to the world community and the world's cultures has been almost impossibly difficult. Of course, science and technology do result in useful knowledge with regard to the careers of scientists and even to some members of some social strata. Nevertheless, Veblen and Baudrillard seem to be right that huge segments of the world's population are written off – as if they "must exit" – and do not benefit from scientific breakthroughs. With these reservations in mind, let us proceed with an analysis of how one might test Veblen's bold hypothesis through the use of modern science.

PROGRESS, BARBARISM, AND EMPIRICISM

Pitirim Sorokin claims that "the highly literate, scientific, and technological twentieth century has been thus far the bloodiest, the most turbulent, and the most belligerent of all the twenty-five centuries of Western history" (1948: 39). Sorokin's empirical evidence for this claim might be construed as support for Veblen's thesis. Furthermore, it is typical of Sorokin's career-long critique of Western civilization and so-called progress. For example, Sorokin did not believe that democracy results in greater peace, but that the "most democratic century has proved to be the most belligerent and bloody" (ibid.: 10). He believed that he had disproved the hypothesis that free enterprise is "a sure antidote for war and a builder of peace" (ibid.: 25). Much like Veblen, he argued that the capitalist "spirit of mutual struggle rather than of mutual aid, the ethos of aggressiveness instead of love" leads to war (ibid.: 28). He noted that communism, fascism, and socialism were all touted as radical cures for war, but that they all resulted in genocide, war, and barbarism (ibid.: 35). All these assertions are in line with his overall theory that Western civilization is now in its death throes or what he calls its sensate phase (Sorokin 1957).

To be sure, Sorokin invokes empirical and notably statistical data to support his claim that "criminality, war, revolution, suicide, mental disease and impoverishment" are the symptoms and consequences of sensate crisis (1943: 204). For example, he collected data on "all the wars and revolutions of the Greco-Roman and Western cultures from about 500 BC to the present time" (ibid.: 212). "Taking for the measure of war the size of the casualty list per million of the corresponding population," Sorokin found that for Greece "in the fifth century BC the indicator of war magnitude is 29" whereas "when we come to the twentieth century, the indicator for the first quarter alone stands at 52" (ibid.: 213). A master of using multiple indicators, Sorokin also used the size of armies (ibid.: 215), the number of revolutions (ibid.: 217), suicide (ibid.: 224), and the brutality of punishments (227), among many other variables.

In each test, Sorokin proves his hypothesis to his satisfaction. But it is easy to question his data, methods, and conclusions. The most obvious objection is that early societies did not keep the sorts of records and "hard" data that are required for these sorts of analyses. And even when data are kept meticulously, as regarding suicide since the nineteenth century, for example, no final conclusions have satisfied all critics. For example, Jack Douglas's (1967) devastating critique of Durkheim's ([1897]

1951) and other studies of suicide centers on the proposition that the determination of suicide depends upon the opinions of coroners or other officials whether a given death is a homicide, suicide, accident, or natural death. Douglas concludes that so many variables are involved, the final determination is always suspect, so that he dismisses all quantitative studies of suicide.

Or take Sorokin's study of brutal punishment: he seeks to disprove the "common belief in the nineteenth century [that] as time goes on, the penalties for crime tend to become more and more humane" (1943: 227). His "proof" is "a comparative study of the barbaric and medieval penal codes of the Soviet, Nazi, and Fascist governments," which he regards as testimonials to an "upsurge of cruelty, bestiality, and inhumanity" (ibid.: 227). But again, the detached scientist could raise the possibility that the most cruel punishments were meted out precisely in societies that did not write cruel penal codes, so that the problem is insoluble. For example, the United States is generally regarded as a humane, democratic nation, yet it holds the dubious distinction of leading the Western world in the rate of incarcerating its citizens and executing them.

In contrast to Sorokin, Francis Fukuyama writes in *The End of History and the Last Man* that

> There is substantial empirical evidence from the past couple of hundred years that liberal democracies do not behave imperialistically toward one another, even if they are perfectly capable of going to war with states that are not democracies and do not share their fundamental values.
>
> (1992: xx)

Later he adds that "the fundamentally unwarlike character of liberal societies is evident in the extraordinarily peaceful relations they maintain among one another" (ibid.: 262). All this is part of Fukuyama's revival of George Wilhelm Friedrich Hegel's ([1899] 1965) philosophical claim that some portions of the world have achieved *the end of history*, by which they both meant the triumph of freedom and reason over the barbaric tendencies of the past. Note that Hegel argued that his native, nineteenth-century Germany was tending in this direction, whereas Fukuyama clearly feels that the twentieth-century United States has achieved it in fact. Fukuyama's "substantial empirical evidence" can be questioned easily on the basis of what countries are labeled as liberal democracies. It is true that Canada and the United States have not and probably will not go to war with each other. But the United States has waged plenty of wars on nations that called themselves democratic. And one could argue that Hitler was, in fact, elected democratically. After all, Fukuyama claims that "a country is democratic if it grants its people the right to choose their own government through periodic, secret-ballot, multi-party elections, on the basis of universal and equal adult suffrage" (1992: 43). In that case, one could argue that the war against the Nazis was not one against a non-democratic state, but a war between two democracies. Moreover, the USA would not qualify as a democracy until well into the present century, when women and African-Americans were finally allowed to vote, whereas the former Soviet Union had argued that it was more democratic than the USA, because it allowed all its citizens the right to vote.

Moreover, the way that Fukuyama poses the problem for empirical verification conveniently overlooks the warlike character of democratic nations toward all those who are demonized. If the world is divided between "we" (democratic) and "they" (all the rest), then Fukuyama and his disciples need not bother with counterexamples to the end of history thesis, such as the American bombing of civilians in Iraq during the 1991 Gulf War, the bombing of German cities during World War II, the extermination of Hiroshima and Nagasaki, or the saturation bombing of the North Vietnamese, among other similar instances of what might be termed war crimes (Riesman 1977). Note that Sorokin would count these events and their resultant casualties, but Fukuyama does not. But then, the empirical investigator holds enormous discretionary power in framing the research program.

One can conclude reasonably that like Veblen, Sorokin sought to indict all of Western civilization, whether or not it actually and directly participated in barbaric acts, by virtue of its vicarious participation, whereas Fukuyama exempts the USA and some other countries that he regards as liberal democracies from the barbarism of history. On purely empirical grounds, neither thinker is more convincing than the other. One's conclusions hinge on one's choice of data, methods, assumptions, and interpretive techniques.

BARBARISM TOWARD CHILDREN

Child abuse in its many manifestations, including the sexual abuse of children, has emerged as an important social problem in postmodern societies. Let us compare Durkheim and the positivists on this issue. It is a relevant topic for our discussion because modernists like to believe that their child-rearing practices are more civilized compared to their barbarian ancestors. Yet, Durkheim, like Veblen and Schopenhauer, believed that so-called civilized societies treat their children less humanely than did archaic societies. Can this difference of opinion be resolved empirically?

Anticipating defenders of the Enlightenment such as Norbert Elias (1982) – who claims that civilization softens the barbaric tendency toward physical violence – Durkheim arrives at the opposite conclusion: "The beginnings of culture were signalized by the appearance of corporal punishment," and, "in a word, civilization has necessarily somewhat darkened the child's life" ([1925] 1961: 189). Durkheim reviews punishment in so-called primitive societies, which he finds relatively mild (ibid.: 184–6), and the Middle Ages in Europe, where it was severe:[6] "The lash remained up to the middle of the eighteenth century the preferred instrument of correction" (ibid.: 187). In the *Evolution of Educational Thought* as well, Durkheim claims that "it was only in the sixteenth century, at the very moment when the Renaissance[7] was dawning, that the whip became a regular part of college life" ([1938] 1977: 157). Elaborating on harsh punishments, he adds, "one might almost say that they are the product of the modern era" (ibid.: 158). He asks: "How does it happen that the school, this seedbed of humane culture, has been, as if by some built-in necessity, a source of cruelty?" ([1925] 1961: 188).

He replies that "the make-up of the school is the source of the evil" (ibid.: 197). Teachers and students form two distinct worlds, and teachers consider themselves so vastly superior to their students, that their "megalomania" leads to violence. Durkheim sees the same danger in modern families, and cautions against "the abuses into which the civilized necessarily fall in their dealings with inferior societies" (ibid.: 197). (One thinks of the near-extermination of the Indians in America by European conquerors.)[8] Clearly, Durkheim does *not* believe that civilization, by itself, is a humanizing force. It must be self-consciously offset by the warm feelings of empathy (ibid.: 207). Durkheim offers something that seems to resemble a hypothesis that could be tested:

> Indeed, it seems that one is justified in seeing here a special case of a law, which might be stated this way: whenever two populations, two groups of people having unequal cultures come into continuous contact with one another, certain feelings develop that prompt the more civilized group – or that which deems itself such – to do violence to the other. This is currently the case in the colonies and countries of all kinds where representatives of European civilization find themselves involved with underdeveloped peoples. Although it is useless and involves grave dangers for those who abandon themselves to it, exposing them to formidable reprisals, this violence almost inevitably breaks out. Hence that kind of bloody foolhardiness that seizes the explorer in connection with races he deems inferior . . . A phenomenon of the same sort manifests itself in a civilized country whenever elders and young find themselves in continuous contact and associated in the same life.
>
> ([1925] 1961: 193)

Clearly, Durkheim is comparing the relationship between teachers and students, even parents and their children in a modern setting, to the relationship between colonial Europeans and the evils they inflicted on peoples that they considered inferior. It is a searing indictment. Illustrations of his interpretations are easy to find. Turning to contemporary America, one finds that corporal punishment is still permitted in most schools in the United States. In addition, hazing, harassment, and institutionalized violence of many sorts are encouraged in fraternities, sororities, sports teams, and other groups related to schools. Many schools in large American cities use metal detectors because even young children bring guns and other weapons to school, and often use them on their classmates and teachers. The murder rate in the United States is ten times what it is in Western Europe, and America is awash in fear of crime as well as horrifying statistics of assault, rape, and murder – especially among school-age children. Far from implementing a Durkheimian program to curb this national tragedy, American culture resorts to violence and harsh punish-ments to try to curb violence. America is also the world's largest supplier of weapons. America uses the imagery of violence to treat violence by declaring metaphorical *wars* on drugs, crime, AIDS, sexual abuse, and other social problems caused by violence. Yet, despite all this repression, official crime rates in America continue to climb, sexual abuse remains a potent issue, and unofficial violence is always a danger.

But can one prove or disprove Durkheim's hypothesis? The first, and most formidable, problem is one of obtaining good data. No reliable statistics on child abuse exist because it is not something that offenders are likely to report, and because it is difficult to define. At what point does "spanking" become child abuse? Durkheim was against all corporal punishment, but such is not the case in Western culture, which still permits spanking. Suppose that one relies on reports from victims, especially in cases of sexual abuse of children. Again, there is no certain way to preclude underreporting of this crime. Even when it is reported, the sensational trials that have sometimes followed often fail to convince the public that the guilty parties received a fair trial. For example, defense lawyers contend that children are often coached to say things that their parents want to charge against each other, or that children's fantasies are actually a cover for vicarious, and lewd, adult fantasies. This state of affairs is reminiscent of Freud's own wrestling with the reality versus fantasies of the alleged sexual seduction of his patients – a debate that continues among scholars of Freud to this day.

Nor is the problem of accurate data collection unique to child abuse. Criminologists contend that from rape to attemp-ted murder, they can never be certain of the validity of their data. Suppose that we bracket this problem, and move to the next one, correlations among variables. Whatever data is used, it is deemed noteworthy if it correlates mathematically with other variables, usually gender, social class, income, education, and race (among others, of course). Suppose that a study finds that men are more abusive of their children than women. Invariably, some other study will arrive at the opposite con-clusion, and still another study will question the mathematical techniques used in such studies. Typically, such studies end with a plea for further research, which is never conclusive. This is the neo-Kantian trap from which there is no exit: all findings are contingent and can be superseded at any time.

Suppose that one uses data from the Holocaust, especially Nazi crimes against children, to support Durkheim's hypothesis. One might argue that the Nazis suffered from megalomania relative to Jews and others they deemed inferior. But there are voices in postmodern culture who either question the data pertaining to the Holocaust, or deny outright that it ever occurred. Closer to our times, charges were levelled at the Serbs in 1992 for running death camps in Bosnia-Herzegovina that were reminiscent of the Nazi concentration camps. By some estimates, over half the victims in this brutal war were children. Again, eyewitness testimony existed, but it was discounted by the United States' State Department for being unreliable because it did not come from an "independent" source such as the International Red Cross (*New York Times*, 5 August 1992: A6). Yet, when such supposedly objective sources of information are admitted into discourse, they are subject to criticism from other sources and other points of view. For example, how can one expect inmates in death camps to give honest accounts of what they witnessed or experienced when such honesty might result in punishment, even death, after the objective researchers leave the camp?

Even the postmodern video image does not constitute hard data. When television crews gained access to one of the alleged death camps in Bosnia, the grisly images were disputed and rationalized by various sources such that, in the end, their meaning was not clear. Or consider the famous videotape of four Los Angeles policemen in the act of beating Rodney King that was broadcast throughout the world in 1991 and 1992. Despite the video evidence, the officers were acquitted. Ironically, the acquittal coincided with the worst race riots in the USA in this century. Strict Kantianism precludes concluding that the acquittal "caused" the riots.

In sum, contemporary science is unable to either prove or disprove conclusively Durkheim's hypothesis, or any other hypothesis. The contingency of meaning uncovered by Kant has matured into the fragmentation of meaning described by postmodernists. As a result, no method, fact, or interpretation is immune from criticism. Postmodern social life implies that persons are confronted daily with instances as well as media representations of various types of barbarism that are consumed vicariously if not directly, at the same time that one has been socialized to believe that twentieth-century humanity is more civilized than our ancestors.

ALTERNATIVE MEANINGS OF SCIENCE

The Cartesian, neo-Kantian, post-Humean, Enlightenment trajectory in science leads to the unwelcome conclusion that the scientist cannot find truth, only correlations and associations among phenomena that are contingent and susceptible to revision. Arthur Schopenhauer had exposed this limitation to science in his critique of Kant over a century ago:

> Science in the real sense, by which I understand systematic knowledge under the guidance of the principle of sufficient reason, can never reach a final goal or give an entirely satisfactory satisfaction. It never aims at the inmost nature of the world; it can never get beyond the representation; on the contrary, it really tells us nothing more than the relation of one representation to another.
>
> ([1818] 1969a: 28)

The epistemological poverty and bias of the modern scientific method stems from the fact that it sets an isolated researcher against the whole of culture in a vain effort to derive universally held truths based on neo-Kantian assumptions that are not up to the task. This is an unsatisfactory state of affairs. Moreover, science cannot speak for itself. It must refer to culture in order to obtain faith in its methods and findings. Because modern science took on this impossible goal of seeking universal truths independent of culture, it finds itself in the predicament of being out of touch with the general population, and reacting to that predicament by further entrenching itself in habits pertaining to the corporate and leisure classes (Mills 1959; Veblen [1899] 1967). Veblen's colleague from the previous *fin de siècle*, Emile Durkheim, presents an alternative view of science that is based on culture:

> A collective representation presents guarantees of objectivity by the fact that it is collective: for it is not without sufficient reason that it has been able to generalize and maintain itself

with persistence. If it were out of accord with the nature of things, it would never have been able to acquire an extended and prolonged empire over intellects. At bottom, the confidence inspired by scientific concepts is due to the fact that they can be methodically controlled. But a collective representation is necessarily submitted to a control that is repeated indefinitely; the men who accept it verify it by their own experience. Therefore, it could not be wholly inadequate for its subject. It is true that it may express this by means of imperfect symbols; *but scientific symbols themselves are never more than approximate.*

On the other hand, it is not at all true that concepts, even when constructed according to the rules of science, get their authority uniquely from their objective value. *It is not enough that they be true to be believed. If they are not in harmony with the other beliefs and opinions, or in a word, with the mass of the other collective representations, they will be denied; minds will be closed to them; consequently it will be as though they did not exist.* Today it is generally sufficient that they bear the stamp of science to receive a sort of privileged credit, because we have *faith in science. But this faith does not differ essentially from religious faith.*
(Durkheim [1912] 1965: 486; emphasis added)[9]

One might add that in the present *fin de siècle*, the privileged credit that science used to enjoy has run out, or at least that it is operating on a deficit. Not just religious fundamentalists, but ordinary middle-class university students today seem to agree that faith in science is not appreciably different from religious faith. But the most important aspect of Durkheim's characterization is that it illuminates a fruitful alternative way to apprehend Veblen's central claim that modern civilization is actually a latter-day barbarism.

From Durkheim's cultural perspective, one might summarize Veblen's position as follows: if we examine the totality of the habits or collective representations in modern culture as found in the family, government, corporations, religion, universities, and other social institutions, they tend to bespeak the persistence of barbaric traits from our past. Thus, we have followed Veblen's linkages between the middle-class high esteem for the manicured lawn as a throwback to the feudal pasture; government waste and inefficiency to the prestige associated with conspicuous waste; corporate piracy as a direct outgrowth of *bona fide* piracy; contemporary religiosity with the traditional association of the priestly functions with war; the pomp and circumstance of the modern university with the barbarian's penchant for pageantry and leisure; the continued abuse of women and children as essentially the male's property; and so on. Veblen's point seems to be that the cultural consistency of these and other barbaric throwbacks bespeaks a barbaric temperament that lies beneath the surface of cultivated manners, lawns, treatises, and ceremonies that characterize modern life. Because Veblen's focus is on the cultural *habit*, not the *event* studied by positivists, he is not concerned with establishing a direct causal link between specific barbaric behaviors and other specific barbaric consequences. We have seen that such studies cannot move beyond neo-Kantian contingencies and associations between variables. Rather, his point seems to be that the persistence of the barbaric temperament is in harmony with the persistence of gnawing social problems that the modernist project has not been able to control, among them, drugs, crime, violence, the dissolution of the family, infinite consumption, the destruction of the environment, and continual wars, among others.

The modernists and the positivists, on the other hand, would have us believe that the modern society is a rational, self-sustaining system that promotes social order (Parsons 1937). They admit that deviance exists, but they attribute the deviance to small subcultures, not the core of society, and they claim that the "right" technique of social engineering will finally bring the deviants under control. Never mind that these promises seem as hollow as the promises made by politicians that peace and prosperity are just around the proverbial corner. From Durkheim's and Veblen's perspectives, the major objection to modernist claims is that they are out of synch with the rest of culture. When the average citizen experiences daily fear of becoming a victim of crime, losing his or her pension to government or corporate mismanagement, or passing on a world and family life to his or her children that is much worse than today, then the promises made by modernists will simply not be believed. Hence, the cynical postmodern rebellion against the narratives and legacies of the Enlightenment that has been documented by scores of contemporary writers.[10]

However, I have stressed all along that Veblen, Durkheim, and their *fin de siècle* contemporaries were not just pessimists in the usual, contemporary sense of the term. They believed that along with the barbaric temperament there persist vestiges of a benign temperament as well. Veblen referred to habits left over from a matriarchal culture that he felt preceded the onset of barbarism (Riesman 1953). Durkheim felt that altruism is the other side of human nature, and is a compulsion every bit as powerful as barbaric egoism. But I cannot repeat often enough that they were against the neo-Kantian, rational, systematization of these benign traits. The moment that one tries to systematize compassion into socialism, for example, one has converted a benign trait into its opposite. This is because, according to Durkheim, any time we act from duty, fear, or any sort of compulsion, we are really acting on the basis of egoistic self-interest, which is the basis for barbarism. Durkheim claims over and over again in his writings that genuine human goodness must be sought spontaneously, for its own sake. Spengler concurs: "In spite of its foreground appearances, ethical socialism is *not* a system of compassion, humanity, peace and kindly care, but one of will-to-power. Any other reading of it is illusory" ([1926] 1961: 361). But here we arrive at the classical, Western problem of good and evil, refracted in writings from Plato to Christian dogma: If virtue cannot be taught, how can it be instilled?

We shall not rush headlong into a neat and tidy solution to this problem that has plagued humanity for centuries. The problem may well be insoluble. The important point, for our purposes in this chapter, is that Veblen's and Durkheim's depiction of the problem of human good and evil is commensurate and in harmony with the broad outlines of what passes for cultural wisdom in the West as refracted in the writings that it holds in highest esteem, from the Bible to books by Plato and Freud. It is this harmony with the rest of Western culture that makes Veblen's assertion seem convincing, not the impotent positivistic program of proving hypotheses false. A distressing corollary follows as well: The positivistic program and the Enlightenment project on which it is based are an aberration in Western cultural development. We agree with Gellner (1992)[11] and others who locate the modernist project in a specific culture peculiar to Northern European Protestants from the seventeenth and eighteenth centuries. There is no good reason to believe the delusion that the cultural assumptions of this small group should hold good for all time and for all humanity. Thus, we move on in our search for cultural referents in the present discussion.

Chapter 3

Barbarism and the idea of progress

> The peculiarities of sociology may be understood as distortions of one or more of its traditional tendencies.
>
> (C. Wright Mills 1959: 24)

"It seems incredible that there should have been a time when mankind had no conception of progress," Park and Burgess (1921: 953) write in the world's first sociology textbook. Instead of the idea of progress, the ideas of providence, fate, nemesis, and deterioration ruled humanity's cultural world-views up until the eighteenth century. Herbert Spencer, Henri de Saint-Simon, Auguste Comte, Immanuel Kant, G.W.F. Hegel, Descartes, Condorcet, Leibniz and the Enlightenment *philosophes* began writing about progress in earnest, but their rule over intellectual life was short-lived. In the previous *fin de siècle*, in which Veblen wrote, the idea of progress was already under attack. Park and Burgess summarize aptly some of these criticisms:

> Progress, in so far as it makes the world more comfortable, makes it more complicated. Every new mechanical device, every advance in business organization or in science, which makes the world more tolerable for most of us, makes it impossible for others.
>
> (1921: 954)

To the inferior, incompetent, and unfortunate, unable to keep pace with progress, the more rapid advance of the world means disease, despair, and death. In medicine and surgery alone does progress seem wholly beneficent, but the eugenists are even now warning us that our indiscriminate efforts to protect the weak and preserve the incompetent are increasing the burdens of the superior and competent, who are alone fit to live.

(Ibid.: 955)

Just as the human body generates the poisons that eventually destroy it, so the communal life, in the very process of growth and as a result of its efforts to meet the changes that its growth involves, creates diseases and vices which tend to destroy the community.

(Ibid.: 957)

The connotations of the term *fin de siècle* carry these and other meanings of a perfumed decadence, hectic decay, and effervescent corruption (Grunwald 1992). Although it was given its name by Auguste Comte, sociology lay dormant after the eighteenth century, and was reborn at the turn of the previous century in a mood of criticizing the alleged fruits of progress, as exemplified by the works of Emile Durkheim, Thorstein Veblen, Georg Simmel, Ferdinand Tönnies, and Max Weber. Park and Burgess are right to claim that the conception of progress is a "superstition [of] recent origin" and that, "it was not until the eighteenth century that it gained general acceptance and became part of . . . popular religion" (1921: 960).

More incredible than the sudden eruption of the concept of progress is its current revival in postmodern America and Western Europe. Francis Fukuyama (1992) revived Hegel's concept of *the end of history*, by which Fukuyama means the alleged triumph of liberal democracy over totalitarianism, imperialism, and other forces inimical to the long-awaited establishment of complete freedom and rationality in the world. A quick survey of the globe suggests that Hegel and Fukuyama simply fail to account for the reality of modern-day totalitarianisms, Serbia's current imperialist war against its neighbors, and ethnic conflict that hit as close to home as the Los Angeles riots of 1992, among many other events that contradict the claims for an end of history. Auguste Comte is hailed as the founder of sociology in contemporary sociology textbooks, even though that is a debatable point. Comte invented the term sociology, but Durkheim ([1928] 1958, [1925] 1961) criticized him, along with Rousseau, Descartes, and Saint-Simon for promoting an oversimplified rationalism that could not sustain genuine sociology. Durkheim's *fin de siècle* colleagues in sociology have been sanitized by Parsons (1937) and others who misrepresent them as disciples of Comte and Hegel rather than the *fin de siècle* critics of the Enlightenment that they were. We have suggested in the previous chapter that this issue – whether sociology is a narrative typical of the Enlightenment or of the previous *fin de siècle* spirit – as all other issues, cannot be resolved neatly through the use of the empirical method. Empiricism is part of the Enlightenment and its attendant ideas, including progress. To be sure, many books and articles exist that argue for and against the influence of the Enlightenment versus the previous *fin de siècle*. But in the end, it comes down to interpretation and judgment. In this, as in other regards, the facts do not and cannot speak for themselves.

Of course, the central issue for our purposes here is the idea that progress entails a lessening of the barbaric propensity in the human animal. Central to the modern idea of progress is the belief that the human animal has established "control over external nature and over himself" (Park and Burgess 1921: 958). This control is supposed to extend to the barbaric, violent, and other anti-social tendencies. I agree with Park and Burgess that belief in the idea that progress can tame the human animal "is an act of faith" (ibid.: 959). It cannot be proved or disproved empirically. If we point to high rates of murder, rape, assault, and carnage in so-called progressive societies, the proponents of progress will claim that the *right* forms of social control have not been used, and that progress is right around the proverbial corner.

In *Modernity and Ambivalence,* Zygmunt Bauman (1991) attacks precisely this ambivalent aspect of the modernist notion of control. Bauman argues that modernity originated in the eighteenth century and has been guided by the spirit of imposing intellectual, social, and political order onto perceived chaos. Modern culture in all its aspects – political, sociological, philosophical, and otherwise – aims to *conquer Nature* and subordinate it to human needs. "Anything that spoils the order, the harmony, the design, and thus refuses purpose and meaning, is Nature" (ibid.: 40). Bauman likens the ideal type modernist to a gardener who tries to grow only sweet plants while he or she poisons, roots out, and otherwise destroys the weeds (ibid.: 30–9). Hence, modernity leads to extreme intolerance, including genocide. In this work, as well as *Modernity and the Holocaust* (1989), Bauman is right to link the modernist dream of progress through rational control to efforts to eliminate Jews, Gypsies, other minorities that came to be regarded as "weeds" in the modernist garden.[1]

Bauman admits that the central problems in his books are "firmly rooted in the propositions first articulated by Adorno and Horkheimer in their critique of Enlightenment" (1991: 17). Yet like his predecessors, Bauman ends his books on the hopeful note that the postmodern rebellion against modernity will finally produce what the Enlightenment could not: tolerance, coexistence, human choice, and the celebration of human diversity. This is a fond hope, and nothing more.

This is because postmodernity may *extend* modernist barbarism much more than rebel against it – we have observed this with regard to Baudrillard's writings. Moreover, why would tolerance suddenly replace the modernist quest to control Nature, which is still strong? Such a change would entail a moral revolution of the highest order. For such a revolution to occur, one should be able to point to cultural roots of tolerance, kindliness, compassion, and other peaceable traits. This is a worthwhile endeavor, yet its absence is conspicuous in the current postmodernist discourse.

THE AMBIVALENCE WITHIN CRITICAL THEORY

Except for the Jungians, perhaps the only twentieth-century thinkers who kept the anti-Enlightenment spirit of the previous *fin de siècle* alive in any sort of systematic form were the critical theorists. For example, in their controversial *Dialectic of Enlightenment*, Horkheimer and Adorno posited (1972) that enlightenment contains within itself opposing tendencies, benign as well as highly destructive, that are exacerbated by progress. Along with other critical theorists, they assume that highly democratic, liberal, modern, and otherwise civilized cultures are capable of extreme barbarism. Jürgen Habermas is often referred to as the successor to the tradition of the critical theorists, yet he disagrees with his predecessors precisely on the connection between barbarism and Enlightenment. Habermas (1987) stands for the optimistic doctrine that the Enlightenment "project" (as he calls it) must be completed despite the serious objections raised by Horkheimer, Adorno, the other critical theorists, and lately, Zygmunt Bauman (1987, 1989, 1991).

Despite the fact that *Dialectic of Enlightenment* is well-known, it is controversial, and still poorly understood. Some of this misunderstanding stems from the very difficult philosophy inherent in the work, and some of it may be due to the unhappy union between Adorno and Horkheimer – and the incompatible assumptions that they held. Adorno was partial to Hegel and Marx (Freedman and Lazarus 1988), whom Horkheimer (1978) criticized, while Horkheimer (1980) admired Schopenhauer (Estrada 1988; Korthals 1985), whom Adorno (1991) criticized (Jay 1982). The problem is that Hegel and Schopenhauer stand for diametrically opposed doctrines regarding progress, rationality, history, and modernity (Tertulian and Parent 1985). They simply cannot coexist in the same theoretical matrix without producing contradictions. The result has been that critical theory can be read as an impossible hodgepodge of Marx, Hegel, Schopenhauer, Kant, Freud, Nietzsche, and other thinkers who were for *and* against progress, Hegelian ideas on the end of history, the Enlightenment, and utopian visions of social order.[2] Because of this intellectual confusion, critical theory has been criticized severely, and at present, is mostly passé.

Let me make it clear that given the strong stand taken on behalf of cultural interpretation in this work, I am not referring to the aforementioned philosophers as philosophers *per se.* Rather, every one of them is part of a *cultural nexus* that inspired their works in the first place, that made them objectionable or acceptable to a wider audience, and that makes their works relevant due to affinities with the cultural problems and diversity of our contemporary times. And, one should keep in mind Veblen's ([1915] 1964) jarring explanation for the preeminence of Germany in philosophy: philosophy is a luxury that involves thinking about thinking, and such luxuries are highly valued in barbaric cultures.

For example, Arthur Schopenhauer's *The World as Will and Representation* was published in 1818 in a time and place that were nurtured by Romanticism in opposition to French and British concerns with civilized progress. Outside Germany, Schopenhauer wrote against the tide of the times in which he lived, which were still inspired by Enlightenment assumptions concerning progress, so that he was practically ignored until his death. Even within Germany, Schopenhauer's arch-rival, G.W.F. Hegel, basked in the sunshine of the glory that Schopenhauer felt should have been his (Luft 1988, Magee 1983). It was not until the 1890s that the *fin de siècle* rebellion against the Enlightenment reached its zenith, and Hegel was forgotten just as suddenly as Schopenhauer's posthumous writings were discovered. Hegel was revived again by the Bolsheviks, and kept alive by Kojeve's (1969) lectures in France between the wars. With the end of the cold war and the resulting euphoria in the United States, Fukuyama (1992) revived Hegel once again. Schopenhauer was all but forgotten again except for Max Horkheimer (1980), although he is enjoying another, much smaller wave of revival in the present *fin de siècle*.[3] The important point is that we are proposing a cultural reading of these philosophers and their significance for the sociological issues being discussed.

Similarly, I have no intentions of reviving critical theory or rescuing it from its critics. Rather, my intent is to sort out critical theory's philosophical ingredients in the cultural sense discussed above, and to analyze the implications of casting one's lot with Hegel versus Schopenhauer. This will set the stage for a reconstituted critical theory that can explain barbarism in the midst of modernity, and that might point to its resolution in the future.

Why Hegel and Schopenhauer, and not Kant, Nietzsche or some other philosopher from the time-periods and cultures being discussed? These other philosophers are important, and can and should be compared and contrasted as well. But in the interest of space, we shall focus on Schopenhauer's rebellion against Hegel because their opposition is dramatic. Hegel was the grand optimist who thought he had seized upon a plan in history that tended toward progress. Schopenhauer believed the exact opposite, that Nature is chaos and only chaos, and that there is no plan to it whatsoever.

What needs to be emphasized is that Hegel and Schopenhauer were rivals in the strongest possible terms, from the cultural perspectives that each represented to personal dispositions. This is because Schopenhauer, in direct opposition to Hegel, taught that the heart is stronger and more important than the mind glorified by the Enlightenment. In fact, Schopenhauer did not hide his great personal contempt for Hegel. For example, Schopenhauer often referred to "that miserable Hegelism, that school of dullness, that center of stupidity and ignorance, that mind-destroying, spurious wisdom" ([1818] 1969b: 616). Unlike Hegel, Schopenhauer taught that the State could never be trusted to make persons moral, only to punish lawbreakers. Contrary to Hegel, Schopenhauer insisted that the individual person is far more important than the State. Schopenhauer took seriously the ethical message preached by all the world's major religions, that the essence of morality is *empathy*, derived from the heart, not egoism derived from the mind and glorified by the Hegelian State. Schopenhauer concluded that utopia could never be reached, and that history would never come to an end. Instead, human evil and irrationality would have to be managed within tolerable limits, because they could never be eliminated completely.

The critical theorists drew upon these and various other refractions of the polemic between Hegel and Schopenhauer, even if they did not always refer to it directly. For example, Erich Fromm (1962) was an important critical theorist who tried to depict both Freud and Marx as disciples of Hegel who tried to liberate humanity from "the chains of illusions" into a more rational state.[4] That is certainly a legitimate way to read Freud and Marx, although one could just as easily note Freud's own contempt for Marx, and account for Schopenhauer's influence on Freud versus Hegel's influence on Marx (Ellenberger 1970). For Schopenhauer, the will (formerly Kant's "thing-in-itself") and mind glorified by the Enlightenment exist as an antagonistic unity, but the heart or will holds the upper hand. Hegel assumes the very opposite in his elaboration of Kant. This means that for Schopenhauer, the will is the ground for enlightenment and its fruits (rationality, the mind, abstraction), and that heightened enlightenment must necessarily inflame the ruthless will, resulting in greater barbarism as humanity "progresses." But for the Hegelians, Marxists, and other modernists, progress entails the gradual control by the mind over the ruthless will.

The polemic between Hegel and Schopenhauer is important in our *fin de siècle*, now that communism, regarded as one version of the Marxist, Hegelian dream, has crumbled in the former Soviet Union and Eastern Europe. As noted by Bauman

(1992: 222), communism was a modernist doctrine, *and it failed.* Its failure should make one ponder the fate of the Marxist and Hegelian versions of modernity in Western nations. Is the West moving toward greater freedom, as predicted by Hegel, or greater barbarism, as predicted by Schopenhauer? This is the key issue. But because the critical theorists tried to fuse Hegel's with Schopenhauer's influence, they were never able to reconcile their Marxist and Hegelian quests for liberation with their Freudian and Schopenhauerian critiques of mass conformity and mass barbarism in modern nations.

SCHOPENHAUER AS THE TEACHER FOR MODERN TIMES

In the remainder of this chapter, we shall pay less attention to Hegel for the simple reason that Francis Fukuyama (1992) has already made a strong case for using Hegel's philosophy as the blueprint for the alleged triumph of liberal democracy in the modernist project. It is more important, for the sake of balance, to highlight Max Horkheimer's opinion that "Schopenhauer is the teacher for modern times" (1980: 32).[5] This is because Schopenhauer's doctrine of "blind will as an eternal force removes from the world the treacherous gold foil which the old metaphysics had given it" (ibid.: 32). Schopenhauer does not promise that tolerance, justice, or kindness are supposed to flow from an enlightened social order, and he began exposing these Enlightenment narratives as hypocrisies long before postmodernists began their purported, albeit confused, rebellion. In this regard, Horkheimer is correct to conclude that "Schopenhauer's thinking is infinitely modern," in the sense that he predicted the fragmentation of meaning that would result from the disruption of social order caused by the enlightened will. Schopenhauer anticipated the Frankfurt School when he criticized the positivistic tendency to treat serious thought as business, as well as the postmodern short-circuit that one need not worry about philosophic truth. Horkheimer praises Schopenhauer for teaching that the individual can try to cut through Enlightenment hypocrisies and practice, as far as he or she is able in private life, and try to imitate the saints and genuine artists through self-abnegation and asceticism. But for Schopenhauer, as for Horkheimer, there can be no saintly mass society, and no plan for social engineering that will eliminate barbarism. Schopenhauer taught, and Horkheimer apparently concurs, that virtue cannot be taught.

There can be no doubt that Horkheimer was influenced by this Schopenhauerian "solution" to the problem of human wickedness, even if Adorno (1991) was not. For example, Horkheimer writes:

> As to poverty and slavery, he [Schopenhauer] says in *Parerga*, "The fundamental difference is that slaves owe their origin to violence; the poor, to cunning." The reason for this perverted state of society, he continues, for "the general struggle to escape misery, for sea-faring that costs so many lives, for complicated trade interests, and finally for the wars resulting from all this," is at bottom greediness for that superabundance which does not even make men happy." At the same time, *such barbarism cannot be abolished, for it is the reverse side of refinement, an element of civilization.* Schopenhauer did not remain behind the sociological knowledge of his day.
>
> (1980: 24; emphasis added)

Schopenhauer influenced Horkheimer more deeply than Adorno, who tended to draw on Marx and Hegel, and this fact needs to be included in analyses of the implicit tensions found in critical theory (see Jay 1982).[6] Imagine how different Horkheimer's version of critical theory might have been without the influence of Marx and Adorno. Marx's Hegelian optimism is incompatible with Schopenhauer's pessimism, so that the particular blend of Freud, Marx, and German philosophy that went into critical theory was ill-fated from the start. We shall elaborate on this implicit contradiction in subsequent chapters. For now, we wish to plant the seed of a reconstituted critical theory that would involve the blend of Freud, Durkheim, Veblen, and Schopenhauer's pessimistic version of German philosophy.

Nietzsche, who is frequently cited by critical theorists as well as postmodernists, describes his first encounter with Schopenhauer's writings:

> I am one of those readers of Schopenhauer who when they have read one page of him know for certain they will go on to

read all the pages and will pay heed to every word he ever said. I trusted him at once and my trust is the same now as it was nine years ago. Though this is a foolish and immodest way of putting it, I understand him as though it were for me he had written ... And, to say without more ado the highest thing I can say in regard to his style, I cannot do better than quote a sentence of his own: "a philosopher must be very honest not to call poetry or rhetoric to his aid." That there is something called honesty and that it is even a virtue belongs, I know, in the age of public opinion to the private opinions that are forbidden; and thus I shall not be praising Schopenhauer but only characterizing him if I repeat: he is honest even as a writer; and so few writers are honest that one ought really to mistrust anyone who writes ... That such a man wrote has truly augmented the joy of living on this earth. Since getting to know this freest and mightiest of souls, I at least have come to feel what he felt about Plutarch: "as soon as I glance at him I grow a leg or a wing." If I were set the task, I could endure to make myself at home in the world with him.

([1874] 1983: 133)

Nietzsche could hardly contain himself in expressing his "joy and amazement" at having discovered Schopenhauer. He found the same pessimistic appraisal and the same humble "solution" to the problem of human evil that impressed Horkheimer. But contrary to many depictions of Nietzsche as well as Schopenhauer as nihilists, Nietzsche found a humanity, a genuinely moral project to pursue in Schopenhauer's philosophy:

Here I have arrived at an answer to the question whether it is possible to pursue the great ideal of the Schopenhauerian man by means of a practical activity. One thing above all is certain: these new duties are not the duties of a solitary; on the contrary, they set one in the midst of a mighty community held together, not by external forms and regulations, but by a fundamental idea. It is the fundamental idea of *culture*, insofar as it sets for each one of us by task: *to promote the production of the philosopher, the artist and the saint within us and without us and thereby to work at the perfecting of nature.*

(Ibid.: 160; emphasis in text)

Later in his career, Nietzsche turned on his master with a

vengeance, particularly on the issue of compassion. However, certain Schopenhauerian assumptions continued to permeate Nietzsche's works, and these need to be acknowledged (see Copleston 1980). The most important affinity is the concern by both philosophers with maintaining the mind–heart distinction as a dialectical unity. In other words, both Schopenhauer and Nietzsche were involved in a deep-seated polemic against Kant's and Hegel's reductions of the knowable world to mere phenomena. Postmodernists in particular, have neglected this Schopenhauerian element in Nietzsche's philosophy, even though they purport to be inspired by him in part.

Thomas Mann elaborates on the probable reason why Schopenhauer had such a powerful effect on Horkheimer and Nietzsche: "The history of Schopenhauerian thought goes back to the sources of the life of thought in our Western world, whence issue European science and European art, and in which the two are still one. It goes back to Plato" (1939: 2). Mann makes one aware of the possibility that Schopenhauer offers a crystallized and refined version of the resumé of wisdom as well as evil found in Western culture.

This is because Schopenhauer regarded enlightenment in general as nothing more than a survival technique that arises out of the defenseless human animal's "will to life" (Nietzsche agreed). It is a conceit to regard enlightenment as something that sets humans apart from animals or the rest of Nature. Thus, even enlightened, so-called civilized humans are subject to the same will to life that can be perceived in the Universe, and its results include not only the modern world order, but also unrest, the incessant striving for something new after every achievement, want, craving, demand, and suffering. Because Schopenhauer unmasked the brutal struggle for existence beneath the facade of civilization, Mann regards him as the "father of all modern psychology" (ibid.: 28). Schopenhauer influenced Nietzsche, Freud,[7] and all *fin de siècle* thinkers who pursued the unconscious: "Nietzsche's anti-socratism and hostility to mind are nothing but the philosophic affirmation and glorification of Schopenhauer's discovery of the primacy of the will" (ibid.: 28).

Even though one is used to linking hostility to the mind with barbarism, Mann insists that Schopenhauer was a humanist. This is because Schopenhauer taught that barbarism is part of the human condition, a permanent disposition that connects humans with animal nature, and that can be controlled within barely tolerable limits through insight and asceticism, but that explodes when it is denied. A similar formula found its way into Jung's explanation of civilized evil (see Stevens 1983, 1989).[8] Anticipating Bauman's (1989) analysis of the Holocaust as the natural result of the modernity project, Mann concludes his essay with a penetrating insight into Nazism and its aftermath:

> The twentieth century has in its first third taken up a position of reaction against classical rationalism and intellectualism. It has surrendered to admiration of the unconscious, to a glorification of instinct, which it thinks is overdue to life. And the bad instincts have accordingly been enjoying a heyday. We have seen instead of pessimistic conviction deliberate malice. Intellectual recognition of bitter truth turns into hatred and contempt for mind itself. Man has greedily flung himself on the side of "life" – that is, on the side of the stronger – for there is no disputing the fact that life has nothing to fear from mind, that not life but knowledge, or rather, mind, is the weaker part and one more needing protection on this earth. Yet the anti-humanity of our day is a humane experiment too in its way. It is a one-sided answer to the eternal question as to the nature and destiny of man. We palpably need a corrective to restore the balance, and I think the philosophy I here evoke can do good service. I spoke of Schopenhauer as modern. I might have called him a futurist . . . What I called his pessimistic humanity, seems to me to herald the temper of a future time. Once he was fashionable and famous, then half-forgotten. But his philosophy may still exert a ripe and humanizing influence upon our age. His intellectual sensitivity, his teaching, which was life, that knowledge, thought and philosophy are not matters of the head alone but of the whole man, heart and sense, body and soul; in other words, his existence as an artist may help to bring to birth a new humanity of which we stand in need, and to which they are akin: a humanity above dry reason on the one hand and idolatry of instinct on the other.
>
> (1939: 29)

Simmel, Tolstoi, Hardy, Freud, and many other illustrious thinkers from the previous *fin de siècle* join Horkheimer,

Nietzsche, and Mann in their praise for Schopenhauer's rebellion against Kant and Hegel, and in pointing to Schopenhauer's philosophy as a viable alternative to neo-Kantian social order and its end-point, postmodern nihilism (see Magee 1983). Without delving further into their tributes at this point in the discussion, it is evident that we have found a philosopher who is relatively neglected today but who evoked heartfelt emotion and faith from thinkers who are still esteemed greatly. This fact, alone, is worthy of notice.

The key point is that Schopenhauer dared to rebel against Kant and Hegel. By contrast, neither the modernity project nor the postmodern rebellion at this project evoke any faith or inspiration, because they maintain discourse on a neo-Kantian plane. Consider Habermas's (1970, 1979, 1984) dutiful and uninspiring resolve that despite all the charges levelled at the Enlightenment project by Horkheimer and Adorno, the Enlightenment project must be completed. One is compelled to ask – why? Similarly, Lyotard, Baudrillard, Derrida and the other postmodernists really add nothing new to the same, old and problematic, fragmented universe of appearances created by Kant. They merely take Kantianism to its logical and Hegelian conclusion: the end of culture, history and philosophy.

The system left by Kant and taken up by Hegel seems stale when perceived against the backdrop of our turbulent *fin de siècle*. Kant restricted scientific endeavors to finding relationships among phenomena in relation to time, space, and causality, but forbade absolutely any attempts to grasp essences, absolutes, or anything as permanent as truth. All the effort exerted by positivists in finding relationships among phenomena amount to little, in the final analysis, because they are meant to support the dismal conclusion that the world is contingent, and that all findings can be superseded by the discovery of new relationships. But if that is true, then how should one feel inspired by Hegel ([1899] 1965) or Fukuyama's (1992) re-reading of Hegel that liberal democracy is the "right" system of government? If one is to be true to the Kantian assumptions that inspired Hegel, then the conclusion that liberal democracy is superior to all other forms of government is equally contingent, peculiar to some nations that partake in so-called Western culture, and can be superseded.

In the moral realm, Kant established a rationalistic ethics

that focuses on obeisance to moral rules and the performance of moral actions whose morality can never be proven or ascertained with certainty. True, Kant's legacy "lives" on in mainstream positivistic sociology, and in the works of the rational moralists, from Piaget (1926, [1932] 1965) to Kohlberg (1981). And Hegel's worship of human rationality continues to inspire these same university academics. But who *really* believes that because modern persons are more rational than their ancestors, they are more moral?

Schopenhauer (1970, 1985) had already challenged Kant on epistemological, metaphysical, and ethical grounds. For Schopenhauer, morality consists in being a certain type of person, possessing a certain type of character, exhibiting particular sorts of *habits* (Atwell 1990). Compassion (but not pity or charity),[9] is the distinguishing mark of moral goodness. Character is the ground for moral action. The focus on what a person *is* – not the Kantian, what a person *does*, nor the Hegelian State control of the individual, nor the postmodernist, what a person *appears* to do – binds Schopenhauer to moral teachings that the world recognizes instantly, from Buddhist to Christian. After all, in all the centuries that Christianity ruled Western culture, no one held it against Jesus that his worldly achievements were minimal, that he did not hold a college degree, or that he possessed minimal prestige (from Veblen). Can one imagine Jesus giving a TV press conference, in the style envisaged by Baudrillard? Schopenhauer's vision breathes life into Veblen, Durkheim, Freud, and other great scientific moralists from the previous century, because all of them were concerned with good versus evil character, not the alleged control of behavior by Kantian duty or the Hegelian State that could never be justified with any degree of finality in a contingent world.

Consider the contemporary relevance of this debate. Ever since the so-called Reagan Revolution, the United States has been moving steadily to the political Right. As of this writing, the United States incarcerates more of its citizens per capita than any other nation on earth, and is the world's biggest arms dealer. But in 1992, the crime rates went up despite all this State control, and this led to calls for more State control. What the politicians (as well as many intellectuals) fail to see is that society cannot exist solely on the basis of social control. No amount of policing can act as a substitute for the spontaneous goodwill that makes citizens *want* to obey the law and preserve the social order.[10] But it is Schopenhauer, not Kant or Hegel, who accounts for the presence of this spontaneous moral goodness that offsets barbarism.

Quite apart from the fact that Schopenhauer's philosophy seems to encapsulate Western wisdom prior to Kant and Hegel, it has an immediate appeal. Simply contrast the Kantian and Hegelian belief that morality consists of and can be known only as moral behavior, or good appearances – still a widely held belief in contemporary universities – with Schopenhauer's penetrating insight that

> A man can go to work rationally and thus thoughtfully, deliberately, consistently, systematically, and methodically, and yet act upon the most selfish, unjust, and even iniquitous maxims. Hence it never occurred to anyone *prior* to Kant to identify just, virtuous, and noble conduct with *reasonable* or *rational*, but the two have been clearly distinguished and kept apart ... Reasonable and vicious are quite consistent with each other, and in fact, only through their union are great and far-reaching crimes possible. In the same way unreasonable and noble-minded can very well coexist.
>
> (Schopenhauer [1841] 1965: 83)

It is easy to see why Mann (1939) would insist that Schopenhauer speaks directly to all of us. Everyone knows that evil intentions are easy to hide beneath a facade of rational duty. If this were not the case, one would not witness looting and a general return to barbarism whenever a long power outage occurs, and the police are not called out immediately to contain the emergence of human wickedness. One should add the postmodernist twist that such looting was televised live during the Los Angeles riots in 1992: Americans were treated to non-rehearsed barbarism, and one should add, compassion as well. And when one thinks of the most far-reaching crimes in this century, like the Holocaust, one has to admit that Nazi extermination was carried out in a most rational manner – organized, professional, and scrupulously mindful of appearances – and that it occurred in one of the most enlightened and reasonable nations in the world at that time (Bauman 1989, 1990). In sum, there exist good intuitive reasons to pursue Schopenhauer's lead, and to try to find an alternative in explaining human barbarism that goes beyond modernist hypocrisy, the call for still more State control, and postmodern nihilism.

It is necessary to reassure the reader that in reviving Schopenhauer, Nietzsche, Horkheimer, and Adorno, I am not advocating a vulgar, neoconservative version of essentialist thinking. In no way would Schopenhauer agree with the us–them distinction that is the basis of the conservative solution to criminals and other evil persons, to segregate and punish *them*, treat *them* as outcasts who are fundamentally different from so-called respectable persons.[11] Schopenhauer taught the exact opposite: The wise person and the saint realize that there exists a commonality between "us and them," because we all share the same will to life. This is what he meant by compassion, the realization of co-suffering, and co-responsibility in human evil. For this reason, the cynical Schopenhauer praised the Christian doctrine of original sin as a profound piece of cultural wisdom. Again, to try to appreciate Schopenhauer in this regard is not to advocate a vulgar version of neoconservative Christian ethics, which is often pugnacious and punitive, and which worships a militant Jesus who battles Satan for supremacy of the world. Rather, Schopenhauer, as well as Veblen, Durkheim, and many of the other founding fathers of sociology regarded the focus on self-abnegation and compassion as the kernel of Christian morals as cultural artifacts or habits that are essential to understanding the other side of the barbarism within Western culture (Hall 1987; Riesman 1953). But, it should be added that Schopenhauer felt that this kernel of Christian wisdom is to be found in Buddhist and Hindu traditions as well. In other words, we shall be striving to uncover the pessimistic humanism in *fin de siècle* social thought with the overall aim of attempting to establish a new ground for liberalism. If liberalism cannot be established on a neo-Kantian, neo-Hegelian, rational basis, for all the reasons already noted, it should not be abandoned to either postmodernism or a return to *status quo* defense of social order.

Of course, understanding how the Schopenhauerian trajectory leads to nonsystematic compassion and humanism even seems enigmatic and difficult to comprehend. We are so used to the habit of associating traditionalist thought with oppression, and liberalism with freedom, that it is very difficult to challenge this habit, like any other habit. But given the social crisis objectified in the debate between postmodernists and modernists, and given the near unanimity by Schopenhauer's interpreters, from Thomas Mann and Max Horkheimer to contemporary philosophers, that he was a humanist, I hope the reader will grant me the benefit of the doubt in pursuing this difficult project.

RETRIEVING THE GROUND FOR THE SOCIOLOGICAL PROJECT

Suppose that one regards Schopenhauer's revival as another manifestation of the revival of the previous *fin de siècle* spirit in our *fin de siècle*. No doubt, we are too close to the action in our *fin de siècle* to make out clearly the outlines and direction of the debate, but this difficulty is not greater than the situation that confronted Veblen, Durkheim, Freud, and their contemporaries as they tried to make sense of their *fin de siècle* by launching sociology. The concerns of contemporary philosophers who are engaging Schopenhauer a century after his fame expired center on unravelling Schopenhauer's seemingly enigmatic claims that the world is will *and* idea, that character is inborn and unalterable, that the actions which are grounded in one's character occur with inexorable necessity, and that a person is nevertheless morally responsible for his or her moral conduct (see especially Atwell 1990). And the Kantian-Hegelian world-view that Schopenhauer had already challenged is being reexamined by philosophers of science as well as postmodern philosophers: Knowledge is necessarily restricted to mere appearances and contingencies; freedom lies in the ego's limited ability to make connections among these appearances; and morality consists of behavior according to rational self-interest on the basis of rules. Postmodernist philosophers have taken each of these propositions and either exaggerated them or claimed the very opposite – the contradictions in post-modern discourse are well-known (Rosenau 1992). Yet all this intellectual ferment is occurring without a sense that it is not new, but is another instance of Nietzsche's eternal recurrence of the same (a doctrine that Baudrillard rejects, of course, 1986: 72),[12] and that can be traced back to the polemic among Schopenhauer, Kant, and Hegel, and before them, to the debates between Plato and the Sophists.

These philosophical debates shall serve as the backdrop for our discussion, which is sociological. What is directly relevant is how twentieth-century social thought followed Kant's and Hegel's trajectory, whereas Veblen and his *fin de siècle* colleagues in the social sciences – Freud, Durkheim, Tönnies, Pareto, Simmel, and Weber, among others – refracted Schopenhauer's pessimistic humanism in their social thought. For example, Freud ([1905a] 1974) also taught that one's character is "set" in the first five years of one's life, and cannot be altered appreciably after that. Veblen's (1948) notion of "habits of thought" are a refraction of Schopenhauer's philosophical legacy, in that Veblen did not believe that these habits, whether peaceable or barbaric, could be changed drastically by deliberate and rational social engineering. Durkheim ([1893] 1933) interpolated the notion of character to include societal and national character, the collective tendencies of a group toward good or wickedness. Similarly, Simmel (1971) insisted that "life" would always break through society's "forms," and life's legacy could be variously barbaric or benign – without regard for human intervention. In sum, one can find the Schopenhauerian legacy of pessimism, including the theme of civilization and its discontents, in the works of all the *fin de siècle* founding fathers of the social sciences (Bailey 1958).

No doubt, our aims shall be criticized as being unscientific by the positivists, and as seeking an essentialist explanation that is held suspect by the postmodernists. But we have already shown that the alternatives presented by these two camps are unsatisfactory, and have pointed to good reasons for pursuing this project despite them. We shall carefully dismantle the assumptions and objections from both camps at every step of this analysis as it proceeds. But we shall proceed, not with the aim of establishing another set of oppressive narratives, but with the aim of exposing the existentialism that lies at the heart of the project that inspired the establishment of the social sciences over a century ago. Some of our conclusions shall be that of the founding fathers of sociology, that a certain degree of tension between barbarism and virtue is the price one pays for the human condition and so-called progress. While these conclusions do not offer the consolation of boosterish faith in Hegelian progress, they shall reflect more honestly than is the case at present the apparent aims of sociology as it was born in the previous turn-of-the-century, as well as the resumé of collective wisdom in Western culture that these founding fathers of sociology attempted to incorporate into their analyses. They did not find only oppression and barbarism in the grand narratives, but hopeful signs of benign narratives as well, a point that is missed by some modernists and postmodernists.

Chapter 4

Finding a ground for discourse

You may perhaps shrug your shoulders and say: "That isn't natural science, it's Schopenhauer's philosophy!
(Sigmund Freud, [1933] 1965: 107)

It is not the discovery of local customs that counts, but discovering the immorality of the space you have to travel through.

(Jean Baudrillard, 1986: 9)

Postmodernism has placed a tremendous strain on the traditional obligation that falls upon the author to lay out the method that shall be followed in an analysis. Baudrillard claims that the best method is to travel – especially on America's highways, because they symbolize infinite circulation – or to watch a lot of TV. But Baudrillard is being disingenuous: his claim that there is no ground or referent to discourse is itself grounded in the Kantian legacy that holds that the thing-in-itself, the essential truth of any debate, is out of reach. Yet Kant ([1788] 1956, 1963) did not have the last word in philosophy, and there is no good reason to let Baudrillard have the last word in postmodernism.

Freud's lines, above, are arresting in that they point to a philosophical ground or referent for his psychoanalysis that many contemporary scholars would find astonishing, namely, Schopenhauer's philosophy. Really, this is not surprising, because Freud's era was saturated in Schopenhauer.[1] At the beginning of his career, Freud would not have had to defend using Schopenhauer, Nietzsche, Plato or any number of other metaphysicians as the philosophical ground that he used to construct psychoanalysis. But the present century is so thoroughly positivistic – at least with regard to appearances and ideology, for Horkheimer (1972b) is correct that all sorts of metaphysics thrive alongside positivism – that many readers are likely to agree with Freud's audience: psychoanalysis isn't science, it's Schopenhauer's philosophy. My point is that Baudrillard's postmodernism is every bit as metaphysical and rooted in philosophy as Freud's approach, albeit they subscribe to vastly different philosophies. Baudrillard draws upon a hyper-Kantian set of assumptions that the universe is a mess of contingent appearances, whereas Freud drew upon Kant's bitter critic, Arthur Schopenhauer, who held that Kant's thing-in-itself, renamed the will, *is* accessible to intuition even if not to conscious knowledge. This difference in starting-points and subsequent trajectories makes an importance difference in comprehending barbarism in modern times.

Let us examine the scene in greater detail. The postmodernist theorists in France, such as Baudrillard, have constructed a theoretical scheme that defies Tocqueville, Veblen, Freud and Durkheim, who stood for seemingly permanent, essentialist entities like habits and culture. Thus, the central thrust of postmodernism is a dialogue of contemporary French scholars with their intellectual history that spills over into American, German, and Western intellectual history in general. And this intellectual history is highly selective: It draws on Kant and Hegel, but not Schopenhauer or Plato. It draws on Nietzsche's will to power, but not the young Nietzsche's tribute to his self-proclaimed "master," Arthur Schopenhauer. With regard to American intellectual history, it denatures Veblen. It takes up Freud, *minus* the Schopenhauerian concept of the unconscious, and ignores Durkheim completely.

But there is more: a neo-Kantian, Enlightenment version of Freud and Durkheim lies at the core of American social science, thanks to Talcott Parsons and his disciples. American modernist theories *also* draw on the German and French *fin de siècle* tradition to construct a typically American, optimistic, rationalist vision of progress and social order. The centerpiece of this American ideology is the Parsonian fiction that social norms are "internalized" – a term that Parsons attributes to Freud, who used it in a wholly different context, and that never became central to psychoanalytic theory – by individuals so that they shall contribute to the social order and not become "deviant."[2] This American "systems model" is also embraced by Jürgen Habermas, at least in part, in opposition to Hork-heimer and Adorno's critical theory, and in recent years, constitutes an effort to reconcile Marxism with functionalism. And Anthony Giddens, in turn, was inspired by Habermas, wrestled with Parsons, and was highly influenced by the South-ern California school of ethnomethodology (Bryant and Jary 1991). The important point is that these and other modernist theories regard with disdain the cultural approaches to social phenomena that were typical of writers in the previous *fin de siècle*, including Freud.

Baudrillard turns his attention to America, and mocks the modernist Parsonian vision even as he falls in love with America's primitive barbarism. For Baudrillard, "America is the only remaining primitive society" (1986: 7). It is "a primary, visceral, unbounded vitality, springing not from rootedness, but from the lack of roots, a metabolic vitality, in sex and bodies, as well as in work and in buying and selling" (ibid.: 7). There are no norms, deviants, or internalization in Baudrillard's scheme of things, only rootless circulation. In the distant background we have Veblen, Freud, Durkheim, and Tocqueville who ascribed these same, barbaric traits to a rooted predisposi-tion, to habits of the heart and mind that are offset by other, "good" habits. Thus, the postmodernist critiques apply beyond the contemporary French scene to include other intellectual traditions and cultural settings. The scene has become cross-disciplinary, cross-national, and oblivious to the constraints of history. Scholars move freely backward and forward in time, even though time is one of the Kantian categories that is called into question by this discussion.

In this mind-boggling situation, we shall move from Thorstein Veblen to include two of his distinguished colleagues from the previous *fin de siècle*, Emile Durkheim and Sigmund Freud. I shall argue that Durkheim and Freud still apply and can capture, if not help explain, the barbarism found in the post-modern condition mobilized by the electronic revolution and interstate highways. The thrust of our project is a challenge to the postmodernist claim that humanity has witnessed the end of culture and the end of history. The historical transformations which are said to mark off the postmodernist period are not as clear and uniform as Baudrillard, Lyotard, and other postmodernists make them out to be. Additionally, Freud and Durkheim were conceptually sensitive to these transformations.

But to pull this off, we have to reach deep into the historical past. It is necessary to cover nearly the same ground in philosophy that Horkheimer, Baudrillard, and Habermas cover, but to arrive at different conclusions. For this reason, we shall invoke Kant, Hegel, Schopenhauer, Nietzsche, and Plato as actors in this fiction who looked at history as more than a series of unconnected events, and who perceived an intent and will to history. Our focal point throughout this discussion shall be barbarism, conceived as omnipresent yet rootless violence by the postmodernists and modernists, and as a habit, a character structure, a temperament, by traditional, metaphysical thinkers.

Unlike Baudrillard and the postmodernists, our theoretical scaffolding shall be more extensive than their overemphasis on hyper-Kantian versions of Freud, Nietzsche, and Marx. We follow Horkheimer's (1972b, 1973, 1974) critiques of Marx and Nietzsche on epistemological as well as moral grounds. Our analysis shall also be in line with Horkheimer's criticisms of positivism as well as his affection for Schopenhauer's philosophy. Against Habermas and Parsons, we reject systems theory and all contemporary forms of functionalism as rationalizations for maintaining the *status quo*, and because these theoretical systems cannot explain the persistence of barbarism within modernity.

The scope of the postmodernist discourse is so wide that it lends itself easily to parody. We see no sure way to avoid the possibility that our intentions shall not be taken seriously.

RETURNING TO THE PATH THAT WAS NOT TAKEN

A good strategy in trying to account for the many factors that are involved in this far-ranging discussion is to turn to notable previous attempts to achieve similar aims. Allan Bloom's *Closing of the American Mind* (1987) comes to mind immediately. Bloom's book was a best-seller in France prior to achieving notoriety in America, and deals with the same stage and many of the same characters that concern us, Habermas, and the other participants in this discourse: Plato, Freud, Weber, Nietzsche, Heidegger, the French postmodernists, and American social character as reflected in the works of Tocqueville and Riesman.[3] It is important to deal with Bloom, not ignore him, because he influenced Francis Fukuyama (1992), whose end of history thesis flows out of Bloom's overestimation of human rationality. Bloom represents the shadow of the liberal neo-Marxist, Jürgen Habermas, in that Bloom's libertarian political views flow from the same overestimation of the Enlightenment that inspires Habermas and other liberals.

Bloom criticizes American naiveté and superficiality as much as Baudrillard admires these traits in the Americans: "This is the only country which gives you the opportunity to be so brutally naive: things, faces, skies, and deserts are expected to be simply what they are. This is the land of the just as it is" (Baudrillard 1986: 28). Bloom's many critics and reviewers turned out to be as naive and gullible as Bloom and Baudrillard claim. Bloom's conservative politics were attacked bitterly – even though he, like Habermas, defends the same Enlightenment projects against the French postmodernists who are inspired by Nietzsche and Heidegger – but his philosophical message got lost in the indignation expressed by liberals over his exposure of sexism, racism, and immorality found in contemporary American life.

Bloom argues that some important turn-of-the-century thinkers have been misunderstood, and their thought has been vulgarized in the process of incorporating them into contemporary American thought, a thought that he treats as nearly equivalent to the modern mind-set. In this regard, he is in good company: Tocqueville, Riesman, H.G. Wells, Veblen, Henry Adams, Baudrillard, and a host of other serious thinkers have hinted that in its naiveté, America symbolizes the modern, if not the postmodern, world-view. For example, Freud despised what little he saw of America during his lectures at Clark University. Bloom writes:

My professors, many of whom were to become very famous, did not tend to be philosophic and did not dig back into the sources of the new language and categories they were using . . . I do not believe any of these professors noticed the darker side of Freud and Weber, let alone the Nietzsche–Heidegger extremism lying somewhere beneath the surface . . . It is amazing to me that the irrational source of all conscious life in Freud, and the relativity of all values in

Weber, did not pose a problem for them and their optimism about science. Freud was very dubious about the future of civilization and the role of reason in the life of man. He certainly was not a convinced advocate of democracy or equality. And Weber, much more thoughtful than Freud about science, morals and politics, lived in an atmosphere of permanent tragedy.

(1987: 149–50)

Bloom has a point, even if one rejects his conservative politics. Freud is still regarded in America primarily as a "doctor of the mind" whose psychotherapy will make individuals happy. Even a thinker as intelligent and well-known as Christopher Lasch (1979) rejects the Schopenhauerian essence of Freud's thought – his libido theory – and derives a theory of narcissism on the object-relations version of Freud: American narcissism is purported to be a defense mechanism against the complexity of modern living. Actually, Freud felt that, at best, psychotherapy could make neurotics insightful, but never "normal." According to Freud, no one is wholly normal, and he insisted that each of us crosses the border between normalcy and psychosis *every day* – some of us more than others. This regression occurs in our dreams as well as the daily host of slips of the tongue and pen, repression, misreadings, bungled actions, and superstitions that he describes in *The Psychopathology of Everyday Life* ([1901] 1965).

As for Weber, sociologists still debate whether he should be understood in the context of the Enlightenment belief in progress versus the extent and significance of Nietzsche's influence upon him (Whimster and Lash 1987). Alan Sica (1988) argues convincingly that Weber's stand on the irrational aspects of life is still not clear. Positivists still peruse Freud and Weber to glean testable hypotheses that can be falsified, even if, following Nietzsche, Freud and Weber would probably have mocked such efforts. For example, regarding the many efforts by modern scholars to prove that Protestantism somehow "causes" capitalism, Max Weber wrote:

We have no intention whatever of maintaining such a foolish and doctrinaire thesis as that the spirit of capitalism (in the provisional sense of the term explained above) could only have arisen as the result of certain effects of the Reformation, or even that capitalism as an economic system is a creation of the Reformation.

([1904] 1958: 91)

However, Bloom could be accused of closing the very discussion he thus opens because he – like the professors he criticizes – does not dig deeply enough into the philosophical underpinnings of the thinkers he treats, and omits a host of others. Bloom's apparent aim is to set up Freud, Nietzsche, and Heidegger as straw men that he can knock over easily in his efforts to defend the Enlightenment against the irrationalist philosophies that they represent. And the conservative Bloom is not the only one who harps on these philosophers: on the opposite end of the political spectrum, one finds that Foucault, Derrida, Lacan, Baudrillard, and in reaction to them, Habermas, also fail to examine the other, more benign roots of German irrationalism.[4] Irrationalism does not have only one face, the extreme, Nietzschean, dangerous, anti-rational tendencies that ordinary Americans, Bloom, Habermas, and the French postmodernists automatically associate with it. Irrationalism also has a benign side: compassion, sympathy, and affection, addressed by Schopenhauer, that both sides of the political spectrum ignore.

Bloom does not take up Schopenhauer's philosophy – which was acknowledged by Nietzsche ([1874] 1965) to be the bedrock upon which he built his critique of the Enlightenment – and he completely ignores the other precursors of the social sciences, among them Simmel, Durkheim, Tönnies, Veblen, Horkheimer, and James, who swam in the waters of Schopenhauer *and* Nietzsche. Despite his penetrating insights, Bloom exposes his bias when he writes that "with the possible exception of Weber and Freud, there are no social science books that can be said to be classic" (1987: 345). It is a pity that instead of pushing his thesis to include the closing of the American mind in the social sciences, Bloom fails to develop the very important discussion he began.

Thus, the thrust of Bloom's book is to castigate the mindless, naive acceptance on the part of Americans of the dark side of German irrationalism – albeit without any awareness that this has occurred – and to replace it with an ethnocentric defense of the alleged superiority of the Enlightenment narratives that the postmodernists and cultural relativists have criticized. But Habermas shares some of this reaction, and surely he is not naive. In any event, our aim is to show the benign side of German irrationalism *vis-à-vis* Nietzsche's self-acknowledged master, Schopenhauer, and to demonstrate that the post-modernists and neo-Kantians have not really rebelled at the Enlightenment narratives, because they have not rejected the core of the Kantian project: Kant forbade any venturing into the domain of the thing-in-itself, what Schopenhauer renamed the will, and restricted all knowledge to the manipulation of appearances. This means that the modernists as well as the postmodernists share a disdain for any vocabulary that hints at essences as derivatives of the will – habits, customs, mores, social character – and accept the world as mere phenomena and mere fiction that are constrained loosely by time, space, and causality. This polemic between Kant and Schopenhauer lies at the bottom of the fragmented postmodernist discourse and the contradictions that have ensued from it. It needs to be addressed head-on.

THE FRAGMENTATION OF CONTEXT

Schopenhauer's philosophy is widely acknowledged to be the antithesis of Kant and the source for Nietzsche. There is something odd in the fact that the disciple Nietzsche is refer-enced frequently by intellectuals engaged in the discourse on postmodernism, while the master is ignored, and the obvious drawbacks of Kantianism have not been overcome after so many years of criticizing his ideas. Magee writes that "within a short time of discovering Schopenhauer, Nietzsche was describing himself to his friends as a Schopenhauerian" (1983: 266). Similarly, Freud was deeply influenced by both Schopenhauer and Nietzsche (see Ellenberger 1970; Jones 1981). One of sociology's founding fathers, Georg Simmel, wrote a book in 1907 entitled *Schopenhauer and Nietzsche*, in which he makes explicit the importance of the divergence between Schopen-hauer and Nietzsche, despite their overall affinity, to the origin of the social sciences. And Simmel claims that Schopenhauer was the more important philosopher compared to Nietzsche. Yet this particular book by Simmel has been almost completely ignored by social scientists for most of the present century, and was not translated into English until 1986. Simmel has already isolated the insights that are missing in the postmodernist discourse, and these insights need only to be incorporated, not achieved anew: Both Schopenhauer and Nietzsche rebelled at the high status that Kant attributed to reason with a capital R, and both gave this lofty status to the irrational will – with a capital W. They differ mainly in that Nietzsche saw only the dark side of an unleashed will, namely the barbaric quest for unlimited power, and mocked his master's exposition of the tender side of the will – compassion. Because this movement from Kant to Schopenhauer to Nietzsche is still understood imperfectly and in a fragmented way, one finds the post-modernists clinging to the Kantian vocabulary of appearances and Nietzsche's Marxist rhetoric of power, while they simply ignore Schopenhauer's doctrine of compassion. We have noted already that Baudrillard, in particular, often comes across as cruel and heartless (cf. Gane 1991; Kellner 1989b).

It seems that the intellectuals who were closer in time and space to this polemic apprehended its import more clearly. In addition to Simmel, Durkheim grasped its significance. Durk-heim was apparently so enamored with Schopenhauer's philo-sophy that his students nicknamed him "Schopen" (Lalande 1960: 23). Like Schopenhauer, Durkheim sought an alternative to the impasse reached by Kant, and perpetuated by Hegel, that universal Reason exists as an *a priori* phenomenon, self-referential and grounded in itself. Durkheim sought the ground and referents for Reason in society and its collective representations. In addition, Durkheim grasped the import-ance of Schopenhauer's focus on compassion: he made compas-sion, sympathy, and other refractions of affection – not Niet-zsche's derivatives of the will to power – among humans the essential ingredient of his version of social solidarity. Yet Durk-heim continues to be misaligned with positivism and Kantianism (La Capra 1972; Lukes 1985; Wallwork 1972). The Parsonians twisted his open pronouncements on "mystic sympathy" as the "glue" that holds society together into a Kantian vocabulary of cognitive, internalization of norms. It must be remarked that this alignment of two thinkers, Kant and Durkheim, who oppose each other with regard to every major philosophical premise, is incredible, and constitutes an aberration. There is simply no way that *a priorism* can be made commensurate with Durkheimian doctrine, so that one must wonder how and why intelligent sociologists can persist in making such a colossal error.[5] The Marxists and conflict theorists who rebelled at Parsons's account merely substituted a Nietzschean focus on power, and missed again the Schopenhauerian element of compassion as an important ingredient in social relations (see Horkheimer 1978). Finally, we have demonstrated in Chapter 1 that Veblen also felt that peaceable, matriarchal habits really make social life possible, and serve to tame and oppose barbaric habits.

In short, at the present time, there exist only bits and pieces of insights into the relationship of portions of *fin de siècle* thought upon certain precursors of the social sciences, all of whom tend to be misread by mainstream sociologists as exclusive positivists: Baudrillard (1981) cites portions of Veblen's thought, Habermas (1987) harps on Nietzsche, the Frankfurt School debates how one should appreciate Freud and Marx (Adorno 1991; Fromm 1962), Frisby (1986) resuscitates Simmel, Bell (1976) finds contradictions in Weber, Bloom (1987) focuses on Freud and Weber in the context of Nietzsche, Ellenberger (1970) emphasizes Freud and Schopenhauer, and so on. But Durkheim is still misaligned with *status quo* functionalism (Alexander 1988), the conflict theorists are still trying to resuscitate Marx, Nietzsche is cited frequently while Schopenhauer tends to be ignored, and the positivistic program continues to dominate mainstream sociology – despite the intellectuals engaged in postmodern discourse who tend to invoke various fragments of selected geniuses from the previous *fin de siècle*. The overall conclusions reached by most discussants in this discourse fail to move beyond the unwelcome alternative uncovered since Nietzsche that the will to power is the essence of social life. If Nietzsche is correct, then any and all claims to civilized, enlightened social life are hollow and hypocritical.

Rather than bemoaning this state of fragmentation in the contemporary discourse, many postmodernists revel in it. According to Lyotard (1984), postmodernism is a liberating philosophy, in that it subverts and destroys the neat divisions among academic boundaries that have dominated the twentieth century. Suddenly, it is permissible to "mix and match," let us say, a Baudelaire with a Simmel, and perhaps this newfound freedom is a good thing to some extent. But if it fails to search for a ground or referent to justify the connections, the affinities that are found may be regarded as arbitrary. Actually, this postmodernist strategy does not appear to be significantly different from modernist fragmentation and disregard for context whose origins can be traced back to Kant. Postmodernism is not unequivocally liberating. It carries its own dogmatism and contradictions, even as it projects these traits onto the Enlightenment narratives that it pretends to rebel against. An overwhelming problem in finding affinities among thinkers from the previous *fin de siècle* and their relevance to the postmodern discourse that is accompanying our *fin de siècle* is that postmodernism delights in deconstructing and otherwise denying narratives that could unify diverse thinkers and themes. Bloom (1987) assumes that an original version of *fin de siècle* thoughts exists, and that the "copy" that has made its way into twentieth-century university courses is flawed (even if his version of the original is also questionable). But for cultural relativists and postmodernists, the notions of an original, objective truth and "distortion" are anathema. Yet, if it is true that nothing is true because everything is culturally relative, then even that is not true, because it is culturally relative. In that case, it is a position that negates itself. A similar logic applies to the postmodernist narrative of rebelling at all narratives: by denying a ground or referent for all objective discourse, postmodernism destroys its own ground or referent, even the possibility of engaging in meaningful discourse, because all decentered discourse is ultimately subjective.

It follows that sociology is crippled: either it upholds the narratives spun from positivism and the faith in *a priori* universal reason that is not grounded in culture, in which case rationality is reduced to an inexplicable ideology, or it weds itself to the cultural relativist position, and thereby becomes nothing but a complex social activity that can never produce truths that are worthy of notice.[6] Indeed, like so many others, Bloom dismisses the social sciences in relation to the natural sciences, which allegedly do deliver absolute truths that are valid in every culture.

Our aim is to find an exit from this impasse, to find a narrative of sorts that will withstand the criticisms made by postmodernists, namely, that it will not be based on oppressive assumptions, but that can also serve as a ground or referent for discourse.

THE FIN DE SIÈCLE SPIRIT

We shall seek the ground or referent for the present discussion in the *fin de siècle* spirit, which can answer some of the objections raised on both sides of the debate described above. Like postmodernism, the *fin de siècle* spirit rebelled at the notion of an *a priori*, Universal Reason, but found a ground or referent for discourse that is non-rational. That ground was given many names, from Schopenhauer's will to life to Durkheim's society, but in all cases, the ground for rationality was presumed to be irrational. Moreover, this irrational ground for Reason was assumed to be Janus-faced, barbaric as well as compassionate. It encompassed the "highest" as well as the "lowest" traits in humanity. This move enables the intellectual to discuss barbarism within the heart of the Enlightenment project, because it assumes the existence of irrational forces and their dialectical relationship to rationality. This is what Horkheimer and Adorno were hinting at in their *Dialectic of Enlightenment*, but the message was diluted by their clinging more to the Enlightenment narratives that constitute Marxism and to Nietzsche's critique of those narratives at the expense of Schopenhauer's contribution.

Anyone who is familiar with *fin de siècle* thought will probably agree that Arthur Schopenhauer's philosophy, as well as the Romantic and pre-Romantic forces that led up to it, constituted the starting-point for much of what has come down to us as great literature in the humanities or the social sciences from that era.[7] And Schopenhauer's thought is directly inimical to the assumptions of positivism and the Enlightenment faith in reason as forces that are more powerful than human passions, and that exist on a plane that is separate from irrationality. Ellenberger summarizes Schopenhauer's achievement well:

> Kant distinguished the world of phenomena and the world of the thing in itself, which is inaccessible to our knowledge. Schopenhauer called the phenomena representations, and the thing in itself will, equating the will with the unconscious as conceived by some of the Romantics; Schopenhauer's will had the dynamic character of blind, driving forces, which not only reigned over the universe, but also conducted man. Thus, man is an irrational being guided by

internal forces, which are unknown to him and of which he is scarcely aware.

(1970: 208)

For Schopenhauer, the will is blind, tyrannical, and all-powerful, and reason is its instrument. The consequence of Schopenhauer's bold move is that human progress can be perceived as a blind, irrational process that rationalizes, after the fact, the growth as well as the degeneration and destruction that it produces. The will stands for passion and desire, what Schopenhauer sometimes calls the "heart," and all that is obscure, unconscious, irrational and emotional – good *and* evil. By contrast, Enlightenment assumptions concerning human progress lead to the impossible task of explaining how and why enlightenment in general can lead to barbarism, a task taken on by Horkheimer and Adorno (1972), and others, with mixed results. And the postmodernist discourse takes as its starting-point Nietzsche's claim that the will is beyond good and evil, while neglecting Durkheim's sociological refraction of Schopenhauer's original claim.

But even Schopenhauer's thought had philosophical roots. The philosopher he praises the most and credits with first perceiving the distinction as well as dialectic unity between the will and representation, albeit in an imperfect form, is Plato.[8] Even some of the scholars who recognize Schopenhauer's importance have failed to incorporate Schopenhauer's extensive admiration for Plato into their analyses. It must be noted that Schopenhauer devotes more pages to Plato than to Kant, and that the pages devoted to Plato are favorable and important. For example, he writes that he finds "Kant's thing-in-itself and Plato's Idea to be, not exactly identical, but yet very closely related" ([1818] 1969a: 170). He believes that his own doctrine of perceiving the will or thing-in-itself is similar to Plato's doctrine on "perception of the universal in the particular" ([1818] 1969b: 475). And of course, Freud, Durkheim, Simmel and the other precursors of the social sciences exhibit a similar high regard for Plato. However wide and deep the differences that separate the modern era from Plato's time, the similarities between Schopenhauer's and Plato's philosophies are far greater. With regard to epistemology and metaphysics, both philosophies seek truth beneath appearances.

Both Schopenhauer and Plato posit powerful irrational forces that can and often do overwhelm reason. Both are critical of utilitarian, optimistic sophistry, and in general, both measure life by its depth, not its surface phenomena, the measuring sticks used by Baudrillard and the postmodernists.

With regard to their moral programs, both Plato and Schopenhauer warn that virtue cannot be taught like any other science, arithmetic or chemistry, for example. The mere adherence to moral rules, which constitutes morality for Kant, is *not* morality for Plato, Schopenhauer, or Durkheim (Cartwright 1987). This insight allows one to appreciate how Durkheim's *Moral Education* ([1925] 1961) is revolutionary with regard to Kant at the same time that it is classical with regard to Plato and in keeping with Schopenhauer's contribution to the *fin de siècle* spirit.[9]

In his neglected *Evolution of Educational Thought*, Durkheim ([1938] 1977) uses the Renaissance to demarcate what he perceives to be a dramatic shift in cultural development from Plato's time to our century. According to Durkheim, genuine, integrated reason (similar to Horkheimer's 1947 discussion of non-alienated rationality)[10] flourished in Plato's time because the ancient Greeks stressed the unity and importance of forces external to the individual. They explained the entire universe with reference to Eros. Eros acted very much like Schopenhauer's will to life, as a dualistic force that is both good and evil and that works *through* individuals, societies, and physical matter to produce order as well as chaos. But following the Renaissance, Western culture began to accentuate the individual's ego and mind as the center of the Universe (a move that Nietzsche mocked bitterly). This movement found its highest expression in Kant's and Hegel's philosophies, which located the focal point of all knowledge in the human animal's subjective perceptions, and the human's alleged superiority with regard to other animals *vis-à-vis* the allegedly superior mind. In this manner, Durkheim links contemporary *anomie* to the Renaissance overestimation of the alleged power of the rational individual over Nature.[11] It is certain that Nietzsche, Veblen, Henry Adams, and many of his other contemporaries agree with Durkheim's assessment of history in this regard.

Thus, the previous *fin de siècle* attempts at synthesis between subject and object as well as fact and value that found their most powerful expression in Schopenhauer's philosophy, can and ought to be linked with Plato's philosophy. Linking Schopenhauer and Plato enables one to challenge the neo-Kantian approaches to the precursors of the social sciences and to challenge the limited focus on the origins of the social sciences to the past one hundred years or so. Granted, something like the social sciences as we know them today blossomed at the previous turn-of-the-century, but it must not be forgotten that most of the precursors of the social sciences smuggled their new disciplines into respectability under the rubric of philosophy, and they were all trained in classical philosophy. This is especially true for Durkheim and Simmel: the former was almost appointed to a chair in social philosophy that was changed to "education and sociology" at the last minute, whereas Simmel steadfastly preferred to call himself a philosopher rather than a sociologist (Frisby 1986). The classical philosophical background of the founding fathers of sociology tends to be neglected in contemporary times, and most contemporary social scientists are not trained in any sort of philosophy.

Moreover, *fin de siècle* philosophy, despite the fact that it openly rebelled against Kant and Hegel, drew much of its sustenance from Plato's philosophy. This holds true even for Nietzsche and his opposition between Apollonian and Dionysian forces, despite his attacks on Socrates. The Platonic connection, so to speak, may explain why the *fin de siècle* rebellion against the Enlightenment did not degenerate into nihilism and the other intellectual dead-ends that plague postmodern discourse.

FOLLOWING THE TRAJECTORY ESTABLISHED BY THE EARLY MAX HORKHEIMER

It is obvious that we regard Marx Horkheimer's attempt at establishing critical theory on a primarily Schopenhauerian base as a sound strategy. However, we take the following exceptions to Horkheimer's program: We shall not link the Freudian tradition with Marx (the two are incommensurable)[12] but with Durkheim. We shall not agonize about metaphysics versus science. Metaphysics is an inescapable aspect of the human condition, and one must choose between vulgar or sophisticated metaphysics. But we do agree with Horkheimer that neo-Kantianism traps the investigator in a world of appearances, only we extend this critique beyond positivism to include postmodernism. We agree completely with Horkheimer (1972b: 38) that:

> In maintaining this [Kantian] doctrine of the necessary limitation of knowledge to appearances or rather in degrading the known world to a mere outward show, positivism makes peace, in principle, with every kind of superstition. It takes the seriousness out of theory since the latter must prove itself in practice . . . in addition, it usually overlooks the contradiction between its own metaphysical description of known reality as appearance and externality, on the one hand, and its ostensible power of prevision, on the other (the latter already containing the undialectical separation of subject and object).

One might add that Baudrillard also fails to justify his collapse of the whole of reality into the category of appearances or fictions. We shall also be following the trajectory of Horkheimer's (1986) philosophical humanism, already linked by other scholars to Schopenhauer's philosophy and the kernel of Christian doctrine.[13] In line with Schopenhauer, the early Horkheimer was highly critical of Marx and Nietzsche for their cruel dismissal of the suffering of the masses if it served a "higher" end. Martin Jay (1982) suggests that these starting-points in Horkheimer's philosophy conflicted with Adorno's Marxism and neo-Kantian acceptance that science stays with appearances, and led to tensions within critical theory that led eventually to its demise. Jay may be correct, but in any event, we shall be following the trajectory of the early Horkheimer, who does not conceive of capitalist society as a mere instance of reification (Adorno 1991 does), but, like Schopenhauer, sees it as a meaningless, anarchic, and egoistic reality.[14]

Our central problem for analysis is Horkheimer's central problem: the postindustrial return to barbarism. We shall single out the original Schopenhauerian premise that animated Horkheimer's vision of the aims of critical theory: to uncover the tendency in Western civilization to separate intellect from nature, and to point to ways to restore the organic unity between heart and mind. We agree also with Horkheimer's understanding of dialectical sociology as one that is conscious of being a part of society, that tries to be the medium by which society is made conscious of its own situation. All these goals are commensurate with the thrust of Schopenhauer's rebellion against Kant and Hegel, and the ways in which his philosophy opposed Marx and Nietzsche.

It is beside the point, for the purposes of the present analysis, how and why these original starting-points in Horkheimer's critical theory conflicted with Adorno's aims, or how and why the Frankfurt School eventually dissolved and lost its once-high stature. The more important point, for understanding our intentions here, is that we shall apply the same Schopenhauerian starting-points that Horkheimer discovered to an area that he neglected: the confluence among Durkheim, Freud, Veblen, and the rest of the *fin de siècle* spirit that took seriously Schopenhauer's philosophy. Really, Horkheimer could have found a strong ally in Durkheim's sociology, which is resolutely anti-Kantian[15] and Schopenhauerian in its aims. Our aim is to launch the Schopenhauerian sociology that Horkheimer might have inaugurated had he not become entwined in the Marxism that he criticized.

We shall be following the authentic methodology laid out for sociology by its founding fathers during the previous *fin de siècle*, among them, Veblen, Simmel, Durkheim, and Freud. This is an interpretive, inductive methodology that regards culture as a system of signs that must be interpreted and decoded to yield insights concerning the underlying social consciousness. By contrast, the positivists and the postmodernists both collapse culture into society conceived as a system of abstract, rootless fictions. Both regard reality naively as something that speaks for itself, and both begin with deductive assumptions that are dreamed up subjectively by investigators, and then applied as fictions against a world that is assumed to be nothing but neo-Kantian appearances. The positivists test hypotheses with the aim of proving that they are false, which is not a strategy far removed from assuming that everything is a fiction anyway. The previous *fin de siècle* thinkers relied on the notion of habit and its associated concepts (mores, customs, representations, folkways, etc.) while contemporary thinkers deal with norms and fictions. Habits reach down into an unconscious will, a historical past, an essential reality, and they imply a tension between centrifugal forces that move humanity forward even as centripetal forces act as inertia. By contrast, norms and fictions exist only in the present, and imply the Kantian world-view in which humanity is free from the effects of the thing-in-itself.

It would seem that because our strategy appears to be traditional, we could be accused of the very conservative tendencies that Veblen finds in the decadent leisure class. Why in the world would we want to seriously revive a seemingly old-fashioned methodology and criticize the positivistic and post-modern methods and assumptions that are at hand? We have implied an answer all along, but seek to make it explicit here: We wish to avoid Habermas's extension of the neo-Kantian errors established by Parsons in this century, and criticized by Horkheimer. And postmodernism stays within the boundaries of this same neo-Kantian world-view. Thus, we must go back to the crossroads at the turn of the previous century, and revive the original intent of the founding fathers of sociology. And far from being traditional, the trajectory we are following is the revolutionary one.

Appearances are deceptive. If one's perspective stays within the confines of the past hundred years, it would seem that the founding fathers of sociology represent the conservative tendency in social theory. But if one goes back to the Enlightenment and beyond, then Veblen and his colleagues will seem radical, and our contemporaries will be perceived as perpetuating a Kantian world-view that was already criticized and left for dead at the previous *fin de siècle*. Thus, in harking back to the previous *fin de siècle*, we hope to resume a radical cultural and moral development in sociological theory that has been arrested since then.

The positivists have tried to make science a substitute for religion, and reason a substitute for faith. But in the first place, this quest is not unique to the twentieth century, and can be traced to Marx, Comte, Hegel, and Kant. Second, and more importantly, these thinkers were denounced in the previous *fin de siècle* by other thinkers who realized that knowing is one thing, and living is another. From Bachofen in the 1860s to Bergson at the beginning of the twentieth century, the *fin de siècle* legacy was to try to reconcile intellectual necessities with the necessities of the heart and will. And this seems to have been Max Horkheimer's intent as well, the most important unifying strand in the diverse thought of intellectuals who comprised the Frankfurt School.

This recognition that the human person is heart and mind, a totality, is precisely what the postmodernists and positivists deny. Lyotard attacks total explanations and metanarratives out of fear that they might lead to totalitarianism. The positivists follow Kant in assuming that since one cannot fathom the heart, it is not worthy of consideration. Horkheimer and Adorno have already argued that in denying the heart, reason itself becomes total and totalizing, and that excessive rationalism is the culprit in totalitarianism. Nazism, communism, the cruel capitalism of the Thatcher and Reagan era – how much more proof does one need that Horkheimer and Adorno (1972) were right to indict any system that tries to get everything from the mind while ignoring the heart?

Habit, the central sociological concept from the previous *fin de siècle*, should be perceived as part of the revolution against and critique of neo-Kantian efforts to extend the domain of one-sided science too far. This is why we shall rely upon it, and its derivatives, in the present analysis, not because it seems like a quaint concept. Habits imply the involvement of both heart and mind. This is why Veblen and Durkheim (among their other colleagues) regarded even "the spirit of progress" as a habit. This connection seems as much an oxymoron as the notion of barbaric habits. For the positivists, progress means departure from and a radical break with habits and tradition. The previous *fin de siècle* thinkers remind us, however, that every innovation eventually becomes a habit, and that it is an extension of previous habits. Thus, a residue of the past is always carried along into the present and future.

If Veblen and his colleagues were completely on the wrong track, one would be at a loss to explain contemporary addiction to sports, gambling, violence, intoxicants, lawns, pets, and other barbaric throwbacks. According to the positivists, we should have outgrown all this irrationalism long ago. The postmodernists write as if all contemporary concern with useless and *kitsch* phenomena (but not habits) was something new, a radical departure from the modernity project. Veblen is certainly more convincing.

We shall not enter the ill-fated debate on whether postmodernism constitutes a rebellion against or an extension of the modernity project. Our approach is more radical, in that it seeks the ground and referent for both postmodernism and positivism in the neo-Kantian attempt to sever the heart or will from discourse. We shall be deconstructing and subverting both the postmodernist and modernist projects, because both are archaic throwbacks to philosophical assumptions that had already been soundly criticized in the previous turn of the century.

The remainder of this book shall fill in the details of this argument. Here, we wish merely to lay out the foundations for the argument, and to defend our starting-points for analysis.

NARROWING THE FOCUS TO DURKHEIM AND FREUD

Although we began with Veblen, we shall shift the focus to Freud and Durkheim, but we shall invoke some of their other *fin de siècle* contemporaries as well. We shall continue to refer to Veblen where appropriate. The justification for this strategy is as follows: Veblen has been labeled as a satirist, an outsider, and a cynic, so that linking him to the German Romantic tradition is neither original nor very useful. The end results of the fruits of our misplaced labors in reviving Veblen would be that the *status quo*, neo-Kantian version of sociology would remain intact, because Veblen is no longer taken seriously. But Durkheim is still perceived in mainstream sociology as the prince of positivism and *status quo* functionalism. And Freud, despite the adulation accorded him by novelists, humanists, and cultural interpreters of all sorts, including the Frankfurt School, is still regarded by social scientists primarily as a doctor of the mind, the forerunner of the positivistic program whose aims are to impose rational order onto the chaos of the id. For us to subvert (from Lyotard) these comfortable, bourgeois images of Freud and Durkheim into the images conjured up by Veblen would have an immense pay-off: we would be challenging the core narratives that are used to prop up mainstream, positivistic sociological theory. This is what we intend to do.

If we were loyal disciples of Lyotard, there would be no need to justify this effort at sabotage. Lyotard commends such subversive efforts to cross traditional turf barriers (in this case, among psychology, sociology, philosophy, and cultural studies), no questions asked. But our aim is not to contribute further to intellectual fragmentation for its own sake. Rather, the aim is to challenge directly the Parsonian effort to link Freud and Durkheim *vis-à-vis* the Enlightenment narrative of rational social action, and supplant it with the original, Schopenhauerian, *fin de siècle* basis for what Freud and Durkheim have to teach us about barbarism. By extension, we are also challenging Habermas's efforts to assimilate the thrust of critical theory into a Parsonian version of systems theory, and Giddens's own efforts to extend Habermas and Parsons.[16]

Some readers will balk at the detailed analysis that follows, the seemingly tedious dismantling of current habits of thought, and the equally detailed analysis of Freud's and Durkheim's actual theoretical scaffolding. Hasn't every serious sociologist already read Durkheim and Freud? Yes, but they have been read from perspectives derived from the Enlightenment. Our aim is to read them in their original *fin de siècle* context, the same context that nurtured Veblen's thought, and this is quite new. It will take a long time and much careful reading to arrive, finally, at the discussion of barbarity and its relationship to modernity, and to return, at long last, to Veblen. But the topic is serious – everyone knows that barbarism must be comprehended if humanity is to survive, let alone progress – and the postmodern impulse of play is not really an appropriate response to such a serious task (even though we invoked it at the beginning as subterfuge in order to convince the reader to give Veblen and his contemporaries a chance to be heard). The intricate analysis of an intricate problem is justified by the prize that is sought.

Others will protest that the effort is not worthwhile because it is not original: Parsons (1948, 1962, 1971) has already linked Freud and Durkheim, while others will note that Parsons has been criticized so many times since the 1960s, further criticism is something on the order of "beating a dead horse." Didn't Habermas as well as the Frankfurt School already achieve something of this sort? We have already made explicit our criticisms of Parsons and Habermas *vis-à-vis* their extension of the Kantian world-view, and obfuscation of Schopenhauer's challenge to this world-view. Nevertheless, because the starting-point for an analysis is its most important part, we shall elaborate further.

With the demise of the Chicago School of sociology in the

1920s and the ascendancy of the Harvard School in the 1930s, the previous *fin de siècle* spirit was eclipsed almost completely by a revival of the very, hyper-abstractionist systems of thought that the founding fathers of the social sciences criticized vehemently: utilitarianism, pragmatism, behaviorism, positivism, and all sorts of "rational action" theories. The primacy of the will was simply forgotten, and the Kantian model was revived quickly. In the Kantian universe, one cannot find truth, essences, or the will. Instead, all knowledge is conditioned by the knowing subject and his or her *a priori* categories, whose origins are unknown and unquestioned. All known objects are categorized in terms of time, space, and causality, and all knowledge is reduced to appearances. Science is given the task of classifying these appearances and explaining changes in terms of time, space, and causes, but is forbidden to venture into questions of habit, essence, truth, or anything else that posits a reality beneath appearances. Morality is reduced to rational conduct according to rules whose essence is never questioned.

Thus, Parsons succeeded in assimilating Freud and Durkheim (among the other founding fathers of the social sciences, with the notable exception of Veblen and Simmel, who proved too tough to handle) into this neo-Kantian framework. Parsons invented a vocabulary of norms, beliefs, values, sanctions, internalization, social order, and other concepts that reproduced the Kantian world of glib appearances. And he was not alone. Piaget, Kohlberg, Habermas, and their many disciples all went along with this revival of an archaic and outmoded way of thinking that had already been dismantled by Schopenhauer, Nietzsche, Freud, Veblen, and others in the previous *fin de siècle*. Twentieth-century social science hardly ever asked whether any of these Parsonian propositions were true – for it was assumed that questions of truth are illegitimate. It simply assumed that anyone who does not go along with this system is a deviant, a breaker of norms, and went on to theorize how deviants should be controlled or assimilated. The ancient philosophical problem of understanding human evil was transformed into the trivial and silly problem of predicting and controlling deviance – as if that were possible. It is worth recalling here Durkheim's ([1895] 1982) awesome and typically *fin de siècle* claim that crime is normal, and that no matter how perfect a society becomes, it will *always* regard some things as criminal. And the standard Parsonian definition of deviance as the breaking of social norms applies equally to Einstein as well as any psychopath. This moral and intellectual pedantry occurred in a century that had witnessed barbarism on a grand scale – the Gulags, the Holocaust, Hiroshima, the Great War, among others – and this seemingly unprecedented eruption of evil was mostly passed over in silence, as argued by Bauman (1989).[17]

Parsons was criticized by Mills (1959) and others on ideological, not philosophical grounds. Thus, "conflict theory" came on the scene to challenge the Parsonian assumption of "social order." But conflict theory is equally shallow and trivial: implicitly, it equates war with family disagreements in its assumption that conflict is more basic than order. Like functionalism, conflict theory never probes into essentialist issues. Like Kantianism, it never makes qualitative distinctions between transgressions of norms, and never ventures into the problem of compassion. Its grand achievement was the realization that society exists on a microscopic scale, in which conflict often holds relationships together, in opposition to Parsons's exclusive focus on "macro" systems. And the trend in the 1990s is to find linkages between "micro" and "macro" social theories, led by Jeffrey Alexander (1982, 1988) and his followers. None of these challenges to or revisions of Parsonian functionalism have penetrated into or questioned the Kantian world-view that Parsons revived. None of these criticisms have taken seriously the tough criticisms of rational social order based on Enlightenment narratives that are found in the works of Nietzsche, Thomas Mann, Max Horkheimer, and Veblen that we have already reviewed.

Horkheimer captures well how it is possible to engage in a long-winded discussion without making radical progress:

> If one wishes to prove the validity of a tenet that clearly contradicts experience and is historically discredited, it should be made the subject of the most difficult and learned investigations. This will create the impression that the things one discusses with so much ingenuity cannot possibly be chimeras . . . Particularly when one has the power to make them the topic of lectures or treatises, they will appear relevant. All direct formulations must be avoided . . . the

laymen will then readily believe that reality, this world, is only one among many, and the experts will have a new or, rather, their old problematics. The mist in which they lose themselves may not be a beyond, but it is a dream – and spirit realm. Anyone who has not mastered the subtle and quickly changing conceptual apparatus these people use will seem ignorant and unimportant. He has no say.

(1978: 99)

Baudrillard (1988, 1990) and some other postmodernists also assume a neo-Kantian world-view even as they pretend to criticize the grand narratives of the Enlightenment. They impose the trick that Horkheimer describes, above. Notice how faithfully Baudrillard's work remains on the Kantian plane of concepts, appearances, images, and perceptions. He ignores the will or the forbidden thing-in-itself as completely as Kant did. His controversial claim that the world is nothing but a mess of circulating fictions, without ground or referent, is really just the end-point of Kant's philosophy. Similarly, Habermas's entire discussion remains on this level of communicative, rational action, and never penetrates beyond the ego or the self, discovered by Kant, to the tumultuous will that lies beneath the surface of rationalizations.

The only notable exception to this neo-Kantian program is the Frankfurt School – albeit its legacy is ambiguous at best, for reasons already discussed. These scholars took seriously Freud's libido theory, recognized the unresolved contradictions that permeate modern living, and questioned whether happiness can or should be a goal for humans. Horkheimer took Schopenhauer very seriously (although Adorno did not, except for his writings on music). But the Frankfurt School never achieved the popularity enjoyed by mainstream functionalism or the success of Habermas and Giddens. And critical theorists glorified Marx at the expense of Durkheim, whom they ignored. As such, they always remained on the left-wing fringes of academia. Moreover, Marx bought into some of the Kantian and Hegelian assumptions that Schopenhauer and Nietzsche criticized, among them, that consciousness is the prime moving force in societies, that consciousness can be changed through social engineering, and that progress is the underlying blueprint in historical change. Freud held to the contrary Schopenhauerian assumption that the chaotic will, not consciousness, moves the universe, and that the locus of the will is *the body*, not society. Freud's *Civilization and Its Discontents* ([1930] 1961) is a typically *fin de siècle* statement. The marriage between Freud and Marx in critical theory proved to be irreconcilable from the start. By contrast, the proposed marriage between Freud and Durkheim should be a good one, if one bases this prognosis on their mutual, Schopenhauerian background (Mestrovic 1988).

Thus, to seek out Freud and Durkheim in their original *fin de siècle* context, prior to their vulgarization at the hands of Parsons, Habermas, and other twentieth-century revivals of Kantianism, is new and worthwhile. And it is a project that is in keeping with the aspirations of postmodern philosophy, for if one truly challenges Enlightenment narratives, one is seeking an alternative to theories that glorify the mind, the ego, and a world of appearances. That alternative has been laid out for us by Schopenhauer, Nietzsche, and other *fin de siècle* luminaries. It is the will, Kant's forbidden thing-in-itself. Our aim is to link two of the most important figures in the social sciences, Freud and Durkheim, with this *fin de siècle* spirit in order to draw fresh conclusions concerning the problem of how barbarism relates to modernity. In Schopenhauer's words, Kant laid out the table and established the rules of etiquette, but never delivered the meal. At this late date, it is high time to serve the meal.

The conjunction of Plato, Schopenhauer, Freud, and Durkheim, along with other *fin de siècle* luminaries, is meant to throw new light on dilemmas and philosophical issues that continue to beset the modern social sciences, up to and including the postmodern discourse. We do not use the metaphor for illumination lightly. Schopenhauer devotes many pages to the phenomena of illumination and light as metaphors for quieting the obscure, egotistical, and tyrannical will so that the genuine power of the mind as integrated with the will can be exposed. By ignoring the philosophical roots and interrelatedness of the thinkers mentioned thus far, the positivistic social sciences are still mired in darkness and obscurity.

We shall preclude from the outset any positivistic evaluation of the metaphysics found in the thought of Plato, Schopenhauer, Freud, Durkheim, and other *fin de siècle* thinkers. *Fin de siècle* continental German philosophy challenged the Enlightenment faith in reason, so that such an evaluation would negate the analysis, and would be nothing but an exercise in tautology. Perhaps one reason why Durkheim's affinity with Schopenhauer's philosophy has not been developed in contemporary sociology is the prevailing bias in favor of positivism and the Enlightenment. But this fact should not prevent an analysis of Durkheim's intellectual milieu which suggests that he, like so many of his contemporaries, was engaged in large measure in reversing the most fundamental assumption of the Enlightenment, that reason is in firm control over the passions.

Moreover, as Schopenhauer correctly points out, metaphysics is unavoidable. Positivism, especially Comte's version, is no less metaphysical than Schopenhauer, only Comte was intellectually dishonest about this fact (see Horkheimer 1972a). The very positivistic assumption that humankind is subject to the invisible law of progress from metaphysical to rational societies assumes a metaphysical faith in reason. After all, "progress" cannot be operationalized and falsified, because it always involves degeneration, and the human subject's interpretation of how many gains offset the losses to constitute progress. And Veblen (1973) has a point when he claims that backwardness can often be advantageous (see Elster 1984). When contemporary social scientists claim they want to avoid metaphysics in favor of empiricism, they overlook the obvious point uncovered by Kant that the faculty of judgment is required to make the huge leap from raw data to concepts. Freud, Durkheim, Veblen, and many of their contemporaries definitely incorporated metaphysics into their versions of social science, and we shall be as open about this fact as they were. It is not fruitful to try to deny it, and to force them into an ill-conceived positivistic mold. And regardless of how fruitful it might be to try to change the fact that they absorbed Schopenhauer's metaphysics, it would be dishonest. It is time to face up to the fact that the modern social sciences were born in the *fin de siècle* that was itself drenched in pessimism and metaphysics.

CHOOSING AND DEFENDING THE STARTING-POINTS FOR ANALYSIS

Arthur Schopenhauer was one of those philosophers who felt that the most important aspect of an argument is its starting-point, not the logic that supports it. It is interesting that Plato, too, always devotes the opening pages of his dialogues to finding the true as opposed to the false starting-point. This is the Socratic signature in philosophy. Schopenhauer ([1813] 1899) also insisted that one's choice of the starting-point is not really a rational decision, but is intuitive, although reason should be used to follow through on it. The starting-point for most of the postmodern discourse as well as the positivistic readings of the origins of the social sciences is derived from Enlightenment culture: that the mind is stronger than the will. Schopenhauer's importance is that he reversed this starting-point, and thereby set an entirely new course for *fin de siècle* thought relative to the Enlightenment.

But in his influential study of Durkheim, Lukes quotes a historian to the effect that in 1884 France, "one attitude of mind, one doctrine dominated and excited French intellectual life: scientific positivism, issuing from Auguste Comte" (1985: 67). Lukes adds that "this attitude of mind was certainly shared by Durkheim" (ibid.). Scores of twentieth-century *sociologists* before and after Lukes have uncritically adopted this starting-point in reading Durkheim's works, the most influential being Talcott Parsons (1937). But their starting-point is contradicted by other intellectuals who write in disciplines that border on sociology. One cannot prove or disprove a starting-point, for it involves metaphysical choice. But one can justify or discredit these choices, and this is what we shall attempt here.

Evidence abounds that Schopenhauer's philosophy had supplanted positivism at the turn of the century, especially in France (Baillot 1927).[18] Schopenhauer's influence could have reached both Freud and Durkheim from any number of indirect sources that surrounded a fledgling sociology and psychology in the previous *fin de siècle*. Magee (1983) has demonstrated Schopenhauer's influence on Nietzsche, Wittgenstein, and William James in philosophy, and both Freud and Durkheim cite Nietzsche and James. Magee also includes Tolstoy, Conrad, T.S. Eliot, Proust, Zola, Maupassant, Hardy, and Thomas Mann in Schopenhauer's sphere of influence. Incidentally, all of these novelists, and others,[19] were concerned with the problem of how evil and barbarism are nurtured by bourgeois living and derivatives of the Enlightenment project. Similarly, Ellenberger (1970) adds to this list Henri Bergson, who was Durkheim's colleague at the Sorbonne; Carl Gustav Jung, who corresponded with Lucien Lévy-Bruhl; as well as a host of others who are now less illustrious than they were in Durkheim's time. For example, one finds degeneration as the main theme in the writings of Nietzsche, Lombroso, Henry Adams, H.G. Wells, and D.H. Lawrence, among many others.[20] Ellenberger adds: "In the last decades of the nineteenth century, the philosophical concept of the unconscious, as taught by Schopenhauer and Von Hartmann, was extremely popular, and most contemporary philosophers admitted the existence of an unconscious mental life" (1970: 311).

The philosopher turned part-time sociologist, Georg Simmel, deserves special mention. In his *Schopenhauer and Nietzsche*, this founding father of sociology (admitted very late into the sociological club) gives us one more reason why Schopenhauer's philosophy should be considered a good starting-point for analysis: "During the past several dozen years, the absolute preponderance of suffering over happiness in life is the definitive portrait of life's value that gave Schopenhauer's philosophy its general significance and signature" ([1907] 1986: 53). Simmel appreciated the fact that "Schopenhauer destroyed the dogma that rationality is the deep-seated and basic essence of man that lies beneath the other ripples of life" (ibid.: 28) whereas "all philosophers prior to Schopenhauer conceived of man as a rational being." Simmel posited the antagonism between "life" (an abbreviation of the will to life) and its "forms" that ultimately results in Simmel's own version of "civilization and its discontents" because the will "condemns [all] to eternal dissatisfaction" (ibid.: 5). To repeat, the *fin de siècle* was a pessimistic era, and the origins of sociology did not escape it. Simmel could hardly foresee the extent of the barbarism that erupted in the West after his death in 1917, a barbarism that was fueled by the discontent he prophesied, but he outlined the referents for apprehending it.

Freud was honest about his intellectual affinities with Schopenhauer. In his *Autobiographical Study*, he wrote that to a large extent "psychoanalysis coincides with the philosophy of Schopenhauer – not only did he assert the dominance of the emotions and the supreme importance of sexuality, but he was even aware of the mechanism of repression" ([1925] 1959: 59). Yet these are among the cornerstones of the psychoanalytic conceptual apparatus. Ellenberger (1970) and Ernest Jones (1981) join in Freud's own rather long list of the affinities between Freud and Schopenhauer: the concept of the unconscious, the focus on death as the problem that stands at the outset of every philosophy, the psychoanalytical omnipotence of thoughts, and the general proposition that man is not "master of his own house" – among *many* others. In the middle of his *New Introductory Lectures*, Freud paused and said to his audience:

> You may perhaps shrug your shoulders and say: "That isn't natural science, it's Schopenhauer's philosophy!" But, Ladies and Gentlemen, why should not a bold thinker have guessed something that is afterwards confirmed by sober and painstaking detailed research?
>
> ([1933] 1965: 107)

Yet none of these connections are obvious. Again, Bloom has a point when he claims that notwithstanding Freud's philosophical starting-points, Americans have concluded that "psychotherapy would make individuals happy, as sociology would improve societies" (1987: 149). Freud was handed over to the psychologists, and Durkheim to the sociologists. David Riesman has remarked that while Freud's concept of the id and focus on the irrational are well-known, he is still considered to be a "doctor of the mind" who left us a rational legacy that would solve problems.[21] How in the world can one apprehend barbarism with these rose-colored glasses? American optimism has co-opted Freud's legacy so that despite Ellenberger, Mann, Jones, and Freud's own terribly gloomy admissions – Dr Freud has found an ambiguous place in American society as well as academia (see also Kurzweil 1990). One must reckon with Schopenhauer's un-American claim that "there is only one inborn error, and that is the notion that we exist in order to be happy" ([1818] 1969b: 634).

No one will ever know for certain whether Durkheim explicitly acknowledged his intellectual debt to Schopenhauer's philosophy, because most of Durkheim's papers and lectures were destroyed in World War II.[22] But anyone who is familiar with Schopenhauer's philosophy will probably come to appreciate the import of Lalande's remark that Durkheim was nicknamed "Schopen."

Thus, despite substantial evidence that the starting-points chosen for this analysis are commensurate with existing knowledge about the importance of the *fin de siècle* spirit – at least in academic disciplines outside sociology – this work is nevertheless pursuing new territory. Despite scholarly knowledge of the previous *fin de siècle*, contemporary thought among laypersons as well as many social scientists continues to be dominated by pragmatism, cultural relativism, and naive, ideological optimism, which have distorted the origins of the social sciences. Moreover, they make it impossible to comprehend evil, deep-seated unhappiness, and barbarism as the sources for philosophical astonishment, whereas Freud, Durkheim, and their *fin de siècle* contemporaries were concerned directly and passionately with these dark phenomena that erupted so forcefully in the West after their careers had expired.

The preceding context for apprehending Freud and Durkheim leads to an unexpected, but extremely relevant, reappreciation of their thought relative to the problem that concerns us here, the relationship of barbarism to the modernity project. Both Durkheim and Freud refer to all sorts of behavior, impulses, thoughts, and currents based on egoism that lead to many sorts of wickedness. Their discussions range across the topics that our neo-Kantian age has classified under the headings of murder, suicide, accidents, cunning, fraud, etc. But they never devote a work exclusively to barbarism *per se*. True, Durkheim wrote *Suicide*, but both thinkers use murder and suicide throughout their writings as vehicles for a much wider, moral and philosophical discussion, and never arrived at an "operational" theory that could be tested by the positivists. And like Schopenhauer, they both regarded modern aggression as something that is derived from the emancipated will, moreover, a will whose blind fury could be channeled against the self or others, depending upon circumstances.

We must set aside immediately the neo-Kantian tendency to limit discussions of Freud's and Durkheim's works to carefully circumscribed methodologies, concepts, and other conceptual limits. Given the exposition that has been presented thus far, it should be obvious that this approach does violence to their intentions to offer a cultural interpretation of barbarism. For example, when read in the broad context presented here, Durkheim's *Suicide* is *not* just an empirical study about suicide *per se*. Rather, it is an interpretive work that invokes metaphysical, moral, and epistemological issues that pertain to all sorts of destruction of self and others. Given our aims, it is more fruitful to compare Durkheim's *Suicide* to Plato's many references to the philosopher as one who seeks death or Schopenhauer's far-ranging but scattered discussion of suicide in relation to the will. We have little choice but to invoke Durkheim's *Suicide*, because it has attained the level of a sociological classic, and because it deals with the issues that are essential to our discussion. But the reader would be ignoring our entire exposition thus far by reverting back to the old-fashioned, positivistic and Parsonian misreadings of this classic. Despite the lengthy, careful and detailed deconstruction of these mainstream misreadings offered thus far, we continue to worry that our intentions shall be misconstrued, because the Parsonian, positivist tendencies are so deeply ingrained. They have attained the status of habits.

The positivists have been trying to digest Durkheim's *Suicide* for nearly a century now. Literally thousands of studies that correlate suicide with a plethora of other variables have failed to arrive at a universal, positivistic law that will enable scientists to predict and control suicide *per se*. But from the metaphysical starting-points used in our discussion, it appears that such rational, modern aims may not have been Durkheim's intentions. Instead, if one reads Durkheim's *Suicide* as a piece of literature, a masterpiece of writing and thought, even an existential treatise, a coherent and disturbing message emerges: in the wide range of phenomena exhibited by suicide *and* murder (and most commentators neglect his discussion of murder) one finds the exaggerated form of virtues that society requires for its well-being. For example, anomie, as a state of unlimited desires, is absolutely essential for social progress, for without it, humans would not question authority. But anomie, which is a modern virtue, easily leads to states of exasperated weariness that can lead to anomic suicide or murder, as well as all sorts of twilight states of pathology that irritate positivists (because these states cannot be measured or "observed" scientifically), but that continue to be found in postmodern societies, from neurosis to the deranged rule that success is open-ended, so that no one can ever be fully satisfied with one's progress. The functionalists have tried to assimilate Durkheim into their antiseptic. modern version of social theory in which suicide *per se* – suicide as an alleged "hard fact" – is merely an act of deviance that stems from "normlessness" (a word that Durkheim never used), and that can be controlled. Durkheim's message is actually far more horrifying, and profoundly relevant.

Similarly, Freud never arrived at a final statement on murder or suicide, and treated both as phenomena that range so far and wide in social life, that he, too, has exasperated the positivists. Freud found murderous-suicidal wishes in children against their parents and against themselves, and vice versa, and he regarded these wishes – which are sometimes unconscious, to complicate matters further still – as seriously as the "acts." He found these wishes in his patients, in himself, and in practically everyone. This is still a disturbing vision, despite all the followers, revisionists, and critics who have commented upon and tried to assimilate Freud into some sort of Enlightenment narrative that will help one predict and control these wishes.

There is still another aspect of Freud's and Durkheim's legacy on barbarism that has been missed, remarkably, after all these years of studying them. This is that they derive the wishes to kill and be killed from the will to life, not an urge to cause death in oneself or another. True to the *fin de siècle* spirit, they were always unmasking surface reality, so that contemporary concerns with reifying and distinguishing dangerous versus non-dangerous individuals would have seemed silly to them.[23] Similarly, Schopenhauer derives suicide from the will to life, which is a refraction of Plato's Eros. Freud, whose concept of the death wish is ultimately fueled by Eros (see Laplanche 1976) or *the life instinct*, remains remarkably close to the Schopenhauerian and Platonic model. And when Durkheim associates egoistic and anomic suicide with egoism and anomie, which are virtues in modern societies, he is assuming that the border between normality and pathology is *not* hard and fast, but is crossed by everyone routinely every day – only some people stray further than others on particular days.

Chapter 5

Choosing philosophical trajectories regarding barbarism

[America] is a world completely rotten with wealth, power, senility, indifference, puritanism, and mental hygiene, power and waste, technological futility and aimless violence, and yet I cannot help but feel it has about it something of the dawning of the universe.

(Jean Baudrillard 1986: 23)

The vehemence of the will keeps pace with the enhancement of the intelligence, just because in reality this enhancement always springs from the will's increased needs and more pressing demands.

(Arthur Schopenhauer [1818] 1969b: 280)

What sets our study apart from most contemporary studies is that we are seeking the secret connection between civilization and barbarism. We challenge the widespread assumption expressed from Descartes, Kant, and Hume to Parsons, Elias, Giddens, and Habermas that the Enlightenment project refines, or is at least able to control, the base tendencies of the human animal. On the contrary, we have aligned ourselves with the trajectory that runs backward from Horkheimer and Adorno's *Dialectic of Enlightenment* through Jung to Veblen, Durkheim, Freud, Tocqueville, Nietzsche, Schopenhauer and the previous *fin de siècle* spirit all the way back to Plato. These thinkers hold that enlightenment exacerbates the will, heightens the tension that is part of the human condition, and yields an ideal-type civilized human who is simultaneously more polished *and* potentially more savage compared to our ancestors. Moreover, and despite their rhetoric of rebellion, we regard Baudrillard and the postmodernists as writing in the neo-Kantian trajectories derived from the Enlightenment.

But our aim is to push further still, past this Nietzschean assessment to the Schopenhauerian formula that preceded it, and has been forgotten: along with heightened barbarism, there occurs a heightened, genuinely human capacity to experience compassion. This insight found its way into Tocqueville's sketch of good America that opposes the bad, Veblen's focus on Christian ethics to offset the predatory habits found in the business world, Jung's Great Mother archetype, and especially Durkheim's insight that only modern societies characterized by organic solidarity are held together by communal affection. This means that barbarism *cannot* be brought under rational social control, as taught by disciples of the Enlightenment, but can be offset – and then only partially – by virtuous or benign aspects of the irrational will. We shall aim at resolving the unfinished problem left over from the previous *fin de siècle*: how in the world does one cultivate the "good" habits of the heart, given that virtue cannot be taught?

This is a formidable problem. Before we attempt to tackle it we shall devote many chapters to deconstructing further orthodox functionalist theories of social order as well as postmodernist theories of apparent disorder. It might seem that the postmodernists would be our allies, for they too purport to rebel at the oppressive, grand narratives of the Enlightenment. But as we have demonstrated already, the postmodernists share the neo-Kantian assumptions of their enemies, especially that the world is nothing but a mass of contingent appearances and that whatever constitutes morality, it is nothing more than a rootless set of cognitively known rules and duties. Only the postmodernists do not take the rules and duties seriously, but then even orthodox Kantians could not ground their categorical imperative in anything other than *a priori* wishful thinking. Postmodernism may be likened to a bastard child of Kant and Nietzsche: It revels in a world that is nothing but fiction, and tries to move to a position that is "beyond good and evil." Like Nietzsche's philosophy, postmodernist philosophy is pitiless and hard when confronted by human suffering. (Refer to Baudrillard's admonitions, already cited, that the poor "must exit.") The main difference is that instead of Nietzsche's aristocratic hardness, it teaches a plebeian hardness – but it is a tough philosophy nevertheless.

An excellent way to detect these contradictions within the

postmodernist narratives, as well as to make the connection with neo-Kantianism, is to simply compare and contrast Baudrillard, Kant, Nietzsche, and Schopenhauer on the issue of barbarism. Schopenhauer rebelled against Kant whereas Baudrillard assimilates Kant. Nietzsche kept Schopenhauer's focus on the will, but disagreed with his master about the viability of compassion as an ethic. By contrast, Baudrillard's postmodern philosophy is a shallow imitation of Nietzsche's attempt to move "beyond good and evil," minus Nietzsche's Schopenhauerian faith that there exists a will beneath phenomena. In sum, Baudrillard bastardizes Nietzsche in a manner that is similar to his shallow reading of Veblen.

Our aim in this chapter is to present an overview of the large, philosophical fissures that we shall be following in this project. We shall align Baudrillard with Kant, to suggest that postmodernist philosophy shares many of the neo-Kantian assumptions found in orthodox functionalism. Against them, one finds Nietzsche and Schopenhauer criticizing the Kantian universe of appearances, and differing primarily on the issue of Christian ethics.

BAUDRILLARD AND SCHOPENHAUER ON AESTHETICS AND CULTURE

Allan Bloom (1987: 68–81) connects the postmodern generation's obsession with round-the-clock music, and especially Music Television (MTV), with Plato's teaching that music is the "barbarous expression of the soul." This is a significant observation in any discussion of contemporary barbarism. Veblen omits music from his long list of modern, barbaric habits, probably because in his era, the listener still chose the time and place that one would give in to the barbaric power of music. Besides, they did not have transistor radios in Veblen's day. Schopenhauer would probably have agreed with Bloom, for he cites Plato and Aristotle to make the claim that "music is the language of feeling and of passion, just as words are the language of reason" ([1818] 1969a: 259). To the degree that one cannot escape popular music in our contemporary culture – for it is everywhere, in elevators, shopping malls, dentist's offices, homes, lobbies, you name it – educators have been bemoaning a dramatic drop in literacy and basic language skills in the MTV pop generation.

In contrast to Plato, Bloom, and Schopenhauer, Baudrillard is not troubled by music. For him, MTV is less a phenomenon that involves music but rather Music *Television*, the translation of the soul's barbaric passions into visual images. For Baudrillard (1986: 56), television images "are a system of luxury prefabrication, brilliant syntheses of the stereotypes of life and love" that embody one single passion only, "the passion for images, and the immanence of desire in the image." In this radical departure from the Platonic model, the distinction between image and reality vanishes into the dream of hyperreality, and America's love for the television screen makes it "the world centre of the inauthentic" (ibid.: 91). Today, "all that fascinates us is the *spectacle* of the brain and its workings" (ibid.: 36). And, Baudrillard concludes, "without this perpetual video, nothing has any meaning today" such that "the mirror phase has given way to the video phase" (ibid.: 37).

Schopenhauer taught that in the long process of evolution, the brain and its hook-up with the visual apparatus pertaining to the eyes developed last, whereas the sense of smell and the ability to hear developed first. Thus, the triumph of the visual can be interpreted as the triumph of the enlightenment process overall (not just the specific period known as the Enlightenment). But Schopenhauer elaborates on Plato that the so-called enlightened person's ability to tolerate noise in general indicates reversion to barbarism. Noise distracts mental activity, and is a counter-enlightenment phenomenon. One should add to Bloom's analysis that the MTV generation likes its music loud – *extremely* loud, to the point that attendance at rock concerts has been found to correlate with increased deafness. But Schopenhauer condemns noise in general, for example, the noise of barking dogs (another aspect neglected by Veblen in his fascinating analysis of keeping dogs as a barbaric habit). In general, according to Schopenhauer:

> The man who habitually slams doors instead of shutting them with the hand, or allows this to be done in his house, is not merely ill-mannered, but also coarse and narrow-minded . . . we shall be quite civilized only when our ears are no longer outlawed, and it is no longer anyone's right to cut through the consciousness of every thinking being within a circuit of a 1000 yards, by means of whistling, howling, bellowing,

hammering, whip-cracking, letting dogs bark, and so on. The Sybarites banished all noisy trades from their city; the venerable sect of the Shakers in North America tolerated no unnecessary noise in their villages.

([1818] 1969b: 30)

Schopenhauer's examples are quaint compared with the noise pollution we all suffer today. What would he have said concerning the noise caused by lawn mowers, airplanes, cars, and the general but steady background hum of noise found in all major Western cities? From the ritualized din of lawn mowers on Saturday mornings to the distressing middle-class habit of leaving the television on for most hours of the day, even when no one is watching, postmodern humans betray the fact that for them, absolute quiet and serenity are intolerable. The crucial point is that Baudrillard ignores music and noise in his exaggeration of the dominance of the visual, whereas Schopenhauer alerts us to the paradox that the hyper-visual postmodern human tolerates an incredible amount of noise, and thereby betrays his or her latent barbarism. Schopenhauer's insight into noise is conspicuously absent in Elias's (1982) acclaimed study of the civilizing process. This is because Elias's starting-point for analysis is the assumption that etiquette is an adequate index for institutionalized self-constraint. Noise is relevant to his view of things only to the extent that individuals are supposed to be quiet in libraries, churches, and other specific settings – but Elias's theory does not account for the institutionalized and background noise found in all postmodern cultures. Schopenhauer begins with the empirical observation that nothing startles our mental concentration more than noise (he elaborates that we can enjoy lightning but thunder is always disconcerting), and ventures into an analysis of social habits with regard to noise tolerance that is reminiscent of Veblen's strategy. Schopenhauer seems to have a point.

But again, Baudrillard (1986: 65) delights in the fact that the TV is constantly on, and even though he agrees that "Americans are barbarians" (ibid.: 67), he defends their lack of culture: "If it is the lack of culture that is original, then it is the lack of culture one should embrace" (ibid.: 101).

Another connection that Schopenhauer ([1818] 1969b: 61) draws is between the life of the animal as a continual present and the lives of the great majority of modern, so-called enlightened humans. Indeed, Frisby (1986) draws on Georg Simmel's philosophical sociology to assert that modernity institutionalizes the sense of an eternal present. From Tocqueville ([1845] 1945)[1] to Baudrillard (1981), scores of intellectuals have commented that modern persons are losing the sense of history as well as a future. Baudrillard (1986: 80) delights in the fact that America "was created in the hope of escaping from history." Nevertheless, Schopenhauer hits hard when he questions how this ahistorical sense is different from the life-experience of animals.[2] He cites empirical examples drawn from architecture, that the ancients built structures to last for hundreds if not thousands of years, and that blended with the surrounding environment, whereas modern human animals build anti-ecological structures that scarcely survive a generation. By contrast, Baudrillard (1986: 17) praises the wild, inhuman type of anti-architecture found in New York, "without considerations of setting, well-being, or ideal ecology." He adds that eco-architecture and eco-society constitute "the gentle hell of the Roman Empire in its decline" (ibid.: 17).

Schopenhauer does not believe that so-called enlightenment has really succeeded in making most persons cultured. He writes that

> purely intellectual pleasures are not accessible to the vast majority of men. They are almost wholly incapable of the pleasure to be found in pure knowledge; they are entirely given over to willing. Therefore, if anything is to win their sympathy, to be *interesting* to them, it must (and this is to be found already in the meaning of the word) in some way excite their *will*, even if it be only through a remote relation to it which is merely within the bounds of possibility. The will must never be left entirely out of question, since their existence lies far more in willing than in knowing; action and reaction are their only element. The naive expressions of this quality can be seen in trifles and everyday phenomena; thus, for example, they write their names up at places worth seeing which they visit, in order thus to react on, to affect the place, since it does not affect them. Further, they cannot easily just contemplate a rare and strange animal, but must excite it, tease it, play with it, just to experience action and reaction.

But this need for exciting the will shows itself particularly in the invention and maintenance of card-playing, which is in the truest sense an expression of the wretched side of humanity.

([1818] 1969a: 314)

Horkheimer (1947) as well as Adorno (1991) substantiate Schopenhauer's claims that modern persons mainly act and react to and upon their environment rather than contemplate. Contemplation presupposes the state of will-less-ness that Schopenhauer describes as the hallmark of the cultured human animal. Indeed, everyone knows that for anything to sell these days – even serious books – it must be "exciting," which means, typically, associated in some way with the barbaric ideas of prestige, sex, and violence. Even Schopenhauer's empirical examples still ring true: graffiti are such an enormous problem in these postmodern times, that they have been assimilated, institutionalized as an art form. Anyone who has been to a zoo knows that humans behave as savagely toward animals as Schopenhauer claims. And Las Vegas has become the Mecca of card-playing and gambling in general, because gambling and cards create artificial excitement in an otherwise insipid life.

But for Baudrillard, Las Vegas, the "great whore" in the desert that he likens to a modern TV screen, is magnificent in its immorality. For him, graffiti are a manifestation of the "I did it!" mentality that leads postmodern persons to enter marathons and to want to go to the moon. "Graffiti carry the same message. They simply say, I'm so and so, and I exist! They are free publicity for existence" (1986: 21). The Platonic, Schopenhauerian art of contemplation is completely absent in Baudrillard's postmodern philosophy.

This is because for Schopenhauer, one experiences the sublime when one is able to quiet the imperious will momentarily, and can thereby contemplate an object as Plato's pure Idea, as something that exists independently of one's desires: "For at the moment when, torn from the will, we have given ourselves up to pure, will-less knowing, we have stepped into another world, so to speak, where everything that moves our will, and thus violently agitates us, no longer exists" ([1818] 1969a: 197). Nietzsche agreed with his master that art is the sole, albeit temporary, deliverance from an all-devouring will, a state in which "we celebrate the Sabbath of the penal servitude of willing; the wheel of Ixion stands still" (ibid.: 196). Even Adorno (1991) insisted that only "high" art is true art, because it allows for this sort of contemplation. But Baudrillard holds to no notion of a will that must be made still and quiet. In a world of mere appearances, nothing can be sublime. Instead, Baudrillard and the postmodernists regard highly the *kitsch* that Schopenhauer would dismiss as the undisciplined expression of will.

For Schopenhauer, "everything is beautiful only so long as it does not concern us" ([1818] 1969b: 374). For this reason, Schopenhauer argues that all natural scenery is beautiful – it reminds us that humans do not matter in Nature's grand scheme of things. Baudrillard is also sensitive to Nature's grandeur, but for different reasons. For Baudrillard, Nature is a mirror of human creations, and he cannot contemplate any aesthetic scene without connecting it in some fashion with the human ego. For example, he writes that "the unfolding of the desert is infinitely close to the timelessness of film" (1986: 1). Contemplating the beauty of the setting for Salt Lake City, he writes: "It is the capitalist, transsexual pride of a people of mutants that gives the city its magic, equal and opposite to that of Las Vegas, that great whore on the other side of the desert." Summing up his travels in *America*, he remarks:

> Extraordinary sites, capitals of fiction become reality. Sublime, transpolitical sites of extraterritoriality, combining as they do the earth's undamaged geological grandeur with a sophisticated, nuclear, orbital computer technology.
>
> (Ibid.: 4)

In stark contrast to Baudrillard, Schopenhauer abhors the mixing of human culture with Nature. Schopenhauer writes:

> How aesthetic nature is! Every little spot entirely uncultivated and wild, in other words, left free to nature herself, however small it may be, if only man's paws will leave it alone, is at once decorated by her in the most tasteful manner, is draped with plants, flowers, and shrubs, whose easy unforced manner, natural grace, and delightful grouping testify that they have not grown up under the rod of correction of the great egoist, but that nature has here been freely active. Every neglected little place at once becomes beautiful.
>
> ([1818] 1969b: 404)

Whereas Schopenhauer recommends travel to the scholar because every new setting jars the will, shakes up its prejudices, and thereby allows objective, *authentic* insights to pass through the barriers created by habits and other routine, Baudrillard always finds the inauthentic. He feels that "even nature in California is a Hollywood parody of ancient Mediterranean landscapes: a sea that is too blue, mountains that are too rugged, a climate that is too gentle or too arid, an uninhabited disenchanted nature, deserted by the gods" (1986: 103). If one starts with the premise that everything is appearance and nothing but appearance, then one fake "scene" is as good as another. Baudrillard's philosophy is the credo of the vulgar, postmodern tourist in search of a spectacle who, when he or she arrives at the Grand Canyon, is disappointed that it doesn't look like it did on TV. Schopenhauer's philosophy is the old-fashioned and now quaint credo of the genius and the saint within us all who, when he or she is finally able to escape the grind of making a living day in and day out, realizes, in the midst of a forest or some other gift from Nature, what life is really about.

Schopenhauer asks a poignant question that affected Freud profoundly and that reverberates in Baudrillard's philosophy: "We have dreams; may not the whole of life be a dream? or more exactly: is there a sure criterion for distinguishing between dream and reality, between phantasms and real objects?" ([1818] 1969a: 16). Baudrillard's answer is negative, and the thrust of his postmodern philosophy seems to be that life might as well be a dream: "America is neither dream nor reality. It is hyperreality" (1986: 28). Freud's answer is unclear, and his struggle with distinguishing fantasies from reality in his patients is still being discussed. Schopenhauer's answer is complex: there is no distinct difference, because "life and dreams are leaves of one and the same book" ([1818] 1969a: 18). This is a metaphorical way of stating that the world is will and idea. But contrary to Baudrillard, Schopenhauer does not dispense with life, an objective reality, as the ground and referent for "dreams." Instead, he seeks their unity and connectedness.

Following Baudrillard and other postmodernists, the notion of hyper-reality – the institutionalized substitution of fantasy for reality – has been sanctioned as an integral aspect of hyper-civilization. Postmodern culture has been likened to a post-tourist or post-museum search for spectacle in which no-one cares about what is "really" represented (Featherstone 1988). Disney World is probably the greatest tribute to hyper-reality, but there are plenty of others (see Rojek 1990). Schopenhauer would have us consider that this constant search for new images devoid of context is infantile and barbaric, like "the childish delusion that books, like eggs, must be enjoyed while they are fresh" ([1818] 1969b: 147). Baudrillard agrees that it is barbaric, but so what? According to him:

> When Paul Getty gathers Rembrandts, Impressionists, and Greek statues together in a Pompeian villa on the Pacific coast, he is following American logic, the pure baroque logic of Disneyland. He is being original; it is a magnificent stroke of cynicism, naivety, kitsch, and unintended humour – something astonishing in its nonsensicality. Now the disappearance of aesthetics and higher values in kitsch and hyper-reality is fascinating, as is the disappearance of history and the real in the televisual. It is in this unfettered pragmatics of values that we should find some pleasure. If you simply remain fixated on the familiar canon of high culture, you miss the essential point (which is, precisely, the inessential).
>
> (1986: 101)

One could argue that Baudrillard's postmodern philosophy is a hyper-exaggeration of Kant's circumscription of knowledge to a game of concepts. This is because Baudrillard merely extends Kant's claim that the thing-in-itself as the ground or referent for conceptual knowledge is unknowable. Schopenhauer ([1818] 1969b: 474) referred to this as Kant's "monstrous assertion that without thought, and hence without abstract concepts, there is absolutely no knowledge of an object, and that, because perception is not thought, it is also not knowledge at all, and in general is nothing but mere affection of sensibility, mere sensation!" This is an apt, albeit partial summary of Kant's as well as Baudrillard's epistemology, but why does Schopenhauer refer to it as "monstrous"? Because the institutionalized severing of the connection between a concept and the perception that gave rise to the concept (fiction) in the first place leads to the animal state in which everything seems to be a matter of course (ibid.: 161). Nothing seems puzzling or mysterious anymore, and curiosity itself is blunted, unless it excites the desiring will directly, as in animals. Schopenhauer would have us consider that the state of humans passively receiving concepts through the media is not far removed from our pets "watching" television (Horkheimer and Adorno would surely agree). For Schopenhauer, the ability to trace a conception to the perception that gave rise to it in the first place is a uniquely human capacity that stems from integrating the superior mind of humans with the will shared by all animals. From Schopenhauer's perspective, one would conclude that Kant and Baudrillard have robbed humans of this capacity.

The end result of severing the idea from the will – enshrined by Kantians as well as postmodernists – is that the human person becomes, in Schopenhauer's words, a mass of "vehement desires, passionate, violent character, with weak intellect" (ibid.: 203). Schopenhauer adds that "this is a phenomenon as common as it is repulsive; it might perhaps be compared to the beetroot" (ibid.: 203). Far from regarding that period known as the Enlightenment as a tribute to the power of the human mind, Schopenhauer regards that whole period as "one of constant massacre and murder, now on the battlefield, now on the scaffold, now in the streets – all over metaphysical questions!" (ibid.: 187).

Many contemporary commentators, from Adorno (1991) and Riesman (1950) to Christopher Lasch (1991), would agree with Schopenhauer that narcissistic, modern persons have lost their capacity for astonishment, philosophical wonder, and curiosity. But Schopenhauer thrusts deeper, claiming that "it is wickedness, evil, and death that qualify and intensify philosophical astonishment" ([1818] 1969b: 172). These are the very things that postmodernists avoid confronting. Wickedness, evil, and death are parodied, turned into fun, or otherwise transformed into the optimistic ethos that characterizes the Enlightenment project. For example, in the postmodernist cult film, *Bill and Ted's Bogus Journey*, Bill and Ted die, and play "Battleship" with the Grim Reaper in order to get out of Hell. No doubt Baudrillard would approve.

SCHOPENHAUER AND BAUDRILLARD ON MORALITY

Up to now, even if the reader agrees with us that Baudrillard and the postmodernists have exalted habits that serious thinkers from Schopenhauer to Adorno would have regarded as barbaric, the impact on the reader may be minimal. "So what?" might be the characteristic reply. The postmodernists have their frame of reference, and the serious "dead dudes" (from Bill and Ted) that we are invoking have a different frame of reference. But the epistemology in the postmodernist frame of reference is an extension of Kant's philosophy, and leads to the same dead-end when applied to ethics that Schopenhauer and Nietzsche discovered.

Baudrillard's pitiless ethics flow logically from his epistemology: if the world is nothing but fiction, if America "is the world centre of the inauthentic," then image alone counts (1986: 109). Thus, "no one keeps count of the mistakes made by the world's political leaders any more, mistakes which, in days gone by, would have brought about their downfall: no one much minds these now within our present system of simulation of government and of consensus through indifference" (ibid.: 109). Baudrillard depicts Ronald Reagan as the penultimate postmodern President who ruled on the basis of fiction, not democratic or any other sort of ideals.

The Reagan generation painted by Baudrillard is the same shallow, indifferent, narcissistic one found in the writings of Bloom, Lasch, Bellah, and other commentators. The difference is that Baudrillard approves:

> Reagan has never had the faintest inkling of the poor and their existence, nor the slightest contact with them. He knows only the self-evidence of wealth, the tautology of power, which he magnifies to the dimensions of the nation, or indeed of the whole world. The have-nots will be condemned to oblivion, to abandonment, to disappearance pure and simple. This is "must exit" logic: "poor people must exit." The ultimatum issued in the name of wealth and efficiency wipes them off the map. And rightly so, since they show such bad taste as to deviate from the general consensus.
>
> (Ibid.: 111)

The ex-CIA chief turned President, George Bush, has kept to the Reagan project. And why not? The CIA and Hollywood both deal with hyper-reality, called disinformation by the former and art by the latter. The Gulf War was added to Lebanon, Grenada, and Vietnam, all "unreal" wars to Baudrillard, because the TV screen told Americans and the world what to think and believe (ibid.: 108).[3] An ethnocentric version of Bellah's American Civil Religion was revived. America would usher in the New World Order, which would be capitalist, unlike the old version of the New World Order that H.G. Wells thought would be socialist. Baudrillard gives his seal of approval: "Americans are not wrong in their idyllic conviction that they are at the centre of the world, the supreme power, the absolute model for everyone" (ibid.: 77).

Despite Baudrillard and the postmodern generation's indifference, anyone who practices contemplation for even a few seconds in this regard will realize that "real" people suffer and were killed off the TV screen as a result of this movement to the far Right. But here we arrive at a fundamental problem. Even if one accuses Baudrillard and the postmodernists of being pitiless and inhuman, what are the referents for the notions of being fully human and humane? Organized religion does not come to mind, for it continues to align itself with the predatory, barbaric habits found in the rest of culture – Veblen ([1899] 1969) has already shown that. Bloom and Habermas point to the Enlightenment project, but this project is anything but humane – Horkheimer and Adorno (1972) must be taken seriously in this regard. In fact, the epistemological poverty of the neo-Kantian frame of reference exposes the abyss of the modernist lack of a moral frame of reference. If the world is nothing but appearance and fiction, then morality is just another appearance and fiction.

With the exception of Plato, the only major philosopher who grounded morality in something other than moral rules as fictions was Arthur Schopenhauer. For Schopenhauer ([1818] 1969a: 331), egoism is the starting-point of all conflict and human wickedness, whereas for Kant, the utilitarians, and the postmodernists, egoism is the starting-point for all theories of human conduct that are supposed to lead to "the greatest good." For Schopenhauer, all humans are condemned to struggle for existence, but breaking through the boundary of another's affirmation of will is evil (ibid.: 334). Cannibalism,[4] murder, cunning, fraud, the lie, the broken contract, the refusal to help another in dire distress, the calm contemplation of another's death (ibid.: 339) – these, among others, are manifestations of the barbaric temperament in the human animal. Whereas contemplation leads to the realization that all of us co-suffer in life, and that therefore no-one has a right to add to someone else's suffering, the egoist feels superior to the suffering that he or she witnesses in others, and either ignores it or adds to it.

In Schopenhauer's philosophy we find two sides to the irrational will, egoism as well as compassion. Neither phenomenon is amenable to rational control. In fact, human rationality is the culprit, for it is the natural ally of egoism. The greatest crimes require cunning, supplied by reason, as well as a barbaric character. According to Schopenhauer:

> All true and pure affection is sympathy or compassion, and all love that is not sympathy is selfishness. All this will be in direct contradiction to Kant, who recognizes all true goodness and all virtue as such, only if they have resulted from abstract reflection, and in fact from the concept of duty and the categorical imperative, and who declares felt sympathy to be weakness, and by no means virtue.
>
> (Ibid.: 376)

Kant restricts morality to the same narrow confines of phenomenalism in which one finds knowledge. Morality is to be rational, even though from Plato through Christianity up to Kant, "rational action and virtuous action are two quite different things" (ibid.: 86). Contrary to Kant, everyone knows that we can go through the motions of a deliberate, methodical, prudent, Sunday school morality – follow all the right "Thou shalt's" and "Thou shalt not's" – and still be acting on the basis of egoism, still be looking out for our own benefit and prestige. The moral message in Plato's *Republic* is that virtue should be chosen for its own sake, even if it does not result in happiness. Similarly, original Christianity places a premium on the pure heart, on the intentions that go into moral conduct.

The Schopenhauerian, Platonic, and Christian models suppose that there is a secret part to human character, a will that lies beneath the appearances. In other words, all these models presuppose metaphysics. By contrast, the Kantian and postmodernist models deal only with the world of appearances, and deny any reality that might lie beneath the surface. Even if one rejects the former and opts for the neo-Kantian models, one's decision does not result in any sort of firm moral resolve or conviction, because one cannot have faith in fictions. Thus, the epistemological nihilism that we have traced from Kant to Baudrillard results in a moral nihilism.

Like Veblen, Schopenhauer was highly critical of the misuse of Christian ethics for egoistic purposes and prestige. But also like Veblen ([1910] 1943), he looked favorably on the kernel of Christian ethics as the embodiment of the same turning away from the will that was the basis of his theory of aesthetic appreciation: "Christianity is nearest at hand, the ethics of which is entirely in the spirit we have mentioned, and leads not only to the highest degree of charity and human kindness, but also to renunciation" ([1818] 1969b: 386). He regards Adam as the symbol for the will to life – which is good and evil – and Christ as the symbol for the denial of the will, grace, salvation (ibid.: 405). Schopenhauer and Horkheimer regarded the myth of original sin as the most sublime teaching found in the Judeo-Christian tradition: the underlying meaning of the doctrine of original sin, for Schopenhauer, is that the human animal recognizes evil in affirming its will to life at the expense and suffering of another's will to life.[5]

If we extrapolate from Schopenhauer's philosophy to sociology, we arrive at an interesting connection that has been hitherto obfuscated: Durkheim made charity, self-abnegation, and "mutual sympathy" the very basis for organized social life in modern societies characterized by organic solidarity. This is so obvious to anyone who has read and contemplated Durkheim, it requires no substantiation. But the functionalists have misread Durkheim from the Kantian perspective, which will not allow any talk of charity and love, and twisted the essentially Christian portrait of social integration in Durkheim into the neo-Kantian vocabulary of normative consensus, values, beliefs, sanctions, and duties. Not only is this a caricature of Durkheim, who agreed with Plato and Schopenhauer that mere obeisance to duties will not result in social order, it leads to the same nihilistic conclusion. For the functionalists, social order must be maintained with reference to fear of sanctions, which is to say, with reference to egoism, which Durkheim regards as the root of all evil. Durkheim envisioned a modern social order based on humans desiring to be virtuous citizens and, in this regard, was following an ancient and distinguished philosophical legacy.

Let us note another neglected aspect of Durkheim's sociology of morals. Like Schopenhauer, he felt that civilization and progress result in heightened barbarism *as well as* heightened sympathy. In *The Division of Labor in Society* ([1893] 1933), he portrays mechanical solidarity in harsh terms, as based on cruel punishments, laws that are not mindful of the individual, and on similarities in customs that easily break down in times of stress. By contrast, organic solidarity is to be based on the refraction of love among dissimilar persons, on an erotic component that is stronger than the basis of primitive solidarity. Schopenhauer favored the New Testament over the Old because it replaced the punitive God the Father with the loving Jesus. One can detect a similar sentiment in Durkheim's *Division of Labor*, a similar bias in favor of the softer, restitutive law characteristic of modern societies compared with the punitive laws of mechanical solidarity.

But like Plato, Schopenhauer, and the original Christians, Durkheim does not believe that virtue can be taught. To teach virtue is to reduce it to a Kantian formula that can have only egoism as its basis. To systematize virtue is to transform its spontaneous quality into something oppressive, the feeling that one *must* behave in a certain way from fear of punishment, guilt, or other derivatives of neo-Kantian duty. Durkheim ([1925] 1961) stays within the boundaries of the Platonic and Schopenhauerian assumptions we are tracing, in that he hopes to cultivate – in a non-systematic and non-oppressive way – the child's *natural* propensity toward altruism, and discourage the equally natural tendencies toward egoism. Like Tocqueville and Veblen, he sought to cultivate "good" habits in opposition to "bad" habits. Even when Durkheim uses the Kantian concept of duty, he adds quickly that to be genuinely moral, the duties must be sought spontaneously and with heartfelt emotion (see Meštrović 1991: 108–35).

Freud exhibits a Christian unconscious (Vitz 1988). He also saw that the human capacity for barbarism, egoism, and narcissism could be offset, at least in part, by the capacity to love.[6] We shall be seeking out this relatively neglected aspect of Freud's legacy, which found its way into Erich Fromm's *The Art of Loving*, but not into the fictional Freud of Elias and Parsons, a Freud obsessed only with control of anti-social impulses. Our project of uncovering the pessimistic humanism that flows from

Western culture and that was crystallized in Schopenhauer's philosophy means that Freud should not be read as just another Nietzsche, a debunker and cynic who saw nothing but evil in the human heart.[7]

RECONCILING NIETZSCHE'S CRITICISMS OF CHRISTIANITY

One major obstacle remains: the legacy of Friedrich Nietzsche, especially his focus on the will to power as a self-conscious and deliberate rejection of Schopenhauer's focus on compassion. Nietzsche ([1901] 1968) abhorred Christian ethics. In this regard, he is not far from the position of his *fin de siècle* colleagues, Veblen (1943), Durkheim ([1912] 1965), Freud ([1927] 1955), and others, as well as Schopenhauer, who were highly critical of all organized religion and organized Christianity in particular as a hypocritical phenomenon that often encourages the very egoism it purports to constrain. But Nietzsche's criticisms extend deeper, into the kernel of Christian dogma, and in particular, the Christian rule to love one's neighbor. One becomes suspicious that this is a profound disagreement when one considers that Nietzsche loved the Old Testament that Schopenhauer despised, and vice versa for the New Testament. In the Old Testament, God is often the cruel judge who metes out justice on his terms, and is hardly ever compassionate. By contrast, the New Testament Jesus is the God of love. From a sociology of knowledge perspective applied to itself, it is highly significant that Habermas, Baudrillard, and the postmodernists draw their inspiration from Nietzsche (Kroker and Cook 1986), and by implication, the cruel Old Testament, whereas they ignore Schopenhauer and the story of love found in the New Testament. Equally telling is the fact that Protestantism, which Max Weber ([1904] 1958) aligned with modernity and capitalism, draws more of its inspiration from the Old Testament than the New. Nietzsche's will to power, not Schopenhauer's ([1841] 1965) compassion, is the hallmark of modernity as well as the postmodernist discourse.

Max Horkheimer offers an interesting sociological analysis of the import of Nietzsche's philosophy that is relevant to our discussion:

Nietzsche derides Christianity because its ideals derived from impotence. By calling them virtues, the weak deliberately misinterpret love of mankind, justice, mildness because they cannot avenge themselves, or, more precisely, because they were too cowardly to do so.

He despises the mass, yet wants to preserve it as such. He wants to preserve weakness, cowardice, obedience, so that he may have room for the breeding of his utopian aristocrats. There must be those who sew togas for these men so that they don't walk about like beggars, for if they could not live off the sweat of the mass, they themselves would have to operate the machines, and there no one intones Dionysian dithyrambs. Actually, Nietzsche is extremely pleased that the mass should exist. Nowhere does he appear as the real enemy of a system based on exploitation and misery. According to him, it is therefore both just and useful that men's gifts atrophy under wretched conditions, however strongly he may advocate their development in the "superman." Nietzsche's aims are not those of the proletariat.

(1978: 32)[8]

By contrast, Schopenhauer's philosophy is widely acknowledged to be socialist in its core, because of its extreme emphasis on compassion and the breaking down of the artificial barriers among individuals (Magee 1983). It is interesting in this regard that the main thrust of the previous *fin de siècle* intelligentsia was socialist: H.G. Wells's (1906) original version of the New World Order was socialist, and was based on the premise that capitalism would eventually collapse. Veblen, Bellamy, Freud, Simmel, and yes, Durkheim, were all socialists or socialist sympathizers in this regard.[9] But the New World Order in our *fin de siècle*, touted by President Bush, gloats in the purported victory of oppressive capitalism over socialism. Is it a coincidence that the revival of Nietzsche's cruel dismissal of Christian ethics by the postmodernists is occurring in the midst of a widespread movement to the far Right in the West? Veblen thought that habits of thought must always "fit" with the habits of life in the general population.

Horkheimer began his criticisms of Marxism following the widespread recognition that Stalin was applying a Nietzschean formula to Marx's socialist ideals. Horkheimer remained faithful to his Schopenhauerian leanings, and criticized the Marxists who rationalized widespread human suffering in the name of the idealized Marxist utopia. This cruelty is captured by the famous maxim, "To make an omelette, you have to break a few eggs." Horkheimer would have nothing to do with any system that condoned human suffering. It is an open question whether Marxism contains within itself the germs of the cruelty that eventually thrived in communism. Horkheimer wavered, but Veblen, Freud and Durkheim were suspicious of Marx from the start, and on Schopenhauerian grounds. If one takes Schopenhauer seriously, one will not be convinced that human compassion can be engineered socially. This is why the end-point of our discussion, the revival of compassionate habits of the heart, is something quite different from using rational methods to inculcate compassion. To repeat: this is a complete impossibility for Schopenhauer, as for Plato, for whom virtue cannot be taught.

Chapter 6

Deconstructing the problem of social order

In its origin, function, and relation to sexual love, the *Eros* of the philosopher Plato coincides exactly with the love-force, the libido of psychoanalysis.

(Sigmund Freud [1921] 1961: 30)

Conceiving something is both learning its essential elements better and also locating it in its place; for each civilization has its organized system of concepts which characterizes it. Before this scheme of ideas, the individual is in the same situation as the *nous* of Plato before the world of Ideas.

(Emile Durkheim [1912] 1965: 484)

Anthony Giddens (1976a) is probably correct that at least since Parsons, the so-called "problem of social order" is not *a* problem in contemporary sociology, but *the* problem. Giddens observes correctly that "Durkheim specifically, though rather casually, dismissed the 'Hobbesian problem' [of social order] as being of no significance for sociology" (ibid.: 707). C. Wright Mills also criticized Parsons in this regard, and concluded that the problem of social order is not based upon any "conception of the nature of man or upon any particular facts about them" (1959: 55). Nevertheless, an overview of dominant themes in twentieth-century sociological theory reveals a preoccupation with functionalist social order and social integration based on normative consensus and the alleged internalization of norms. Mills may be correct that these functionalist assumptions are not supported even by any dominant Western conceptions of human nature. Nevertheless, they flow from Enlightenment narratives that stress assimilation and control of the individual. Little effort has been made to distinguish just from unjust social order – a distinction that concerned Durkheim greatly – so long as it is order. Furthermore, modern sociology tried to assimilate Freud, Durkheim, and other *fin de siècle* thinkers into its assimilatory paradigm. It is as common as it is false to regard Freud and Durkheim as proponents of social programs that should control the individual in order to minimize *all* sorts of deviance, from alcoholism to suicide and murder.

Actually, both Freud and Durkheim conceived of human nature as fundamentally dualistic, and they thought of these dualisms primarily in terms of Schopenhauer's and Plato's concepts of the *idea* (or representation) versus various metaphors for the will. This means that the thinkers that concern us here thought that the individual is a potential enemy of society and civilization at all times, but additionally, they also thought that society and civilization were potentially detrimental to the individual. This latter aspect of their thought gets lost in modernist accounts of their legacy. Dualisms abound in contemporary as well as ancient thought, of course, but what sets Freud and Durkheim apart is their Schopenhauerian assumption that will and idea are *mutually* antagonistic, yet constitute a dialectical unity, such that they result in inescapable tension, and, above all, that the will is more powerful than the mind. By contrast, modernists follow the Enlightenment narratives in assuming that the mind can rule the passions that stem from the will, while postmodernists seek to jettison the entire vocabulary of dualisms as an oppressive narrative. Interesting but widely different consequences follow, depending upon which of these assumptions one pursues in analysis: Freud, Durkheim and many of their *fin de siècle* colleagues will find *more*, not less, aggression and other manifestations of the will in modern, so-called civilized societies. The modernists develop positivistic models for controlling and predicting human aggression, which have been largely unsuccessful so far. And postmodernists do not trouble themselves with violence, aggression, or barbarism as primary concerns. They admonish us to be comfortable with uncertainty.

Thus, in his "Dualism of Human Nature and Its Social Conditions," and elsewhere, Durkheim ([1914] 1973) likens his notion of *homo duplex* explicitly to Plato's conception of the person as torn between body and soul, the lower appetites and reason, forms and Ideas.[1] Durkheim also specifically criticizes

Kant's version of this dualism.[2] Ultimately, Durkheim, like Schopenhauer, depicts the dualism of human nature in terms of society's representations versus "the body" and its tyrannical appetites. Throughout his writings, Durkheim expresses this dualism in various forms, so that in *Division of Labor in Society* ([1893] 1933) he posits the antagonism between two consciences within us[3] as well as centripetal versus centrifugal forces acting on persons as the division of labor develops, in stark contradistinction to the unilateral emphasis on centrifugal progress found in modernist visions. In *Suicide* ([1897] 1951: 319), he makes use of the observation that humans lead a "double existence" simultaneously to explain how and why suicide becomes the "ransom money" of civilization. In *Moral Education* ([1925] 1961: 224) he discusses egoism and altruism as two expressions of human consciousness, whcih is simultaneously oriented in two opposing directions.[4] Again, by contrast, both modernists and postmodernists assume that self-interest is the primary motive in humans. In *Elementary Forms of the Religious Life* ([1912] 1965: 29), he points to the distinction betwen the sacred and the profane as the underlying dimension of *homo duplex* which ultimately leads to the antagonism between collective and individual levels of existence.[5] And in "The Dualism of Human Nature and Its Social Conditions," he complains that he has not been understood in these other writings, and summarizes the many forms the dualism can take ([1914] 1973: 152–7 passim). Ultimately, they can all be better understood as refractions of Schopenhauer's will versus idea better than in terms of Enlightenment narratives that continue to be debated by postmodernists.

Freud ([1905a] 1974) frequently likens his use of sexuality to the extended use of Eros found in the writings of Plato, and he also credits Schopenhauer with the emphasis upon sexuality as the primary expression of the will. The order produced by Eros is hardly the Parsonian social order based on normative consensus. It is well known that in his final version of this dualism, Freud sets Eros in opposition to the death instinct. Various interpreters of Freud have already related this final dualism to his many other dualisms between Primary and Secondary Processes, Binding and Unbinding, the Pleasure Principle versus the Reality Principle, and so on (see Laplanche and Pontalis 1973). What remains to be done is to further trace the unity in Freud's thought and then compare and contrast these dualisms with those of Durkheim in the context of Schopenhauer extended to Plato.

What sets Freud and Durkheim apart from some disciples of the Enlightenment who also use dualisms – thinkers as diverse as Descartes, Hegel, Kant, Rousseau and Nietzsche – is that the tension that results from these dualisms can never be resolved ultimately in favor of either the higher or lower pole in humans, although the lower is supposed to be more powerful than the higher. This means that the possibility of attaining a permanent social order is out of the question for Freud and Durkheim. In contrast to Kant's focus on submission to the universal, rational principle that found its way into Hegel's works, and others who resolve the tension in favor of the higher, as well as with Rousseau and Nietzsche who recommend that the higher principles be overthrown in favor of the lower, Freud and Durkheim seek a dynamic equilibrium between the higher and the lower that is never static but always changing as humans change and as civilization develops. Moreover, even though they display Schopenhauer's pessimistic belief that the will is stronger than the idea, or that the heart is stronger than the mind, they are not ready to follow Nietzsche and others who favored overthrowing the idea in favor of the will. Freud and Durkheim, like Schopenhauer, wanted to maintain some sort of faith in rationalism, albeit a renovated, complex rationalism,[6] which acknowledges the power of human irrationality and desire.

The similarity between the dualisms found in Freud and in Durkheim is not exact, of course. That is why this discussion will point to differences as well as similarities. But given the context of Schopenhauer and Plato, that Durkheim conceived of unconscious motivations and that Freud wrote that he saw himself primarily as a student of culture, the venturing forth into this discussion is justified. To repeat, Freud and Durkheim have been chosen as primary protagonists in this discussion in order to illuminate aspects of the thought of one relative to the other that might not otherwise become apparent – ultimately, to expose the artificiality of the present-day compartmentalization between psychology and sociology.

For example, Durkheim's philosophically wondrous notion of representations as phenomena that bridge the mind–body dualism in the form of mental facts, and as phenomena that bridge the individual–society distinction in the form of social facts, illuminates the perplexing nature of Freud's use of "instincts" as forces that are psychical representatives of bodily demands with regard to individuals and as forces that affect groups and civilization itself. In the context of Schopenhauer's attempt to bridge Kant's gap between phenomena and noumena, these moves by Freud and Durkheim take on an entirely new meaning compared to positivistic readings which conclude simply that Freud and Durkheim lapsed, at times, into non-science in their alleged quest to establish a blueprint for social order. And of course, scores of their *fin de siècle* contemporaries, from Veblen to Pareto, referred to all sorts of "instincts," but did not mean to imply "real," biological instincts that can be "observed."

Similarly, Freud's extensive treatment of the idea of unconscious intentions illuminates Durkheim's perplexing discussion of suicide as well as murder and other violent acts that do *not* refer to intentions. Again, Schopenhauer's focus on the imperious will that discounts the human person's rational intentions makes these moves intelligible. Many other aspects in the thought of one thinker are put into a fresh perspective relative to the other, pointing to a resolution of problems that beset their contemporary interpreters.

Clearly, the present work is only an interpretation, so that there is no need to be dogmatic about it on the level of interpretation. But it must be emphasized that its starting-point is significantly different from most other interpretations of Freud and Durkheim because of the context that is invoked for its starting-points: the *fin de siècle* spirit as exemplified in Schopenhauer's philosophy which in turn crystallizes Plato's philosophy and the ambivalence of Western thought in general. These new cultural starting-points make this interpretation different from many others, not the ground that shall be covered.

While this work is in many ways pursuing untrodden paths, the paths have been broken, at least at the entrance, by some previous thinkers, already reviewed. There can be no doubt that, as Henri Ellenberger (1970) and many others have pointed out, the *fin de siècle* ethos focused on pessimism, decadence, degeneration, and the limitations of human reason relative to the passions. This ethos was mindful of the costs of civilization and social order. The contemporary social sciences were born, in large measure, in this gloomy period. How this fact came to be overlooked, forgotten, or distorted in favor of the positivistic and assimilatory narratives of the social sciences is a mystery I do not intend to pursue here. No one can read seriously the works of Wundt, Tönnies, Ribot, Herbart, Simmel, Veblen, Durkheim, Guyau, Freud, and their contemporaries and deny that the *fin de siècle* spirit leads to something quite other than the assimilatory spirit of modernism and its excessive emphasis on social order. The important point is that I see myself as pursuing paths that are clearly relevant to sociology and the social sciences in general, and for which precedents exist, but that need to be unearthed and distinguished from the positivistic paths.

Nevertheless, this work is highly critical of some previous theoretical understandings of Durkheim's and Freud's relevance to sociology. The critical stance is consciously chosen, and, hopefully, stems from more than arrogance and an unappreciative attitude toward the work of others. To repeat, most commentators tend to ignore the *fin de siècle* starting-points that Freud and Durkheim used, and impose their own, positivistic and other enlightenment starting-points onto Freud and Durkheim without justification or elaboration. They simply assume that positivism is unequivocally superior to metaphysics, and that any social order – seemingly even unjust order – is preferable to chaos. Thus, Durkheim's concept of anomie is generally misunderstood by contemporary sociologists as the overly rational normlessness, when, in fact, Durkheim referred to it as a state of infinite desires which afflicts the core of society, not its deviant subcultures. He used this concept in its full range of *fin de siècle* meanings to denote a strange and paradoxical condition of progress as well as Nietzschean degeneration which results in pessimism, disenchantment and sorrow in society. His usage is commensurate with similar concerns by his *fin de siècle* colleagues, including Veblen's use of the term "conspicuous consumption." All of these connotations reverberate in Schopenhauer's philosophy. By contrast, the term normlessness is extremely recent, lacks an etymology (there can be no such thing as normlessness), assumes the modernist position that lack of norms leads to social disorder – which is assumed to be unequivocally bad – lacks any dimension of psychological feeling, and most important of all – Durkheim never used it.

Despite these facts, Merton's (1957) dictum that, as initially developed by Durkheim, the concept of anomie referred to a condition of relative normlessness in a society or group, continues to be widely quoted today. And this, despite postmodern pretense to rebel at narratives spun from the Enlightenment. It is important to disengage Durkheim's *fin de siècle* version of anomie, and other key concepts, from the false and fruitless modernist versions that perpetuate an anachronistic model of social order.

Similarly, Freud continues to be attacked for his alleged overemphasis on sexuality, which is misunderstood in the modern sense of genital contact, even though he made it clear that he used this concept in the context of the etymology and historical usage of Schopenhauer and Plato's Eros. Simmel (1971), Bloom (1987), and others have already criticized how modernists tend to obfuscate Eros, how modern "love" has been reduced to its lowest denominator, narcissism.

Finally, I do not mean to criticize the moral or professional intentions of some of Durkheim's and Freud's commentators. Every scholar is entitled to his or her starting-point in an analysis. However, it is another thing to reproach Freud and Durkheim simply because their starting-points are different from the dominant starting-points today, without trying to understand why they began as they did, and without the ability to criticize the *status quo*. For "genuine" understanding to occur – a possibility that some postmodernists deny, because of their overemphasis on decentering discourse – the starting-points of thinkers whose thought seems incomprehensible to us must be identified, compared and contrasted with our starting-points. The terribly oppressive paradigm of social order must be deconstructed. In the criticisms that follow, the intent is to recover the kernel of insight from the previous *fin de siècle* that can help one make sense of the present, not to engage in pugnacity for its own sake.

DECONSTRUCTING THE OVERSOCIALIZED CONCEPTION OF THE HUMAN PERSON IN SOCIOLOGY

Our target is the oversocialized conception of the human person that Parsons attributes falsely to Freud and Durkheim, and then applies to the kernel of sociological theory: that social order is maintained through the socialization of individuals such that they internalize social norms and do what they are supposed to do automatically, albeit not habitually or based on culture. Where did this notion of internalization come from? Parsons (1937) attributes it to Freud, but Freud never made much use of it. Freud did use the term introjection, but he used it in the sense of a defense mechanism that is the opposite of projection, which is quite different. Dennis H. Wrong (1961) has already criticized the works of Parsons, Merton and other functionalists in this regard. He points out that Freud held a dualistic view of humans as torn by bodily and social impulses so that "to Freud, man is a social animal without being entirely a socialized animal" (ibid.: 193). Durkheim makes a remarkably similar argument in "The Dualism of Human Nature and Its Social Conditions" ([1914] 1973). But despite Wrong and the huge *fin de siècle* literature, the modernist, fictitious model of "internalizing" norms, invented by Parsons, continues to operate in the social sciences.

A notable example is Norbert Elias's reliance on one troublesome passage by Freud ([1927] 1955: 13): "It is in keeping with the course of human development that external coercion gradually becomes internalized – for a special mental agency, men's super-ego, takes it over and includes it among its commandments." This became the basis of Elias's (1982) theory that self-constraint replaces external constraint in the civilizing process. It is also the basis for the divergence between Elias's optimistic theory of the civilizing process and the Frankfurt School's faithfulness to Freud's concept of the libido (discussed by Bogner 1987). No doubt Freud referred to the idea of internalizing social demands, but the notion of internalization never became a cornerstone of orthodox – libidinal – psychoanalytic theory. Both Parsons and Elias independently took Freud's reference to internalization out of context. That context is the Schopenhauerian idea that the body is the reservoir of libido that always opposes socialization. Because Wrong's (1961) critique failed to make an impression on sociologists, we mention it, but shall proceed with our own attempt to deconstruct the oversocialized conception of the human person. It is the cornerstone of the widespread belief among sociologists that social order, envisaged as normative consensus, is *the* problem of sociology.

Most contemporary attempts at understanding Durkheim tend to be positivistic, and focus on the only book by him that involves quantitative data, his enigmatic *Suicide*. Despite Pope's (1973) and other criticisms of Parsons for misreading Durkheim as a positivist, the functionalist emphasis on social order has remained intact. Durkheim's *Suicide* continues to be misread as a defense of the *status quo*, of maintaining social order at any cost. The Marxists and conflict theorists who rebelled at Parsonian functionalism threw out Durkheim with the bathwater of functionalism, because they never bothered to separate Durkheim's intentions from Parsons.

One of the most common misinterpretations of Durkheim's *Suicide*, along the trajectory established by Parsons, is the following made by Gibbs and Martin (1958: 141): "Running throughout Durkheim's comments on the nature of integration is the suggestion that the concept has to do with the strength of the individual's ties to his society." Gibbs and Martin are referring to the following general conclusion drawn by Durkheim ([1897] 1951: 209): "Suicide varies inversely with the degree of integration of the social groups of which the individual forms a part."

On the face of it, it appears that Durkheim is referring to the *integration of groups*, not the supposedly quantifiable attachment of individuals to groups, even though he does not make it immediately clear how a group can be conceived as being integrated versus disintegrated. But Gibbs and Martin (1958: 141) offer a different understanding:

> While Durkheim's study provides the most promising point of departure for an attempt to formulate a theory of suicide, it must be emphasized that his assertion of an inverse relationship between social integration and the rate of suicide has never been subjected to formal test and is not testable in its present form. At no point in Durkheim's monograph is there an explicit connotative definition of social integration, much less an operational definition.

Notice how Gibbs and Martin have shifted Durkheim's wording from "integration of social groups" to Parsonian "social integration" as social control over individuals. And in keeping with modernist narratives, they imply that social integration – as the control of individuals – will ameliorate all deviance, not just suicide, of course. Without argument, and without the use of any evidence, Gibbs and Martin claim that Durkheim meant that

> the stronger the ties of the individual members to a society the lower the suicide rate of that society . . . The suicide rate of a population varies inversely with the stability and durability of social relationships within that population.
>
> (Ibid.: 141)

Note the modernist assumption that social control can and should ameliorate the barbarism of suicide. But this is simply not true. Nowhere does Durkheim claim that integration refers to the ties of individuals to society, and nowhere does he claim that the stronger the ties of the individual members to a society, the lower the suicide rates – or any other rates of deviance. Quite the contrary, he claims that altruistic and fatalistic suicides are the result of society holding the individual in "too strict tutelage . . . where the ego is not its own property, where it is blended with something not itself" ([1897] 1951: 221). And positivists do not know what to do with Durkheim's paradoxical claim that suicide occurs "likewise when social integration is too strong" (ibid.: 217). More on that later.

Actually, Durkheim seems to have adopted the Schopenhauerian view that exposure to a decadent and barbaric society is pathogenic – that "integration," in the sense intended by Gibbs and Martin, is a culprit in suicide, not a prophylactic. For example, he showed that women were shielded from suicide precisely because they participated less than men in society – internalized fewer of its sickly norms. And Durkheim claimed that suicide rates increase with the lengthening of the day because longer days enable greater exposure to social interaction – but he does *not* refer to these examples of over-exposure to society as integration (discussed in Meštrović 1988). Thus, to pick one example out of many, child-suicide is numerous in large cities, according to Durkheim, because "nowhere else does social life commence so early for the child, as is shown by the precocity of the little city-dweller" ([1897] 1951: 100). Similarly, the aged have higher suicide rates than the young, because they were exposed longer to decadent society. In general, Durkheim repeatedly argues against the most dominant misinterpretation of this thought, the idea that social contacts, integration, and internalization are always beneficial.[7] Other sociologists have noticed that Durkheim appears to say that suicide varies directly *and* inversely with integration – whatever that is – and have come up with peculiar explanations for what is purported to be a contradiction. For example, in his *Social Forces in Urban Suicide*, Ronald W. Maris (1969: 12) claims that Durkheim made a foolish mistake:

> The suicide rate cannot vary indirectly and directly with social integration at the same time. Being a great man, Durkheim realized this and put his comments on fatalism in a footnote, apparently hoping that this rather obvious contradiction would be overlooked.

In fact, it is entirely possible for any phenomenon to vary indirectly and directly with another phenomenon. This happens frequently in medicine with drugs, for example, such that drugs have contrary effects depending upon whether they are given in extremely small or large doses.

But in general, sociologists have ignored Durkheim's claim that too much integration can be pathogenic, and have focused mainly on the claim that too little integration is harmful. Why? Based on our starting-points, an answer seems to be that adherents of modernist narratives find it an offensive affront to their project to admit the possibility that excessive assimilation, social control, internalization, and social order can be pathogenic. Their starting-points dictate that assimilation into an enlightened, rational social order is an unqualified good. Similarly, many so-called mainstream theorists have assumed that social contacts and resources are always beneficial, and they have attributed this misunderstanding to Durkheim. For example, this assumption finds its way into the large literature on stress, which takes the moral tone that stress is always ameliorated by social supports. These investigators hardly consider the possibility that too many social supports and contacts can be – and often are – stifling and pathogenic in their own right. Consider the added stress on the newborn baby and mother caused by the social support offered by in-laws, for example. This is such an obvious problem, that Lamaze classes now instruct expecting couples to simply tell in-laws *not* to visit immediately, and to keep some of their support to themselves.

In any event, there is no good reason to continue misinterpreting Durkheim's thought in this oversocialized vein.

Durkheim never claimed that collective representations, alone, account for any phenomenon. His explanations always involve the dualism of human nature, in terribly complex ways. For example, Durkheim writes:

> To be sure in so far as we are solidary with the group and share its life, we are exposed to their influence; but so far as we have a distinct personality of our own we rebel against and try to escape them. Since everyone leads this sort of double existence simultaneously, each of us has a double impulse. We are drawn in a social direction and tend to follow the inclinations of our own natures . . . Two antagonistic forces confront each other. One, the collective force, tries to take possession of the individual; the other, the individual force, repulses it. To be sure, the former is much stronger than the latter, since it is made of a combination of all the individual forces; but as it also encounters as many resistances as there are separate persons, it is partially exhausted in these multifarious contexts and reaches us disfigured and enfeebled.
>
> ([1897] 1951: 318)

In subsequent chapters I shall develop further how this tension based on *homo duplex* is important to understanding modern barbarism. Furthermore, the dynamic equilibrium of forces that comprise the dualism of human nature corresponds to what Durkheim calls integration. Such an explanation is commensurate with Schopenhauer's assumption that although will and idea are mutually antagonistic, they remain a unity.

Even Durkheim's definition of suicide invokes *homo duplex*, follows in the wake of Schopenhauer, and parallels the work of Freud. Durkheim wrote: "The term suicide is applied to all cases of death resulting directly or indirectly from a positive or negative act of the victim himself, which he *knows* will produce this result" ([1897] 1951: 44; emphasis added). Strictly speaking, Durkheim does not define suicide with reference to the intentions – his followers, Bouglé (1938), Halbwachs ([1930] 1978), and Mauss ([1950] 1979) insisted on that fact.[8] One could argue that knowing is one kind of intentionality, but Durkheim distinguishes sharply between knowing the outcome of one's act and intending it. After all, one *knows* the outcome   .

of all sorts of bodily processes, from respiration to perspiration, but one does not really intend these things, even if one can interfere with their "normal" functioning. These things are set in motion and maintained by the Schopenhauerian will to life. Thus, Jacobs (1980) has not addressed the context of Durkheim's remarks in *Suicide*, nor in Durkheim's other writings. And Schopenhauer's philosophy explains Durkheim's move: The will is a striving without aim or end that does its work despite or against rational, conscious motives. So, for example, the will operates even when we are asleep and not conscious of digestion, the body's self-repairs, and so on.

Of course, another theorist who is able to define suicide without reference to rational, conscious intentions is Freud. Freud makes use of the concept of the unconscious even though modernist interpreters regard such a notion as absurd. (Not comprehending an opponent's starting-points in discourse frequently makes them seem absurd.) Ellenberger (1970) and Ernest Jones (1981) have already established affinities between Freud and Schopenhauer in this regard, so I will not pursue the matter further at this point.

One should also consider the statement by Durkheim's follower Maurice Halbwachs in *The Causes of Suicide*: "We notice that when Durkheim defines suicide as an act which the victim knows must produce death, he does not say that this act is voluntary" ([1930] 1978: 294). Halbwachs agrees with Durkheim that "nothing proves intentions," because the full extent of a human's motives are always obscured and veiled by defense mechanisms and other forces that obfuscate reality (ibid.: 294). Moreover, Halbwachs specifically cites Schopenhauer's notion of the will to make the point that the human agent does not abandon the will to live when he or she contemplates suicide:

Schopenhauer quite properly remarked that the will to die, seeing that it is a desire, presupposes that one is still attached to life. An unconscious being would be incapable of taking this step . . . All of the collective sadness and melancholy becomes embodied in him and rises through him to a higher awareness of itself . . . not until one is no longer capable of seeing the other aspects of the world are the discouraging ones so plainly uncovered. It is in society, not in himself, that the suffering person best perceives the image of his own destiny.

(Ibid.: 314)

This summary by Halbwachs goes completely against the modernist grain, and seems to be a complex refraction of Schopenhauer's enigmatic claim that because the suicide cannot give up willing, he or she gives up living. Halbwachs seems to agree with Schopenhauer and Durkheim that the will to life is the source of suffering which in turn can lead to suicide in complicated ways that involve society as well as the individual, intentionality as well as unconscious forces:

> It is not enough to know how many people kill themselves or to ascertain that this is, after all, only a limited loss of a substance which may not be healthy. Suicide is also a symptom. What is the extent and the nature of the social trouble it reveals to us? "If life were in itself a blessing to be prized," wrote Schopenhauer, "and decidedly to be preferred to non-existence, the exit from it would not need to be guarded by such fearful sentinels as death and its terrors. But who would continue in life as it is if death were less terrible?" A man must have reached a rather high degree of suffering for him to decide to pass through these doors [to non-existence] ... We can assume that the number of suicides is a rather exact indicator of the amount of suffering, malaise, disequilibrium, and sadness which exists or is produced in a group. Its increase is the sign that the sum total of despair, anguish, regret, humiliation, and discontent of every order is multiplying.

(Ibid.: 314)

Halbwachs is faithful to Durkheim's complex understanding of the intimate tie between society and the individual, and the pathos that this understanding inspires. Durkheim was not pursuing the modernist project of trying to predict and control the deviance of individuals, but was indicting society, civilization, and the modern order as harboring barbaric proclivities that cause individuals to suffer. Individual deviants – suicidal or otherwise – are a sign that the entire social body is sick. What an affront to Enlightenment narratives! And one has to wonder: do postmodern individuals suffer any less despair, anguish, regret, humiliation, and discontent since Halbwachs wrote these lines?

The Durkheimians took a ponderous position on the problem of human agency. Overall, the problem of interpreting Durkheim on the issue of intentions and suicide stems from an incomplete understanding of his notion of the dualism of human nature. If the human person is two beings, then the determinism versus free will controversy is irrelevant to Durkheim because for him, humans are always partly determined and partly free. This statement is a logical error for positivists, of course, and anathema to modernists, who seek to liberate the individual from supposedly oppressive tradition and culture as well as Nature. But my aim is to understand Durkheim's cultural mythology in the context of similar Western cultural myths, not to impose a modernist version of logic onto his thought.

In general, the so-called phenomenological approach to Durkheim's treatment of suicide (and by extension, all deviance) is not superior to functionalism: it leads to the dead-end conclusion that all statistical studies of suicide are irrelevant because they cannot capture the agent's conscious intentions and point of view. It perpetuates the same kind of sociological nihilism found in extreme positivism: in both cases, intellectuals seek total control of the will, but cannot achieve it, because the will is stronger than the mind. Neither the statistical, hard data cherished by positivists nor the subjective accounts of the agent's motives found in suicide notes, interviews, and qualitative data are to be taken at face value. Both are representations of reality that involve *homo duplex*, and reality will not speak for itself in either case. "Pure" data will always be "contaminated" (a terrible fear to modernists) by the imperious will. Surely the history of Western thought, up to the twentieth century, suggests that the human agent's intentions are often clouded from witnesses and the agent by the unconscious and other factors.

STRESSFUL LIFE-EVENTS AS CAUSES

The concept of stress is one of the most frequently used concepts in postmodern culture. In our postmodern culture, it is common for persons to blame stress for all sorts of barbaric acts: child abuse, spouse abuse, homicide, rape, drug abuse, assault, and suicide, among others. We shall continue to concentrate on suicide as a vehicle for the larger discussion that concerns us in the interest of conserving space, and because this topic invokes key elements of Durkheim's and Freud's writings. What can be learned from comparing the cultural trajectory we are following with the positivistic program we are criticizing?

The problem of stress is commonly interpreted through the stressful life-events school of thought, but these also betray their Enlightenment assumptions and Parsonian starting-points. Not surprisingly, the proponents of this school invoke the false, modernist, and Parsonian version of Durkheim that we are attempting to deconstruct. For example, Bruce P. Dohrenwend, in his essay entitled "Egoism, Altruism, Anomie, and Fatalism: A Conceptual Analysis of Durkheim's Types" (1959) claims that the study of the links between "environmental factors and mental illnesses" has been predominantly psychological because very few sociologists could offer a theoretical basis for such a study. Dohrenwend apparently believes that in sociology, "perhaps the single most important source of these (theoretical guideposts) is Emile Durkheim's study of suicide" (ibid.: 466). Dohrenwend elaborates: "For in this study (of suicide), Durkheim locates diverse social conditions or states as major sources of stress for individuals exposed to them."

But Durkheim seems to have been following in the footsteps of Schopenhauer's belief that as life gets better and easier due to progress and the conveniences of civilization, it gets worse because the insatiable, now liberated will causes humans to suffer more, not less, than they did before. Thus, the typically modernist life-events interpretation of Durkheim must reckon with Durkheim's devastating claim that "Facts thus are far from confirming the current idea that suicide is due especially to life's burdens, since, on the contrary, it diminishes as these burdens increase" ([1897] 1951: 201). Durkheim's claim is in harmony with findings that so-called developing countries have much lower suicide rates compared with modern countries.

Because Durkheim's intellectual and cultural milieu has been generally ignored, the result has been a potpourri of interpretations that are extremely different from each other.

Durkheim's work has been approached from a purely modernist vantage point, and has been reduced to a game of concepts. Scholars amputate from Durkheim's thought what does not fit their modernist assumptions, and add what they think is needed. For example, Barclay Johnson claims that altruism and fatalism "really do not belong" in Durkheim's scheme, and that Durkheim really posited one cause of suicide:

> A closer look at *Suicide* suggests, however, that altruism and fatalism really do not belong in Durkheim's scheme, and that egoism and anomie are identical. Thus, his four causes of suicide can be reduced to one, so that all variation in suicide rates is attributed to a single cause.
>
> (1965: 875)

Elwin H. Powell also reduces all of Durkheim's conceptual categories to one category: "Behind the diverse manifestations of the act of self-destruction . . . there is a common sociological ground – anomie" (1958: 133). Gibbs and Martin, in turn, reduce anomie to integration: "Nearly all the properties Durkheim ascribes to anomie can be subsumed under the concept of social integration" (1964: 7). Dohrenwend laments this "preoccupation with anomie," but even he adopts the position that anomie is the supposedly quantifiable "normlessness" (1959: 466). These and other interpretations are based, not on finding harmony in Durkheim's thought or in relation to his cultural context, but on making his theory more suitable to quantitative analyses and commensurate with modernist assumptions of progress and social order.

To repeat: Durkheim never used the term normlessness. The end result of this pragmatic approach is intellectual confusion, because no point of view, least of all Freud's and Durkheim's, is examined in its historical context. Rather, in pretending to be objective, Durkheim's positivistic interpreters merely perpetuate the modernist myth that barbarism – conveniently renamed deviance – can be brought under social control. By contrast, Durkheim's horrifying message is similar to Freud's and Schopenhauer's: enlightenment merely exacerbates the all-devouring will, which can never be fully controlled. The modernists miss completely the connection between Freud's writings on the id and Durkheim's writings on anomie.

THE ASSIMILATION OF FREUD INTO ENLIGHTENMENT NARRATIVES

With regard to assimilating Freud into the positivistic, modernist program, consider Fisher and Greenberg's *The Scientific Credibility of Freud's Theories and Therapy* (1977). The authors state at the outset that "the time has come to face up squarely to the scientific sparseness of what has generally been offered as support for Freudian formulations" (ibid.: 6). One suspects that Fisher and Greenberg approach Freud like Gibbs and Martin approach Durkheim: give us intellectually testable propositions, or don't call yourself a scientist. Fisher and Greenberg hold that "Freud and many other analysts seem to believe sincerely that they have no choice but to reject traditional scientific methodology in approaching psychoanalytical issues" (ibid.: 7) – as if positivism were "traditional"! – but they do not elaborate.

Just what is "traditional scientific methodology?" I would argue that Freud's Schopenhauerian approach is far more traditional than modern positivistic approaches, which self-consciously cut themselves off from philosophy as well as culture. For Fisher and Greenberg, when Freud writes in a way that does not lend itself to their understanding of a "testable" model, they conclude that Freud is not being a scientist. Fisher and Greenberg do not refer to Freud's writings on what science, theory, and testable propositions meant to Freud or his contemporaries.

Bauman (1991) helps to explain Freud's stance in this regard by arguing that Freud felt that he had to challenge the entire modernist edifice, and had to guard jealously any attempts to assimilate his project into the Enlightenment project. Durkheim and Freud were concerned with insights, not just hypotheses to be tested, and insight – in Schopenhauer's view – involves heart and mind. Insight can never really be replicated because it involves collective representations in a cultural context, not hard facts. As such, each time representations are approached, the object and human agent performing the analysis have changed. Each representation is relative to the configuration of object, subject and witnesses. For Durkheim, Freud, and many of their *fin de siècle* contemporaries, hypotheses are not discarded just because they cannot be "verified" repeatedly – as if the universe were static, frozen in time and space, a monstrous, modern artifact. Rather, each analysis yields knowledge which is useful in some fashion so long as it is perceived with the heart and mind. Both art and science deal with representations, not "reality," and both involve the will and its emotional, intuitive manifestations. Just as there can be no last and lasting interpretation of any artistic work, so also any scientific description can be superseded at any time.

Instead of trying to understand the unifying theoretical structure of Freud's psychoanalysis, namely, the *fin de siècle* spirit, Fisher and Greenberg and other positivists approach his work as a collection of disjointed propositions that must be forced into the modernist project. In the array of propositions Fisher and Greenberg have collected as testable, we do not find one on suicide. This is not because Freud does not write about suicide – hardly a case study does not refer to it in some form – but because Freud never gave a final, testable (in terms of cause and effect) hypothesis regarding suicide. It is well-known that in the one paper that addresses suicide in its title, "Contributions to a Discussion on Suicide" ([1910b] 1974: 232), Freud concludes: "We have not reached a decision on the problem that interests us."

Other interpreters of Freud have tried to make use of Freud's statements to the effect that no person thinks of harming his or her self who does not harbor murderous wishes against another. This has resulted in the popular, and unfortunate, misunderstanding that suicide is inverted murder (Freedman and Kaplan 1967: 1172; Shneidman 1969, 1972: 11; West 1967: 113). One unfortunate result of this characterization has been the simplistic understanding that suicide and the murderous wish are uniquely related, implying that Freud was reductionistic and closed to other causes of suicide.[9] Another unfortunate interpretation has been that all suicides are potential murderers. What is incorrect in these, and other misinterpretations, is the belief that suicide and the murderous wish are uniquely related – that only suicidal persons harbor murderous wishes against others. These positivistic misreadings of Freud's intentions lend themselves to the hope for social control, of course. In fact, Freud is consistent in maintaining that *all* persons harbor murderous wishes against others, only for most persons these wishes arc unconscious and if effectively "worn away," do not result in violence. This will be discussed later, but at this point in the discussion, even a cursory glance at a relevant passage by Freud indicates the truth of this claim:

> Analysis has explained the enigma of suicide in the following way: probably no one finds the mental energy required to kill himself unless, in the first place, in doing so he is at the same time killing an object with whom he has identified himself a death-wish which had been directed against someone else. Nor need the regular discovery of these unconscious death wishes in those who have attempted suicide surprise us (any more than it ought to make us think that it confirms our deductions), since the unconscious of all human beings is full enough of such death wishes, even against those they love. Finally, the discovery that several quite different motives all of great strength, must have co-operated to make such a deed possible is only in accordance with what we should expect.
>
> ([1920] 1974: 163)

The more pressing problems generated by Freud's comments on the relationship of murder and suicide, when read in the context of Schopenhauer's focus on the will, include the following questions: Why is it that we do not all kill those we love? Why is it that we are not all suicidal or otherwise barbaric? What happens to these murderous wishes? These are threatening questions, for they address the possibility that our husbands, wives, mothers, fathers, children, and friends sometimes wish to kill us, and vice versa. All these signify a terribly chaotic state of affairs to the modernist mind! Clearly, for Freud, society prevents the fulfillment of some of these murderous wishes, but not without the cost of making the individual sick, in some cases. Also, some of these murderous wishes are "worn away" – to use Freud's own phrase, so that their strength is diminished, transformed into art and other creative acts, and in some cases eliminated. But one cannot address these problems generated by Freud without invoking the entire edifice of his theory, including the cultural assumptions and philosophies that informed it.

The frightening conclusion drawn by Freud – yet to be addressed seriously by his modernist interpreters – is that:

Impeded aggressiveness seems to involve a grave injury. It

really seems as though it is necessary for us to destroy some other thing or person in order not to destroy ourselves.

([1938] 1969: 94)

But this statement, as horrifying as any found in Schopenhauer's and Nietzsche's texts, applies to *all* humans, not just those who are suicidal or otherwise deviant. Yet modernists cannot accept such a chaotic view of the social universe, one in which the dangerous will lurks beneath and behind peaceable, orderly facades. Hence, great efforts have been made to assimilate Freud's thought into a modernist paradigm of any sort.

Chapter 7

Moving beyond hermeneutics

Nor was I then aware that in deriving hysteria from sexuality, I was going back to the very beginnings of medicine and following up a thought of Plato's.

(Sigmund Freud [1925] 1959: 24)

In our Western world, it was with the great thinkers of Greece that it [humankind] first became clearly conscious of itself and of the consequences which it [*homo duplex*] implies; when the discovery was made, it caused an amazement which Plato has translated into magnificent language.

(Emile Durkheim [1912] 1965: 436)

The theory of the instincts is so to say our mythology. Instincts are mythical entities, magnificent in their indefiniteness.

(Sigmund Freud [1933] 1965: 84)

According to our hypothesis human instincts are of only two kinds: those which seek to preserve and unite – which we call erotic, exactly in the sense in which Plato uses the word Eros in his *Symposium* . . . and those which seek to destroy and kill and which we class together as the aggressive or destructive instinct.

(Sigmund Freud, from "Why War?" [1933] 1963: 200)

It is from myths and legends that science and poetry have arisen.

(Emile Durkheim, from Preface of 1899 *L'Année Sociologique*)

Suppose, for the sake of argument, that the reader wants to agree with our claims that the social-order paradigm is a modernist aberration relative to the rest of Western culture;

that it cannot be derived from Veblen, Freud and Durkheim when they are read in the context of their *fin de siècle* cultural milieu; and it cannot succeed in its misguided quest to tame and control Nature. What are the implications of these claims for comprehending modern barbarism?

Baudrillard would probably make the counter-claim that Veblen, Freud and Durkheim were just three hermeneutic interpreters among many whose interpretations are on a par with any TV commentary. And if the individual is the enemy of civilization, why do we not live perpetually in Hobbes's state of war? (Some might suggest that humanity is approaching Hobbes's vision.) The answers to these and other questions based on our philosophical and cultural starting-points are that there is a reality beneath the Kantian world of appearances, and that reality is the irrational will. Moreover, the will is constructive as well as destructive. Hobbes and the modernists forgot Plato's myth, in which Eros binds, builds, and holds peoples as well as the Universe together through affinity and other derivatives of love.

Veblen, Freud and Durkheim seem to have been building their theories on a similar interpretation of Plato's myths. What use do myths have in social science, and how do we interpret them? In this chapter, we shall focus on the issue of hermeneutics. Most contemporary efforts to interpret a work or theorist make no claims toward finding truth or reality. For Baudrillard especially, postmodernism signals the end of the real (Smart 1992: 139), so that one interpretation is as good, or bad, as another. Positivists are also scornful of myths, but the truths at which they arrive are every bit as contingent and susceptible to revision as any myth. In the end, both positivists and postmodernists reduce the world to neo-Kantian, circulating fictions. By contrast, Veblen, Durkheim and Freud regarded the consistent myths, habits, and collective representations that make up Western culture as signifying something true and real about that culture. These mythical representations mean something, refer to something, and are grounded in something, even if that something can never be known with full and complete clarity.

Thinkers from the previous *fin de siècle* remind us that even so-called hard facts are still representations that must be evaluated critically, and that must not be taken at face value.[1] But again, representations are not just surface realities: they have a hidden side to them that points to the collective will that objectified them in the first place. Thus, Veblen, Freud and Durkheim should be ranked among the existentialist philosophers, not just as precursors of the social sciences. Commensurate with our previously established strategy, we shall concentrate more directly on Freud and Durkheim than Veblen because they made their sources clear whereas Veblen did not.

DURKHEIM'S AND KIERKEGAARD'S ELABORATION OF PLATO

Durkheim turned to the same fictions that interest Baudrillard and found a referent and ground for them that he often traced back to Plato's mythical account of the forces that animate the Universe. For the time being, let us not evaluate these meta-physical moves by Durkheim. Let us first seek them out, and convince ourselves that Durkheim was engaged in a sort of hermeneutics that is unfamiliar to neo-Kantians. I would like to demonstrate that Durkheim's classical education explains more of his enigmatic moves than any positivistic, structuralist, or postmodern reading.

The reader will recall from the previous chapter that the positivists are still debating how to make sense, in a neo-Kantian framework, of Durkheim's seemingly strange accounts that involve egoism, altruism, anomie, and fatalism. Let us switch context completely for the moment, and compare Durkheim's account with Søren Kierkegaard's *The Sickness Unto Death* ([1849] 1954). In *The Sickness Unto Death*, Søren Kierkegaard cites Plato's *Philebus* as the basis of some startling claims that he makes. These are of interest because, according to Magee (1983: 26), Kierkegaard wrote in his diary that encountering Schopenhauer's philosophy was a major event in his life, and Schopenhauer claimed that the kernel of his philosophy is Platonic. It is a fascinating coincidence that two important precursors of modern existentialism, Kierkegaard and Schopenhauer, both derive their pessimism from Plato's philosophy, and these in turn bear a striking resemblance to Durkheim's and Freud's own struggles with the dualism of human nature.

For Kierkegaard, the essence of being human is to be in despair, not to pursue happiness! And he depicts four types of despair, treated as pairs. In each pair, one type of despair is always defined in terms of its opposite. As Kierkegaard put it: "No kind of despair can be defined directly (that is, undialectically), but only by reflecting upon the opposite factor" ([1849] 1954: 163). He defines these four types of despair as follows:

1 the despair of infinitude is due to the lack of finitude.
2 the despair of finitude is due to the lack of infinitude.
3 the despair of necessity is due to the lack of possibility.
4 the despair of possibility is due to the lack of necessity.

(Ibid.: 163–70)

Kierkegaard makes the Platonic claim that "health consists essentially in being able to resolve contradictions" (ibid.: 173), particularly the contradictions of the types of despair he outlines. Consider how this Platonic claim resonates with previous *fin de siècle* understandings of health as well. All four of the elements that make up the various types of despair are also essential to life. This is in keeping with the Platonic theme that even poison can be beneficial, but anything in excess is harmful, although Schopenhauer and Durkheim wrote much the same thing. Thus, anomie, egoism, altruism, and fatalism – all essential virtues – are pathogenic when excessive, and when they combine in dangerous ways with the other currents. Durkheim frequently refers to anomie and egoism in terms of infinity – a term that Schopenhauer also uses when describing the infinitely striving will – whereas altruism and fatalism constitute excessive finitude.

In *Philebus* (16c), Plato writes that "whatever things are said to be are composed of one and many, and have the finite and infinite implanted in them." This dualism between finitude and infinitude is expressed in several forms: the body (finite) versus the soul (infinite), rationality (finitude) versus pleasure (infinite), and so on. Durkheim explicitly compares his dualisms to those of Plato in his essay "On the Dualism of Human Nature and Its Social Conditions" ([1914] 1973). And any student of Durkheim knows that he treats egoism, altruism, fatalism, and anomie as a chiasmus such that these can be paired in various ways to represent finitude versus infinitude (see especially Durkheim [1897] 1951: 277–94). For example, egoism–anomie is characterized by a "mixture of agitation and apathy," anomie–altruism by "exasperated effervescence," and egoism–altruism by "melancholy tempered with moral fortitude" (ibid.: 293).

We have seen in previous chapters that in the interest of imposing an artificial, modernist parsimony onto Durkheim's thought, some scholars reduce Durkheim's topology to one, two, or three suicidal currents. The only reason for these idiosyncratic maneuvers that are passed off as scientific is to make Durkheim's propositions easier to test by quantitative methods. There is no effort to ground Durkheim's moves into some larger, Western myth of what it means to be human, even though that appears to have been Durkheim's inspiration. Ultimately, the modernists have eliminated the notion of despair in favor of an optimistic faith in progress, forgetting Plato's arresting claim that the aim of life is death.

Our point is that Durkheim's enigmatic topology flows naturally out of the classical philosophical tradition that can be traced from Plato to Schopenhauer and Kierkegaard, among others. For example, Durkheim ([1897] 1951: 276) writes:

> There is a type of suicide the opposite of anomic suicide, just as egoistic and altruistic suicides are opposites. It is the suicide deriving from excessive regulation, that of persons with futures pitilessly blocked and passions violently choked by oppressive discipline.

Moreover, the concept of despair permeates Durkheim's thought, even though he never calls it such. In his *Division of Labor*, Durkheim arrived at the Platonic, Schopenhauerian insight, later reflected in Horkheimer's works, that happiness cannot be the aim of individual or collective life. Much of *Suicide* is devoted to elaborating "the true suicide, the sad suicide" of modern times as compared to the obligatory suicides of primitive societies, first mentioned in *Division of Labor*. Altruistic suicide – characterized by excessive finitude – in primitive societies was normal because the individual was not held in high regard by society. It was not the result of simple unhappiness. But for Durkheim, anomie, which is predominantly a modern phenomenon, and which he calls a disease of infiniteness, is linked to suffering and pain. It follows that the abnormal, anomic suicide – the true suicide – will be sad and despairing (Durkheim [1893] 1933: 247). Of course, Durkheim devotes time to distinguishing how the sadness of excessive finitude is different from the sadness of excessive infinitude. The widespread modernist belief is that to be in despair, one must know that one is in despair. Kierkegaard, on the other hand, goes to great lengths to argue that one form of despair is precisely that of not knowing one is in despair ([1849] 1954: 167):

> This form of despair is hardly ever noticed in the world. Such a man, precisely by losing his self in this way, has gained perfectibility in adjusting himself to business, yea, in making a success in the world. Here there is no hindrance, no difficulty, occasioned by his self and his infinitization, he is ground smooth as a pebble, *courant* as a well-used coin. So far from being considered in despair, he is just what a man ought to be. In general, the world has of course no understanding of what is truly dreadful. The despair which not only occasions no embarrassment but makes one's life easy and comfortable is naturally not regarded as despair.

A thorough comparison and contrast between Kierkegaard and Durkheim on the issue of despair would illuminate aspects of both thinkers, though such an undertaking is not within the scope of this work. Our aim is limited to exposing the existential import of Durkheim's arguments – the depth of his thought, the fact that his roots go back to Plato and resonate with the existentialists – compared to the superficial modernist understandings criticized in the previous chapter. For if one applied Kierkegaard's insights to the ideal-type of the Parsonian individual who has internalized society's norms, one would conclude that such a person is suffering from the despair of excessive finitude – but is not aware of this fact. Parsons's paradigm is incapable of such thought-provoking insight, for it stays on the neo-Kantian surface of things. Nevertheless, to anyone familiar with Schopenhauer's philosophy, it should be evident why Kierkegaard was so struck with discovering Schopenhauer. Both philosophers focus on the theme of unmasking the surface, illusory happiness to discover the inner decadence and barbarism of modern living. And both use Plato's philosophy to achieve this aim.

The links between Plato and Durkheim mentioned in this chapter and book as a whole are obviously not meant to be exhaustive. We are merely opening a door to a new, cultural hermeneutics. Nevertheless, I believe that it is important to suggest that Durkheim may be read as a kind of existentialist, in order to counter the claims by Lyotard (1984) and other post-modernists that all totalistic narratives are always oppressive. On the contrary, Plato's, Kierkegaard's, and Schopenhauer's efforts to find a total vision of the human person are widely acknowledged to be humanistic and existential. The postmodernists and positivists imply an optimism in their varieties of hermeneutics that is every bit as open to the charge of being oppressive. This is because an easy optimism in the face of collective despair associated with modernity is nothing less than cruel.

FREUD'S AND PLATO'S MYTHOLOGIES

With regard to Freud, another one of Plato's concepts, Eros, plays a crucial part in his work. In fact, Freud refers to the battle between Eros and the death instincts (which may be likened to the tendency toward infinitude and finitude) so often that he felt self-conscious about the number of occasions he refers to it. So he writes in *Civilization and Its Discontents*:

> Some readers of this work may further have an impression that they have heard the formula of the struggle between Eros and the death instinct too often. It was alleged to characterize the process of civilization which mankind undergoes but it was also brought into connection with the development of the individual, and, in addition, it was said to have revealed the secret of organic life in general.
>
> ([1930] 1961: 86)

Such bold, truly incredible, Platonic claims have no doubt left Freud open to the charge of wanting to apply one formula to everything. This criticism can be tempered if he is read in the cultural context of Plato and Schopenhauer. For Plato, indeed, everything that is living in the universe *is* subject to this dualism between a tendency toward regression, death, and contraction versus the opposing tendency toward development, greater unity, and expansion. Similarly, Schopenhauer definitely meant his statements on the will to life to apply to everything in the universe, animate and inanimate (cf. Magee 1983). And like Plato, Schopenhauer emphasized the importance of the erotic.

In *Mind and Madness in Ancient Greece: The Classical Roots of Modern Psychiatry*, Bennett Simon (1978) comes up with some marvellous insights that are partially relevant to this study. He not only wishes to trace the roots of psychoanalysis to Plato, he applies psychoanalysis to Plato.[2] To seek the precursors of psychoanalysis while applying the psychoanalytic method (or Simon's interpretation of it) in this search for cultural precursors is a method that carries considerable risks. There is the logical problem of applying a method to itself as well as to another body of thought. Either project, applying psychoanalysis to history or seeking the roots of psychoanalysis, is formidable in its own right, but undertaking them both simultaneously is confusing from the start.

In my project, I will do neither. That is, I am not claiming that Freud and Durkheim have roots in Plato or Schopenhauer as philosophers *per se*, because clearly, Freud and Durkheim established the social sciences, and ventured into territory that Plato and Schopenhauer could scarcely imagine.[3] Nor am I claiming that Plato or Schopenhauer ought to be analyzed in Freudian and Durkheimian perspectives. For example, Alvin Gouldner (1965) commits this mistake by applying functionalism to Plato's social milieu. Nor am I claiming that Freud has roots in Durkheim, nor vice versa, nor will I judge the one relative to the other. All of these claims presuppose modernist, neo-Kantian causal connections and post-Humean dilemmas that I seek steadfastly to avoid. My book involves a safer but hopefully more profitable search for *cultural* affinities between the ideas of Freud and Durkheim in the context of Schopenhauer extended to Plato.

Regardless of the individual spin that each and every thinker, and reader, puts on these cultural myths, we are searching for grounds and referents for discourse, and to escape the post-Humean conclusion that all affinities are mere accidents. We are acting on the hunch that the riddle of how barbarism thrives within the heart of modernity may be found in the résumé of Western thought itself. The ultimate significance of the Platonic legacy in the ideas of various thinkers will be addressed from the viewpoint of the link to Schopenhauer's focus on the primacy of the will as a refraction of Plato's Eros – but not Plato or Schopenhauer *per se* (as if that were possible), nor the Plato or Schopenhauer of scholarly debates. These debates have their own agendas, which – like the positivistic agendas regarding Freud and Durkheim – we do not wish to enter.

Furthermore, there is no certain procedure for demonstrating the roots or origins of any system of thought, be it psychoanalysis or anything else. There will always be the possibility that the two bodies of thought being considered are similar in structure or content or both from coincidence, or for a host of other accidental reasons. My personal stand on this debate, as well as the reader's, is not relevant to the outcome of this project in which the works of Freud and Durkheim are read *as refractions of Western cultural narratives* in the context of *fin de siècle* narratives that refract Schopenhauer extended to Plato. Such a context will merely illuminate the new starting-point that can lead to paths that would not otherwise have been perceived.

To put it another way, there is no effort here to be dogmatic about the choice of Plato's and Schopenhauer's philosophies as a context for analysis. There are good reasons for using them as a context, and these have been discussed. But again, the cultural ideas and their refractions, not the thinkers themselves, are most important. Plato, Schopenhauer, Veblen, Freud, and Durkheim concerned themselves with similar *collective representations*, essences, habits of thought, or whatever name one wants to give to seemingly permanent problems of being human in a Western context. Part of their amazing similarity is that they all thought there was an other, irrational, hidden side to appearances of reality.

Despite these criticisms of Simon with regard to method, I applaud his findings when he simply compares and contrasts Plato and Freud (in Chapter 10 of his book). For example, he notes that Plato's use of Eros and Freud's use of libido are similar. Both Freud and Plato hold a model of the mind as being split between a higher and a lower part; where for Plato this split takes the forms of the rational versus the appetitive part, psyche versus soma, and others, and for Freud it takes the forms of the conscious versus the unconscious, the ego versus the sexual instincts, the ego versus the id, and others. Both Plato and Freud claim that the lower part of the mind thinks in illusions, and both use anthropomorphic language.

Both Plato and Freud hold a model of conflict and emphasize

the need to rule the instincts that is unlike the Enlightenment model of social order and control. In this regard, Simon observes that in *The Ego and the Id* ([1923a] 1974), Freud likens the ego's control of the id to a person trying to control a horse, much like Plato characterizes the soul as a charioteer trying to control a team of wild horses pulling in contrary directions, rational and irrational (in his *Phaedrus* 246a). These models, in turn, are essentially similar to Durkheim's ([1914] 1973) concept of *homo duplex*, and are radically different from the Enlightenment model, in which the team of horses is assumed to be well trained. Both Plato and Freud also stress cooperation between these two parts of the psyche (the higher and lower). For example, Freud's use of sublimation can be likened to Plato's depiction of the progress from carnal love of bodies to the love of abstract beauty in *Symposium*. We find similar apparent paradoxes in Durkheim and Schopenhauer, who assume that will and idea, even if they are contraries, are absolutely essential to each other, and must harmonize to some extent.

Regarding terminology, Simon believes that Plato's use of the concept of appetites can be "equated" with Freud's use of instincts (*Trieb*).[4] Simon writes: "'Instinct' as used by Freud bridges the mind and body; the instinct is the mental representative of the bodily demand" (1978: 205). This is true. But most of the points raised by Simon apply to Schopenhauer's philosophy as well, with only slight modification.

I have by no means exhausted Simon's investigation of the comparison and contrast between Freud and Plato. The intent thus far has been to suggest that the sort of hermeneutics in which Freud and Durkheim were engaged is different than the hermeneutics that has come down to us from the post-modernists.

ART VERSUS SCIENCE

We have seen in previous chapters that some contemporary social scientists are critical of Freud's and Durkheim's allegedly unscientific use of language, by which is meant their tendency to indulge in highly descriptive, suggestive, and at times un-doubtedly metaphysical terminology that allegedly does not lend itself to empirical verification. Even though Lyotard (1984) and other postmodernists argue that scientific narratives are not more privileged compared with artistic narratives with regard to truth, they, like the positivists, deny the existence of metaphysical essences that might lie beneath the surface of things. This leads to the conclusion that one interpretation is as good (or bad) as another. In the context of this debate between the postmodernists and the defenders of the scientific *status quo*, I hope to avoid two extremes in reading Freud and Durkheim. One is the hostility shown to social scientists by literary writers, even by other social scientists who claim that sociology is an art form, and the other is the hostility shown to artists by some social scientists who claim that unless something can be operationalized, it is meaningless. Schopenhauer's *World as Will and Idea* is an important context for this debate, because he definitely treats art and science as a unity.

In *The Savage God* (1970), Alvarez engages in an analysis that is highly relevant to the present discussion of barbarism. He studies the phenomenon of suicide from the point of view of a literary appreciator, and charges that social scientists have killed the chances of genuinely understanding suicide because of their lack of literary talents: "It is as though the procedures necessary to a scientific understanding of suicide had made the subject unreal. In part, this is the doing of the great sociologist Emile Durkheim" (ibid.: 87).

One surmises that Alvarez feels that in the writings of Durkheim one has lost the sense that suicide is about persons who find life intolerable. He goes on to criticize the "Byzantine prose" of Jack Douglas and to conclude that in sociology in general:

> The more that has been written, the narrower the field has become. To wade through even the shallow end of the mass of books and articles on the sociology of suicide is an odd experience. Clearly, the researchers are serious men, well trained and well informed, sometimes gifted and perceptive. Yet what they actually write seems somehow not to be wholly real.
>
> (Ibid.: 89)

Alvarez is not to be dismissed simply because, from the perspective of the Byzantine social scientists he criticizes, he has not defined the meaning of the term real. He has a point.

Despite the mountains of research articles that have been written on suicide since Durkheim's time, we do not necessarily understand this phenomenon better than he did. And I should note that Alvarez does not quote Durkheim to substantiate his criticism that Durkheim originated this Byzantine approach to suicide. (Obviously, I would argue the opposite, that Durkheim writes with great pathos.) Perhaps he read the secondary sources on Durkheim, and these seem to deserve the criticisms Alvarez makes.

In any event, one social scientist who seems to support the position of Alvarez, albeit only implicitly, is Robert Nisbet. Nisbet claims that the great sociologists were, in fact, artists, and that the lesser sociologists have failed to appreciate this, and have thereby obscured the importance of the initial insights. In *The Sociological Tradition*, Nisbet writes: "Consider one example: the view of society and man that underlies Durkheim's great study of suicide. Basically it is the view of the artist as much as that of the scientist" (1966: 19). The same holds true for the other great sociologists. For example, regarding Simmel, Nisbet writes: "Remove the artist's vision from the treatments of the stranger, the dyad, and the role of secrecy, and you have removed all that gives life" (ibid.: 20).

In *Sociology as an Art Form* (1976) Nisbet makes some convincing comparisons between art and sociology. For example, he claims that the great sociologists portrayed "landscapes" in everything they did:

> A great deal of what is most important in sociology consists of, in effect, landscapes of the social, economic, and political setting in nineteenth- and early twentieth-century Western Europe. What Tocqueville and Marx, and then Tönnies, Weber, Durkheim, and Simmel, give us in their greatest works ... is a series of landscapes, each as distinctive and compelling as any to be found among the greater novels or paintings of their age.
>
> (Ibid.: 7)

I agree. And I would add that the novels and paintings of their age bore the imprint of Schopenhauer's philosophy to a large extent (see Baillot 1927; Magee 1983; Simmel [1907] 1986). Nisbet goes on to lament the ways in which the spirits of graduate students in sociology are crushed because their teachers ignore the artistic quality of the great sociologists and demand a more arid operationalization of relevant concepts.

There is something to be said for Nisbet's claims. But it is not clear that this obscuring of great insights is due entirely to a neglect of art. Artists may write well, but they frequently display total ignorance of sociology's most important principles. So, for example, in *The Myth of Sisyphus* Albert Camus writes:

> Suicide has never been dealt with except as a social phenomenon. On the contrary, we are concerned here, at the outset, with the relationship between individual thought and suicide. An act like this is prepared within the silence of the heart, as is a great work of art. The man himself is ignorant of it. One evening he pulls the trigger or jumps . . . Society has but little connection with such beginnings. The worm is in man's heart. That is where it must be sought.
>
> (1955: 4)

But where did the worm come from? The person? Or something external to the person, like society? To repeat, Halbwachs ([1930] 1978: 294) takes up exactly this issue of society's role in the individual's role to kill his or her self, and does so in relation to Durkheim's sociology and Schopenhauer's philosophy. Camus should not be allowed to dismiss so casually one of the most basic premisses of sociology, particularly Durkheim's sociology, no matter how eloquently he expresses himself. At least Durkheim resorts to arguments for his position in addition to his beautiful writing – that sets him apart from the artist.

In sum, the postmodernist rebellion at the grand narratives of modernity has dissolved the distinction between art and science, but has not pointed to grounds or referents for apprehending truth through either medium. Scientific discourse and narratives are no more privileged than artistic discourse. Rather than become embroiled in the debate that these claims have unleashed between those who find such radical deconstruction liberating versus the defenders of the *status quo*, our aim is to pursue a third alternative. It does not follow that representations are merely circulating fictions, as claimed by Baudrillard (1981) and others. Instead, representations are objectifications of the will, and are grounded in cultural reality even if they are not to be taken at face value, because all reality is always veiled and obscured. For Durkheim especially, science, art, and even religion consist of collective representations, but these representations represent social forces and realities.

Thus, one can pursue the "landscapes" of Freud and Durkheim at the same time that one can muster evidence for or against interpretations of that landscape. We shall not sit in judgment on Freud and Durkheim, demanding that they provide us with something like a computerized list of empirically verifiable definitions and hypotheses – that is simply not their style nor the style of writing in the previous *fin de siècle*. But the very fact that one can find commonalities in the *fin de siècle* spirit suggests that common experiences gave rise to their collective representations of reality.

Consider the alternatives. If one criticizes Freud and Durkheim harshly for not offering so-called empirical definitions of terms – wherein the modernist grounds for such definitions of empiricism are assumed to be universally valid – one will end up like Gibbs and Martin, Douglas, and others reviewed in previous chapters. One will have to say that Freud and Durkheim cannot be tested, and therefore much of what they have written is useless. That is a dead end. If one takes Lyotard's (1984) approach, and does not care about arriving at any semblance of a true interpretation of their terms, one has contributed one more subjective fiction to a fragmented world drowning in subjective fictions. But, based on the starting-points chosen for this analysis, art and science are not necessarily incompatible with each other, and relative truths grounded in the will can be found. Only these truths are limited to a particular time and place, and can be superseded at any time.

What would be the point of searching for such relative truths? We indicated at the outset that many authors find compelling similarities between our *fin de siècle* and the previous *fin de siècle*. Others, from Bloom (1987) to Simon (1978) and Kierkegaard ([1849] 1954), find commonalities between their times and some of Plato's representations of reality. Just because science cannot claim to find universally valid truths, it does not follow that it cannot find insights drawn from other times and places that might help illuminate contemporary issues.

STRUCTURALISM AND HERMENEUTICS

At first glance it may seem like our mode of reading Freud and Durkheim is related to the diverse works of the following thinkers whose works are frequently subsumed under the rubrics of structuralism or hermeneutics: Chomsky, Foucault, Lacan, Lévi-Strauss, Lewin, Parsons, Saussure, Piaget, Laplanche, Pontalis, Ricœur, and others. But there are important differences between our mode of reading and of what passes for hermeneutics and structuralism. For some of the authors mentioned above, hermeneutics and structuralism are methods of analysis that carry rigid criteria and standards of adequacy, and presuppose modernist narratives at the outset. Many of them seek a universal, timeless social order that exists beneath appearances. In a sense, they are seeking an appearance beneath an appearance, because they subscribe to the neo-Kantian tenets that time, space, and causality cannot be anything but contingent.

By contrast, in our hermeneutics inspired by Schopenhauer, Durkheim, and Plato, we admit from the outset that any truth or reality that is found will decay and change the moment that it is plucked from the stream of life. There are no universal, positivistic truths. We reject the assumption that any social order at any cost is desirable, even if we agree with the structuralists that some minimal order is preferable to anarchy. Also, in contrast to many of the thinkers listed above, we are searching for degeneration, chaos, and derangement as they accompany all semblance of order. In these and other ways, we are using the previous *fin de siècle* spirit as the ground for the present analysis, whereas most structuralists use modernist narratives for starting-points. We are attempting to steer a middle course between modernist narratives and postmodern, anti-narrative narratives that often lead to nihilism.

It is highly debatable whether the method one uses in interpreting a Biblical text – which is how hermeneutics began (Schleiermacher 1977) – can be the same sort of exegesis one uses on texts that are supposed to be scientific. Both Freud and Durkheim examined religious texts as part of their overall projects, but they always tried to draw scientific conclusions from their analyses. Likewise, no matter how sensitive the exegesis of Freud and Durkheim, it will make a difference whether one is approaching their works as random narratives, mere fictions, or as scientific works that happen to be particularly difficult to comprehend because of their landscaping and metaphorical use of language, not to mention the grounds and referents they use for their discourse.

For example, Paul Ricœur claims that: "The essence of psychoanalytic interpretation consists in the relation between the semantics of desire and the syntax of distortion" (1970: 168). Similarly, Ellenberger (1970) has argued that many of Freud's colleagues writing in the *fin de siècle* spirit were obsessed with these two themes. Nevertheless, Freud steadfastly maintained that he was a scientist, and even his harsh critics concede that some of his claims "ring true" with regard to postmodern realities, even if they are not all testable by strict, positivistic standards. Otherwise, the many authors who invoke Freud – Bloom, Adorno, Bellah, Lasch, Riesman, and others – to make a point about postmodern social reality would not have bothered. Clearly, there has to be something "objective" in Freud's fictions for these fictions to be invoked so often. Presumably, "the semantics of desire" means that Freud is concerned with refractions of the Schopenhauerian will as they objectify themselves in human agents, and that these wants and needs are expressed through language, as well as other psychic representations (slips of the tongue, symptoms, dreams, etc.). Presumably, "the syntax of distortion" has to do with all the means by which persons misunderstand what other persons want and need. Presumably, the relation of "the semantics of desire" and "the syntax of distortion" has something to do with the scientific concern with "What is true?"

To put it another way, for Schopenhauer, as for Freud and many of his colleagues, science must take into account the other side of reason, the will, and it must unmask what the consciousness distorts. Thus, there is no good reason to dismiss Freud or his colleagues for being unscientific because of these *fin de siècle* concerns. I would suggest the contrary, that much of contemporary science is only pseudo-science because it assumes a kind of felicity and naiveté regarding reason and the objectivity of the world. This felicity makes an easy target for postmodern criticisms.

INSTINCTS AS MYTHOLOGY

Like Veblen, Pareto, and many of his contemporaries, Freud refers to various sorts of mythical instincts that are not biological.[5] The relationships among these instincts, by positivistic standards, are curious. At one time in Freud's writings the instinct of self-preservation was opposed to the sexual instinct, but later, both of these instincts are subsumed under Eros. The Platonic Eros comes to fuel the life *and* death instincts at another point. For a while Freud entertains the idea of the ego-instincts in opposition to sexual instincts as well. This grand mythology on the part of Freud is simply too ambiguous, illogical and contradictory to satisfy positivistic standards. But it is commensurate with Schopenhauer's own grand speculations on the various manifestations of the will found in *The World as Will and Representation.* "It is the sexual instinct *par excellence* which exemplifies certain characteristics of the Freudian instinct that distinguish it from instinct in the biological sense," according to Laplanche and Pontalis (1973: 417). Yet Schopenhauer preceded Freud in claiming that "the sexual impulse is the most vehement of cravings, the desire of desires, the concentration of all our willing" ([1818] 1969b: 580) and that the genitals are the focus of the will (ibid.: 514). This is because for both Schopenhauer and Freud, the object or aim of the sexual instinct is *not* pre-determined, and its modes of satisfaction are various.

Moreover, in his later writings, Freud tended to equate the sexual instincts with Eros, and thereby to relate his notion of sexuality explicitly to Plato. (And one must keep in mind Schopenhauer's own self-conscious efforts to extend Plato.) According to Freud:

> What psychoanalysis called sexuality was by no means identical with the impulsion towards a union of the two sexes or towards producing a pleasurable sensation in the genitals: it had far more resemblance to the all inclusive and all pre-serving Eros of Plato's *Symposium.*
>
> ([1925] 1974: 220)

Elsewhere, Freud wrote:

> And as for the "stretching" of the concept of sexuality which has been necessitated by the analysis of children and what are called perverts, anyone who looks down with contempt upon

psychoanalysis from a superior vantage-point should remember how closely the enlarged sexuality of psychoanalysis coincides with the Eros of the divine Plato.

([1905a] 1974: 134)

I have by no means exhausted Freud's many references to Plato in the context of his usage of the terms Eros, libido, sexuality, and instinct. But my point is that if we take Freud seriously that his notion of instincts – in some forms – resembles Plato's terms more than what is literally or biologically understood as instinct by modernists, then we are on a track to relate Durkheim to Freud in the context of Schopenhauer and Plato. This is because Durkheim, like Freud, relates his dualisms to Plato's to capture a source of inexorable tension between higher and lower aspects of the human condition.

Freud admits: "The theory of the instincts is so to say our mythology. Instincts are mythical entities magnificent in their indefiniteness" ([1933] 1965: 84). The modernist understanding of myths is that they represent illusion, something unreal and ungrounded in fact. But like Freud, Durkheim ([1924] 1974) regards myths as representations that have as their substratum something real. Schopenhauer regarded myths and Plato's Ideas as the highest forms of representing the will objectively. Similarly, it is clear that Freud does not understand his notion of the instincts literally.

Freud, Durkheim, Veblen, and Jung, among others, were concerned with the problem of collective memory (Halbwachs [1950] 1980): how the past – and particularly remnants of the barbaric past – persists into the present. This problem plagued Freud throughout his career, as in his *Totem and Taboo* ([1912] 1950), wherein he had to try to explain how collective guilt that stems from killing the father operates in civilized life. Veblen also assumed, but never explained in a satisfactory manner, that barbaric habits of thought persist in modern life. Durkheim, too, wrestled with the fact that past representations (memories, for instance) may coexist with present ones. Thus, Freud appears to claim that various phases of libidinal development exist as representations – permanently, which is to say, independently of time, space and causality – even as the individual changes. But Schopenhauer preceded all these thinkers in claiming that the character (will) that shows itself in childhood is set and relatively unalterable. To the extent that both Freud and Durkheim seem to believe that human heritage, individual and collective, is stored in the unconscious, this is a topic worthy of analysis as it merges into Jungian thought – itself a refraction of Schopenhauer's philosophy, according to Ellenberger (1970) – and straddles both Freud and Durkheim.

Ernest Jones writes that "Freud seemed to have landed in the position of Schopenhauer, who taught that death is the goal of life" (1981, vol. 3: 273). In addition, Freud claimed that the death and life instincts are both fueled by Eros, a move that has baffled psychoanalysts (see Laplanche 1976). But in this case Freud is actually describing Schopenhauer's equivalent of the dualistic will (again, a sort of dualism within a dualism) and what Durkheim came to call *anomie*, a longing for infinity that is simultaneously pathogenic and benign, the basic ingredient of all social progress as well as destruction. Yet all these sociological and cultural myths relate to Plato's myth, that life is an accidental adventure on the road to death.

In the opening pages of *Civilization and Its Discontents*, Freud brings up this problem again:

> But have we a right to assume the survival of something that was originally there, alongside of what was later derived from it? Undoubtedly. There is nothing strange in such a phenomenon, whether in the mental field or elsewhere.
>
> ([1930] 1961: 15)

There is much that is strange in such a move by positivistic and modernist standards, yet the modernists are unable to account for the persistence of traditions. If the memory trace no longer exists, how can the memory exist? Freud continues, in a manner remarkably similar to Durkheim's ([1924] 1974) reasoning:

> Since we overcame the error of supposing that the forgetting we are familiar with signified a destruction of the memory-trace – that is, its annihilation – we have been inclined to take the opposite view, that in mental life nothing which has once been formed can perish – that everything is somehow preserved and that in suitable circumstances (when, for instance, regression goes back far enough) it can once more be brought to light.
>
> (Freud [1930] 1961: 15)

Though he does not say so explicitly here, Freud is clearly taking up Schopenhauer's assumption that the will exists independently of time, space, and causality.

Freud's next move is that "the purpose of life is simply the programme of the pleasure principle. This principle dominates the operation of the mental apparatus from the start" (ibid.: 23). This is simply another version of Schopenhauer's will to life. But if the organism were allowed free rein in this manner, it would destroy itself: "An unrestricted satisfaction of every need presents itself as the most enticing method of conducting one's life but . . . it soon brings its own punishment" (ibid.: 24). We may liken an unrestricted pleasure principle as an anomic "disease of the infinite" in Durkheim's terms. For Freud, as for Durkheim and Schopenhauer, the organism needs some kind of *règlementation*, or the will to life destroys itself.

For Freud, civilization is one of the regulatory mechanisms. The German word Strachey has translated as "civilization" is *Kultur*, which can be translated as either culture or civilization. This controversy has a long history and has been dissected by many intellectuals, but stems from the fact that the Germans preferred the word culture to the French and English civilization.[6] This is due, in part, to the fact that Germany was tardy in experiencing the Enlightenment, and also to the hostile reactions of the Germans to the French Revolution.[7] In any event, in *The Future of an Illusion*, Freud wrote "I scorn to distinguish between culture and civilization" ([1927] 1955: 2). Freud defines *Kultur* as follows:

> The word "civilization" [*Kultur*] describes the whole sum of the achievements and the regulations which distinguish our lives from those of our animal ancestors and which serve two purposes – namely to protect men against nature and to adjust their mutual relations.
>
> ([1930] 1961: 36)

Freud claims that "love is one of the foundations of civilization" (ibid.: 48), but love may be fully sensual (individual) and aim-inhibited (social). Freud's use of "love" is clearly another creative elaboration upon Schopenhauer's will.[8] Thus, "on the one hand love comes into opposition to the interests of civilization; on the other, civilization threatens love with substantial restrictions" (ibid.: 48). If we compare sensual love with egoism and aim-inhibited love with altruism, a parallel with Durkheim's ([1897] 1951) thought is immediately apparent. This is particularly true with reference to Durkheim's ([1914] 1973) discussion of the body, the senses, instincts, and so on. Even in his early essay on incest, Durkheim ([1897] 1963) actually preceded Freud in claiming that sexual love is threatening to civilization (discussed in Meštrović 1988).

With reference to these two kinds of love, Freud writes that "this rift between them seems unavoidable" ([1930] 1961: 50) and continues:

> It expresses itself at first as a conflict between the family and the larger community to which the individual belongs. We have already perceived that one of the main endeavors of civilization is to bring people together into large unities. But the family will not give the individual up.

Notice that collective and individual tendencies are at war with each other – this is an essential component of Durkheim's thought.

In addition to controlling sexuality, civilization forces humans to control their aggression. Freud writes: "In consequence of this primary mutual hostility of human beings, civilized society is perpetually threatened with disintegration" (ibid.: 59). Referring specifically to Marx, Freud rejects the idea that "man is wholly good and is well-disposed to his neighbour; but the institution of private property has corrupted his nature" (ibid.: 59). No, writes Freud:

> In abolishing private property we deprive the human love of aggression of one of its instruments . . . but we have in no way . . . altered anything in [human] nature. Aggressiveness was not created by property.
>
> (Ibid.: 60)

No matter how far humans develop civilization, Freud believes that love, aggression and other forces that threaten civilization will follow. In Schopenhauerian terms, the will is stronger than the idea. Durkheim criticizes Marx in *Socialism and Saint-Simon* ([1928] 1958) on similar grounds. Durkheim's and Freud's absorption of Schopenhauer's philosophy separates them from Marx and other optimistic followers of Enlightenment narratives as well. Freud and Durkheim believe that humans are fundamentally torn between a benign and barbaric component, and will therefore always be subject to more or less tension. The next move is crucial in the context already established. Freud writes:

> I may now add that civilization is a process in the service of Eros, whose purpose is to combine single human individuals, and after the families, then races, peoples and nations into one great unity, the unity of mankind. Why this has to happen, we do not know; the work of Eros is precisely this. These collections of men are to be libidinally bound to one another.
>
> ([1930] 1961: 68)

So we see that Eros is the culmination of the centrifugal force acting on humans. It literally seems to hurl humans into greater and greater forms of association, spontaneously and of its own accord, not due to rational or utilitarian calculation. It is important to note that Durkheim describes the progress of the division of labor and civilization similarly in his *Division of Labor in Society* ([1893] 1933). Durkheim believed that the division of labor is fueled spontaneously by a will of its own independently of human agents, and that it ultimately brings forth less, not more happiness for individuals. Indeed, both Freud and Durkheim held versions of the theme of civilization and its discontents, though this has been completely overlooked for Durkheim. Finally, Durkheim's own focus on variants of "libidinal" attachments – the sympathy and love that society's members feel for each other and for society – is among the most neglected aspects of his thought, eclipsed completely by Parsons's cerebral notion of normative consensus.

However, for Freud, the work of Eros is offset by the aggressive instinct and the death instinct. Freud writes:

> And now, I think, the meaning of the evolution of civilization is no longer obscure to us. It must represent the struggle between Eros and Death, between the instinct of life and the instinct of destruction, as it works itself out in the human species. This struggle is what all life essentially consists of, and the evolution of civilization may therefore be simply described as the struggle for life of the human species.
>
> ([1930] 1961: 69)

If one interprets the death instinct as used above – as the centripetal element – in opposition to Eros as the centrifugal, then one may reasonably compare and contrast the above statement with Durkheim's ([1912] 1965) notion that collective and individual aspects of human existence are fundamentally separate and are in perpetual, ever-growing tension that increases as civilization progresses. And Durkheim applies this opposition between centripetal and centrifugal forces in his discussion of civilization in *Division of Labor*. We shall make this clearer in the next section. In sum, according to Freud:

> Just as a planet revolves around a central body as well as rotating on its own path, so the human individual takes part in the course of development of mankind at the same time as he pursues his own path in life. But to our dull eyes the play of forces in the heavens seems fixed in a never-changing order; in the field of organic life we can still see how the forces contend with one another, and how the effects of the conflict are continually changing. So, also, the two urges, the one towards personal happiness and the other towards union with other human beings must struggle with each other in every individual: and so, also, the two processes of individual and of cultural development must stand in hostile opposition to each other and mutually dispute the ground.
>
> ([1930] 1961: 88)

I believe that Freud's memorable lines above are a reflection of Plato's as well as Schopenhauer's philosophies, and that one finds a similar reflection in Durkheim's many dualisms.

FREUD'S USE OF EROS

Plato's Eros, Schopenhauer's will to life, and Freud's life instinct – these similar depictions of the secret of life all contradict the Enlightenment's glorification of rationality with a capital R. It is well known that Freud introduced the concept of the death instincts working in opposition to Eros in *Beyond the Pleasure Principle* ([1920] 1961). Let us reexamine this work. In general, instinctual renunciation comes about because of culture and the social world. Thus Freud brings up the example of a child who is momentarily left by his mother and proceeds to play a game in which a lost object is retrieved. According to Freud, the child is repeating and mastering a perceived loss through the game: "The interpretation of the game then becomes obvious. It was related to the child's great cultural achievement – the instinctual renunciation (that is, the renunciation of instinctual satisfaction) which he had made in allowing his mother to go away without protesting" ([1920] 1961: 9). We are back to Durkheim's individual–social and Schopenhauer's will–idea dichotomies in different forms.

What Freud extracts from the example of the child, as well as other examples, is the compulsion to repeat. The idea of compulsion is an important bridge to Veblen's use of the concept of habits and Durkheim's notion of constraint. All these concepts challenge the Enlightenment's supposition that the human agent is capable of freeing his or her self from culture and other constraints (Gellner 1992). Why do persons repeat past experience, even unpleasant experience, in various forms? Freud answers that it is an instinct or

an urge inherent in organic life to restore to an earlier state of things which the living entity has been obliged to abandon under pressure of external disturbing forces; that is, it is a kind of organic elasticity, or, to put it another way, the expression of the inertia inherent in organic life.

([1920] 1961: 30)

Freud claims that all instincts except the sexual instincts have as their aim this restoration to an earlier state of things, ultimately death (ibid.: 32). The instinct of self-preservation is no exception; it merely provides a roundabout path to death. The only exception is the sexual instinct, in its wider sense as Plato's Eros. But we have already raised the suspicion that for Freud, sexuality had more to do with culture than the organism.

Freud's pessimism pours through when he takes time to reject the notion of an "instinct towards perfection at work in human beings" which has brought us our present level of culture. Here is one modernist instinct of progress that Freud will not allow into his conceptual scheme. "I cannot see how this benevolent illusion is to be preserved" Freud writes (ibid.: 36). Rather, human achievements through culture are the result of instinctual repression and the dualistic, tension-filled work of Eros which ultimately brings forth unhappiness as the price for progress. The rough similarity between this claim and

Durkheim's thought is that Durkheim ([1893] 1933) criticized Herbert Spencer and the utilitarians *vis-à-vis* the notion of progress, and did not perceive advanced cultural development as due to a progressive, rational force, but as the gradual outcome of a sort of tug of war between two opposing forces that are part of one collective will to life – for Freud, Eros. Science has little to say about Eros in this sense, Freud confesses, and so he turns to Plato again:

> What I have in mind is, of course, the theory which Plato puts into the mouth of Aristophanes in the *Symposium*, and which deals not only with the origin of the sexual instinct but also with the most important of its variations in relation to its object . . . Shall we follow the hint given us by the poet-philosopher, and venture upon the hypothesis that living substance at the time of its coming to life was torn apart into small particles, which have ever since endeavored to reunite through the sexual instincts?
>
> ([1920] 1961: 51)

Freud traces his dualisms to an original unity (but so does Schopenhauer). The urge toward greater and greater unity, including the unity of mankind (which corresponds to Durkheim's cosmopolitan religion of humanity in *Moral Education* [1925] 1961 and elsewhere), belongs to the sexual instincts, the life instincts, and Eros. To put it more precisely, Freud writes:

> What are commonly called the sexual instincts are looked upon by us as the part of Eros which is directed towards objects. Our speculations have suggested that Eros operates from the beginning of life and appears as a "life instinct" in opposition to the death instinct which was brought into being by the coming to life of inorganic substance. These speculations seek to solve the riddle of life by supposing that these two instincts were struggling with each other from the very first.
>
> ([1920] 1961: 55)

To repeat, Freud frequently claimed that by "sexual" instincts and sexuality in general he did not mean to refer to the genital functions. But as so many of my colleagues continue to misunderstand Freud in this regard, one cannot repeat it often enough. Laplanche and Pontalis explain (1973: 153):

Those criticisms which claim that Freud brings everything down to sexuality (as commonly understood) do not stand up once this confusion has been dispelled: "sexual" should be used according to Freud "in the sense in which it is now commonly employed in psychoanalysis – in the sense of Eros".

Laplanche and Pontalis further observe that Eros and libido are related. Freud indeed wrote that "the libido of our sexual instincts would coincide with the Eros of the poets and philosophers which holds all living things together" ([1920] 1961: 50). The idea that libido is the energy of the sexual instincts which do the work of Eros was never modified by Freud. Rather, shortly before his death, he wrote in his *Outline of Psychoanalysis* ([1938] 1969: 149) that "the total available energy of Eros . . . henceforward we shall speak of as 'libido'".

There is another aspect of Plato's *Symposium*, to which Freud refers, that is relevant to this discussion concerning Eros. In the *Symposium*, Diotima tells Socrates that he who would proceed correctly in the steps of the god of love, Eros, must begin with the love of beautiful forms, including bodies, but not stop there. One must gradually come to love beautiful forms in general until one comes to understand the science of beauty everywhere. At this point, the soul, and not only the body, will be pregnant. In a sense, there are two dualisms at work here: Through seeking beauty, at first in a carnal fashion, the lover is actually seeking to return to an "earlier state of things," the original unity of lovers. Gradually, however, he or she comes to love the "higher," noncarnal, spiritual beauty that is concerned "with the ordering of states and families," among other things.

Similarly, Durkheim emphasizes the dualism between the body and soul, profane and sacred, imperfect and perfect, ultimately individual and society. Durkheim realized that this conflict is refracted and expressed through many different representations, most of which he subsumed under the headings centripetal–centrifugal, inward–outward and the sacred–profane. Freud emphasized that even the urge toward perfection, the higher things in life, toward unity, is ultimately carnal, ultimately tainted with the urge to return to an earlier state of things. On the level of myth, Plato, Schopenhauer, Freud and

Durkheim recite nearly the same myth, with slightly different emphases. Or, to put it more precisely, Freud and Durkheim recite nearly the same myth of Western culture. Schopenhauer was self-conscious of the fact that he, too, was elaborating upon Plato's myth. For Schopenhauer, the will is also ultimately bodily, carnal, sensual and primary. Higher forms of love as well as everything that we commonly subsume under the rubric of culture follow in the wake of the will. Schopenhauer, Plato, Durkheim and Freud were all making arguments in a tradition that is directly inimical to the remnants of the Enlightenment and positivism in our time, and various overly intellectualist philosophies in Plato's time.

Chapter 8

Reconstructing *homo duplex*

> The old formula *homo duplex* is therefore verified by the facts. Far from being simple, our inner life has something that is like a double center of gravity. On the one hand is our individuality – and more particularly, our body on which it is based . . . On the other is everything in us that expresses something other than ourselves.
>
> (Emile Durkheim [1914] 1973: 152)

> One has, I think, to reckon with the fact that there are present in all men destructive, and therefore anti-social and anti-cultural trends . . . There are countless civilized people who would shrink from murder or incest but who do not deny themselves the satisfaction of their avarice, their aggressive urges or their sexual lusts, and who do not hesitate to injure other people by lies, fraud and calumny, so long as they can remain unpunished for it.
>
> (Sigmund Freud [1927] 1955: 14)

After one has deconstructed the contemporary versions of the dualism of human nature, one realizes that modernists tend to resolve this ancient problem along the simplistic lines that the higher pole is stronger and more "natural" than the lower pole. Hence, the oversocialized conception of the human person found in orthodox functionalism merges into the postmodernist world-view. It is a false dualism (like false labor), in that it claims really that the human animal is not only one-dimensional, but has overcome "the body." In both modern frames of reference, the "higher" aspects of human culture – concepts, rationality, rules, "fictions," norms, and so on – are supposed to be able to overwhelm and control the will to life that rages uncontrollably in the rest of Nature. In the two previous chapters, we have sought to disengage Freud and Durkheim from this modern (and postmodern) world view. They felt that the lower pole is stronger than the higher, and equally "natural," so that they were concerned with the tension that ensues when social rules confront the individual's will and its derivatives, among them, libido, egoism, greed, Eros, sex, and other forms of desire. Our aim in this chapter is to elaborate upon and reconstruct Freud's and Durkheim's concepts of *homo duplex*, and their relevance to sociology.

In the case of Freud, the discussion of basic concepts easily merged into the discussion of the dualism of human nature. Freud defines his "instincts" as being almost wholly antagonistic and contrary to each other. One can hardly discuss his basic concepts without becoming involved in his understanding of what it means to be human. This chapter will necessarily emphasize the dualism of human nature in Durkheim's thought more than Freud's (though both will be considered) because the connection between Durkheim's concepts and his understanding of human nature is more problematic. The reason it is problematic does not necessarily have to do with whether or not the connection may be made. It is more likely that sociologists are not used to examining a founding father of sociology's views of human nature. This attitude, in turn, may have developed from sociology's emphasis on positivistic methodologies. There can be little doubt that Durkheim's own version of *homo duplex* is a faithful refraction of Schopenhauer's opposition between the will and idea – down to the detail that "the body" is the ultimate seat of the will – and that it is built on the Platonic formula of Ideas in opposition to the body and its "appetites."

One of our aims is to show, first of all, that Durkheim's version of social facts is related to some of his dualisms. For example, the distinction between individual and collective representations may be related to his distinction between the profane and the sacred, respectively. Indeed, by focusing on Durkheim's essay "The Dualism of Human Nature and Its Social Conditions," this connection will become clearer. But if one speculates, one may imagine that Durkheim's distinction between "true" social facts and social facts as they appear to society (previously discussed) is also related to the "truth versus illusion" dualism, which, in turn, he relates to the sacred and the profane. In short, we wish to guard against simply cataloging dualisms and conceptions in a one-to-one, factual sort of way. Our aim is to elucidate and shake up old misconceptions. As such, there is no expectation that at the end of this chapter one will be able to neatly categorize Durkheim's conceptions and dualisms. But that is far from our aim in any event. The hope is that questions and problems will have been raised that have not been put forth in the previous literature, and that will be considered important.

It would be missing the point, as well, to expect a one-to-one correspondence between Freud's version of the dualism of human nature and Durkheim's, or a listing of the exact ways in which they are similar and dissimilar. In the first place, we do not wish to reduce the thought of one thinker to that of the other. To a certain extent, sociology and psychoanalysis, Durkheim and Freud, are left in place, their own place. Our aim is to elucidate and focus on the importance of the connection between concepts and understandings of human nature in both thinkers in the context of Schopenhauer and Plato.

A critical reader may remark that is the same as saying that apples and humans are similar because they have skin, in other words, that it is not significant that they appear to have something in common with Schopenhauer and Plato. One can only hope that a thinker's wrestling with Schopenhauer and Plato, or his or her conscious comparison with them, is more important and worthier of study than the fact that apples and humans have skin. This problem merges into a question of values – why this work is or is not important – and we have no intention of becoming entangled in a desperate desire to prove that this work is valuable.

THE DUALISM OF HUMAN NATURE IN DURKHEIM'S THOUGHT

Sociologists frequently assume that for Durkheim, all human activities originate in society. Hence, the frequent charge levelled at Durkheim is that he reified society and despised psychology (a charge he and his followers refuted; see especially Bouglé 1938). It does not appear to be the case that this was what Durkheim meant. In order for all human activity to

originate in society, human nature would have to be completely
or predominantly social. Even so, it is not clear whether such an
oversocialized human is an artificial creation or "natural" –
here we are touching on issues raised by Rousseau, Locke, and
other Enlightenment thinkers that have still not been resolved
completely. In contrast, consider Durkheim's opening lines in
"The Dualism of Human Nature and Its Social Conditions":

> The work that we recently published, *The Elementary Forms of
> the Religious Life,* offers an example of this general truth
> [concerning *homo duplex*]. In attempting to study religious
> phenomena from the sociological point of view, we came to
> envisage a way of explaining scientifically one of the most
> characteristic peculiarities of our nature. Since the critics
> who have discussed the book up to the present have not – to
> our great surprise – perceived the principle upon which this
> explanation rests, it seemed to us that a brief outline of it
> would be of some interest to the readers of *Scientia.*
>
> ([1914] 1973: 150)

Because Durkheim felt misunderstood even by some of his
contemporaries, let us take careful note of what he has to say in
this essay. Before we proceed to that task, it is equally important
to emphasize that he regarded the 1914 essay on *homo duplex* as
a sequel to his 1912 work on religion. The 1912 book on
religion is not read in such a context today, and continues to be
misunderstood, as it apparently was in Durkheim's time. Durkheim felt that both works were moves against Kant's formal *a
priorism,* though Durkheim continues to be read as if he
remained trapped in that Kantian formalism (see La Capra
1972). It is extremely interesting that these were exactly
Schopenhauer's anti-Kantian intentions in his *World as Will and
Representation,* and that Schopenhauer, like Durkheim, ended
his speculations by focusing on the penultimate importance of
religious representations.

The opening moves in the 1914 essay are immediately disturbing to those who have misunderstood Durkheim as the
founder of "extreme sociologism." Durkheim writes:

> Although sociology is defined as the science of societies,
> it cannot, in reality, deal with the human groups that are
> the immediate object of its investigation without eventually

touching on the individual who is the basic element of which these groups are composed. For society can exist only if it penetrates the consciousness of individuals and fashions it in "its image and resemblance." We can say, therefore, with assurance and without being excessively dogmatic, that a great number of our mental states, including some of the most important ones, are of social origin.

([1914] 1973: 149)

Durkheim's next step is to claim that in *The Elementary Forms of the Religious Life* he had uncovered "one of the most characteristic peculiarities of our nature." Durkheim continues:

The peculiarity referred to is the constitutional duality of human nature. In every age, man has been intensely aware of this duality. He has, in fact, everywhere conceived of himself as being formed of two radically heterogeneous beings: the body and the soul.

(Ibid.: 150)

Anyone familiar with philosophy will immediately be able to trace the importance of this distinction to the writings of Plato, Schopenhauer and a host of other philosophers for whom "the body" is the focal point of the will. Whereas Kant argued that we could never know the thing-in-itself or the will, Schopenhauer replied that we may not be able to conceive of it, but we can perceive it, directly, through our bodies. Human desires, passion, the appetites – all these things are kin to the will to life that animates the entire Universe. Durkheim continues:

A belief that is as universal and permanent as this cannot be purely illusory. There must be something in man that gives rise to this feeling that his nature is dual, a feeling that men in all known civilizations have experienced.

(Ibid.: 151)

The fact that Durkheim regards *homo duplex* to be the central point of his *Elementary Forms* stands in sharp contrast to the misreadings of this classic in the Parsonian straightjacket of social integration and social control. Durkheim claimed that,

At the foundation of all systems of beliefs and of all cults there ought necessarily to be a certain number of funda-mental representations or conceptions and of ritual attitudes which, in spite of the diversity of forms which they have taken, have the same objective significance and fulfill the same functions everywhere.

([1912] 1965: 17)

He added that "Religious representations are collective representations which express collective realities" (ibid.: 22).

It is interesting that Schopenhauer, too, regarded religious beliefs as empirical realities that reflect back to humans their existential situation. Schopenhauer was among the first to distinguish religions not on the basis of monotheism versus polytheism but on the continuum optimism–pessimism. In other words, religious representations reflect consciousness of the objectification of the will in one's society. According to Durkheim:

The old formula *homo duplex* is therefore verified by the facts. Far from being simple, our inner life has something that is like a double center of gravity. On the one hand is our individuality – and more particularly, our *body* in which it is based.

([1914] 1973: 152; emphasis added)

Schopenhauer, too, claims that the "body itself is only concrete willing, objectivity of will" ([1818] 1969a: 175), that humans come to know the will through their bodies, and that "the whole body is the will itself" ([1818] 1969b: 250). And this is an old formula, as Durkheim claims, when one considers that Saint Augustine made the hatred of the body fashionable in early Christianity, and in this regard was following in the footsteps of the neo-Platonists. Durkheim finishes: "On the other is everything in us that expresses something other than ourselves" ([1914] 1973: 152).

If this line is to be used to support a notion of internalization, note that for Durkheim, the individual internalizes two opposing forces. Consistent with his claims in *Sociology and Philosophy* ([1924] 1974), Durkheim writes:

Not only are these two groups of states of consciousness different in their origins and their properties, but there is a true antagonism between them. They mutually contradict and deny each other. We cannot pursue moral ends without causing a split within ourselves, without offending the instincts and the penchants that are the most deeply rooted in our bodies.

([1914] 1973: 152)

There is an unmistakable similarity between the above passage and Freud's notion that the "higher" aims of life, like morality, are based upon a renunciation of instincts.

Durkheim's next step in his essay is to argue against the philosophical doctrines of empiricism and idealism. If Durkheim is going to propose that human nature is dualistic, he almost has to take this position. What is important to note at this point is that for Durkheim, empiricism and idealism are false because they do not acknowledge the fundamental dualism he is proposing, only one-dimensional slices of it. But in this case, too, Durkheim is merely following in the footsteps of Schopenhauer, who rages against both doctrines in the opening pages of his *World as Will and Representation,* and reconciles them into his philosophy of "transcendental idealism." Thus Durkheim makes his next move:

> If we reject the theories which eliminate the problem rather than solve it, the only remaining ones that are valid and merit examination are those which limit themselves to affirming the fact that must be explained, but which do not account for it.

([1914] 1973: 157)

One of these theories that affirm the problem, but do not explain it, for Durkheim, is that of Plato. As Durkheim put the matter:

> First of all, there is the ontological explanation for which Plato gave the formula. Man is double because two worlds meet in him: that of non-intelligent and amoral matter, on the one hand, and that of Ideas, the spirit, and the good, on the other.

(Ibid.: 157)

This passage suggests crucial links among the writings of Plato, Schopenhauer, Freud, and Durkheim, as explored in part by Ellenberger (1970) and Simon (1978). Yet some readers may object, with some justification, that Durkheim's interpretation of Plato is too extreme. On the other hand, Durkheim's interpretation of Plato is commensurate with Schopenhauer's and Freud's assessments. Moreover, at least Plato's *Phaedon* offers unambiguous support for Durkheim's claim, as Plato claims therein that the philosopher seeks death as release from a body that is perceived as nothing but a burden.[1] Durkheim continues: "Because these two worlds are naturally opposed, they struggle within us; and, because we are part of both, we are necessarily in conflict with ourselves" ([1914] 1973: 157).

The reader must appreciate the extremity of Durkheim's position in order to appreciate the significance of its similarity to the thought of Freud, who characterized the individual as the enemy of civilization, and certainly as being in perpetual conflict within the self. A more "reasonable" claim would be that being human entails living in greater or lesser degrees of tension based upon human organismic and social needs being in conflict at times. But Durkheim's position is, by contrast, "unreasonable," and highly dramatic: the organism and social being are by nature opposed to each other at all times.[2]

Durkheim goes on to credit Plato with apprehending the problem correctly, but to fault him for being unable to explain it. The explanation, for Durkheim, is that all previous characterizations of *homo duplex* can be summarized as the dichotomy of the "sacred" versus the "profane," and that this dichotomy corresponds to something real. At least with regard to the dichotomy sacred–profane, this is a departure from, if not a creative elaboration of Schopenhauer's philosophy. Durkheim explains:

> The duality of our nature is thus only a particular case of that division of things into the sacred and the profane that is the foundation of all religions, and it must be explained on the basis of the same principles. It is precisely this explanation that we attempted in the previously cited work, *The Elementary Forms of the Religious Life*, where we tried to show that sacred things are simply collective ideals that have fixed themselves on material objects.
>
> ([1914] 1973: 159)

The sacred always pertains to what is "higher" and moral. And these collective representations of the sacred versus the profane, in turn, correspond to the actual state of affairs. Or

as Durkheim put it, in another apparent return to Schopenhauer's system:

> It is not without reason, therefore, that man feels himself to
> be double: he actually is double. There are in him two classes
> of states of consciousness that differ from each other in
> origin and nature, and in the end toward which they aim.
> One class merely expresses our organisms and the objects to
> which they are most directly related. Strictly individual, the
> states of consciousness of this class connect us only with
> ourselves, and we can no more detach them from us than we
> can detach ourselves from our bodies. The states of conscious-
> ness of the other class, on the contrary, come to us from
> society; they transfer society into us and connect us with
> something that surpasses us ... It is, therefore, quite true
> that we are made up of two parts, and are like two beings,
> which although they are closely associated, are composed of
> very different elements and orient us in opposite directions.
>
> (Ibid.: 161)

For Freud as well, the organismic aspect of humans is the
source of perverse and destructive impulses as well as benign
and constructive ones. In this sense, Freud and Durkheim agree
with Schopenhauer that the unrestrained will is the source of
all wickedness, egoism, immorality and the barbarism that
concerns us. (But also that the will is the source of compassion,
as we will see later.) Durkheim writes, quite similarly:

> In brief, this duality corresponds to the double existence
> that we lead concurrently; the one purely individual and
> rooted in our organisms, the other social and nothing but
> an extension of society. The origin of the antagonism that
> we have described is evident from the very nature of the
> elements involved in it. The conflicts of which we have
> given examples are between the sensations and the sensory
> appetites, on the one hand, and the intellectual and moral
> life, on the other; and it is evident that passions and egoistic
> tendencies derive from our individual constitutions, while
> our rational activity – whether theoretical or practical – is
> dependent on social causes.
>
> (Ibid.: 162)

Note Durkheim's departure from Kant's *a priorism*. The ground for human rationality, in Durkheim's view, is society. Reason does not, and cannot, beget itself. But for Durkheim, rationality is *not* derived from the body, whose focal point is the will. Thus, rationality opposes barbarism as well as compassion.

The extremity of Durkheim's position may be construed as being dependent upon his outlandish distinction between individual and collective representations. This is an important point because it suggests the logical consistency of Durkheim's thought. Had he held, as some contemporary sociologists do, that society evolves from individual representations, Durkheim would not have been in a position to posit his fundamental dualism. Similarly, had he felt that the two poles of *homo duplex* were equal in strength, or that the "higher" pole was stronger than the "lower," Durkheim could not have adopted his own pessimistic stance. He would have been just another Enlightenment thinker. But in fact Durkheim, like Schopenhauer, assumes that the "lower" pole of *homo duplex* is the stronger one, despite the fact that both are equally "natural," and consequently that human desires are by nature insatiable, and lead to suffering. In Durkheim's words:

> The painful [*douloureux*] character of the dualism of human nature is explained by this hypothesis. There is no doubt that if society were only the natural and spontaneous development of the individual, these two parts of ourselves would harmonize and adjust to each other without clashing and without friction: The first part, since it is only the extension and, in a way, the complement of the second, would encounter no resistance from the latter.
>
> (Ibid.: 162)

But for Durkheim, "society has its own nature, and, consequently, its requirements are quite different from those of our nature as individuals: the interests of the whole are not necessarily those of the part" (ibid.: 163). Durkheim's next sentence is particularly Freudian: "Therefore, society cannot be formed or maintained without our being required to make perpetual and costly sacrifices" (ibid.: 163).

By sacrifice, Durkheim is clearly referring to the sacrifices of egoistic, hence organismic, individual, desires and motives, to the social:

Because society surpasses us, it obliges us to surpass ourselves, and to surpass itself, a being must, to some degree, depart from its nature – a departure that does not take place without causing more or less painful tensions.

(Ibid.: 163)

To live a civilized life necessarily implies discontent and tension – Freud made this argument in *Civilization and Its Discontents*. Like Freud, who believed that the tension between civilization and human biological impulses can never be overcome, Durkheim believes that these tensions are a given of being human, never to be resolved. In fact, Durkheim goes further than Freud in his pessimism, to predict that the tensions will get worse, and in this sense Durkheim is more Schopenhauerian than Freud. For Schopenhauer believed that enlightenment serves to unleash the will and causes greater suffering.[3] Durkheim concludes:

Since the role of the social being in our single selves will grow ever more important as history moves ahead, it is wholly improbable that there will ever be an era in which man is required to resist himself to a lesser degree, an era in which he can live a life that is easier and less full of tension. To the contrary, all evidence compels us to expect our effort in the struggle between the two beings within us to increase with the growth of civilization.

(Ibid.: 163)

Looking back on the writings of Freud and Durkheim, with the hindsight of two world wars, the ever-present threat of nuclear holocaust and a daily diet of wars somewhere on the globe, one can scarcely fail to appreciate the keen insight of their claims. In a very real sense, all of the human animal's profound education, so-called culture, and technical competence has not bettered nor tamed his or her aggression, brutality, and destructiveness. And, one could make a case for the claim that things are getting progressively worse. Such an argument would be futile, however. One can claim that at present, humanity can destroy itself several times over with nuclear weapons. But despite the end of the cold war, there are those who are planning strategies for nuclear "victory" apparently believing that their version of civilized life will prevail after the holocaust.

In any case, Durkheim ends his essay on this chilling note. The reader familiar with the works of Freud has probably already thought of the id versus superego distinction as a parallel to Durkheim's dualism. And of course, Freud's chilling pronouncement that at best, all we can hope for is discontent is well known. As stated previously and shown throughout, the fit among Freud, Durkheim and Schopenhauer in this regard is not exact. But the key point here is that *homo duplex* carries with it the attendant idea that pain and suffering are the sacrifice and price individuals must pay to society because the will is stronger than the idea. Indeed, Durkheim had made this claim explicit in his *Elementary Forms*, although it continues to be ignored in mainstream sociological research: "If there is any one belief which is believed to be peculiar to the most recent and idealistic religions, it is the one attributing a sanctifying power to sorrow [*douleur*]" because "society itself is possible only at this price" ([1912] 1965: 354). Durkheim continues:

> Though exalting the strength of man, it [society] is frequently rude to individuals; it necessarily demands perpetual sacrifices from them; it is constantly doing violence to our natural appetites, just because it raises us above ourselves. If we are going to fulfill our duties towards it, then we must be prepared to do violence to our instincts [it is] inherent in all social life.
>
> (Ibid.: 356)

In his 1914 essay, too, Durkheim concludes that the pessimism in modern religions reflects back to humanity the unwelcome truth that

> Human malaise continues to increase. The great religions of modern man are those which insist the most on the existence of the contradictions in the midst of which we struggle. These continue to depict us as tormented and suffering, while only the crude cults of inferior societies breathe forth and inspire a joyful confidence. For what religions express is the experience through which humanity has lived.
>
> ([1914] 1973: 156)

Durkheim asserts that "we are thus condemned to live in suffering," and that compared to animals, "man alone is normally obliged to make a place for suffering in his life" (ibid.: 154). He had made similar claims concerning religion earlier in his career, in *The Division of Labor* ([1893] 1933: 243) and *Suicide*: "It is a quite remarkable fact that the great religions of the most civilized peoples are more deeply fraught with sadness than the simpler beliefs of earlier societies" ([1897] 1951: 366). There exists an unmistakable affinity between Durkheim's pessimistic appraisal of modern religions, and Schopenhauer's ([1818] 1969b: 603–46) many allusions to the pessimism reflected in Christianity, the New Testament, and Protestantism compared with the Old Testament, Judaism, and other, earlier religions.

COMPREHENDING ANOMIE

Kant viewed progress through the rosy glasses of the Enlightenment, and if Durkheim was really a disciple of Kant, how can one explain his gloomy prediction that human malaise will increase with progress? On the other hand, this claim is Schopenhauer's signature in philosophy. The Schopenhauerian version of the dualism of human nature, in which the "lower" pole is more powerful than the "higher" pole, is embedded in all of Durkheim's works. I agree with Bellah (1973: xiii) that Durkheim was one of those intellectuals who write essentially one book, though in a number of versions (Schopenhauer was another such thinker).

Durkheim's concept of anomie flows from his understanding of *homo duplex*, in which he assumes that the will is stronger than the idea. For Durkheim ([1897] 1983: 281), anomie is a state of *dérèglement* or derangement among the individuals solidified imperfectly by an abnormal division of labor. The derangement stems from society's efforts to structure moral rules upon human desires – upon the classical utilitarian doctrine that self-interest leads to felicitous consequences – as in classical capitalist theory. Because Durkheim assumes that the will is inherently insatiable, he believes that such undertakings are contradictory and unstable, even dangerous. At no point in *Division of Labor*, *Suicide*, or any other work in which he addresses anomie does Durkheim equate regulation with some sort of magical conformity or integration to society as claimed by Gibbs and Martin (1958) and others who write in the oversocialized tradition. On the contrary, he portrays the sympathetic, desiring, and otherwise emotional forces that flow from the lower pole of *homo duplex* as being so strong that they always threaten society, because society is the *weaker force* in his Schopenhauerian version of *homo duplex*, compared with the will. Thus, for Durkheim, *règlementation* pertains to the balance between the centripetal and centrifugal forces necessary at each stage of society's evolution such that the lower pole is counterbalanced by the higher. But, because the lower is stronger than the higher, Durkheim claims in *Professional Ethics and Civic Morals* ([1950] 1983) and elsewhere that *many* secondary groups – the State, family, Church, nation, corporation, etc. – must weigh upon the individual's will to restrain it adequately. Even so, the individual will breaks through all these barriers, so that in modern societies, the "cult of the individual" becomes enshrined by society, a collective state wherein "man is a God to mankind" ([1897] 1951: 363).

Moreover, and again in keeping with Schopenhauer's philosophy, the *dérèglement* of anomie implies immorality. For Schopenhauer as for Durkheim, motives that stem from egoism – and anomic motives are essentially egoistic – can never serve as the basis for moral actions. In this regard, both thinkers challenge utilitarian social theory directly. Moreover, contemporary philosophers criticize both thinkers for holding to this inflexible rule, and try to find a moral basis for self-centered action (see Atwell 1990; Hall 1987). Nevertheless, Durkheim's extreme position is consistent with his career-long discussion of a "science of moral facts" (discussed in Meštrović 1988). Thus, in the introduction to *The Division of Labor*, he refers to anomie as evil, not as some bland, value-free state of normlessness ([1893] 1933: vi).

Durkheim elaborates: "We repeatedly insist in the course of this book upon the state of juridical and moral anomie in which economic life actually is found" ([1893] 1933: 5). It is important to note that in this work as well as in *Suicide*, Durkheim regards the economic sector of society as the major source for egoism and anomie. He does not criticize the business professions alone, but is mindful of how the economic *habits* of looking at the world in terms of mere self-interest spill over into other social institutions and the rest of social life:

If in the task that occupies almost all our time we follow no other rule than that of our well-understood interest, how can we learn to depend upon disinterestedness, on self-forgetfulness, on sacrifice? In this way, the absence of all economic discipline cannot fail to extend its effects beyond the economic world, and consequently weaken public morality.

([1893] 1933: 5)

In these regards, his discussion of economic anomie complements Veblen's ([1899] 1967) mocking treatment of the quest for unlimited prestige that also permeates virtually all sectors of social life, even though Veblen also focuses on the business professions, too. It also complements the Frankfurt School's many critiques of the modern treatment of persons by each other as commodities. According to Durkheim: "It is this anomic state that is the cause, as we shall show, of the incessantly recurrent conflicts, and the multifarious disorders of which the economic world exhibits so sad a spectacle" ([1893] 1933: 5).

Durkheim thought that the social pole of *homo duplex* is unable to contain the lower pole in order to achieve the social order posited by the neofunctionalists. Thus, and in line with Veblen and Schopenhauer, he points to other strong aspects of the lower pole of *homo duplex* to offset the egoistic ones that lead to barbarism. Compassion, sympathy, and other refractions of Christian morals constitute some of these *irrational* forces. It is for this reason that Durkheim advocates the revival of guild-like associations and the family to offset anomie, and never refers to anything like normative consensus as a solution.

Whereas Parsons, Giddens, Lukes, Alexander and other proponents of the Enlightenment model of social order follow Kant in considering dry duty, conformity, and obedience to norms as the glue that holds societies together, Durkheim follows Schopenhauer and Nietzsche. Durkheim's disciple, Bouglé (1926: 34), stresses that for Durkheim, society is not a "super policeman" that merely constrains individuals. Rather, society is a "fiery furnace," a magnet that surrounds social values with the non-Kantian quality of desire. Thus, "values are not so many dead weights which oppress us, burdening our breasts; far rather are they magnets which draw out, and are worthy to draw out, our convergent effort" (ibid.: 37). But desire pertains to the will and the heart, not the mind, the fictional internalization of social norms that affects only the

mind. Durkheim tells us that society's members are held together by love and its derivatives, such that in all religions,
primitive as well as modern, members of a society are intimates,
associates, and friends ([1912] 1965: 175). For Durkheim, as
for Schopenhauer, the will is the ground for enlightenment,
and not the other way around:

> The influence of society is what has aroused in us the
> sentiments of sympathy and solidarity drawing us toward
> others . . . To play our social role we have striven to extend
> our intelligence and it is still society that has supplied us with
> tools for this development by transmitting to us its trust fund
> of knowledge.
>
> ([1897] 1951: 211)[4]

In general, Durkheim entertains a psychological discussion of
human nature as well as a sociological one. Thus, in *Moral
Education* ([1925] 1961), he is concerned with the problem of
educating children so that their true natures are fulfilled, so that
they are neither all selfish nor all selfless. In the context of *Moral
Education*, one can better understand Durkheim's claim in *Suicide*
that every society requires the four currents of egoism, anomie,
altruism and fatalism, and that "where they offset one another,
the moral agent is in a state of equilibrium which shelters him
against any thought of suicide" ([1897] 1951: 321). These
currents are normal refractions of the Schopenhauerian opposition between the will and idea. Durkheim makes this claim
because egoism and anomie stand for the centripetal forces and
altruism and fatalism stand for the centrifugal forces he mentions
in *Division of Labor*. Humans are by nature torn, and can survive
only by achieving the proper balance required by their organ-
isms and society's stage of evolution.

I have by no means exhausted all of Durkheim's works nor
have I thoroughly discussed the works cited. But I hope to have
demonstrated that the dualism referred to in Durkheim's 1914
essay is not an isolated incident in Durkheim's intellectual
history. Rather, one can trace the concept of *homo duplex* from
Division of Labor ([1893] 1933) to *Elementary Forms of the
Religious Life* ([1912] 1965) and the last years of Durkheim's
career. Ultimately, this dualism rests upon Durkheim's extreme
position on the subject of individual versus collective representations – the two enjoy philosophically separate levels of

existence, but the lower, organismic pole is stronger than the higher, social pole. And this peculiar approach to *homo duplex* explains his depiction of anomie as a state of unlimited desires that is exacerbated, not contained, by progress and general enlightenment. It bears more resemblance to Schopenhauer's philosophy than Kant's, Comte's or the other Enlightenment traditions typically cited with regard to Durkheim. Because of this extreme position, Durkheim is logically forced to come back to a tension inherent in human existence again and again, an ultimately inextinguishable tension.

The reader will perhaps better appreciate the importance of this dualism in Durkheim's thought by imagining that he had allowed that individual representations come from collective representations, or vice versa. The first position would have led him to an extreme sociologism whereby individuals would be literally determined by society. This is a typical misunderstanding of Durkheim's position, but it is false, as we have demonstrated with numerous examples. The second position would have led him to an extreme psychologism whereby societies would be mere reflections of the individuals comprising them. This is a view in contemporary sociology that is gaining in popularity, or at least serves as an alternative to the over-socialized view (see Giddens 1976b). But it is a position that Durkheim vehemently and consistently rejects, as it undercuts, in his view, the essential reason why sociology is a science distinct from other social sciences, and because he regards the unrestrained ego – enshrined by utilitarian and contemporary economic theory – as dangerous to civilization.

LINKS TO FREUD

Laplanche and Pontalis (1973) link the concept of binding with Freud's discussion of the compulsion to repeat and its relationship to Eros in *Beyond the Pleasure Principle* ([1920] 1961). Recall that for Freud, Eros binds and unifies everything from particles to individuals into ever greater associations, in opposition to the work of the death instinct. The death instinct may be said to be an "unbinding" force – it wants to return to what was, namely a chaotic state – and Eros is a "binding" force. Freud is explicit: "The aim of Eros is to establish even greater unities and to preserve them thus – in short, to bind together; the aim of the destructive instinct is, on the contrary, to undo connections and so to destroy things" ([1938] 1969: 148).

Note the span of years from when the notion of "binding" was introduced, in 1895, and its final expression as the notion of Eros in 1938. This connection is one of the most powerful pieces of evidence for a unity in Freud's works.

Laplanche and Pontalis (1973: 436) point out that the superego, as heir to the Oedipus Complex, is not so much a representation of parental agency but of an entire culture. Moreover, the cultural–individual dichotomy involved here has already been investigated, as Laplanche and Pontalis note:

> The Oedipus Complex is not reducible to an actual situation – to the actual influence exerted by the parental couple over the child. Its efficacy derives from the fact that it brings into play a proscriptive agency (the prohibition against incest) which bars the way to naturally sought satisfaction and forms an indissoluble link between wish and law (a point which Jacques Lacan has emphasized). Seen in this light, the criticisms first voiced by Malinowski and later taken up by the "culturalist" school lose their edge . . . In practice, when confronted with the cultures in question, psychoanalysts have merely tried to ascertain which social roles – or even which institution – incarnate the proscriptive agency, and which social modes specifically express the triangular structure constituted by the child, the child's natural object and the bearer of the law. Such a structural conception of the Oedipus complex conforms to the thesis put forward by Claude Levi-Strauss who, in his *Structures elementaires de la parente*, makes the prohibition against incest the universal law and the minimal condition of the differentiation of a "culture" from "nature".
>
> (Ibid.: 286)

For example, in *Civilization and Its Discontents*, Freud writes:

> Whether one has killed one's father or has abstained from doing so is not really the decisive thing. One is bound to feel guilty in either case, for the sense of guilt is an expression of the conflict due to ambivalence, of the eternal struggle between Eros and the instinct of destruction or death. This conflict is set going as soon as men are faced with the task of living together.
>
> ([1930] 1961: 80)

Note the connection to our previous discussion: The Oedipus Complex is literally heir to the dualisms we have been discussing. Freud continues:

> So long as the community assumes no other form than that of the family, the conflict is bound to express itself in the Oedipus Complex. When an attempt is made to widen the community, the same conflict is continued in forms which are dependent on the past . . . What began in relation to the father is completed in relation to the group. If civilization is a necessary course of development from the family to humanity as a whole, then – as a result of the inborn conflict arising from ambivalence, of the eternal struggle between trends of love and death – there is inextricably bound up with it an increase of the sense of guilt.
>
> (Ibid.: 80)

Apparently, even if one grows up without a father, or in a culture where parental agency is minimized, the Oedipus Complex is bound to come up because of the struggle between Eros and the death instinct, which is itself a refraction of Schopenhauer's opposition between the idea and the will, respectively. In effect, the Oedipus Complex is a form of the individual versus the collective conflict we found even in Durkheim's concept of *homo duplex*.[5] The German word for "guilt" can also be translated as "debt," and is used as such by Freud to denote the debt that is owed to society. Durkheim, too, frequently refers to the debts that individuals owe to society and civilization, and argues that the notion of self-sacrifice, as one form of repaying this debt, is an essential manifestation of the tension between the individual and society.

A thread of continuity appears to run through Freud's multivarious dualisms. It is the single theme of processes based upon the organism at war with processes based upon society and culture. Like Durkheim, Freud distinguishes, at times sharply, between biological processes and psychical representatives of those processes. By contrast, the epistemologies of some of his contemporary interpreters are not that elaborate, because they try to make him out to be an Enlightenment thinker. And as in Durkheim's version of *homo duplex*, in Freud's scheme, too, the antagonism between these processes does not diminish with evolution, and the end product of evolution is not necessarily better than the original.

Durkheim's ([1924] 1974) discussion of individual and collective representations illuminates the peculiarities in Freud's mythology that have perplexed his positivistic interpreters. One can understand how the notion of instincts in Freud's usage presupposes that they are based upon bodily demands, but are not biological phenomena, by invoking Durkheim's concept of representation. And one can trace the continuing theme of the battle between two types of forces in Freud's vast mythology that bears some resemblance to the dualisms found in Durkheim's thought. To be sure, Freud did not have all of these dualisms, like the sacred and the profane. But both thinkers overlap in the use of other terms: instincts, higher, lower, egoism, bodily demands, conscience, and so on. As the aim of this project is not an attempt to translate the mythology of one thinker into the other's, no great effort will be made to resolve their similarities and differences. These have been noted as the discussion proceeded.

What stands out and can hardly be emphasized enough, given the distortion of Freud's and Durkheim's views, is that they did not believe that the tension between the two beings in the human person could ever be resolved, and that this tension increases as civilization progresses. There is no way out of the dilemma, no Kantian submission to some abstract, universal, categorical imperative, self-begotten and unfit for the mighty task of controlling the all-powerful will that Kant ascribes to it. For Freud and Durkheim, the tension based on *homo duplex* will always be there, and the task is to find the right balance between will and idea before humans destroy themselves, individually and collectively, knowing that any balance they find will be temporary.

Chapter 9

Civilized barbarism: the nature of psychic wounds

Facts thus are far from confirming the current idea that suicide is due especially to life's burdens, since, on the contrary, it diminishes as these burdens increase.

(Emile Durkheim [1897] 1951: 201)

It is not the latest slight – which in itself, is minimal – that produces the fit of crying, the outburst of despair or the attempt at suicide, in disregard of the axiom that an effect must be proportionate to its cause; the small slight of the present moment has aroused and set working the memories of very many, more intense, earlier slights.

(Sigmund Freud [1896c] 1974: 217)

Then virtue, seemingly, will be a kind of health and beauty and good condition of the soul, vice a disease and ugliness and weakness.

(Plato, *The Republic* 444b)

Running throughout Durkheim's and Freud's works is the message that the civilized, human animal is more likely to engage in and is more vulnerable to suffering from psychic wounds compared with our ancestors, and compared with animals. Freud and Durkheim enable us to see through Norbert Elias's felicitous account of the civilized person: it is true that he or she exhibits polished manners, and no longer spits on the sidewalk, passes gas in public, belches loudly, or engages in other acts that used to be routine but are now considered disgusting. But this ideal-type civilized person is also highly skilled in sarcasm, at camouflaging one's contempt in cleverly constructed jabs, cuts, slurs, and insults. A certain chic bitterness is found routinely in so-called civilized social interaction (Sloterdijk 1987). Civilized manners have not diminished human aggression, only transformed it – Freud was a master at uncovering it. On the receiving end, the civilized person seems more vulnerable than our ancestors to humiliation, derision, and all sorts of psychic wounds – Durkheim was a master at uncovering this vulnerability. If the civilized type is less likely to engage in "naked aggression" – "punching someone's lights out" in response to an insult – he or she is just as likely, if not more likely, to resort to fraud, calumny, hypocrisy, and other forms of "breaking through the boundaries of another's affirm-ation of will" – which is Schopenhauer's definition of evil ([1818] 1969a: 334).

In private as well as public life, the average modern day is filled with stories of deception, scandals, tongue-lashings, and psychic brutality. Even on TV, one finds more than Bau-drillard's bland fictions: one's favorite television characters spend a lot of time shouting at, lying to, and hurting each other in every conceivable way. Soap operas chronicle adultery, extortion, divorce, and other varieties of human evil, with the apparent aim to entertain. The barbaric, predatory habits of the fight ooze out seemingly from every pore of modern and postmodern culture. They have even become the staple of the formerly hallowed halls of higher education. If in past genera-tions, students at least pretended to be absorbing wisdom for life, today's students will admit, with minimal prodding, that they are aiming only "to get by" a professor's course so that they can join the "rat race" outside. An implicit mutual contract operates in most university courses: the professor won't make too many demands on the students if they don't make too many demands on the professor. Otherwise, the relationship is understood to be antagonistic, even if externally polite.

How quaint Elias's theory of the civilizing process seems compared with Freud's, Durkheim's, and Veblen's cynicism. At least one feels redeemed by intellectuals from the previous *fin de siècle*. They felt that beneath the gracious conventions of everyday interaction, life was becoming more subtly savage than ever. Their explanation was that the dialectic between will and idea had resulted in the peculiar state in which the human animal has become simultaneously more clever and willful.

One needs the concept of *homo duplex* to arrive at this insight. Without it, one pretends that reason has succeeded in taming the passions.

THE STRESS CONCEPT: THE LAST BASTION OF HEROISM

A widespread "fiction" in modern life is that it is stressful. Baudrillard does not even take note of this fiction, and if he did, he would no doubt dismiss it as being as groundless as all other fictions. By contrast, laypersons as well as intellectuals at the previous turn of the century became self-conscious of the fact that compared to their ancestors, they were suffering more from "nervousness" and neurasthenia – and that these spiritual diseases were a mark of distinction (see Lutz 1990; Weber 1987). Veblen ([1899] 1967), in particular, cited nervous disorders as a sign that the victim was sufficiently refined to be able to suffer from them and that he or she could afford to indulge in the symptomatology by not being forced to work for a living. Freud turned from a career in research medicine when he became interested in these nervous disorders of the middle class, and Durkheim ([1897] 1951) also devotes many pages of *Suicide* to "neurasthenia" as a mark of distinction. Walter Benjamin (1973) cited Baudelaire for being among the first to note that modernity makes heroes out of all of us by exacting such a heavy toll of suffering.

The positivistic schools have tried to assimilate the stress concept into the Parsonian, oversocialized conception of the human person. They have reduced the problem of stress to one of establishing something like a laundry list of stressful life-events that serve as the causes for all sorts of effects, from migraines to murder. And they have come up with an unimaginative, even narcissistic solution to the problem of stress: avoid stressors, and seek social supports. As if stressors can be avoided, and as if certain types of "social supports" could not act as stressors. The thousands of empirical studies on this topic betray an astonishing lack of sociological imagination.

One must wonder why our ancestors did not blame stress (or any equivalent of inner, psychic tension) for their health problems, bad moods, murder, and suicide, when we know that their lives were much more difficult than ours *vis-à-vis* the technical fruits of civilization. In the present *fin de siècle*, we possess more technical gadgets and conveniences than our ancestors could imagine, yet stress is on everyone's lips. Stress has become the new, insidious brutality and savagery in our daily lives, the inhuman force that the ancient Greeks ascribed to barbarians. But this reality, felt intimately by everyone, is obfuscated by an anachronistic faith in progress and the Enlightenment project.

Freud and Durkheim did not use the concept of stress, of course. It was invented by Hans Selye in this century. But they did write about a psychic tension based on *homo duplex* that increases with the development of civilization. One of the consequences of supposing that humans are actually two beings, one pushed by the will and the other pulled by the idea, is that "external" events should not have an automatic effect upon persons, and that the distinction between "inner" and "outer" disappears. What is at stake here is the highly ambiguous understanding of causes and events that sometimes goes by the name of the "life-events" school that has become the staple of current literature in medical sociology, related fields, and pop culture. The reader need only pick up any issue of the *Journal of Health and Social Behavior* or any popular magazine, like *People*, to be convinced that scholars and laypersons return to the most fundamental dilemmas of the life-events explanation again and again: Do "life-events" cause "illness" or does "illness" cause life-events? Do "life-events" derive their stressfulness by causing change or by being undesirable or through some other unknown quality of being a "life-event?" Why is it that some people are relatively unaffected by stressful life-events that allegedly produce undesirable effects in others? What is the effect of "social dislocation" – and what does that mean – in terms of a person's response to life-events? The many other questions, problems, and the confusion that surround the probably thousands of studies subscribing to the "life-events" school cannot possibly be accounted for in this work.

I do not mean to beg the question of what is wrong with the life-events school and therefore what can be somewhat remedied by the new, *fin de siècle* reading of Veblen, Freud and Durkheim being proposed here. Nor do I wish to contribute to a renovation of the stress concept. The aims in this chapter are to expand the narrow, contemporary understanding of stress to its wider context of psychic *trauma*, a word used by Plato to denote "wound." I plan to use the reconstructed Freud and Durkheim to discuss the mechanisms by which modern humans wound each other and themselves psychically even as civilization imposes upon them constraints against physical violence and aggression. The life-events school shall be used as an entry point into a much larger discussion.

THE ORIGINAL STRESS CONCEPT

Hans Selye and Walter Cannon are widely regarded as the precursors of the stress concept. Selye and Cannon, who were still saturated with the *fin de siècle* spirit exemplified by Freud, Durkheim, and Veblen, taught that a stressor is anything that produces stress, such that "normal life-events may turn otherwise inconsequential conditioning factors into potent stressors" (Selye 1978: 370). Anything can *become* stressful, and this seems to be especially true in modern societies. Selye and Cannon even went as far as to claim that society as a whole can act as a stressor depending upon the ways that society is arranged.[1] In his *Wisdom of the Body*, Walter Cannon (1963: 313) claimed that: "The homeostasis of the individual human being is largely dependent on social homeostasis." Their understanding of "homeostasis," another Greek concept, implies Freud's and Durkheim's understanding of a tension-filled equilibrium that is temporary, and can turn into a stressor at any moment.[2]

Incidentally, the title as well as the contents of Cannon's book, "the wisdom of the body," imply the Platonic, Schopenhauerian insight into *homo duplex* that we are following throughout this book. The body's "wisdom" is superior to reason: "it" knows how to heal itself even though "it" is responsible for the symptoms of stress by seeking to defend itself against dangers perceived by the mind (see Wulf 1987).

By contrast, contemporary stress research relies on the individualistic, cerebral, subjectivist version of "stressful life-events" coupled with a Parsonian assumption that many social contacts and supports promote well-being. Stress is determined largely by asking subjects to recall specific events that have been listed on something that resembles a laundry list, from death of a loved one to vacations. But it is well known that events that are stressful for one person may be beneficial to another, whether that event is marriage, divorce, death, or anything else on the official list of stressful life-events. For example, in the introduction to their often-cited work, Dohrenwend and Dohrenwend (1974: 1) write:

> Stress is a term that has been linked to varied concepts and operations . . . For some researchers it is a stimulus, sometimes more, sometimes less complex; for others it is an inferred inner state; and for still others it is an observable response to a stimulus or situation. Thus the use of the term is somewhat hazardous because of the lack of consensus that prevails in stress research.

The Dohrenwends attempt to give some unity to the various concepts that comprise the life-events school of thought by claiming that researchers

> Focus on a class of stressful stimuli or situations to which everyone is exposed to a greater or lesser extent in the natural course of life. These stimuli or situations, which we call "life-events," include experiences such as marriage, birth of a child, divorce, and death of a loved one.
>
> (Ibid.)

But what is it about a particular stimulus or situation that makes it allegedly stressful, and then, only for some persons? Why did our ancestors not find these common events, from marriage to childbirth, stressful? These questions are not addressed sociologically nor philosophically by this school. Nevertheless, in the background of the life-events paradigm one finds the modernist, Parsonian, model: if only you will assimilate, belong to many groups, be a joiner, adjust, and otherwise get into the swing of the Enlightenment project, you shall ameliorate the stress process (whatever it is). It does not even occur to contemporary positivists that enlightenment and civilization might be the culprits in the stress process.

I will attempt to show that for Freud, in general, events do not produce distressing effects – that is the role of traumas. But for Freud, a trauma is not just an event. A trauma stands midway between the inner and outer dichotomies already discussed, and is resolved by means of a dualistic process of "wearing away" which will be discussed. For Freud, persons succumb to illness because they are unable to resolve traumas adequately. Durkheim has no explicit theory of trauma. But he does have the ingredients that serve for a workable theory of trauma that is similar to Freud's, particularly the concept of anomie as *dérèglement*.

Consider also that Selye's solution to stress was what he called the philosophy of "altruistic egoism," or earning the gratitude of others (1978: 449). It comes very close to being the Christian ethic also espoused by Veblen and Durkheim in particular. One of Selye's home-spun examples is for a professor not to brag about his or her publications to colleagues in order to avoid causing them the stress of envy and the subsequent stress of dealing with their envy. In line with Schopenhauer, Selye felt that a life of self-interest tempered by compassion would minimize the inevitable effects of stress brought on by modernity. Selye's scientific treatise on stress is very much an example of the humanistic pessimism that Max Horkheimer found in Schopenhauer's philosophy.

Contemporary research does not address the issue of moral philosophy as it pertains to stress. Nevertheless, one might characterize the social philosophy of the current paradigm as "raw egoism" (to distinguish it from Selye's altruistic egoism), since persons are seen as objects to be used as supports, and there exists no notion of giving to others, or the therapeutic effects of altruism. In other words, the current paradigm assumes the vulgar Darwinian notion of survival of the fittest: avoid stressors, use other people for social support, and don't worry about compassion. It is an extension of the vulgar, Me-generation aspect of postmodern culture praised by Baudrillard.

Thus, the positivistic approach to stress is hardly value-free, for it implies the egoistic ethic that Schopenhauer, Freud, and Durkheim condemned. They thought that egoism is the root of barbarism, and even though they realized that heightened egoism is an inevitable accompaniment to so-called progress, they sought to temper, not eliminate it. The contrast between contemporary approaches to stress, in which one seeks to avoid stressors (even though that is impossible) and to promote one's self-interest, and that of the originators of the stress concept and *fin de siècle* thinkers, is thought-provoking: it points to the persistence of barbaric traits despite the civilizing process.

MOVING BEYOND THE OVERSOCIALIZED
CONCEPTION OF THE HUMAN PERSON

When one speaks of cybernetics today (a word derived from *kybernetes*, meaning "pilot" or "governor" which is also the root of the word "government") one thinks of robots and artificial intelligence, not Durkheim's ([1950] 1983) analysis of anomic forms of government as sources of collective tension, nor the suggestions by Cannon, Bernard, and Selye. Of course, similar sociological speculation on the social origins of illness can be traced back to Plato, and beyond. These are important ideas because the proper governance of social arrangements such as the economy, education, government, religion and other institutions will obviously have a greater impact on individual health and illness than the management of merely an individual's stressful life-events.

But current stress research ignores the sociological import of the theories of the thinkers it regards as pioneers of such research. Current research focuses almost exclusively on individual experiences of stressful events and social support. In addition, it has wed itself to a subjectivist, positivistic, pragmatist orientation whereas the pioneers in this field were all critical of these philosophical orientations, which are also under attack by some postmodernist philosophers. Current research relies on subjective accounts of events even though orthodox tenets of the social sciences call for strict adherence to objectivity. Stressful life-events are treated as specific causal agents while the forerunners of this research were highly critical of the doctrine of the specific etiology of disease.

The epistemological poverty of the life-events paradigm is betrayed by its lack of solid theoretical scaffolding. For example, bits and pieces of Durkheim are typically invoked, usually out of context, never resulting in theoretical unity, and rarely using verbatim quotes from Durkheim (rather, Parsons and Merton are usually quoted as to what Durkheim allegedly meant). Thus, it is typically alleged that Durkheimian anomie theory assumes that psychological well-being is maintained by social integration and that integration, as social norms, contacts and resources, is always beneficial. But we have already demonstrated that, in fact, for Durkheim, "integration" referred to the state of a society or group, not the attachment of individuals to groups; that too much integration can be harmful; and that Durkheim's use of integration is part of his thesis of the dualism of human nature.

Selye's (1978) notion of altruistic egoism and Durkheim's concept of *homo duplex* are amazingly similar. One has to wonder to what extent Selye might have been familiar with or influenced by Schopenhauer's philosophy given the non-positivistic tone of his *Stress of Life*. Nevertheless, researchers continue to "credit" Durkheim with the false, oversocialized version, and to try to make Selye seem positivistic.

Or consider the simplistic references to homeostasis like Pearlin's (1981: 337) allegation that "the organism is fundamentally intolerant of change, an assumption rooted in the pioneering laboratory studies of Cannon and Selye." The forerunners of the concepts of stress and homeostasis never said anything like that. On the contrary, they were mindful of the stress of monotony and lack of change (so similar to Schopenhauer's warnings that boredom is one of the most important problems that plague enlightened persons). Immediately after he introduces the concept of homeostasis, Cannon writes (1963: 24): "The word does not imply something set and immobile, a stagnation. It means a condition which may vary, but which is relatively constant." And Selye wrote (1978: 386): "As we have often said, living beings are constructed for work and if they have no outlet for their pent-up energy, they must make extreme efforts at adaptation to this unphysiological state of inactivity which has been named deprivation stress."

The intellectual milieu of the pioneers of stress research was not pragmatism, positivism or behaviorism, but a complicated stance that included a mindfulness of something like Schopenhauer's notion of the "will to life." I believe Selye's *Stress of Life* is built on a *fin de siècle* scaffolding that served as the ground for Freud's and Durkheim's works, that stress is merely the consequence of the will to life that can be controlled to some extent, but never eliminated. If Schopenhauer is right that the aim of life is death, then life must entail "wear and tear," which is what Selye regards as stress. But the more important point is that for both Selye and Schopenhauer, enlightenment adds more wear and tear to the organism's journey to death, because it complicates his or her psychic life, and thereby promotes anxiety and subjective terrors that simpler creatures do not know.

Similarly, Freud and Durkheim sought to break out of the neo-Kantian subjectivism–objectivism debate. The original "myth" that informs Freud's and Durkheim's thoughts on sickness and health may be traced to the writings of Plato. For Plato, the physician does not merely cure the body, but body and soul (will and idea). The health of the individual is dependent upon the health of society. Health is a kind of beauty and harmony within the soul, and also between the soul and the community. Yet, death is understood to be a release from the constraints of the body. Death and suicide, in one way of reading Plato, are the natural end of a life based on the idea that health is harmony and beauty. To this terse summary of Plato one can relate Freud's enigmatic statements concerning the interplay of the life and death instincts, and Durkheim's ideas concerning *homo duplex*, and of course, Schopenhauer's own abundant references to Plato.

The Platonic idea that health is not merely the absence of disease but the ability to function effectively in harmony with one's environment is actually quite up to date. It is the definition of health cited by the World Health Organization, although it is not typically attributed to Plato. Socrates, that son of an Athenian sculptor who did not follow his father's craft but preached the search for virtue and truth, and who ended his life by committing suicide, claimed in *Phaedon* that the entrance of the soul into the body at birth is a sort of disease which is the beginning of dissolution. This is similar to Schopenhauer's focus on death as the problem that must be confronted at the outset of every philosophy. A pessimistic metaphysics is an integral part of Western culture that can be traced from Plato up to the positivistic paradigms that ignore the philosophical problem posed by death.

This Platonic myth is echoed even in the writings of another important precursor of the stress concept, Claude Bernard, who writes in his *Lectures on the Phenomena of Life Common to Animals and Plants* (what a Schopenhauerian title!) that "existence [is] nothing more than a perpetual alternation of life and death, of composition and decomposition" (1974: 94). It follows that "every manifestation of life is necessarily associated with an organic destruction" (ibid.: 114). Every time a muscle is flexed, movement, volition or any constructive act of life occurs, destruction, "wear and tear" also occurs. To repeat, Selye (1978) also used the phrase "wear and tear" as a synonym for stress (one wonders if he derived it from Bernard), to drive home the point that stress is a part of life which cannot be avoided, but must be managed.

By contrast, the life-events paradigm in stress research teaches that stressors *can* be avoided and that homeostasis is lack of change. What philosophy or narrative can possibly supply the ground for such an alien, artificial view of life? We have been tracing it throughout this book. It is the modernist, Enlightenment narrative that approaches life as a mechanical problem, something to be solved for the sake of progress and social order, whose metaphysics never confronts death.

In *Charmides*, Socrates taught that: "Just as one should not attempt to cure the eyes apart from the head, nor the head apart from the body, so one should not attempt to cure the body apart from the soul." Of course, modern medicine denies the existence of a soul, the metaphysical essence of the human person. Herein lies the vast difference in the positivistic versus the previous *fin de siècle* understandings of the tension that constitutes stress. For Freud, hysteria was a disease that had no physical causes, whose origins were psychic. Initially, Freud tried to explain hysteria in physicalist language, but found that the symptoms of hysteria did not make sense anatomically. As Freud put it, "Hysteria behaves as though anatomy did not exist or as though it had no knowledge of it." Freud drew ridicule from his colleagues for suggesting that hysteria, as a physical ill-ness, could be alleviated symptomatically through "talking cures." But Freud's suggestion is strangely similar to Plato's idea that the soul is bared through speculation and made well through knowledge. And Durkheim pursued this Platonic trajectory even further, by suggesting that society is the con-sciousness of consciousness, as an important ingredient in the communication that occurs between the healer and the patient. Indeed, Freud's ideas have still not been accepted by the scientific community, and no analyst dares call himself strictly Freudian. Nor is it safe to call oneself a total Durkheimian in this Platonic sense.

Obviously, the terms principle of constancy, equilibrium, self-regulation, homeostasis, stability, constancy of the internal milieu, cybernetics, and other terms used by stress researchers as well as by Freud and Durkheim all bear some resemblance to each other. It is beyond the scope of this book to delve into an analysis of all the similitudes. But what set Freud and Durkheim apart is that because of their particular understanding of *homo duplex*, any equilibrium is a tension-filled truce that can easily dissolve into pathology. This follows from Schopenhauer's understanding of the antagonistic relation between the will and idea. Thus, illness is not the opposite of health. Rather, health and illness lie on a continuum.

FREUD AND THE CONCEPT OF TRAUMA

Consider Laplanche and Pontalis's (1973: 465) definition of trauma: "An event in the subject's life defined by its intensity, by the subject's incapacity to respond adequately to it, and by upheaval and long-lasting effects that it brings." Clearly, a trauma is more than just an event. Freud wrote: "We apply it [the term trauma] to an experience which within a short period of time presents the mind with an increase of stimulus too powerful to be dealt with or worked off in the normal way" ([1916] 1966: 275). Similarly, Freud writes in "Further Remarks on the Neuro-Psychoses of Defence" that: "It is not the experiences themselves which act traumatically but their revival as a memory after the subject has entered on sexual maturity" ([1896b] 1974: 164).

Furthermore, some of these experiences *become* traumas through social interaction, and do not come prepackaged as traumas. Thus in the "Sketches of the Preliminary Communication of 1893" Freud writes: "Any impression which the nervous system has difficulty in disposing of by means of associative thinking or motor reaction becomes a psychical trauma" ([1893a] 1974: 154).

There is another complication to Freud's notion of trauma not previously discussed in psychoanalytic literature. Notice, in the passage above, that the impression is to be disposed in two radically different ways, "associative thinking" (along the path of ideas) or "motor reaction" (along the avenue established by the will). In other words, the "disposal" of impressions for Freud is by means of the dualisms already seen in Freud's work: Binding and Unbinding, Free and Bound Energy, Primary and

Secondary Processes, ultimately will and idea. In their discussion of "abreaction," Laplanche and Pontalis merely state
that for Freud "Abreaction is thus the normal way for the
subject to react to an event and to ensure that is does not keep
too great a quota of affect" (1973: 1) and that abreaction allows
the "subject to get rid of the memory of a traumatic event." I
do not agree that memories are gotten rid of; in Freud's
language, they are "tamed." Let us start from scratch in trying
to understand Freud's meaning of "trauma," always addressing
it in the context of the dualisms previously discussed.

In his "Comparative Study of Organic and Hysterical Motor
Paralyses" Freud writes:

> Every event, every psychical impression is provided with a
> certain quota of affect of which the ego divests itself either by
> means of a motor reaction or by associative psychical activity.
> If the subject is unable or unwilling to get rid of this surplus,
> the memory of the impression attains the importance of a
> trauma and becomes the cause of permanent hysterical
> symptoms. The impossibility of elimination becomes evident
> when the impression remains in the subconscious. We have
> called this theory *Das Abreagieren des Reizzuwachses* (the Abre-
> action of Accretions of Stimulus).
>
> ([1893d] 1974: 171)

Let us dissect the above passage: (1) The divesting of affect (not
memories) occurs bodily and mentally. *Homo duplex* is implied.
(2) Freud allows that the subject cannot *or will not* divest himself
or herself of the surplus affect. Part of this process of abreaction
is intentional and part is unintentional. (3) The memory
charged with surplus affect that came from the ego *becomes* a
trauma. The objective event as well as the subject participate in
this process. Freud elaborates:

> It may therefore be said that the ideas which have *become*
> pathological have persisted with such freshness and affective
> strength because they have been denied the normal *wearing-
> away* processes by means of abreaction and reproduction in
> states of uninhibited association.
>
> ([1893b] 1974: 11)

Note that in this passage, abreaction is part of the larger
process of "wearing away." Uninhibited association, the other

type of "wearing away," appears to be dominated by primary processes.

In fact, the wearing-away processes appear in many varieties: crying, anger, forgetting, conversion, etc. Thus Freud summarizes the concept of trauma as follows: "This can only be explained on the view that these [pathological] memories constitute an exception in their relation to all the wearing-away processes which we have discussed" ([1893b] 1974: 10).

In *Studies on Hysteria*, Breuer and Freud write:

> The strength of the affect which can be released by a memory is very variable, according to the amount to which it has been exposed to "wearing-away" by different influences, and especially according to the degree to which the original affect has been "abreacted."
>
> ([1893–1895] 1974: 205)

Unfortunately, there is some confusion about what is worn away. Thus far, it appears that affect is worn away. Elsewhere, Freud makes it seem like memories are worn away:

> Thus hysterics suffer mainly from reminiscences. If the traumatic scene which has been arrived at in this way is reproduced vividly accompanied by a generation of affect, the symptom which has hitherto been obstinately maintained disappears. We must therefore suppose that the forgotten memory has been acting like a foreign body in the mind, with the removal of which the irritating phenomena cease. This discovery, first made by Breuer in 1881, can be made the basis of a therapy of hysterical phenomena which deserves to be described as "cathartic". . . . It seems that by thus remaining unconscious they escape the wearing-away process to which psychical material is normally subject.
>
> ([1896c] 1974: 244)

However, the notion that memories act like "foreign bodies" in the mind hardly sounds like a biological understanding of memories. It seems, rather, that "memories" are representations, something concocted from affect generated by the ego and certain scenes, which persist with a life or Schopenhauerian-like "will" of their own unless worn away. The Freudian claim that we suffer from reconstructed memories is a far cry from the positivistic version in which we fall ill due to specific events. It is also remote from Baudrillard's and other postmodern versions in which the memories are mere fictions that circulate within and external to the human agent, but do not accumulate or cause tension. Baudrillard's fictions just dissolve into nothingness, like the air bubbles in a bottle of soda when it's been opened. But Freud's fictions are as real as material "stuff," and they do not go away of their own accord. If Freud is correct, one has to wonder how modern individuals cope with all these accumulated memories.

THE CONCEPT OF MORTIFICATION

In an essay entitled "On the Psychical Mechanism of Hysterical Phenomena," Freud foreshadows his arguments in *Civilization and Its Discontents*, and relates "wearing away" to the dualisms we have been discussing. He writes:

> The increase in the sum of excitation takes place along sensory paths, and its diminution along motor ones. So we may say that if anything impinges on someone he reacts in a motor fashion. We can now safely assert that it depends on this reaction how much of the initial psychical impression is left. Let us consider this in relation to a particular example. Let us suppose that a man is insulted, is given a blow or something of the kind. This psychical trauma is linked with an increase in the sum of excitation in his nervous system.
>
> ([1893c] 1974: 37)

Notice how Freud blurs the mental and physical aspects of being human. For him, psychical phenomena involve both the mind and body. And "wearing away" is partly social. We are dealing here with Durkheim's total social facts, as well as the Schopenhauerian, antagonistic unity of will and idea. Psychical traumas can be discharged through motor reactions, and these traumas can be caused by insults as well as physical blows. This is an important point to consider for our discussion, because even if Elias is correct that civilization has made it less likely that we shall receive blows, it has not decreased our chances for encountering insults. On the contrary. But let us continue with Freud's engrossing story:

There then instinctively arises an inclination to diminish this increased excitation immediately. He hits back, and then feels easier; he may perhaps have reacted adequately – that is, he may have got rid of as much as had been introduced into him.

(Ibid.: 37)

But just what was introduced into him? Freud is writing more like an artist portraying a colossal battle between "inner" and "outer" fictions, than a biologist. Freud continues:

Now this reaction may take various forms. For quite slight increases in excitation, alterations in his own body may perhaps be enough: weeping, abusing, raging, and so on. The more intense the trauma, the greater is the adequate reaction.

(Ibid.: 37)

Let us summarize: something external impinged on the man, and for various reasons, he responded with great "excitation." His task now is to empty his insides of this intrusion, hurl it back at the external, and be healthy again. However, civilized society imposes restrictions on the public display of weeping, abusing, raging, and so on. According to Freud:

The most adequate reaction, however, is always a deed. But as an English writer has wittily remarked, the man who first flung a word of abuse at his enemy instead of a spear was the founder of civilization.

(Ibid.: 37)

Words are symbols and representations – fictions. Yet, in Freud's view, they literally behave like things. Words can wound humans every bit as grievously as spears, only the civilized wounds caused by insults are invisible. Freud's insulted man can rid himself of trauma by wounding his enemy with words as well as a spear, and may have been wounded by other insults long ago in his childhood, which only compounds the present wound. Is this biology? It cannot be, because animals cannot use language as weapons. Freud is implying *homo duplex*, that humans have a "higher" social capacity that makes them both sensitive to insults as well as capable of inflicting them, at the same time that they never outgrow the "lower," barbaric impulses to avenge a blow with a blow. He continues:

Thus words are substitutes for deeds, and in some circumstances (e.g. in Confession) the only substitutes. Accordingly alongside the adequate reaction there is one that is less adequate. If, however, there is no reaction whatsoever to a psychical trauma, the memory of it retains the affect which it originally had.

(Ibid.: 37)

This is a curious move. Freud is saying that the affect behaves "freely" and in fact will behave as if it had a life and existence of its own, apart from the human agent:

So that if someone who has been insulted cannot avenge the insult either by a retaliatory blow or by a word of abuse, the possibility arises that the memory of the event may call up in him once more the affect which was originally present.

(Ibid.: 37)

It should be noted that Schopenhauer, too, regarded what we now call mental illness but he called madness as being primarily a disease of the memory. The madman is essentially at the mercy of his or her memories instead of being their master. It hardly seems a coincidence that Freud's treatment of the same subject parallels Schopenhauer's so closely. This is an important point to consider, because it enables one to appreciate Freud's implicit metaphysics. For example, simply compare Freud's account thus far with Schopenhauer's explanation that the will prohibits "the intellect from having certain representations, by absolutely preventing certain trains of thought from arising, because it knows . . . that they would arouse in it any one of the emotions previously described" ([1818] 1969b: 208). Like Freud, Schopenhauer believed that the "wearing away" of the unpleasant emotions must occur immediately, and that the accumulation of affect-laden, repressed memories is dangerous:

Every new adverse event must be assimilated by the intellect, in other words, must receive a place in the system of truths connected with our will and its interests, whatever it may have to displace that is more satisfactory. As soon as this is done, it pains us much less; but this operation itself is often very painful, and in most cases takes place only slowly and with reluctance. But soundness of mind can continue only in so far as this operation has been correctly carried out each time. On the other hand, if . . . certain events or circumstances are wholly suppressed from the intellect, because the will cannot bear the sight of them; and then, if the resultant gaps are arbitrarily filled up for the sake of the necessary connection; we then have madness.

([1818] 1969b: 400)

What is clear from Freud's and Schopenhauer's passages, above, is that the affect-laden memories behave like Durkheim's representations, as if they possessed a "will" of their own. The circumstances change, but the fact lives, and may come back to influence the behavior of the subject. One might raise the question whether collective memories might not be subject to similar repression with similar consequences – whether whole peoples and epochs might not be considered "mad" due to a distorted sense of history. In any event, this move enables Freud to describe neurosis as something that happens *to* a person, in part. After all, it is the memory of the event that calls up the affect, but it is not the person himself or herself who calls up the memory of the affect. Freud elaborates:

An insult that has been repaid, even if only in words, is recollected quite differently from one that has had to be accepted; and linguistic usage characteristically describes an insult that has been suffered in silence as "mortification" (*Kränkung*, literally, "making ill").

([1893c] 1974: 37)

Freud uses "mortification" again in *An Outline of Psychoanalysis* ([1938] 1969) to describe the holding in of "aggressive instincts," over forty years after the particular usage above. In this mature work Freud wrote:

When the super-ego is established, considerable amounts of the aggressive instinct are fixated in the interior of the ego and operate there self-destructively. This is one of the dangers to health by which human beings are faced on their path to cultural development. Holding back aggressiveness is in general unhealthy and leads to illness (to mortification).

([1938] 1969: 7)

We have already seen that the aggressive instinct is not a real instinct for Freud; it is part of the inner, centripetal, death trend of being human. Note the emphasis on cultural problems, as if aggressive instincts that are not worn away because of culture result in sickness. This is another one of many clear indicators that Freud was following in Schopenhauer's footsteps.

Let us return to our insulted man in the 1893 lecture. Freud comes to the general conclusion:

> Thus, if for any reason there can be no reaction to a psychical trauma, it retains its original affect, and when someone cannot get rid of the increase in stimulation by "abreacting" it, we have the possibility of the event in question remaining a psychical trauma.
>
> ([1893c] 1974: 38)

But we have seen that "abreaction" is one of many forms of wearing away for Freud. It is no surprise, then, that he adds:

> Incidentally, a healthy psychical mechanism has other methods of dealing with the affect of a psychical trauma even if motor reaction and reaction by words are denied to it – namely by working it over associatively and by producing contrasting ideas. Even if the person who has been insulted neither hits back nor replies with abuse, he can nevertheless reduce the affect attaching to the insult by calling up such contrasting ideas as those of his own worthiness, of his enemy's worthlessness, and so on.
>
> (Ibid.: 38)

Again, notice that the mind–body dualism is crossed over many times in the above passage. Hitting the enemy, cursing the enemy, or thinking bad thoughts about the enemy are all methods of wearing away, methods of cleansing the inner world of this foreign body, the trauma. To put it another way, the primary process directs immediate discharge through the body, but the secondary process directs the psychical excitation through other, more elaborate avenues of discharge if the primary avenues are blocked:

> Whether a healthy man deals with an insult in one way or the other, he always succeeds in achieving the result that the

effect which was originally strong in his memory eventually loses intensity and that finally the recollection, having lost its affect, falls a victim to forgetfulness and the process of wearing-away.

(Ibid.: 38)

In this fantastic lecture, quoted at length above, Freud uses hydraulic language, but he is certainly not faithful to the physicalist tradition. Perhaps some of Freud's contemporaries used words that indicated static equilibrium, but evidence abounds that even his teachers were influenced by Schopenhauer's philosophy (see Jones 1981, vol. 1: 375). And Freud's equilibriums are always dynamic, clearly Schopenhauerian truces in this dualism between the inner and outer already discussed. I will attempt to show, shortly, that even Freud's famous Principle of Constancy has a dual aim, the maintenance of equilibrium and death itself.

For now, I hope to have shown that despite his hydraulic language, Freud's descriptions of trauma, wearing away, and culture point to the dualisms we have already investigated: the individual is impinged by an event from the outside to which he adds his own reaction, creating a new phenomenon, trauma, which he must then expel from his inner world. This description is more like a fairy-tale than a scientific explanation, but from the outset, I have expressed a willingness to follow Freud's myths. What is more significant is that Plato and Schopenhauer preceded Freud's mythology with their own similar myths that center on the evil consequences of failure to be honest with oneself. Following the trajectory from Plato to Freud, the discussion has moved far from the positivistic goal of merely suppressing symptoms in neurotics by means of psychotropic "medications," without bothering to engage them in "talking cures." By contrast, Plato, Schopenhauer, Freud and Durkheim were arguing that sanity is maintained through proper mental hygiene that involves an ongoing, accurate assessment of personal and collective memories, which is to say – history. But the modern and postmodern eras have denied that there is any such thing as accurate memory. Far from rejecting Freud because his explanation seems unfamiliar to modernists, it is useful to consider the relevance of his explanations to the evil consequences of all the insults that postmodern humans are forced to endure.

COLLECTIVE MEMORIES AND TIME

In *Sociology and Philosophy*, Durkheim ([1924] 1974) argued that memories exist permanently as mental facts: they do not disappear when the firings that caused them disappear. One way to paraphrase Durkheim is to say that memories are timeless. Scattered across many of Durkheim's writings are references to collective memories, a portion of which takes material form in monuments, feasts, calendars, and other collective representations, although another portion remains free-floating. In Schopenhauerian terms, memories belong to the realm of the "will," which is independent of the constraints of time and space. But if that is so, does it not follow that consciousness would become a heap of timeless memories that are acting upon the person, especially in the unconscious? Without "wearing away," which literally means "using up" (from the word *Usur*), that would be the case in Freud's system of thought. Freud and Durkheim do not make the exact same argument, but they come close, and both argue that memories are timeless.

Durkheim's disciple, Maurice Halbwachs, extended Durkheim's thought in this regard in *The Collective Memory* ([1950] 1980). Like Durkheim, Halbwachs argues that memory is a social "reconstruction of the past achieved with data borrowed from the present" (ibid.: 69). Like Freud, who assumes that neuroses are antisocial structures, Halbwachs argues that "a man must often appeal to others' remembrances to evoke his own past. He goes back to reference points determined by society, hence outside himself" (ibid.: 51). And these social reference points are not merely extensions of the subjective viewpoints of individuals, but realities *sui generis*, such that the retrieval of any memory involves society and the human agent, will and idea. We are back to *homo duplex*, Schopenhauer and Plato.

Neither Durkheim nor Halbwachs elaborated on the mechanisms by which society and its members become sick due to incorrect remembering and repression. They could not have foreseen the postmodernist movement, which severed all linkages between ideas and referents, and declared that the world is a mass of disconnected, circulating fictions. Yet the Durk-heimians devoted many pages to the importance of rituals, habits, and other mechanisms that keep the past alive in the present, that forge a chain between past and present. The burning questions which emerge from our analysis thus far are the following: Is Baudrillard's vision of circulating fictions one that Freud and Durkheim would have regarded as characteristic of an insane society? What is the "proper" way to handle memories such that an individual and society are deemed more healthy than unhealthy, even if both states exist on a con-tinuum for *fin de siècle* thinkers?

Even in the now famous "Fliess Papers" Freud refers to the timelessness of memories, and to the need to "tame" them:

> What is it then, that happens to memories capable of affect till they are tamed? It cannot be supposed that "time," repetition, weakens their capacity for affect . . . Something must no doubt happen in "time," during the repetitions, which brings about this subjugation; and this can be nothing other than that a relation to the ego or to ego-cathexes which obtains power over the memories.
>
> ([1895] 1974: 280)

The process of "taming" is similar to Freud's "binding" and abreaction as well as Durkheim's usages of the ideas of "inte-gration" and "constraint." Note that in figurative language, Freud recognizes that if memories are not mere epiphenomena, then something must be done to account for them lest they pile up and dominate the person. Durkheim assumed something similar, only part of this process was occurring in the collective consciousness, not just the individual consciousness.

In *The Psychopathology of Everyday Life,* Freud reiterates that: "It is generally thought that it is time which makes memory uncertain and indistinct. It is highly probable that there is no question at all of there being any direct function of time in forgetting" ([1901] 1965: 274). The claim that the memory is not even altered in the passage of time is more important. First, it is a link to Schopenhauer's rebellion against Kant's philo-sophy, which restricts the study of all phenomena to the categories of time, space, and causality. Second, Durkheim went a step further than Schopenhauer and Freud in that he argued in his *Elementary Forms* especially, that the ground or referent for the category of time is society itself. The important point is that for Freud and Durkheim, memories do not just go away with the passage of time. Rather, memories are reconstructed, repressed, or transformed in some other way just as time itself is constructed and transformed. According to Freud:

> In the case of repressed memory-traces, it can be demonstrated that they undergo no alteration even in the course of the longest period of time. The unconscious is quite timeless. The most important as well as the strangest characteristic of psychical fixation is that all impressions are preserved, not only in the same form in which they were first received, but also in all the forms which they have adopted in their further developments.
>
> ([1901] 1965: 275)

Freud seems to assume that most memories are quickly "worn away" and those that have been only partially worn away remain as psychical facts even when the original brain tissue that recorded them changes. Breuer and Freud hint at the automatic tendency to wear away impressions in *Studies on Hysteria*: "As a rule . . . an affective idea is promptly subjected to 'wearing away,' to all the influences . . . which deprive it little by little of its quota of affect" ([1893–1895] 1974: 213).

We can grasp the Durkheimian version of a similar wearing-away process by turning to T.S. Eliot, who was influenced by Durkheim, Schopenhauer, and Freud (see Crawford 1984; Menand and Schwartz 1982; Magee 1983). Eliot read Durkheim's *Elementary Forms* ([1912] 1965) to conclude that the savage lives in two worlds, the one commonplace, practical, a world of drudgery, the other sacred, intense, a fantastic world into which he escapes at regular intervals in order to obtain psychic release (Menand and Schwartz 1982). Eliot's famous poem, "The Wasteland," indicts modernity as not offering persons sufficient means to escape into this other, sacred world, the metaphysical world of the will. Eliot and Durkheim imply Freud and Schopenhauer in every way except the direct mention of the concept of "wearing away," but it takes only a little imagination to infer this final step. We arrive at the uncomfortable conclusion that in severing ties to the primitive past, modernity forces humans to suffer from an accumulation of reminiscences which they cannot place in context and cannot wear away.

It is not difficult to substantiate this conclusion. Tocqueville noted long ago that "in America society seems to live from hand to mouth, like an army in the field" because "no one cares for what occurred before his time" ([1845] 1945: 219). He adds that "if the United States were ever invaded by barbarians, it would be necessary to have recourse to the history of other nations in order to learn anything of the people who now inhabit them" (ibid.: 219). This tendency has been exacerbated in the present *fin de siècle* by the postmodernist circulation of fictive forms, decentering, and the enshrinement of hyper-reality as a valid substitute for old-fashioned "reality." Consider any news broadcast or history book as an illustration: the postmodern person has been reduced to a passive consumer of pastiche, disconnected fragments of history that are never connected into a meaningful context or whole (Adorno 1991). But, whereas some postmodern philosophers regard this condition as liberating, Freud and Durkheim would have us consider that this condition may be responsible for the widespread barbarism – including violence, drug use, and crime – and symptomatology that everyone has noticed in the postmodern social world.

FREUD'S DUALISTIC PRINCIPLE OF CONSTANCY

The most dominant version of the notion of homeostasis in contemporary social theory is the Parsonian notion of social order based on normative consensus, and this is the version that is used, implicitly and sometimes explicitly, by the life-events school. From the preceding discussion, it should be obvious that if Freud and Durkheim followed in Schopenhauer's footsteps, their version of homeostasis will be quite different from the positivistic version. Thus, it is often argued that when he used the concept of wearing away, Freud simply meant that the organism wishes to restore homeostasis understood as a basal level of tension, a static state in which the will to life has been practically eliminated. But that is not what Freud meant by the principle of constancy.

In *Beyond the Pleasure Principle*, Freud characterizes the principle of constancy as follows:

The dominating tendency of mental life, and perhaps of nervous life in general, is the effort to reduce, to keep constant or to remove internal tension due to stimuli (the "Nirvana principle") – a tendency which finds expression in the pleasure principle; and our recognition of that fact is one of our strongest reasons for believing in the existence of death instincts.

([1920] 1961: 50)

Curiously, for Freud, the principle of constancy aims at homeostasis *or* the radical removal of all tension, death. Also, this principle applies to "mental life" (whatever this is, psychic, biological, or both) *or* "nervous life in general" (whatever that is). As for the term "nirvana principle," Freud admits that it is a term coined by Schopenhauer and drawn from Buddhism, "where it connotes the extinction of human desire, the abolition of individuality when it is fused into the collective soul, a state of quietude and bliss" (ibid.: 50).

The nirvana principle, however, is sometimes used by Freud to represent the death instinct as well as the principle of constancy. Thus, in *The Economic Problem of Masochism*, Freud writes that "The Nirvana principle expresses the trend of the death instinct" ([1924] 1974: 160). If the principle of constancy is the death instinct, then we are freed from the constraints of academic biology and thrust into a Schopenhauerian discussion of cosmic proportions. Wearing away seeks to restore the primacy of the inner, individual pole of the dualism previously discussed – of the will.[3]

Freud remarked that some hysterics who commit suicide do so not due to immediate events but due to the transformed memories of distant events. He then asks, "Why do healthy people behave differently?" and, "Why do not all their excitations of long ago come into operation once more when a new, present day excitation takes place?" ([1896c] 1974: 218). The answer is, of course, that healthy people are able to wear away excitations more effectively than neurotics. Yet culture is an integral aspect of this process. Some methods of wearing away may be quite offensive. For example, in a letter to Fliess he asks a similar question, with a slightly different bent: "How does it come about that under analogous conditions, perversion or simple immorality emerges instead of neurosis?" ([1895] 1974:

221). He answers that where there is no shame, no morality, and where disgust is blunted "there too no repression and therefore no neurosis will result" (ibid.: 221). Clearly, repression is one of the chief mechanisms that stand in the way of wearing away, and repression occurs partly against ideas that are offensive to the ego relative to the subject's culture.[4]

In *Jokes and Their Relation to the Unconscious*, Freud writes:

> And here at last we can understand what it is that jokes achieve in the service of their purpose. They make possible the satisfaction of an instinct (whether lustful or hostile) in the face of an obstacle that stands in its way. When we laugh at a refined obscene joke, we are laughing at the same thing that makes a peasant laugh at a coarse piece of smut.
>
> ([1905a] 1974: 101)

Freud never pursues the notions of "lustful" or "hostile" instincts (these are like Veblen's many invented instincts, discussed by Riesman 1953). Rather, the more important point seems to be that society and culture disapprove of "smut" in "refined" circles and so "refined individuals" take a detour in obtaining individual satisfaction that the peasant obtains as a matter of course. And this cultural detour may result in neurosis. It is interesting that in our postmodern *fin de siècle*, comedy has become one of the most important aspects of culture. "Stand-up comics," in particular, dominate popular culture, and become heroes of sorts. This is something that Elias (1982) does not foresee or discuss in his discussion of how the civilizing process constrains the enjoyment of smut: the price for this supposed advance in social order is neurosis, and the automatic remedy is a desperate need to laugh at smut, which is fulfilled by comedy. But Freud would argue that the same barbaric needs are met in postmodern comedy as in peasant smut.

Another expression of the inner–outer dualism and its relationship to trauma is expressed by Freud's many comments on art. For example, in *Five Lectures on Psychoanalysis* he writes:

> If a person who is at loggerheads with reality possesses an artistic gift . . . he can transform his phantasies into artistic creations instead of into symptoms. In this manner he can

escape the doom of neurosis and by this round-about path regain his contact with reality.

([1910] 1974a: 50)

The artist is in a better position to "wear away" the frustration that ensues from society's attempt to block his satisfaction than the typical neurotic. Without this socially approved method of "wearing away," the person is "doomed" to neurosis because the blocked wishes (will) pile up as traumas:

> If there is persistent rebellion against the real world and if this precious gift [art] is absent or insufficient, it is almost inevitable that the libido, keeping to the sources of the phantasies, will follow the path of regression, and will revive infantile wishes and end in neurosis.

(Ibid.: 50)

Part of "regression" is a failure to wear away wishes that have not been satisfied since infancy. But for art to have this therapeutic effect, it must be "high art," a controversial point argued also by Adorno (1991) and other members of the Frankfurt School.[5] Popular art follows more directly the regressive path of infantile wishes, and exacerbates the neurotic process. Many postmodernists have castigated Adorno for his seemingly elitist views in this regard, but if Adorno and Freud are correct, one could accuse the postmodernists of contributing to collective psychopathology.

Durkheim's views on art have been neglected by sociologists, but are remarkably similar to Freud's and Schopenhauer's. Schopenhauer felt that in high art, the individual experiences a sense of the sublime by momentarily suspending the all-desiring will in the act of contemplation. Nietzsche followed Schopenhauer in regarding art as the only release from the daily combat based on the will to power. Similarly, in *Moral Education*, Durkheim writes:

> The love of art, the predilection for artistic joys, is accompanied by a certain aptitude for getting outside ourselves, a certain detachment or disinterestedness . . . We lose sight of our surroundings, our ordinary cares, our immediate interests. Indeed, this is the essence of *the healing power of art*. Art consoles us because it turns us away from ourselves.

([1925] 1961: 268; emphasis added)

But Durkheim was also mindful of the reverse side of the coin, that "the domain of art is not that of reality." Art does not convey percepts or concepts, but images, and images are free to play on our whims and internal dispositions: "The artist's world is the world of images, and the world of images is the world of dreams, of untrammeled mental play" (ibid.: 271). Like Freud, Durkheim assigns to art a secondary importance in his overall scheme of society as the science of morality because art "is not a positive factor in morality" and "morality, we suggest, is life in earnest" (ibid.: 274). The important thing for Freud and Durkheim is to remain in contact with reality – and this was Schopenhauer's view as well, that genuine art connects the perceiver with Plato's Ideas, with realities – and Freud would probably have agreed with Durkheim that "in itself, leisure is always dangerous" (ibid.: 274).[6] Of course, postmodernists have reversed completely this serious approach to art by Freud, Durkheim, and Schopenhauer, and have enshrined the impulse toward play as one of the cornerstones of the implicit liberation theology in postmodern philosophy. If one adopts Freud's and Durkheim's more balanced approach, one would conclude that the results on Western society as a whole have been devastating.

In general, for Freud, society "itself plays a great part in causing neuroses" and for a consistent, basic reason ([1910] 1974a: 147). Society is one of the principal representations of the "reality principle" and as such puts a damper on the many varieties of representations that represent the "pleasure principle": excitations, instincts, phantasies, wishes, memories, cathexes, drives, libido, love, and so on. But this is essentially Durkheim's position. The two thinkers use different terminology, but the Platonic principle stays the same. It is inner versus outer, the primary process versus the secondary and in Schopenhauer's vocabulary, the idea versus the "will."

Compare Freud's 1893 essay "On the Psychical Mechanism of Hysterical Phenomena" in which, as we have seen, Freud is comparing the reflex action of the insulted man who wants to run a spear through his opponent's chest to the demands of civilization that he not do so, with one of Freud's last works, *New Introductory Lectures on Psychoanalysis* ([1933] 1965). In both works, he explicitly refers to the concept of "mortification" as the blockage of the individual's sphere of existence by what is external to him. In both works, the most oppressive external force is the collectivity in the form of civilization. Thus, in the 1933 *Lectures*, Freud writes: "Impeded aggressiveness seems to involve a grave injury. It really seems as though it is necessary for us to destroy some other thing or person in order not to destroy ourselves" ([1933] 1965: 94).

In general, for Freud, the more civilized a person becomes, the more he or she must restrain external aggression toward others: civilized persons ought not shoot and kill whoever angers them. But the price for this civilized restraint seems to be an increase in the tendency toward self-murder and its derivatives, including masochism, stress, and all the other manifestations of mortification. Here is another dimension to the civilizing process that Elias as well as the positivists overlook.

The link to Durkheim is indirect. In *Professional Ethics* and *Suicide* Durkheim wrote that as civilization advances, the tendency toward passionate murder decreases while suicide rates increase. Durkheim does not explain the reasons behind this shift in the direction of aggression. He does not treat the issues of civilization, trauma, and their interrelatedness directly. Nevertheless, his intricate discussions of how murder relates to suicide lead to the conclusion that these two forms of murder have the same anomic roots (Durkheim [1897] 1951: 326–60). Durkheim echoes Freud when he claims that "suicide is, then, a transformed and attenuated homicide" (ibid.: 341). He finds that "suicide sometimes coexists with homicide, sometimes they are mutually exclusive; sometimes they react under the same conditions in the same way, sometimes in opposite ways" (ibid.: 355). Freud traced the vicissitudes of aggression in similarly complex ways. Sociologists have paid undue attention to deriving positivistic laws based on Durkheim's writings on suicide, but have neglected his more complicated, and seemingly Freudian discussion of how murder and suicide are related. Consider the following passage from Durkheim as an example:

Anomie, in fact, begets a state of exasperation and irritated weariness which may turn against the person himself or another according to circumstances; in the first case, we have suicide, in the second, homicide . . . This is why there exists today, especially in great centers and regions of intense civilization, a certain parallelism between the development of homicide and that of suicide. *It is because anomie is in an acute state there.* The same cause prevents murders from decreasing as rapidly as suicides increase.

(Ibid.: 357; emphasis added)

The last thing on Durkheim's mind is to find a positivistic explanation for how anomie can produce both suicide and murder. The more important point is that Durkheim seems to be implying Freud's dictum that it is necessary to wear away aggression. Otherwise, the aggressive "instincts" can be expressed as murder or suicide. And, he also seems to parallel Freud's thinking in assuming that aggression can never be eliminated completely in any sort of social order, only maintained within tolerable limits.

In general, civilization imposes privations on humans, and "the individual reacts to the injuries which civilization and other men inflict on him" by developing "a corresponding degree of resistance to the regulations of civilization and of hostility to it" (Freud [1927] 1955: 21). For Freud, the "injury" that civilization imposes on humans is primarily one of "mortification." Persons must check their aggressive, murderous, and lustful "instincts," but when they do so they risk becoming unhealthy. Mortification is a major form of trauma for contemporary persons. It illustrates the tension between the individual and the collective that has already been discussed. But whether trauma is depicted as something that forces persons to hold back a part of their nature or as the introduction of extra "excitations" into their systems, the basic form of Freud's understanding of trauma remains the same in his writings: it is psychical conflict brought about by a particular interaction of *homo duplex* that we are discussing.

OTHER LINKS TO DURKHEIM

Durkheim has no explicit theory of trauma. What he does have are pieces in his writings that would lead to such a concept, and descriptions of the dualism of human nature that lead to Freud's notion of trauma. More importantly, Durkheim does have his own version of civilization and its discontents which has not been acknowledged because he has been misread as a positivist. While it is true that Durkheim did not develop a psychoanalytic theory of the mind, it must be recalled that Durkheim, like Freud, adopted the concept of the unconscious and of unconscious mental processes. In fact, Durkheim held a more elaborate conceptualization of the conflict between the individual and collective levels of representations than Freud. This claim, alone, may surprise some who believe that for Durkheim, there is no conflict between the individual and the collective, that the former is a reflection of the latter.

In a manner reminiscent of Freud, Durkheim takes up the question in his *Suicide* of whether explanations of suicide on the level of what happens to individuals are adequate. In many ways, Durkheim foreshadows what has come to be known as the stressful life-events model. Thus, for Durkheim, the effects of stressful life-events are shaped by collective processes and individual predisposition – but that is essentially Freud's understanding of trauma. As Durkheim put the matter:

> But we know that these individual events, though preceding suicides with fair regularity, are not their real causes. To repeat, no unhappiness in life necessarily causes a man to kill himself unless he is otherwise so inclined. The regularity of possible recurrence of these various circumstances thus cannot explain the regularity of suicide. Whatever influence is ascribed to them, moreover, such a solution would at best change the problem without solving it. For it remains to be understood why these desperate situations are identically repeated annually, pursuant to a law peculiar to each country. How does it happen that a given, supposedly stable society always has the same number of disunited families, of economic catastrophes, etc.? This regular recurrence of identical events in proportions constant within the same population but very inconstant from one population to another would be inexplicable had not each society definite currents impelling its inhabitants with a definite force to commercial and industrial ventures, to behaviour of every sort likely to involve families in trouble, etc.
>
> ([1897] 1951: 100)

Durkheim's reasoning on this issue is compelling. Societies definitely exhibit characteristic rates of many stressful life-events. For example, the rates of marriage, divorce, and bankruptcies are widely different in the USA and India. And societies just as regularly produce specific rates of depression, alcoholism, and other forms of psychopathology that predispose individuals to succumb to life's sorrows. Stressful life-events, alone, do not and cannot account for symptomatology. It should be noted that in contrast to Durkheim, the contemporary stressful life-events school of research does not emphasize the social rates of stressful life-events. The unit of analysis, in general, is the individual. Individuals are said to experience certain events and some of these individuals fall ill. Both extremes of *homo duplex* are missing from this positivistic explanation. One is society's role in the genesis of the events, and the other is society's role in the individual's role in the interaction that leads to the impact of the event, including a predisposition to succumb to illness. In other words, positivistic explanations do not hold to the concept of trauma, but perpetuate a defunct version of the host–pathogen model of disease. By contrast, Durkheim's explanation clearly implies Freud's notion of trauma.

If the individual could learn to ignore the collective world, he or she would not suffer some peculiarly human forms of hurt, such as trauma and insults. On the other hand, if the individual could learn to ignore the realm of the "will" – especially the body and its "appetites" – he or she might become a god of sorts. But in the Platonic myth being followed here, humans are such that they are perched between these two worlds that constitute an antagonistic unity. In fact, religion frequently teaches the myth that the human person is god-like in some ways but also only slightly above the animals in other ways, as Durkheim notes: "The only explanation which has ever been given of this singular necessity (that the two worlds mingle) is the hypothesis of the Fall" ([1912] 1965: 494).

For Durkheim, the myth of man's "original sin" and dual nature contains a kernel of truth: it is a representation of the dualism between the individual and the collective forces that forms the ground for his radically new sociology. Of course, Plato depicted his own version of the Fall in *Phaedrus*. And Schopenhauer serves as a link between Plato and Durkheim, because Schopenhauer felt that

religious teaching regards every individual, on the one hand, as identical with Adam, with the representative of the affirmation of life, and to this extent as fallen into sin (original sin), suffering, and death. On the other hand, knowledge of the Idea also shows it every individual as identical with the Saviour, with the representative of the denial of the will-to-live, and to this extent as partaking of his self-sacrifice, redeemed by his merit, and rescued from the bonds of sin and death, i.e., of the world (Romans v, 12–21).

([1818] 1969a: 329)

Apart from Christianity, which Durkheim, along with Veblen and Schopenhauer, favored, Durkheim found self-sacrifice and self-abnegation to be the kernel of all religious myths, themselves a refraction of the original Platonic myth. "Thus sociology appears destined to open a new way to the science of man," Durkheim adds ([1912] 1965: 495).[7] Durkheim's sociology is rooted in this conflict that stems from *homo duplex*.[8]

Because Durkheim posits an essential human dualism, it follows, as he put it, that if moral activity is "left entirely to individuals, it can only be chaotic and dissipated in conflicts: the society cannot be shaken by so much internal strife without injury" ([1950] 1983: 24). But this does not mean that Parsons was correct to recruit Durkheim as an ally for the social order paradigm. From the primacy of *homo duplex*, it follows also that if moral activity is left entirely to society, the individual must do violence to himself or herself to conform, and cannot continue to do so without injury. These claims are echoed in *Suicide*, wherein Durkheim asserts that too much as well as too little integration is pathogenic.

We have found that Freud has an individual notion of trauma as well as a notion that whole societies may be regarded as sick, as suffering from a "collective trauma" of sorts (an insight pursued especially by Erich Fromm in *The Sane Society*, 1955). On this issue too, Durkheim comes close to conceptualizing a notion of collective trauma. For example, one of the most enigmatic passages in *Suicide* is the following:

No moral idea exists which does not combine in proportions varying with the society involved, egoism, altruism, and a certain anomie. For social life assumes both that the individual has a certain personality, that he is ready to surrender it if the community requires, and finally, that he is to a certain degree sensitive to ideas of progress. This is why there is no people among whom these three currents of opinion do not coexist, bending men's inclinations in three different and even opposing directions.

Where they offset one another, the moral agent is in a state of equilibrium which shelters him against any thought of suicide. But let one of them exceed a certain strength to the detriment of the others, and as it becomes individualized, it also becomes suicidogenetic.

([1897] 1951: 321)

Since Durkheim regards fatalism as the opposite of anomie, I agree with Jack Douglas (1967) that the above passage really means that two sets of opposing forces are at war. It is not immediately apparent what the "equilibrium" of these forces consists of, what disturbs it, nor what maintains it. Nevertheless, in the context of Plato, Schopenhauer and Freud, a fresh reading of this enigmatic passage is possible. Recall that for Freud, equilibrium meant a constancy of excitation as well as the total elimination of tension, death. Durkheim's notion of equilibrium also seems to be a tension-filled truce between two diametrically opposed forces, either of which leads to death, individually and collectively, when unrestrained by the other. Its origin, then, is the dualism of human nature already discussed. Freud also never defined what constitutes the "adequate" level of discharge of this tension, but he made it clear that an "inadequate" level is traumatic. One may speculate that when society is in a state of disequilibrium or anomic *dérèglement* for Durkheim, it is undergoing a collective trauma. One wishes to call it a trauma because of the imbalance among forces that constitute it and because collective trauma affects individuals by predisposing them to illness as well as affecting their individual homeostasis. This is remarkably similar to Walter Cannon's (1963: 313) belief that individual homeostasis is largely dependent on social homeostasis, previously discussed.

Furthermore, Durkheim's last clause, that as this imbalance of forces becomes "individualized," a given "current" will produce suicide, is troublesome. Clearly, the mere existence of societal imbalance does not lead directly to individual suicides. Depending upon various circumstances, the awesome collective representations can be rendered impotent or be substantially neutralized if the individual, or groups of individuals, do not "individualize" these forces.

Durkheim never defined social integration explicitly. He does use the term in a consistent way, however. That is, integration seems to be an adequate balance between the two poles of existence under discussion, and lack of integration is a state of tension between these two poles that I am comparing to trauma. So, for example, Durkheim claims that when the individual thinks more of himself or herself than the common cause, "it is because society is not integrated," adding that

> society cannot *disintegrate* without the individual simultaneously detaching himself from social life, without his own goals becoming preponderant over those of the community, in a word without his personality tending to surmount the collective personality . . . if we agree to call this state egoism, in which the individual ego asserts itself to excess in the face of the social ego.
>
> ([1897] 1951: 209; emphasis added)

The clash between the individual ego and the social ego is an aspect of *homo duplex* under discussion. When the balance between these two forces is upset – as in the contemporary narcissism discussed by Lasch (1979) and others – society disintegrates, and its disintegration produces still more narcissism. What has not been addressed in previous, positivistic interpretations of *Suicide* is that the independent variable is not normative consensus, but the tension between the individual and the collectivity.

In sum, Durkheim holds no explicit notion of trauma. But both Freud and Durkheim share the belief that life's events do *not* cause persons to commit suicide, nor do they cause any other symptoms by themselves. Rather, suicide – and by implication, other sorts of deviance – are the result of some mysterious imbalance of "energy." For Freud, this imbalance occurs when various kinds of phenomena are not "worn away": ideas, memories, instincts, affects, excitations, aggressions, and the like. Durkheim devotes little attention to how this balance of opposing forces is achieved, maintained, or disturbed. For both thinkers, the loss of balance has something to do with the clash between the two levels of existence under discussion.

Most important of all, both Durkheim and Freud posit the existence of a metaphysical will that has been unleashed in modern times, which is the underlying cause of what passes as the concept of "stress." Both Freud and Durkheim held a version of civilization and its discontents, and posited that the individual's will is the enemy of civilization. Curiously, both twentieth-century psychology and sociology have largely ignored these metaphysical moves, but in so doing, have been unable to explain why modernization, indeed, seems to carry a heavy cost in terms of psychic and physical health. If that were not true, the word "stress" and its consequences would not be instantly recognizable in all modern cultures.

Chapter 10

Barbarism and human agency

Intent is too intimate a thing to be more than approximately interpreted by another. It even escapes self-observation. How often we mistake the true reasons for our acts!"
(Emile Durkheim [1897] 1951: 44)

In addition to consciously intentional suicide, there is such a thing as half-intentional self-destruction (self-destruction with an unconscious intention) capable of making skillful use of a threat to life and of disguising it as a chance mishap.
(Sigmund Freud [1901] 1965: 178)

Another consequence of the doctrine of *homo duplex* to which Durkheim and Freud subscribe, and the split of the individual into a conscious and unconscious being, is that our intentions can then never be wholly our own. Freud and Durkheim cannot be made to fit the paradigm that Parsons called "rational social action," because their *fin de siècle* account of human motivation reverses completely the utilitarian assumptions that inform Parsons's work. They also challenge the emphasis on human agency by Anthony Giddens (1976b, 1987, 1990). Contrary to Parsons and Giddens, Durkheim and Freud held that part of the agent's motivational apparatus – whether one wants to admit it or not, whether one can know it or not – comes from society, while other parts come from our conscious and unconscious selves. The Schopenhauerian understanding of human motivation, to which Freud and Durkheim subscribe in large measure, holds that the "will" acts relatively independently of the intellect and our conscious reasons for our acts. Thus, this Schopenhauerian flavor in Freud's and Durkheim's thought will lead to an entirely new understanding of the relation of the intentions in explaining the motivation to engage in barbaric acts relative to contemporary understandings. Indeed, it will lead to a completely different understanding relative to some of the most cherished but unexamined values and institutions in Western societies, from law to psychiatry and medicine.

As stated earlier, Durkheim defined suicide without making direct reference to the intentions: "The term suicide is applied to all cases of death resulting directly or indirectly from a positive or negative act of the victim himself which he knows will produce this result" ([1897] 1951: 44). There are several peculiarities to this definition. One is that it is not immediately apparent how a person may know that he or she is committing suicide without intending to do so. A convenient way to account for this peculiarity is to account for unconscious intentions; thus, persons may consciously know they are killing themselves, but they may not know why, because the intention is unconscious. Durkheim (1908, [1924] 1974) subscribed to the idea of unconscious intentions, as I have already shown. But even in *Suicide*, Durkheim gives good, Schopenhauerian reasons for not pursuing explanations on the basis of intentions:

> How discover the agent's motive and whether he desired death itself when he formed his resolve or had some other purpose? Intent is too intimate a thing to be more than approximately interpreted by another. It even escapes self-observation. How often we mistake the true reasons for our acts!
>
> ([1897] 1951: 44)

By emphasizing that Durkheim believed in the unconscious, one has widened the context for interpreting his problematic definition of suicide, which is used as the basis for understanding other forms of "deviance." For Durkheim, mental and social facts may do their work while the subject is relatively unaware of them, which is something like Freud's notion that intentions within the person behave like persons – and both notions are, in turn, derived from Schopenhauer's understanding of human motivation in which the "will" acts relatively independently of the intellect.

Another peculiarity in Durkheim's treatment of suicide – the one most frequently cited – is that the individual has ostensibly little to do with his own suicide. It is true that to some extent, Durkheim absolves the individual from responsibility in his act of suicide, and places it on society:

At any given moment the moral constitution of society establishes the contingent of voluntary deaths. There is, therefore, for each people a collective force of a definite amount of energy, impelling men to self-destruction. The victim's acts which at first seem to express only his personal temperament are really the supplement and prolongation of a social condition which they express externally. It is not a mere metaphor to say of each human society that it has a greater or lesser aptitude for suicide; the expression is based on the nature of things. Each social group really has a collective inclination for the act, quite its own, and the source of all individual inclination, rather than their result . . . The private experiences usually thought to be the proximate causes of suicide have only the influence borrowed from the victim's moral predisposition, itself an echo of the moral state of society.

([1897] 1951: 299)

Durkheim seems to be substituting "social forces" for the forces that comprise Schopenhauer's "will," which Schopenhauer meant to apply to everything in the universe in any event. Durkheim's argument definitely presupposes the metaphysical assumption that society is a "will" that is much stronger than the "will" as it is objectified in individuals. But that is not the same as the oversocialized conception of the human person adopted by Parsons (1937) and criticized by Wrong (1961), because it is the irrational will that works through society, not the rational form that society takes in "normative consensus," that is the focal point in *fin de siècle* sociology.

A third peculiarity of Durkheim's treatment of suicide in relation to the intentions is that the "knowledge" of the outcome pertains to too many common phenomena to be entirely useful for the positivistic purposes of operationalizing suicide. For example, in Durkheim's view, scholars may "know" they are killing themselves, although their intentions may be the very opposite:

Suicides do not form, as might be thought, a wholly distinct group, an isolated class of monstrous phenomena ... they are merely the exaggerated form of common practices ... thus, the scholar who dies from excessive devotion to study is currently and not wholly unreasonably said to have killed himself by his labour.

(Ibid.: 46)

One of Durkheim's aims appears to be the demonstration that "there are not one but various forms of suicide" (ibid.: 277). Throughout his discourse on suicide he alternates between treating suicide as a collective versus an individual phenomenon, a unified versus multifaceted phenomenon, a phenomenon that has its own "nature" as well as many different characteristics. After suggesting that scholars, daredevils, soldiers, and slaves may all be regarded as suicides merely for doing what is normally required of them, he adds: "All such facts form a sort of embryonic suicide, and though it is not methodologically sound to confuse them with complete and full suicide, their close relation to it must not be neglected" (ibid.: 46).

Reflecting on these observations, Durkheim asks, "But is the fact thus defined of interest to the sociologist?" He does not answer directly. Durkheim apparently recognizes a great variety of acts as being suicidal, some of them being quite "normal," but he selects specific types for sociological analysis. Moreover, intentions are not important to him, presumably because sociology cannot account for intentions and because they are hidden even from the individual. For Durkheim, the essential point seems to be that suicide rates indicate some aberration in the social and individual forces that go into the will to life, the capacity for human morale.

What Durkheim and Freud have in common regarding the definition of suicide in relation to intentions is the idea that this seemingly most private of acts, suicide, is actually influenced, in varying degrees, by forces greater than the individual's consciousness. In fact, even the will acts through the individual: the will is in charge, not the individual.

For Durkheim, these forces are external to the individual as well as internal – what Wilhelm Wundt ([1886] 1902) called the opposition between the individual and social will – but he emphasizes the social forces. For Freud, some of these forces are also social, but he emphasizes the awesome power of the unconscious. This is a difference primarily in emphasis, not conceptual vocabulary. To put it another way, both thinkers seem to be treating intentions in terms of the "total social fact" that Mauss ([1950] 1979) envisaged. One of Freud's most fundamental claims is that we all carry within us secrets that are secret even from ourselves. This claim echoes Platonic concerns with the enigma of knowledge and self-knowledge, but repeated closer to our times in Schopenhauer's writings.

Even if one could convince positivists that it is possible to have unconscious intentions – that this idea is not absurd – it does not follow that suicide must be either an intentional or an unintentional act. It could still be both simultaneously. This is the quagmire, by positivistic standards, that Freud and Durkheim enter, and which makes their thought seem problematic to modernists.

FREUD'S CONCEPTION OF HUMAN AGENCY

Freud's position on human agency relative to suicide as well as other forms of deviance is similar to Durkheim's in the sense that Freud refers to a wide range of behaviors, motives, and processes, but never gives a final, explicit definition of suicide, especially not with regard to the intentions. The following passage from Freud's *The Psychopathology of Everyday Life* is pregnant with meaning in relation to this problem:

It is well known that in the severer cases of psychoneurosis instances of self-injury are occasionally found as symptoms and that in such cases suicide can never be ruled out as a possible outcome of the psychical conflict. I have now learnt and can prove from convincing examples that many apparently accidental injuries that happen to such patients are really instances of self-injury . . . Anyone who believes in the occurrence of half-intentional self-injury – if I may use a clumsy expression – will be prepared also to assume that in addition to consciously intentional suicide there is such a thing as half-intentional self-destruction (self-destruction with an unconscious intention), capable of making skillful use of a threat to life and of disguising it as a chance mishap. There is no need to think such self-destruction rare. For the trend to self-destruction is present to a certain degree in very many more human beings than those in whom it is carried out; self-injuries are as a rule a compromise between this instinct and the forces that are still working against it.

([1901] 1965: 180)

Note that Freud apparently adds another instinct to his long list, but then, I have already tried to show that he never meant to refer to biological drives in his use of instincts. He continues:

And even where suicide actually results, the inclination to suicide will have been present for a long time before in lesser strength or in the form of an unconscious and suppressed trend . . . Even a conscious intention of committing suicide chooses its time, means, and opportunity and it is in keeping with this that an unconscious intention should wait for a precipitating occasion which can take over a part of the causation and, by engaging the subject's defensive forces, can liberate the intention from their pressure.

(Ibid.: 180)

Like Durkheim, Freud blurs the concepts of "intention" and "knowledge" in this and other discussions. Like Durkheim, Freud assumes that anyone and everyone is capable of the barbaric act of suicide, and in many forms, including aggression against others. What is clear is that the intentions act as if they had a life of their own, like Durkheim's representations, and as if they possessed their own Schopenhauerian "will" apart from the human agent. The agent is more a victim of his or her intentions than their author. Both Freud and Durkheim are fond of using the word "pressure" in such discussions.

But how do these unconscious self-destructive wishes become unconscious? No doubt repression is one of many such mechanisms. For Freud, however, repression itself is partly intentional and partly unintentional. This complexity in Freud's use of the term repression has already been investigated by Theodore Mischel and others. Mischel demonstrates that Freud sometimes refers to repression as something the person willfully does, as in deliberate self-deceit, and sometimes as "something that just happens to everyone in the course of development" (1974: 225). Anyone can confirm Mischel's interpretation by referring to passages in Breuer's and Freud's *Studies on Hysteria* such as the following:

We cannot, it is true, understand how an idea can be deliberately repressed from consciousness. We have further found that there is another kind of idea that remains exempt from being worn away by thought. This may happen, not because one does not want to remember the idea but because one cannot remember it.

([1893–1895] 1974: 220)

Note that repression prevents the wearing-away processes. In a sense, a person may unwittingly contribute to the strength of his or her trauma through deliberate repression, *as well as* unintentional repression: "Repression may, without doubt, be correctly described as the intermediate stage between a defensive reflex and a condemning judgement" (Freud [1905a] 1974: 175). Reflexes are usually regarded as unintentional, but judgments are usually regarded as conscious and intentional – hence the dilemma in understanding what Freud meant.

In general, Freud subscribes to the idea that psychical processes happen to and through persons, in part. This is not so much an example of Freud's alleged "strict determinism" – it is anything but strict – as much as it is an expression of the dualisms and aspects of Schopenhauer's philosophy already discussed. That is, if a person is made up of two beings, various versions of the "will" versus the idea, then it must follow that the human person is "lived" as well as that he or she "lives." In Freud's words:

Now I think we shall gain a great deal by following the suggestions of a writer who, from personal motives, vainly asserts that he has nothing to do with the rigours of pure science. I am speaking of Georg Groddeck, who is never tired of insisting that what we call our ego behaves essentially passively in life, and that, as he expresses it, we are "lived" by unknown and uncontrollable forces ... We need feel no hesitation in finding a place for Groddeck's discovery in the structure of science.

([1923a] 1974: 23)

Any theoretical understanding of barbarism will be affected by the final interpretation that is made concerning Freud's general notion that everyone is partly "lived" – no doubt by the "will" – at the same time that one lives one's life under the apparent guidance of rational activity. For example, one is "lived" when repression happens to one, as opposed to deliberate repression. To what extent is suicide, or any other barbaric act of violence, then, something that happens to and through a person, and to what extent is it an act of will performed by a person? This is a scholar's dilemma that affects philosophical as well as empirical approaches to the problem of barbarism. Freud's struggles with this dilemma betray the influences of Plato and Schopenhauer.

Freud portrays suicide – when he refers to it tangentially – as an act that involves massive repression that is partly intentional and partly not, that joins with other psychic forces to result in an eruption of "energy" that may lead to suicide as a general resolution of conflict, which can then not be said to be entirely intentional. Unfortunately, Freud, like Durkheim, never addresses the issue of intentions and suicide directly, so that we cannot be sure that this interpretation of Freud's understanding of suicide applies to all cases of suicide nor to all cases of Freud's discussion of repression.

Nevertheless, much can be learned from examining Freud's many peripheral references to suicide in his writings. Let us seek out the Schopenhauerian aspect of some of these characterizations of suicide. For example, in his "Psychogenesis of a Case of Homosexuality in a Woman" ([1920] 1974) Freud addresses the problem of suicide extensively, though suicide is not the main subject. The patient in question attempted suicide by throwing herself off a bridge when a woman she loved rejected her. Freud comments: "In her despair at having thus lost her loved one for ever, she wanted to put an end to herself" ([1920] 1974: 162).

What appears to be an "impulsive suicide attempt" is actually a very complicated affair, however. Freud continues:

> The analysis, however, was able to disclose another and deeper interpretation behind the one she gave, which was confirmed by the evidence of her own dreams. The attempted suicide was, as might have been accepted, determined by two other motives besides the one she gave: it was the fulfillment of a punishment (self-punishment), and the fulfillment of a wish. As the latter it meant the attainment of a very wish which, when frustrated, had driven her into homosexuality –

namely, the wish to have a child by her father, for now she "fell" through her father's fault.

(Ibid.: 162)

Clearly, at least to Freud, this patient's attempted suicide was the outcome of several forces. In part, the suicidal wish took over the patient's psyche and was enacted through her because it was determined by other wishes. She is described as having limited psychic access to the wishes she enacted; they had to be re-constructed in analysis. Freud then makes this famous yet misunderstood summation:

Analysis has explained the enigma of suicide in the following way: probably no one finds the mental energy required to kill himself unless, in the first place, in doing so he is at the same time killing an object with whom he has identified himself, and, in the second place, in turning against himself a death-wish which had been directed against someone else.

(Ibid.: 162)

If one stopped reading here, one might conclude that Freud's conception of suicide is that suicide is nothing but an inverted murder. But Freud makes an important addition:

Nor need the regular discovery of these unconscious death wishes in those who have attempted suicide surprise us (any more than it ought to make us think that it confirms our deductions), since *the unconscious of all human beings is full enough of such death wishes, even against those they love.*

(Ibid.: 162; emphasis added)

Unconscious death wishes are *not* peculiar to suicides nor to homicides nor any other class of deviants. Contemporary social theories have ignored completely this affront to the Enlightenment assumption that persons are not masters in their own homes (selves). Imagine how different twentieth-century social theory would be if it had taken seriously the Freudian idea that everyone harbors death wishes – even against those that one claims to love. More importantly, these death wishes pertain to the "will," not reflective consciousness. Many persons, scholarly and otherwise, are still offended by Freud's claims that we all harbor incestuous and murderous wishes, but much of the sting of this charge dissipates when one acknowledges that properly speaking, these are the wishes of our imperious "will," not our proper, public selves. Recall that for Freud, individuals are enemies of civilization because of their aggressive, murderous and other anti-social wishes – but in a sense, the individual is actually little more than a host to the tyrannical "will." Here the importance of the wearing-away processes discussed previously becomes apparent. In those persons who do not kill themselves or others, these primary, individual trends get "used up" through a variety of means. Barbarians have the same wishes as everyone else, but their wearing-away processes may be impaired. When these intentions are not worn away, and when they join with other forces, violence is one possible outcome. Freud concludes: "Finally, the discovery that several quite different motives, all of great strength, must have co-operated to make such a deed possible is only in accordance with what we should expect" (ibid.: 163).

Elsewhere, Freud lists some of the healthy, normal ways in which our unconscious death wishes are worn away:

> The dangerous death instincts are dealt with in the individual in various ways: in part they are rendered harmless by being fused with erotic components, in part they are diverted towards the external world in the form of aggression, while to a large extent they undoubtedly continue their internal work unhindered.
>
> ([1923b] 1974: 54)

In the famous "Rat Man" case, Freud again addresses the topic of suicide, though not directly nor exclusively. The "Rat Man" often felt like slicing his throat, and Freud speculates that these suicidal wishes "arose as reactions to a tremendous feeling of rage, which were inaccessible to the patient's consciousness" ([1909a] 1974: 207). The "Rat Man's" thoughts about suicide were accessible to him, but his intentions were not, at least not in the contemporary sense found in rational social action theories. When Freud told the "Rat Man" that his hatred had been buried in his unconscious since childhood, the "Rat Man" flatly refused to believe him. Freud concluded, in spite of these denials, that, "We may regard the repression of his infantile hatred of his father as the event which brought on his . . . neurosis" (ibid.: 238).

The "Rat Man's" unconscious suicidal intentions arose in

association with the repressed hatred, and derived much of their "energy" from the pressure which resulted from the repression. This condition therefore made the "Rat Man's" life precarious, and impaired his social relations with others because of his rage.

In the famous "Case of Dora," Freud refers to several suicidal persons. Dora left a suicide note for her parents, but Freud does not take Dora's suicide intent seriously. Why? Because, Freud tells us, Dora's father once threatened suicide, and part of Dora's symptoms involved mimicking her father. Freud nevertheless refers to Dora's "purpose of self-injury" even though he does not call it suicidal. He also refers to her "craving for revenge" and her intent to frighten her father. He also refers to Dora's "compulsion to repeat" several traumas from her past through destructive behavior. Freud makes it clear that Dora was unaware of the many traumas she was repeating through her symptoms and suicide threats. Because her "excitations" had not been worn away adequately, she was not the author, in the full sense of the term, of her own self-destructive behavior:

> It is impossible to avoid the suspicion that, when the ideas attaching to certain excitations are incapable of being conscious, those excitations must act upon one another differently, run a different course, and manifest themselves differently from those other excitations which we describe as "normal" and which have ideas attaching to them of which we become conscious.
>
> ([1905b] 1974: 114)

The paragraph above links the discussion of intentions to the discussion on trauma and wearing away. Note that ideas are attached to "excitations" which have not been worn away. If some of those ideas have to do with suicide, then the patient may commit suicide not wholly because he or she really wants to, but because the suicide itself is a desperate attempt at catharsis, at wearing away traumas. Thus, for example, one may understand how Dora's suicidal tendency takes on several different forms – suicide threats, self-destructive symptoms, a craving for revenge, etc. – and stems from several different causes and various traumas. The idea of killing oneself may dissipate quickly in a "normal" person, but it may literally possess one incapable of wearing away certain "excitations."

In the *Psychopathology of Everyday Life*, Freud reviews many cases of "indirect attempts at suicide," some of them quite curious. For example, Freud discusses his little son's angry threat to kill himself, and subsequent accident, as an indirect attempt at suicide. In general, Freud holds that "suicide can never be ruled out as a possible outcome of ... psychical conflict" ([1901] 1965: 180). How are suicide and psychical conflict related? Freud explains:

> What happens is that an impulse to self-punishment, which is constantly on the watch and which normally finds expression in self-reproach or contributes to the formation of a symptom, takes ingenious advantage of an external situation that chance happens to offer, or lends assistance to that situation until the desired injurious effect is brought about. Such occurrences are by no means uncommon in cases even of moderate severity, and they betray the part which the unconscious intention plays by a number of special features – e.g. by the striking composure that the patients retain in what is supposed to be an accident.
>
> (Ibid.: 165)

Again, Freud describes wishes, desires, and intentions within the person as if they were persons with a will of their own. Freud's footnote to the above passage is also worth noting:

> In the present state of our civilization self-injury which does not have total self-destruction as its aim has no other choice whatever than to hide itself behind something accidental or to manifest itself by imitating the onset of a spontaneous illness. Formerly self-injury was a customary sign of mourning; at other periods it could express trends towards piety and renunciation of the world.
>
> (Ibid.: 165)

Accident rates are shockingly high in modern societies, although contemporary sociologists have yet to explain this phenomenon theoretically. Among young people in America especially, accidents are the leading cause of death, followed by murder and then by suicide. In general, American adolescents die from violent causes more than from so-called natural causes. Freud would no doubt argue that young Americans suffer from massive psychic traumas, and Durkheim would have concurred. In the opening chapters of *Suicide*, Durkheim ([1897] 1951) also notes that the seasonal variations of accidents follow the patterns for suicide. Why would modern persons – who are more enlightened than our ancestors and work under incomparably safer and more hygienic conditions than they did – suffer from accidents? Freud's answer is Schopenhauerian: the will uses accidents as an excuse to carry out its aggression. This explanation seems particularly relevant to the barbaric habit among American teenagers to drive while intoxicated, and usually with passengers. It is a habit that Veblen surely would have noted.

Freud makes another explicitly sociological comment on suicide in "Contributions to a Discussion on Suicide." He suggests that one way to avert student suicides is for schools to become better substitutes for the family and to arouse interest in life rather than being a game of life. Freud writes:

> If it is the case that youthful suicide occurs not only among pupils in secondary schools but also among apprentices and others, this fact does not acquit the secondary schools; it must perhaps be interpreted as meaning that as regards its pupils the secondary school takes the place of the traumas with which other adolescents meet in other walks of life.
>
> ([1910b] 1974: 231)

Freud implies that suicide is one possible outcome of psychical traumas and conflict. He continues:

> But a secondary school should achieve more than not driving its pupils to suicide. It should give them a desire to live and should offer them support and backing at a time of life at which the conditions of their development compel them to relax their ties with their parental home and their family and of arousing interest in the world outside.
>
> (Ibid.: 231)

Clearly, Freud's harsh criticism of schools and earnest plea that a substitute for the family be found is similar, in some respects, to Durkheim's conclusions in *Moral Education* ([1925] 1961) and *Suicide* ([1897] 1951). Both thinkers also share the view that the educated have higher rates of suicide than the uneducated. Moreover, the many contemporary criticisms of education and the decline of the family, by Bloom (1987) and Lasch (1977), resonate with Freud's and Durkheim's *fin de siècle* predictions.

Note the relevance of Freud's comments on schools and suicide to the present discussion on intentions: schools are a source of trauma which causes psychic conflict which in turn may result in various ideas of self-destruction and other forms of aggression, one of which is suicide. Thus, even for Freud, the intention to commit suicide may have social origins.

Still another mechanism of suicide is referred to in *Totem and Taboo*, which is replete with references to Durkheim, particularly to *Elementary Forms of the Religious Life* ([1912] 1965). Freud writes: "We find that impulses to suicide in a neurotic turn out regularly to be self-punishments for someone else's death" ([1912] 1950: 154). In this context, Freud is discussing the social phenomenon of self-sacrifice as one of suicide's many forms. For example, the celebration of the Eucharist is depicted as a re-enactment of Christ's suicide and the human being's innate propensity to murder:

> We should have to suppose that the desire to murder is actually present in the unconscious and that neither taboos nor moral prohibitions are psychologically superfluous but that on the contrary they are explained and justified by the existence of an ambivalent attitude towards the impulse to murder.
>
> (Ibid.: 70)

We see, again, that for Freud, all humans have murderous wishes, and that if these are not worn away properly, they may take their toll. Furthermore, these wishes are so powerful that the collectivity enacts prohibitions against them as well as rituals and socially approved mechanisms by which they may be enacted safely. So, for example, in the celebration of the Eucharist, an entire congregation may safely wear away its murderous, and perhaps suicidal, wishes by re-enacting the brutal murder of Christ.

Part of the murderous wishes are individual in origin, but – and this is important – part of them are collective in origin. Freud apparently believed that the original killing of the father was a collective act resulting in collective guilt, and that it was "the beginning of so many things – of social organization, of moral restrictions and of religion" (ibid.: 142). The transfer of this collective guilt from generation to generation may be explained with reference to Durkheim's notion of collective representations.[1]

THE ROLE OF HUMAN AGENCY IN AGGRESSION

Representations that have not been worn away are likely to erupt, and suicide is one form these eruptions may take, but many other forms are possible, from murder to accidents. The representations themselves have many forms: wishes, feelings, desires, intentions, memories, etc. Some of them are peculiar to individuals, and some to the fact of being human – they are collective. One of these common representations is the wish to kill, a wish that has various origins.

To some extent, these eruptions clearly happen to a person. What is not clear is the extent to which a person ought to believe that he or she is an agent, in the contemporary sense of the term, when wanting to kill self or others, since his or her intention is grounded in the histories of personal slights and collective guilt. Furthermore, the events in question may have been repressed at a time when the person was not fully aware of his or her motives nor of the problems he or she is "solving" by violence – in childhood.

The process by which the person attaches enormous intensity to seemingly trivial events in one's personal life – the alleged causes of violence – as common in symptoms as in dreams, is a process Freud likens to Nietzsche's writings by calling it a "transvaluation of psychical values" ([1900] 1965: 655). This transvaluation makes it difficult to place final accountability for any other aggressive act. The observer may be struck by the triviality of the event that seems to "cause" a person to lash out in violence. Actually, neither the agent nor the observer may be aware of the meaning of the event responsible for the emotional upheaval that led to the act. It may not be an event *per se* that is responsible for "causing" a person to act, and it may not have been the person who chose the act in the fullest sense of the term. Contrary to this common, Kantian assessment – which is every bit as subject to the charge that it is fictional as Freud's and Durkheim's accounts – Freud would have us consider a metaphysical explanation: it may be a "demonic" affect or a "demonic" intention which is, so to speak, called into action by the event. But this "demonic" aspect is nothing other than Schopenhauer's "will" that has been contaminated by "civilization" and perverted by the "pressure" which kept it from being "worn away" and "used up."

For example, Freud wrote that "hysterical people do not know what they do not want to know" ([1888] 1974: 72). This statement represents perfectly Freud's complicated position on repression and its relationship to later consequences. To what extent does a person choose not to know, and to what extent is his or her not wanting to know something that happened to that person? Freud never gives a definitive answer to this question – it seems to be a little bit of both.

In contradistinction to Bloom (1987) and many others who find little use for Freud because they assume that modern persons are less likely to engage in repression than Freud's patients, I would suggest that repression is more of a social problem in our *fin de siècle* than it was in the previous *fin de siècle*. Elias's (1982) analysis of the civilizing process leads to this conclusion, albeit indirectly, because he demonstrates that civilization entails ever-greater repression and suppression of bodily habits and processes that are deemed disgusting. Despite the facade of openness about love, sex, and their bodies, modern persons are actually quite "hung-up" about these things. For example, even Lamaze instructors note that many contemporary women choose not to breast-feed their babies, despite medical research that suggests that this is healthier for newborns than formula milk, because they regard breast-feeding as disgusting. I have encountered this attitude in discussions with my classes. Consider all the euphemisms that are used in television advertisements with regard to bodily functions, and the aversion to body odor, stained teeth, passing gas, and other bodily functions that were probably more accepted in Freud's day than our own. A strong case can be made for Freud's relevance to our times if one simply reads Elias in a Freudian context.

If one wishes to be faithful to Freud's thought, one may not claim of a suicidal or murderous person, "This person killed due to an unconscious intention." Rather, one should claim, "This person's unconscious intention to kill, itself a refraction of murderous wishes we all hold, joined with other forces, and

was magnified in strength because it was not worn away."
Otherwise, we would all be murderers and suicides because
we all have or have had such intentions in our unconscious. In
this manner, one can account for persons who unconsciously
intend to kill themselves (the intention may manifest itself in
unhealthy or self-destructive habits, for example) but whose
intention does not erupt into a recognizable suicide attempt
because other forces are not present, or because it is being
worn away to some degree of adequacy, or because it is being
cancelled out or at least held in check by other forces.

Third, even if we allow for Freud's "demonic" descriptions
of intentions, a number of things are peculiar about these
"demons." The intention to die, as it is described by Freud,
whether conscious or unconscious, does not only want to die. It
also chooses to wait for the right occasion to die. In Freud's
usage, it has become an agent. It is an agent within the agent.
And, it is a very clever "demon," because it will not press its
case regardless of obstacles. It is not a "demon" that will make
its own occasions for consummation. It does not behave as an
instinct or drive would behave in biological terms. This
"demon" behaves as persons behave. This is a sticky problem
that might be pursued at greater length by others at another
time.

The intention to kill engages the person's defensive forces,
forces that are already intent upon repression. Because of
the primacy of repression, and other defenses, the violent
act cannot be just the result of a conscious decision, nor
just the result of an unconscious decision. The violent act
does not owe the success of its project to intentions alone. So
much resistance must be overcome to kill oneself or others
that the act would not be possible without the help of an
"extra division of troops," one might say, forces that come
from massive repression and presumably other defensive processes.

Finally, the role of society and culture is always present in
Freud's explanations if for no other reason than repression.
Repression, for Freud, is primarily a representative of secondary
processes which have their origins in the environment and
society. Furthermore, some of the unconscious murderous
wishes we all hold are collective in origin.

OTHER LINKS TO DURKHEIM

Can it be claimed that what Durkheim calls "suicide" is the same phenomenon that Freud calls "suicide"? Yes and no. Their respective definitions of "suicide" are not precise enough to justify an exacting "translation." Even within the sphere of his own thought, each thinker adds many shades of meaning to "suicide." So much for the "no." The important similarity between their conceptions of suicide is that for both thinkers it is a phenomenon intimately linked to daily living, to normal processes, and above all – to Schopenhauer's "will to life." According to Durkheim, the devoted scholar knows that he or she is harming himself or herself through excessive study, and is therefore suicidal, in one sense of the term: "The scholar who dies from excessive devotion to study is currently and not wholly unreasonably said to have killed himself by his labor" ([1897] 1951: 46). For Freud, this same scholar may be working devotedly instead of slicing his or her throat. The scholar is wearing away his or her murderous wishes in a relatively constructive fashion, but he or she is committing a form of suicide nonetheless. Creation and destruction, birth and dissolution, life and death, good and evil, and pain and pleasure, are among the many pairs of opposites that play an integral role in suicide and other forms of violence in Freud's and Durkheim's social theories. Freud and Durkheim link what is highest in humans with what is lowest.

I mean that Durkheim wrote "suicide is a close kin to genuine virtues, which it simply exaggerates" ([1897] 1951: 371).[2] The courageous soldier who saves his or her comrades at the cost of his or her life may be regarded as a hero or suicide (ibid.: 45). The devoted mother who gives up most of life's joys to care for a crippled, diseased child may be regarded as saintly, suicidal, or pathological. Who will ever know what her "will" was getting out of this sacrifice? The same can be said for pious monks who literally destroy their health through self-sacrifice, disciplined athletes who reach old age unfit for the quiet life of retirement, obedient workers who sacrifice their health on the assembly lines, the mines, the skyscrapers and so on. The modern worker who retires to a life of despair and isolation after he or she has given society his or her youth and strength has committed a form of altruistic suicide with regard to contemporary society. The individual's most noble intentions and motives, which derive from the seemingly innocent will to life, are easily twisted into the lowest, darkest, most pathological motives imaginable, twisted by and *through* the individual as well as by society, and often largely unknown to both. The scholar to which Durkheim refers may begin with ardent zeal and end his or her career with the most bitter of cynicisms as the result of his unappreciated self-sacrifice. For both Freud and Durkheim, intentions and ideas beget other intentions and ideas – as representations they are capable of such Nietzschean transformations and transvaluations – and as such are relatively inessential to the act of suicide or any other violent act.

But Freud and Durkheim downplay intentions for slightly different reasons. For Freud, it appears that the extreme plasticity of intentions leads him to always seek an intention beneath an intention. For Durkheim, individual intentions are a subclass of individual representations[3] and as such are relatively insignificant when compared to collective representations. But for both Freud and Durkheim, the Schopenhauerian "will" – whether it is the "social will" or the "private will" – is far more important in explaining violence than rational, conscious intentions. To repeat, it is as if the individual and his or her body were mere hosts to the Schopenhauerian will and its derivatives: to Groddick's "it," and Nietzsche's and Freud's "id."

Philosophy is again the most important factor in Durkheim's thinking, however. We need to consider Durkheim's explanation in rejecting the idea that suicide can be defined with reference to intentions:

> An act cannot be defined by the end sought by the actor, for an identical system of behavior may be adjustable to too many different ends without altering its nature. Indeed, if the intention of self-destruction alone constituted suicide, the name suicide could not be given to facts which, despite apparent differences, are fundamentally identical with those always called suicide and which could not be otherwise described without discarding the term. The soldier facing certain death to save his regiment does not wish to die, and yet is he not as much the author of his own death as the manufacturer or merchant who kills himself to avoid bankruptcy?
>
> ([1897] 1951: 43)

This is an interesting refutation of the Kantian theory of motivation which was elaborated by Parsons into the rational social action paradigm. Contrary to Kant and Parsons, Durkheim does not feel that the actor's intentions are essential to grasping the actor's behavior. Durkheim seems to be aware that in Schopenhauerian terms, one is not really permitted to say of someone that he or she intended anything in the fullest sense of the term. The intentions are always subject to illusion and rational camouflage.

Durkheim literally does not bother with intentions, then, and concludes instead that: "The common quality of all these possible forms of supreme renunciation is that the act is performed advisedly . . . no matter what reason may have led him to act thus" ([1897] 1951: 44).

Jack Douglas (1967) and Jerry Jacobs (1980) criticize Durkheim on this issue, and claim that he never checked to see whether or not persons who committed suicide actually "intended" what the outcome would be. But they miss Durkheim's point. Durkheim does not believe the actor can tell us all that he or she knows or intends. Durkheim will deduce the actor's knowledge from other evidence – and that is very much like Freud's disregard for the patient's conscious account of his or her motives, and Freud's deductions of what he thinks the patient knows. In a sense, Durkheim is describing the human agent as watching and partially acknowledging his or her "will" in operation without being able to do much about it.

Let us return again to Jack Douglas's claim that there is the problem of relating the intentions to suicide and then the problem of determining empirically in what ways intentions are involved in suicide. These may be problems for Douglas and other neo-Kantians, but they are not problems for Durkheim. In a real sense, the human agent's intentions are not important to the act of suicide for Durkheim, and secondly, asking people what they intend does not even scratch the surface of the many representations operating upon that person – and these representations are the key issue. Similarly, when Jacobs claims that suicide results from a conscious, rational choice, that has little to do with Durkheim, whom he criticizes in this regard. Both Douglas and Jacobs appear to operating on the Enlightenment assumption that the mind is, or ought to be, in control of the passions, which is a notion that Schopenhauer had veritably destroyed.

And if the mind is not the superintendent of the self, then why should intentions to commit any act be regarded as anything more than rationalization? This was Durkheim's assessment: "Human deliberations, in fact, so far as reflective consciousness affects them are often only purely formal, with no object but confirmation of a resolve previously formed for reasons unknown to consciousness" ([1897] 1951: 297). That is an apt summary of Schopenhauer's position that humans rationalize, after the fact, what they desired in the first place.

Furthermore, what is the ultimate point, for Parsons or Douglas and the phenomenologists, of linking intentions to behavior? Such a procedure will yield one more connection in terms of space, time, and causality, but can never be regarded as anything more than an apparent certainty that can be superseded at any time. The agent's motive may not seem as certain as it once seemed. The circumstances of the event in question may be challenged with regard to space and time. Any of these changes, and others, preclude any sort of certainty in drawing conclusions about suicide or any other event. Freud and Durkheim seem to have realized the ultimate uselessness of these Kantian concerns, and chose to focus on the will, whose motives can be traced regardless of particular configurations of particular events in terms of space, time, and causality.

To pursue the differences between Freud's and Durkheim's treatment of human intentions is to downgrade their more important similarities in the context of some contemporary criticisms of both thinkers as well as the context of Schopenhauer's philosophy which informs their thought. The differences are obvious: Freud has an elaborate theory of defense mechanisms, the unconscious, and subtle workings of the mind. To accentuate these differences is to harden the existing gulf between psychology and sociology. The important similarity between the two thinkers is that Freud and Durkheim deduce the actor's state in relation to individual and collective representations as well as the individual and the collective "will."

The basic ingredients in Durkheim's social theory are egoism, anomie, altruism, and fatalism. These social currents that Durkheim invokes are *habits* or commonly accepted virtues in various societies. Everyone participates in them, and they are not unique in any way to society's deviants. Durkheim believes that egoism exhibits an affinity for anomie ([1897] 1951: 209), but that a certain amount of egoism and anomie is absolutely essential for all social life, and especially modern social life (ibid.: 321). Egoism is part of the will to life, and like Freud's concept of narcissism, is absolutely essential for survival. Egoism is excessive when the "individual ego" defies the "social ego" (ibid.: 209). Its opposite, altruism, corresponds to rudimentary individualism and when excessive, altruism also leads to suicide. But egoism and altruism also correspond to the two poles of human existence, the centripetal and the centrifugal. Thus, to say that a person's suicide or murder was altruistic is to say that one aspect of his or her humanity was under-developed at the expense of the other. Likewise for egoistic and anomic suicide. On the collective level, Durkheim claimed that ancient societies tended to produce excesses in altruism, and contemporary societies tend to produce excesses in egoism. In both cases, one of the two beings that comprise *homo duplex* is overdeveloped.

Similarly, anomie and fatalism are opposites that are concerned with passions and longings. Both "anomic suicide and egoistic suicide have kindred ties" (ibid.: 258). Similarly, altruism and fatalism share a certain excess of *contrainte* with regard to the passions. Anomie is absolutely essential to modern societies, because it entails a questioning of tradition, and without it, all semblance of progress would cease. Thus we see we have come full circle back to the "diseases of the infinite" (egoism and anomie) versus "diseases of over-regulation" (altruism and fatalism) discussed previously. To complicate matters further, Durkheim posits a kind of dualism that cross-cuts the other dualism – a chiasmus, really – such that egoism and altruism, which are opposites regarding regulation, are similar in that both pertain to the mind, whereas anomie and fatalism pertain to the passions, even though they are also opposites in some ways. To be human is to be torn between these conflicting social currents.

Let us now go back to the idea that every society must have various proportions of these currents. On the collective level, then, we have a parallel to what we have already found on the individual level – humans are torn in two. By virtue of being human, the agent is doomed to living with the constant threat of self-destruction and destruction by others. On the collective level, depending upon his or her society, he or she is more or less likely to commit suicide or murder because of society's propensity for the act. A certain amount of violence, even crime, is normal for every society, and other levels are pathological (Durkheim [1895] 1938). On the individual level, depending upon their degree of individualism, humans are more or less likely to kill because of their own propensity for the act.

For example, Durkheim held that anomie and altruism are opposites, yet they may combine forces:

> Anomie may likewise be associated with altruism. One and the same crisis may ruin a person's life, disturb the equilibrium between him and his surroundings, and, at the same time, drive his altruistic disposition to a state which incites him to suicide.
>
> ([1897] 1951: 288)

An example of this type, given by Durkheim, is the bankrupt man who loses his social position, which leads to anomie, but who cannot bear to have his name and family disgraced by bankruptcy, which is an altruistic trait. Another example is the mass suicide of the Jews when the Romans captured Jerusalem; the Jews could not bear that the Romans would disrupt their culture – cause anomie – and they loved their culture too much to allow this – altruism. Another example is the suicide of retired officers:

> If officers and non-commissioned officers readily commit suicide just when forced to retire, it is also doubtless because of the sudden change about to occur in their way of living, as well as because of their general disposition to attach little value to life. The two causes operate in the same direction. There then result suicides where either the passionate exultation or the courageous resolution of altruistic suicide blends with the exasperated infatuation produced by anomie.
>
> (Ibid.: 289)

What are the intentions of persons thus torn apart by anomie and altruism? Each of the examples above places little value on life, but for different reasons. It is not so much that they wish to end life as that they intend to exit an intolerable social situation. When life itself becomes relatively meaningless, suicide is more an escape than a true intention to die.

Thus suicide is one of many possible resolutions of the

trauma induced by the particular configuration of *homo duplex* in an agent's cultural milieu. It is not the only resolution, and its formula takes on many forms, but in general, to be human in any society is to live under the threat of destroying self or others. Note how far removed from Kant's formula is Durkheim's explanation. Instead of treating suicide as a phenomenon whose manifestation must be explained in terms of what caused it in a particular place at a particular time, Durkheim isolates specific *habits* as derivatives of *homo duplex*. These habits stem from the will, which is not mindful of space, time, or causality. For Durkheim, suicide becomes a mere exaggeration, a symptom on a phenomenal level that betrays deeper secrets about an individual and society when the sociologist analyzes the habits and virtues that comprise it. In a real sense, Durkheim posits a "depth sociology" that parallels and complements Freud's "depth psychology" (Staude 1976).

Chapter 11

Conclusions

To turn away from reality is at the same time to withdraw from the community of man.

(Sigmund Freud [1912] 1950: 74)

A man is only a man to the degree that he is civilized . . . Thus to love society is to love both something beyond us and something in ourselves.

(Emile Durkheim [1924] 1974: 55)

Having established that for both Freud and Durkheim, the will is the source of self-destruction as well as the destruction of others that might be exacerbated by general enlightenment, and that both thinkers followed the trajectory of Schopenhauer's philosophy in these regards, we are in a position to examine the rest of that trajectory. In stark contrast to Kant's vision of society dominated by dry, heartless, and supposedly rational *duty*, Schopenhauer opens the possibility that humans can be bound to each other on the basis of *desire*, including compassion, sympathy, and various derivatives of love. The imperious will is Janus-faced: evil and benign, destructive and constructive.

No doubt Freud and Durkheim, as well as Veblen, followed Schopenhauer even in this regard. Neither thinker is content to depict social order as based merely on Kantian duty and its Parsonian derivative, normative consensus. These modernist views of social order reduce society to the role of a policeman, and everyone knows that police tactics cannot maintain genuine, peaceful social order, day in and day out. Society must be cemented by habits pertaining to goodwill. And, thinkers from the previous *fin de siècle* saw the individual will as more than just the enemy of civilization. Rather, and as everyone knows, Freud posited an erotic component to social relations. But the problem is that even this insight has been distorted into an almost exclusive focus on romantic love or in general, the love of an ego for another ego or itself (see Restivo 1991). Freud's Durkheimian claim that the group is held together by love has been relatively neglected. Similarly, heaven knows that Durkheim and Veblen claim over and over again that society is held together by all sorts of love, sympathy, compassion, affection, attachment, devotion, and other derivatives of the heart as opposed to the mind. And yet, mainstream sociology makes no use of these obvious and strong aspects of Durkheim's sociology. Instead, Lukes, Giddens, Habermas, and other main-stream sociologists follow Parsons, who followed Kant, in posit-ing that social order is maintained by the mind more than the heart, and by cognitive, normative consensus. The only major twentieth-century sociologist to challenge Parsons was Pitirim Sorokin (1963), who hired Parsons at Harvard University in the first place. Sorokin (1948) claimed that humanity should turn to Christ's Sermon on the Mount to offset its barbaric ten-dencies. Yet Sorokin's legacy was eclipsed almost completely by Parsons and his disciples. The only major twentieth-century sociological tradition to challenge Parsonian assumptions was the Frankfurt School, but we have seen that its legacy has been ambiguous at best. Jürgen Habermas sees himself as the heir to the Frankfurt School tradition, but he ignores Horkheimer's Schopenhauerian bent, and seeks to complete the Enlighten-ment project. Yet the Enlightenment project may not be up to the task of containing barbarism.

This distortion and contrast between the original *fin de siècle* and contemporary versions of sociology is part of the unques-tioned domination of the Cartesian and Kantian world-view that we have been tracing throughout this book. Yet the Cartesian, Kantian, Parsonian model explains social integration and the miracle of human unity as poorly as it explains evil. If Schopenhauer is correct that the heart is stronger than the mind, then how in the world could cognitive adherence to society's rules and norms be sufficient for explaining inte-gration? Sociologists must confront Schopenhauer's question: how can Kant's duty "have the power to put bridle and bit on the impulse of strong desires, the storm of passion, and the gigantic stature of egoism?" ([1841] 1965: 62). Everybody knows the all-consuming power of human desire, for good or ill, compared with the relatively weak mental rationalizations that are used to justify moral rules. Schopenhauer concluded that only something as powerful as egoism can contain egoism, and that something is compassion, derived from the same will to life that produces egoism. Following Schopenhauer, Freud and Durkheim, as well as Simmel, Veblen, Mead and some of their other colleagues, claimed that various derivatives of empathy, not normative consensus based on rational self-interest, is the glue that holds society together.

One feels a great deal of hesitancy and something like embarrassment writing about feelings as a sociologist, particularly feelings derived from empathy. In contemporary social science, to mention love is to be met with immediate cynicism and suspicion, as if one is going to say something silly, as in love songs, or else something that belongs in cults and newfangled religions. We have stressed throughout this book that the meanings attributed to the concepts of love and compassion by sociologists from the previous *fin de siècle* should not be misconstrued as mere charity, pity, or other condescending versions of love. Rather, these thinkers were informed by Plato's and Schopenhauer's philosophical understandings of love as Eros or will. One of Freud's and Durkheim's strongest allies on the issue of love is the neglected philosopher-sociologist, Georg Simmel who, as we have noted already, proved too formidable to be assimilated by Parsons into the rational social action paradigm. In his essay "Eros, Platonic and Modern," Simmel expressed the poverty of any system that ignores love as a philosophical and sociological phenomenon. Note Simmel's explicit references to Plato and Schopenhauer in this regard:

The history of philosophy reveals the peculiar and not particularly praiseworthy fact that its claim to provide a deeper estimation of life has been left unfulfilled with respect to a number of the most important and problematic elements of life. Apart from occasional observations, philosophy has nothing to tell us about the concept of fate; nothing on the enigmatic structure of what we call "experience"; nothing, before Schopenhauer, about the deep meaning which happiness and suffering have for life insofar as this meaning is morally significant. Perhaps the most neglected of all the great vital issues has been love – as though this were an incidental matter, a mere adventure of the subjective soul, unworthy of the seriousness and rigorous objectivity of philosophical endeavor.

In reality, the preference for the problem of knowledge, which has frequently been treated in depth, over the problem of Eros betrays a certain subjectivity on the part of philosophers. For since they personally are men of a passionate drive for knowledge, but seldom of a passionate drive for love, their subjective nature is reflected in the fact that they continually make cognition the object of their thought, but most infrequently do the same for love. Were they actually to do their job properly – something for which there is still no better description than the somewhat old-fashioned expression, wisdom about life – and thus rank their labors according to the potency of life's elements, the preponderance of these labors would most surprisingly have to shift to the question of the meaning which love has for the soul, for fate, and for being.

The only one of the great philosophers who confronted this question and answered it in a profound way is Plato.

([1921] 1971: 235–36)

Simmel's sentiment is understandable in the context of Schopenhauer's philosophy, itself a refraction of Plato's philosophy: If the unleashing of the "will" has forced cognition to take a back seat to passion, then love, in all its manifestations, has to become more important than rationality for the human person, even if it is neglected by scholars. This is the deeper meaning of Freud's apparent obsession with Eros and "sexuality;" and Durkheim's strongly expressed concerns with anomie, desires, and all sorts of social attachment; and Veblen's focus on peaceable traits that he believed are remnants of an archaic, matriarchal historical tradition. Simmel's admonition to the Kantians in his day applies still to contemporary social scientists, who are still more concerned with cognitive functions than phenomena pertaining to the passionate will. And Simmel's essay on Eros may be read as a faithful refraction of Schopenhauer's influential essay, "The Metaphysics of Sexual Love" (a connection discussed in Meštrović 1991: 59–62).

The more serious sounding "sociology of emotions," as a subdiscipline in sociology, intellectualizes the power of passion and love. It is another attempt to assimilate an affront to the Enlightenment into an Enlightenment narrative. Thus, the sociology of emotions imposes the Kantian program on this most non-Kantian issue by seeking various functions for various emotions for maintaining social order, and making the same, old, tiresome connections in terms of space, time, and causality that amount to nothing but a world of contingent appearances. One learns from such research, for example, that wealthy men tend to marry beautiful women, and that beauty is "exchanged" for status (discussed by Lasch 1977). But one learns nothing about the fate of humanity on the basis of such behavioristic exchange theories, which appeal only to selfishness, not the disinterestedness that Freud and Durkheim felt were essential to understanding love.

One of the most important original concerns of the founding fathers of sociology was how it is that humans can overcome their egoism and better the life of themselves and others. So, for example, Henri de Saint-Simon described critical epochs in society as those in which "egoism dominates; [and] there exists neither conviction in, nor the love for, what one thinks might be duty or general interest" ([1828] 1972: 178). Organic epochs, on the other hand, are those in which feelings of harmony and unity with others dominate. However, Saint-Simon and his noted disciple, Auguste Comte, clung to the Enlightenment belief that organic epochs could be engineered, and mutual sympathy could be legislated in society, with the elegance and simplicity of mathematical formulas. Saint-Simon has been depicted correctly as an unwitting forerunner of fascism in these regards (Carlisle 1988). However, those who mistakenly align Durkheim with the Saint-Simonian project and fascism (Ranulf 1939) should consider Durkheim's searing critique of both Saint-Simon and Comte in *Socialism and Saint-Simon* ([1928] 1958). In sum, commensurate with the *fin de siècle* rebellion against the Enlightenment, Durkheim sought a non-engineered, anti-modernist path toward organic societies.[1]

Freud, Veblen, and Durkheim deal extensively with something that might be called love, in Simmel's sense, and with various aspects thereof: Egoism, narcissism, altruism, unity, goodwill, love of humanity, and so on. Most contemporary interpretations of these thinkers have either ignored these concerns or dismissed them as part of something dismissed as the nineteenth-century moralistic milieu. Exceptions to this rule exist, to be sure. For example, Robert N. Bellah, in an introduction to his book *Emile Durkheim on Morality and Society*, writes that there is no word in Durkheim's writings more difficult than "society" because it stands for a composite of ideas and representations as well as moral ideals: "To love one's society is to love this ideal, and one loves it so that one would rather see society disappear as a material entity than renounce the ideal which it embodies" (1973: ix).

But Bellah is an exception to the mainstream, positivistic program in sociology which leads to narcissism (see also Bellah *et al.* 1985; Lasch 1979; Riesman 1980a). Far from being just moralistic, most turn-of-the-century precursors of the modern social sciences were intent upon finding a "science of morality" as an integral part of the sociological enterprise. This phrase is an oxymoron by Kantian standards, of course. Kant taught that morality is not an empirical phenomenon, and that questions of value cannot be ascertained through science. But Schopenhauer (1841) argued against Kant that morality is as empirical as any other phenomenon in the universe, because it consists of rules constructed by humans that can be analyzed and traced to their metaphysical origins. Against Kant, and in the wake of Schopenhauer, one finds that many other serious, important, *fin de siècle* thinkers were engaged with the "science of morality" project as the underlying aim of their conversions from philosophy to the new discipline called sociology. Not since Plato's *Republic* had an entire age been so preoccupied with establishing a cultural basis for morality. This fact has been obscured by many twentieth-century social scientists, influenced as they were by a quest to make social science "value-free." We pointed out in Chapter 2 that *fin de siècle* conceptions of science were not like modernist versions of science. Thus, it is still a worthwhile project to inquire what was meant at the turn of the previous century with this curious phrase, science of morality.

In any case, Freud, Veblen, and Durkheim were no exception to the interests which dominated their times, but they offered a unique solution for establishing morality scientifically. Durkheim's (1920) quest for a "science of moral facts" was explicit. Veblen made the notion of peaceable habits a cornerstone of his overall theory, yet this aspect of his thought has been dismissed as myth (Riesman 1953). Freud was more implicit. But these thinkers wanted to establish morality on the basis of *homo duplex*, which means that utopian visions and plans for social engineering were out of the question. That is why they were all critical of Marxism, socialism, communism, capitalism, utilitarianism, pragmatism, and so many other modernist "isms" the world has accepted since their death. All these doctrines assume that consciousness, rationality, and other "higher" aspects of *homo duplex* can override the power of the will. But the thinkers that concern us followed Schopenhauer in assuming that the will was stronger than the mind, so that morality cannot be established on the basis of the mind or rationality, but on the basis of the other, benign side of the will – compassion. Even then, it must always contend with egoism and barbarism, which can never be eliminated completely, albeit they might be contained within tolerable limits. In Schopenhauer's philosophy, an irrational, imperious, egotistical will confronts an equally irrational and strong tendency of the will to renounce itself.

The functionalists have distorted Durkheim's stand on morality with the claim that conformity to social norms is automatically moral. This is but another refraction of the oversocialized conception of the human person that will not disappear no matter how little sense it makes. Durkheim realizes fully that not all societies are moral: he rivals Marx in criticizing the injustices, anomie, and various pathologies found in modern societies.[2] Hence, the dilemma: to love society is to participate in the "higher" side of being human, but what if one's society is sick? And if Durkheim truly meant that society is the "real" object to which the word "God" points, then the problem is not only how such a theological view of society can be made acceptable to sociology, but how one can appreciate Durkheim in an era in which it is as gauche to say that one believes in God as it is to say one loves one's society.

Throughout this work we have been investigating the dualisms of higher and lower, outward and inward, sacred and profane, and other derivatives of *homo duplex*. If it is the case that there are two beings in the human person, then this formula shall affect characterizations of modern barbarism. Surely one's "highest" love will always be tainted with perversion and profanity; conversely, one's "lowest" feelings of love will have something noble about them. Freud, Veblen, and Durkheim exhibit the typical *fin de siècle* awareness that love is a disintegrating as well as an integrating force. The "love of self" is particularly difficult to place in relation to these dualisms. Is narcissism sacred or profane? Questions like these must be addressed in order to understand how one is to go about coping with the tensions that these thinkers believed are inevitable as a result of human nature and the conservative drag caused by cultural habits. The uniqueness of their answers is that they call for a balance of the highest and lowest, the sacred and the profane, the two poles of *homo duplex*. All this is in keeping with Schopenhauer's focus on the unity of will and idea.

THE ANTISOCIAL NATURE OF NEUROSES

A careful reading of Freud in the context of Schopenhauer's philosophy reveals that he was mindful of love as a two-edged sword. It has the potential for disrupting social relations at the same time that it is the "glue" that holds societies together. Unlike Christopher Lasch (1991), Freud is aware that even narcissism is simultaneously a social and anti-social phenomenon. Even when the narcissistic neurotic loves his or her self to excess, he or she betrays an unconscious attachment to and love of society.

Thus, Freud introduces a section of his *Totem and Taboo* with the question: "how is it that the study of the psychology of the neuroses is important for an understanding of the growth of civilization?" ([1912] 1950: 73). This is a startling connection:

> The neuroses exhibit on the one hand striking and far-reaching points of agreement with those great social institutions, art, religion and philosophy. But on the other hand they seem like distortions of them. It might be maintained that a case of hysteria is a caricature of a work of art, that an obsessional neurosis is a caricature of a religion and that a paranoic delusion is a caricature of a philosophical system. The divergence resolves itself ultimately into the fact that the neuroses are social structures; they endeavour to achieve by private means what is effected in society by collective effort.
>
> (Ibid.: 73)

Though neuroses are "social structures" for Freud, their nature and aim are anti-social:

> The asocial nature of neuroses has its genetic origin in their most fundamental purpose, which is to take flight from an unsatisfying reality ... The real world, which is avoided in this way by neurotics, is under the sway of human society and of the institutions collectively created by it. To turn away from reality is at the same time to withdraw from the community of man.
>
> (Ibid.: 74)

It is by no means obvious that "reality" has to be social. The neurotic's personal problems, his or her biological urges, the truth of what he or she is repressing, etc., may all be regarded as "realities." For Freud, however, the "real world" is the social world. In the context of the dualism we have been discussing, one may understand Freud as claiming that to become neurotic is to give in to the inward, centripetal force, the individual being of *homo duplex*. "Reality" in Freud's usage apparently stands for the "higher" aspects of humanity, although he is as aware as Durkheim of perverted, sick societies. This move by Freud is essentially like Durkheim's formulation. But because the human person is by nature two beings, when he or she gives in to one being, in this case to the asocial, his or her very asocial acts are tainted with the social. Humans caricature the social – despite themselves – even as they attempt to escape it. And vice versa. Thus dualism of human nature is implied in Freud's thoughts on the social–asocial aspects of neuroses.

Freud's assumption that the neuroses are asocial is not confined to *Totem and Taboo*. For example, in *Obsessive Acts and Religious Practices*, Freud writes:

> An obsessional neurosis furnishes a tragicomic travesty of a private religion ... In view of these resemblances and analogies one might venture to regard the obsessional neurosis as a pathological counterpart to the formation of a religion, to describe the neurosis as a private religious system, and religion as a universal obsessional neurosis.
>
> ([1907a] 1974: 119)

Merging Freud's and Durkheim's vocabularies, one may paraphrase the above to the effect that the individual feels a compulsion to repeat collective representations individually to compensate for the "higher" being that is being denied in neurosis. *Homo duplex* demands that both poles be involved simultaneously in all human action. The particular significance of religion and the feelings it creates in individuals is that it is a representation of society. For both Freud and Durkheim, this feeling is inescapable.

Another interesting passage in the context of religion and the neuroses is the following from *Five Lectures on Psychoanalysis*; Freud writes: "To-day neurosis takes the place of the monasteries which used to be the refuge of all whom life had disappointed or who felt too weak to face it" ([1910a] 1974: 50). Mizruchi (1983) has taken this insight far in his analysis of the role of monasteries in Medieval Europe. Does this mean that neurosis recreates what society creates for its members who cannot or will not be social? Or does it mean that modern humans no longer resort to monasteries as forms of asylum for the asocial being in themselves, and so they individually repeat what is collective by becoming ill?

In *Group Psychology and the Analysis of the Ego*, we find similar claims with a slightly different bent:

A neurosis should make its victim asocial and should remove him from the usual group formations. It may be said that *a neurosis has the same disintegrating effect upon a group as being in love.* On the other hand it appears that where a powerful impetus has been given to group formation neuroses may diminish and, at all events temporarily, disappear . . . Even those who do not regret the disappearance of religious illusions from the civilized world of today will admit that so long as they were in force they offered those who were bound by them the most powerful protection against the danger of neurosis . . . If he is left to himself, a neurotic is obliged to replace by his own symptom formations the great group formations from which he is excluded. He creates his own world of imagination for himself, his own religion, his own system of delusions, and thus recapitulates the institutions of humanity in a distorted way.

([1921] 1961: 74; emphasis added)

Freud pursues this theme in his "Preface to Reik's Ritual: Psychoanalytic Studies":

Thus hysterics are undoubtedly imaginative artists, even if they express their phantasies mimetically in the main and without considering their intelligibility to other people; the ceremonials and prohibitions of obsessional neurotics drive us to suppose that they have created a private religion of their own; and the delusions of paranoics have an unpalatable external similarity and internal kinship to the systems of our philosophers. It is impossible to escape the conclusion that these patients are, in an asocial fashion, making the very attempts at solving their conflicts and appeasing their pressing needs which, when they are carried out in a fashion that has binding force for the majority, go by the names of poetry, religion, and philosophy.

([1919] 1974: 265)

Recall that for Durkheim, too, society is the "higher" reality compared to the individual, and therefore anomie and egoism are contrary to what is "highest." But even when a person turns away from this "higher" reality, it haunts him or her. It cannot be escaped or shunned – it expresses itself through the person. Durkheim writes in *Suicide*:

However individualized a man may be, there is always something collective remaining – the very depression and melancholy resulting from this same exaggerated individualism. He effects communion through sadness when he no longer has anything else with which to achieve it.

([1897] 1951: 214)

EMOTIONAL TIES AND LIVING IN SOCIETY

In *Group Psychology and the Analysis of the Ego*, one finds the famous reference to libido that the Frankfurt School incorporated into their otherwise Marxist analyses of social conflict. Freud writes:

Libido is an expression taken from the theory of the emotions. We call by that name the energy . . . of those instincts which have to do with all that may be comprised under the word "love."

([1921] 1961: 29)

For Freud, libido is the "energy" of Eros and the life instincts.

Love will prove to have something to do with the binding functions of Eros. Freud continues:

> The nucleus of what we mean by love naturally consists . . . in sexual love with sexual union as its aim. But we do not separate from this – what in any case has a share in the name "love" – on the one hand, self-love, and on the other, love for parents and children, friendship, and love for humanity in general, and also devotion to concrete objects and to abstract ideas.
>
> (Ibid.: 29)

That is probably one of the more problematic passages Freud has ever written. Generally, persons have difficulty believing that the manner in which they love their sexual partners has something in common with the manner in which they love humanity or their children (if they do at all). Apparently, these kinds of love are the "extended use of sexuality" borrowed from Plato, and discussed previously. Freud's passage seems to be another refraction of Schopenhauer's claim that all forms of desire are ultimately reducible to the will, which in turn finds its strongest expression in sexual desire. In invoking this most non-Kantian understanding of love, Freud knew that

> Psychoanalysis has let loose a storm of indignation, as though it had been guilty of an act of outrageous innovation. Yet it has done nothing original in taking love in this "wider" sense. In its origin, function, and relation to sexual love, the Eros of the philosopher Plato coincides exactly with the love-force, the libido of psychoanalysis . . . and when the apostle Paul, in his famous epistle to the Corinthians, praises love above all else, he certainly understands it in the same "wider" sense. But this only shows that men do not always take their great thinkers seriously, even when they profess most to admire them.
>
> (Ibid.: 30)

Having shown, to his satisfaction, that "love" works in the service of Eros in relation to individuals, Freud turns to the group:

> We will try our fortune, then, with the supposition that love relationships (or, to use a more neutral expression, emotional ties) also constitute the essence of the group mind . . . A

group is clearly held together by a power of some kind: and to what power could this feat be better ascribed than to Eros, which holds together everything in the world?

(Ibid.: 31)

One can think of all sorts of alternatives to the power of Eros: Kant's duty, Parsons's normative consensus, and various forms of social integration based on the internalization of norms. But notice how far off the mark Parsons was in trying to assimilate Freud into his rational social action paradigm. In addition, Freud's claim above needs to be compared and contrasted with his claims in *Civilization and its Discontents* ([1930] 1961) that civilization is founded upon love. But in that same work he also depicted love as a threat to civilization.

One problem is that it is not immediately apparent whether the destructive aspect of "love" also comes from Eros – which is supposed to be the "binding" and "higher" force – or whether there is a "love" on the side of Eros as well as a "love" on the side of the death instincts. If the former is true, then groups will be held together by positive emotions as well as by destructive ones: suspiciousness, mistrust, and various other shades of enmity. This is something like Simmel's (1971) idea that conflict may unify groups. On the other hand, if the latter is true, then a group will be held together by friendship, goodwill, and any discord will be explained as due to the human being's individual, selfish, centripetal tendencies. A program of social reform based on the former would be cynical about really reforming the human animal. A program based on the latter would attempt at all costs to eradicate individuality, greed, passions, etc. As noted by many commentators, the latter program resembles Marxism, and lends itself easily to totalitarianism.

Jean Laplanche has isolated a portion of this particular problem in *Life and Death in Psychoanalysis* (1976). The problem is: Does Eros have an energy separate from the death instincts, or are both forces "energized" by libido? This is somewhat similar to the problem of whether Schopenhauer's compassionate will is distinct from "bad will," or whether evil is a perversion of the same "will to life" that can be constructive. Laplanche opts for the latter interpretation, presenting us with a dualism within a dualism, or as he calls it, a chiasmus. In other words, the energy associated with Eros (libido) is itself dualistic.

What is clear is that according to Freud, to love is a perilous undertaking. So, for example, in one of his characteristic jabs at Marx, Freud claims that "it is always possible to bind together a considerable number of people in love, so long as there are other people left over to receive the manifestations of their aggressiveness" ([1930] 1961: 114). The human animal's "higher" side is always accompanied by his or her "lower side." There will never be a utopia of social integration based on friendship and love. Freud gives many examples of this phenomenon: Religions typically teach that their members should love some of their neighbors even though they wage "holy wars" and breed enmity against other religions and sometimes whole peoples. A nation may appear to be very peace-loving until one examines its relations with neighboring nations, and its subgroups that it regards as deviant. In general, I believe that Freud leans toward the view that Eros fuels the higher and lower forms of love.

Apart from psychosis, Freud claims that "ego-libido" and "object-libido" are always at war in each other: "The more one is employed the more the other becomes depleted" ([1914a] 1963: 70). It is not clear if these are two types of libido since in 1914, when the essay was written, Freud distinguished between the ego-instincts and the sexual instincts, not Eros and the death instincts. Psychoanalysts are apparently baffled by these two types of libido (see Laplanche and Pontalis 1973: 255–7).

But for the purposes of this analysis, it is significant that the person's emotions of love are torn between the inward and the outward. For Freud, love is always ambivalent ([1915c] 1974: 240). And depending upon which aspect of love is favored, the inward or the outward, the consequences vary. When libido is withdrawn from the world, it is "dammed up" ([1914a] 1974: 76) and the effect is similar to the "damming up" of excitations, aggressiveness, and other "instincts" – mortification ensues and the person is not healthy. It is therefore necessary for the person to direct love outward – toward other people, one's nation, up to and including humanity – so as to avoid this damming up: "At this point we may even venture to touch on the question: whence does that necessity arise that urges our mental life to pass on beyond the limits of narcissism and to attach the libido to objects?" ([1914a] 1974: 76).

Freud's reply is that a strong egoism is a protection against disease, but in the last resort, one must begin to love in order that one may not fall ill, and must fall ill, if, in consequence of frustration, one cannot love. If one fails to love in the outward direction, the libido is dammed up and mortification ensues. Egoism is a protection against disease, because trauma is least likely to occur when the ego automatically binds "excitations." But if the ego binds the excitations too well, then they build up a tension, and so persons must love others in order to "work over" the tensions: "The working over of stimuli in the mind accomplishes wonders for the internal discharge of excitations which are incapable of direct discharge outwards" (ibid). The dualism of human nature we have been discussing is implicit here. Extreme love of self and extreme selfless love are both unhealthy. The two must somehow be balanced, but the resulting equilibrium will always be temporary. Freud does not promise one a rose garden.

It is evident that a careful reading of Freud in the context of the *fin de siècle* spirit cannot lead to the conservative conclusions drawn by Lasch, Bloom, and Bellah – among others – that humanity must somehow return to a primitive sort of tribalism in order to combat the narcissism that accompanies the modernist project. If one takes Freud seriously, one would conclude that primitive societies had their mixtures of love and hate, even if their proportions of these basic ingredients are not the same as ours. And in Freud's sociology, one will not find the modernist or postmodernist promises of liberty, justice, and charity based on careful social engineering. One will find, instead, a resolution to move into the future with the pessimistic knowledge that the contradictions of the human condition will never be resolved completely. This is the pessimistic humanism to which Horkheimer referred, and which apparently proved to be more correct than the Marxist assumptions that Freud criticized, and that have fallen into disrepute in our *fin de siècle*.

LIVING A VIRTUOUS LIFE IN A BARBARIC SOCIETY

As with Freud, a careful reading of Durkheim fails to support the naive felicity concerning social order and social integration that is found in functionalism and functionalist misreadings of Durkheim. It is true that in *The Division of Labor* Durkheim writes:

A group is not only a moral authority which dominates the life of its members; it is also a source of life *sui generis*. From it comes a warmth which animates its members, making them intensely human, destroying their egotisms.

([1893] 1933: 26)

Clearly, Durkheim regards egotism as something harmful for the individual and the group. On the other hand, we have seen that he also regards a certain amount of it as absolutely necessary for social life, much like Freud argued that primary narcissism is essential in order to live. Even though morality, as one of the "higher" aspects of the human animal, belongs to society, morality, in part, bids the person to engage in self-interest: "Morality, in all its forms, is never met with except in society" but "the duties of the individual towards himself, are, in reality, duties towards society" (Durkheim, [1925] 1961: 399). Elsewhere, he asserts that "morality begins at the same point at which disinterestedness and devotion also begin" ([1924] 1974: 52), which was Schopenhauer's starting premise as well.

It is easy to see how the functionalists might have misinterpreted Durkheim as implying the oversocialized conception of the human person if they read passages like the one above out of context. But Durkheim's context is that he had to choose between Kant and Schopenhauer. Kant argued that egoism is the source of all wickedness, and advocated a moral life based on duty and obedience to the dictates of some *a priori* categorical imperative that is exempt from empirical analysis. Schopenhauer agreed that egoism is the root of evil, but he cynically caught Kant in a trap from which there is no apparent exit: mere obedience to rules is still egoism, because the individual is acting morally in order to avoid the pangs of conscience, punishment, or some other external threat. The key point is that Kant's ideal type of the moral person is not motivated by a desire to be moral for its own sake, out of disinterested love. Durkheim ([1925] 1961) must have been aware of this polemic between Kant and Schopenhauer, for he steered a middle course between them: He found, on empirical grounds, that humans do construct rules and duties to which they attach synthetic powers of sanction. But like Schopenhauer, he argued steadfastly that the moral person must be motivated by a sincere desire to relieve the suffering of others, and that this desire must not be egotistical. He argued further that society has a dual role: as a kind of policeman that controls as well as a magnet that draws out benign, moral desires in society's members (see also Bouglé 1926; Hall 1987). Elsewhere, and in remarkably Jungian terms, Durkheim depicted society metaphorically as both mother and father:

> What is discipline, in fact, if not society conceived of as that which commands us, which dictates to us, which hands on its laws to us? As for the second element, the attachment to the group, it is again society that we discover, but conceived this time as a thing desirable and good, such as a goal which attracts us, an ideal to be realized. On the one hand, it seems to us an authority that constrains us, fixes limits for us, blocks us when we would trespass, and to which we defer with a feeling of religious respect. On the other hand, society is the benevolent and protecting power, *the nourishing mother* from which we gain the whole of our moral and intellectual substance and toward whom our wills turn in a spirit of love and gratitude.
>
> ([1925] 1961: 92; emphasis added)

Thus, according to Durkheim, and in contradistinction to Kant, "it is psychologically impossible to pursue an end to which we are indifferent – i.e. that does not appear to us as *good* and does not affect our sensibility. Morality must, then, be not only obligatory but also desirable and desired" ([1924] 1974: 45).

Schopenhauer wrote about a sense of divine justice that operates in the world by which egoism and its resultant immorality are seemingly punished through suffering. Philosophers argue among themselves how they should make sense of these claims (see Cartwright 1988b). But for our purposes, let us note that Durkheim seems to be following Schopenhauer's metaphysics in his overall theory of "deviance." Why immorality – an overly self-centered life – should bring eventual heavy penalties to the individual as well as to society is not clear. What is clear is that Durkheim makes this explicit: "The average number of suicides, of crimes of all sorts, can effectively serve to mark the intensity of immorality in a given society" ([1925] 1961: 50).

In the modern world-view, one is much more used to the notion that immorality is the mere transgression of norms, which has no consequences if it goes undetected and unpunished. But if we remember that morality for Durkheim pertains to the proper balance of egoism and altruism (and the other social currents), then we shall get more out of him than the view that Durkheim is giving a sermon. There can be little doubt that postmodern America in particular, held up by Baudrillard as the model of the postmodern future, is drowning in crime and various symptoms of anomie.

In *Sociology and Philosophy*, in particular, Durkheim makes it clear that the "moral" attachment to groups is not an abstract act, as it is for Kant and Parsons, and it does not pertain to one's specific milieu: "Attachment to a group implies a necessary, if indirect, attachment to individuals . . . When one loves one's country or humanity one cannot see one's fellows suffer without suffering oneself and without feeling a desire to help them" ([1924] 1974: 53).

Here, as elsewhere in his writings, Durkheim uses "attachment" and "love" interchangeably. Durkheim's statement above can be likened to Freud's perplexing passage that love of self, friends, parents, society, and humanity are all in the "higher" service of Eros. For Durkheim, the love of others, for one's country, and humanity are all aimed toward the "higher" service of morality.

This is a side of Durkheim that does not come out in contemporary interpretations of him, and it has significant consequences. For suppose that the society one loves has norms that make some humans suffer or are otherwise unjust. In other words, suppose that one lives in a barbaric culture, even if that culture denies its barbarism. Then clearly one's love of humanity – one cannot see one's fellows suffer without suffering oneself – will be in conflict with one's love of one's immediate society, even though both are or should be, *ideally*, in the service of humanity. Simple "normative" attachment to a group, which is how Durkheim is typically misinterpreted by the functionalists, does not touch upon this dilemma. Let us follow Durkheim's struggles with this important dilemma.

First, one must dispel further the erroneous notion that Durkheim was a disciple of Kant, promulgated by La Capra (1972), Lukes (1985), and other contemporary interpreters. Durkheim criticizes Kant explicitly, and often:

Duty, the Kantian Imperative, is only one abstract aspect of moral reality. In fact, moral reality always presents simultaneously these two aspects which cannot, in fact, be isolated. No act has ever been performed as a result of duty alone; it has always been necessary for it to appear in some respect as good. Inversely there is no act that is purely desirable, since all call for some effort.

([1924] 1974: 45)

Durkheim adds that "Kant's hypothesis, according to which the sentiment of obligation was due to the heterogeneity of reason and sensibility, is not easy to reconcile with the fact that moral ends are in one aspect objects of desire" (ibid.: 46). Overall, Durkheim felt that his sociological account of morality was a departure from "Kantian *a priorism*, which gives a fairly faithful analysis of the nature of morality but which describes more than it explains" (ibid.: 62).

Second, because of the dualism of human nature, the human being's moral obligations must be finely tuned to fulfill the higher as well as the lower demands. In *Moral Education*, Durkheim writes:

Man has an obligation to live, but I say that he does not fulfill a duty, through the sole act of survival, except when life is for him a means of achieving an end that transcends his own life. There is nothing moral in living just for the sake of keeping alive.

([1925] 1961: 57)

Conversely, it is clear from the previous discussions that there is also nothing moral about living just for the sake of society. Durkheim is highly critical of extreme altruism and its complete disdain for the individual. Humanity and civilization ultimately transcend the individual, and the fulfillment of those goals implies a balance of devotion to oneself as well as to others.

In recent years, we have heard much about the debates concerning "value-free science," with one side claiming that science must not be prejudiced by values and the other that scientists totally without values are monsters. For Durkheim, the moral ends which he describes are not inherent in science; they must be consciously brought to the enterprise of science. To put it another way, science must be attached synthetically to morality. He writes:

The search for truth is not itself a moral occupation; all depends upon the reason for which it is sought. It is only really and fully moral when science is revered for its beneficial effects upon society and humanity. On the other hand, the mental process involved in the self-sacrifice of the scientist impassioned by his work resembles so closely those involved in true moral self-sacrifice that it must to a certain extent participate in the feelings which the latter inspire. It is tinged with morality.

([1924] 1974: 53)

One is reminded here of Durkheim's claim that suicide is akin to the virtues, which it exaggerates, mentioned previously. The devoted scientist is participating in a suicide of sorts, but it is a moral sort of "suicide" or self-sacrifice. For Durkheim, motives and feelings are clearly never pure, but they are essential for judging the moral worth of an act. In this regard as well, Durkheim follows Schopenhauer and departs from Kant, for whom duty takes precedence over motive.

Yet the problem remains: the society that is loved when one is "moral" may itself be corrupt, pathological, and barbaric. How is it that one is supposed to love in a "higher" way what is "low"? Should one simply conform to any society, even an unjust one? Durkheim's reply involves a distinction between collective representations *in* versus *by* society: "The society that morality bids us desire is not the society as it appears to itself, but the society as it is or is really becoming" ([1924] 1974: 38).

The society that really "is," exists metaphysically as a Platonic Idea. It is this metaphysically pure society that is loved when one is moral. The society as it appears to itself presumably consists of social facts of the second order, and this society may be pathological. Thus, "It is the 'true' nature of society that is conformed to when the traditional morality is obeyed, and yet it is also the true nature of society which is being conformed to when the same morality is flouted" (ibid.: 65).

This passage touches upon one of Durkheim's most re-markable complexities in thought, namely, that a society's apparent "norms" may not be its actual norms. To love society is not the same thing as slavish conformity to its apparent norms that are perceived from a Kantian perspective, nor is it impetuous rebellion against those norms. It is, rather, a

Schopenhauerian and metaphysical, carefully balanced attempt to respect norms coupled with a love of humanity that may or may not be in keeping with the norms of one's immediate society in its particular phase of development.

Durkheim's major interpreters in this century bypass completely the metaphysics in Durkheim's depiction of morality and love of ideal society. For them, there is no distinction between apparent norms and pure, Platonic norms, because they work from the Kantian perspective in which the social world consists only of appearances. But, not only is their interpretation unfair to Durkheim's intentions, it leads to the unwelcome conclusion that the good citizen must dutifully obey a society even when it imposes inhumane norms upon its members. Jean Piaget is a prominent interpreter of Durkheim who at least noticed this metaphysical aspect in Durkheim's thought, even though he eventually took the Kantian road in this and other regards. According to Piaget:

> One must make one's choice between these two solutions . . . for either society is one, and all social processes, including cooperation, are to be assimilated to pure constraint alone, in which case right is bound to be determined by public opinion and traditional use; or else, a distinction must be made between actual and ideal society . . . [But] how, we would ask, is it possible to distinguish between society as it is and society as it is tending to become?
>
> ([1932] 1965: 346)

We agree with Piaget that this choice is crucial. But we have demonstrated that for Durkheim, because of *homo duplex*, society is not one, and public opinion does not constitute society. Hence, a distinction must be made between actual and ideal society, or in Durkheim's words, "what we have to discover is society as it is, not society as it sees itself, which may produce an erroneous picture" ([1924] 1974: 63). He adds that "the role of science does not stop at throwing a little more light upon the tendencies of public opinion, for the primary object of its investigations is the condition of the society and not that of social opinion" (ibid.: 64). As to how it is possible to make this distinction, a ready reply lies in Schopenhauer's philosophy and in Durkheim's conviction that ideally, modern societies are tending toward a greater respect for the dignity of the human person, what he called the cult of the individual. Any apparent norms that suppress the individual's rights and dignity, that are not mindful of "the characteristic sacredness with which the human being is now invested" (ibid.: 58), are immoral in a modern society, even if they would have been moral in a "primitive" society that is dominated by altruistic and fatalistic currents.

We thus arrive at a conclusion that is surprising in relation to the oversocialized conception of the human person that is wrongly attributed to Durkheim. Despite or because of his Platonic assumptions, he was a metaphysical liberal, and a champion of individual rights. His sociology allows one to criticize any assimilatory tendencies toward rational social order if these trends oppress the individual.

MORE ON THE PLATONIC ELEMENT IN DURKHEIM'S AND FREUD'S SOCIOLOGIES OF EMOTION

As indicated previously, it is not our intention to demonstrate that Freud and Durkheim actually, "objectively" (whatever that could mean) show Platonic elements in their thinking. One reason for this hesitancy is that Platonic scholars themselves are not in complete agreement about Plato. Rather, one wishes to show that Durkheim and Freud contrast and compare themselves with Plato directly, on many issues, and in particular on what is here being called the sociology of emotions. And these self-conscious allusions to Plato expose the metaphysical element in their thinking that cannot be assimilated into positivistic and neo-Kantian narratives. Finally, in their self-conscious search for Plato's pure Ideas, they were either refracting or acting parallel to Schopenhauer's equally self-conscious attempt to use Plato's metaphysics as an antidote to the Kantian conclusion that the world is merely a mass of contingent appearances.

The best evidence for this, relative to Durkheim, and apart from his *Sociology and Philosophy*, can be found in the neglected work *Socialism and Saint-Simon*, published in 1928. It is not only the case that Durkheim hails Saint-Simon as the father of positivism and the father of sociology, specifically reducing Comte to the status of heir of Saint-Simon ([1928] 1958: 104). In addition, he discusses the doctrine of Saint-Simon specifically in the context of Plato's metaphysics. Durkheim glides easily over the distinction between "state" and "society" as used by Plato, because for him both represent the "sacred." The Platonic context is important in understanding Durkheim's criticism of Saint-Simon and all subsequent derivatives of Enlightenment attempts at social engineering, that they wanted to get the most from the least, the superior from the inferior, moral rule from economic matter ([1928] 1958: 240).

According to Durkheim, Saint-Simon and all subsequent systems of socialism as well as capitalism wanted to establish morality on the basis of enlightened self-interest – on selfishness. For Durkheim, as for Schopenhauer, it is impossible to derive morality from self-interest, because morality involves disinterestedness. Durkheim does not state explicitly why this is impossible, because this is a basic, philosophical premise in his thinking, not subject to proof in his opinion. The only support for his position is found in his continual agreement with Plato's sharp differentiation between the sacred and the profane – Durkheim also perceived these as eternally separate. In Chapter 12, Durkheim places moral movements, including religious movements, with the sacred, and economic intellectual movements, including socialism and capitalism, with the profane, because they involve pecuniary self-interest. He then castigates the Marxists and other revolutionary movements:

> What do the neo-religious and socialist movements indicate? It is that if science is a means, it is not an end, and as the goal to be achieved is distant, science cannot reach it except slowly, and laboriously, whereas emotional and zealous beings attempt to lay hold of it instantly. Without waiting for scholars to sufficiently advance their research, they undertake to discover the remedy by instinct, and nothing would be more natural than to convert this method into a unique procedure and exaggerate its importance by denying science. Besides, the latter has much to learn from this two-sided movement which expresses two different aspects of our present state, one considering things from a moral view, the other, in their economic aspect.
>
> ([1928] 1958: 239)

This passage suggests that Durkheim was a new sort of liberal, one that approached economics in a Platonic manner, as the realm of the profane:

What gives strength to the first movement is the feeling that we must believe in an authority which controls passions, makes egoism bend to its domination, and which will require a religion – without its being seen just how it can be constituted. And what gives power to the second is that the condition of moral disorder has economic results which it places in relief.

(Ibid.)

Durkheim praises Saint-Simon for attempting to find the underlying unity between these two opposing forces, the moral and the economic. But ultimately, he regards Saint-Simonianism as a failure. Saint-Simon, according to Durkheim, tipped the balance between these two antagonistic forces in the direction of economics. Let us note that Durkheim's solution to this problem is in line with the preceding discussion, to keep the sacred and the profane distinct as two poles of *homo duplex*, and to envision morality as strictly sacred: "The problem must be put this way: to discover through science the moral restraint which can regulate economic life, and by this regulation control selfishness and thus gratify needs" ([1928] 1958: 240).

Thus the dualism of human nature, which Durkheim links to Plato, is the essential point in his analysis of the significance of the doctrine of Saint-Simon. Durkheim ends the book on this same page, in his consistently anti-climactic style of ending a work.

Freud claims that his use of libido is "exactly" like Plato's use of Eros. One of the more troubling aspects of Freud's thought is that all love has a sensual base. To love one's friends, one's mother, and on to humanity, is to love erotically, in part. This is a highly offensive idea to some. "Aim-inhibited" love is the basis for social ties in Freud's thought, but "love with an inhibited aim was in fact originally fully sensual love, and it is so still in man's unconscious" ([1930] 1961: 102). Offensive or not, the concept may be said to be faithful to Plato's portrait of love in *Symposium*. What is more, Freud was aware that this is the case:

What psychoanalysis called sexuality was by no means identical with the impulsion towards a union of the two sexes or towards producing a pleasurable sensation in the genitals; it had far more resemblance to the all inclusive and all preserving Eros of Plato's *Symposium*.

([1925] 1974: 214)

As for the charge that Freud's early writings do not share this Platonic element, one has to reckon with Freud's claim in *An Autobiographical Study*: "Nor was I then aware that in deriving hysteria from sexuality I was going back to the very beginnings of medicine and following up a thought of Plato's" ([1925] 1959: 24).

Even if Freud was not aware in the 1890s that he was following up Plato's thoughts, his extended use of "love" bears witness to the truth of such a comparison. Apparently, Freud realized what path he was on in 1905, writing in *Three Essays on Sexuality*: "How closely the enlarged sexuality of psychoanalysis coincides with the Eros of the divine Plato" ([1905a] 1974: 134). Plato's Eros is destructive and constructive (as is the case with Freud's usage of this concept) and it includes forms of love ranging from the most egotistical to the most altruistic.

Finally, Plato realized that the lofty, transcendent love of truth, humanity and what is regarded most highly by humankind can itself become grotesque and miscarry. In *Phaedon*, Plato makes shocking statements to the effect that "the life which philosophers desire is in reality death" and that "the true philosophers . . . are always occupied in the practice of dying" (a line that Schopenhauer was fond of quoting). This is because death is the ultimate release from egoism, from the confines of the body, and the true philosopher is always seeking to overcome egoism. The only reason the philosopher does not take his or her own life is that it belongs to the gods and the community. But he is of good cheer when he is about to die. There is a fine line between this noble acceptance of death and a perverse longing to be rid of the distractions of living. Egoism and altruism are linked intimately. The philosopher must seek a mean between these two extremes. In the language of Durkheim, a state of equilibrium between two antagonistic forces must be found. In the language of Freud, one must manage one's libido in such a way that it is not all "dammed up" but also not all depleted.

VEBLEN ON CHRISTIAN MORALS

Not only Freud and Durkheim, but many of their *fin de siècle* colleagues in sociology turned to the Platonic elements in Christian dogma in their search for repositories of Western

wisdom on self-abnegation that might offset the barbaric representations that flow from unrestricted egoism. Veblen was
another such thinker. This strategy is completely different from
Marxist, Enlightenment, or other value-free attempts to establish morality and social order on an exclusively scientific plane.
It is also different from theology in that religious beliefs are
treated as cultural artifacts, not divinely inspired truths.

Veblen was consistently critical of Christianity when it reduced itself to an appendix to the leisure class. Riesman
summarizes well Veblen's feeling that Christianity is "a patri-
archal religion of futile subservience to extravagant earthly
representations of a leisure-laden heavenly hierarchy" (1953:
66). But in his 1910 essay entitled "Christian Morals and the
Competitive System" especially (and less clearly elsewhere),
Veblen ([1910] 1943) isolates and praises ideal Christian
morality as an important habit in Western culture. Christianity
teaches brotherly love, self-abnegation, and humility, the habits
that Durkheim subsumes under altruism and asceticism, the
essential elements of any system of morality that leads to non-
oppressive social solidarity. But "Western civilization is both
Christian and competitive (pecuniary)" according to Veblen
([1910] 1943: 200), so that if these two tendencies seem
contradictory, "the student of this culture might have to face
the question: Will Western civilization dwindle and decay if
one or the other, the morals of competition or the morals of
Christianity fall into abeyance?" Veblen's approach is essentially a refraction of Durkheim's discovery of the coexistence of
altruism and egoism as part of *homo duplex*.

Let us try to answer Veblen's question from the perspective of
our *fin de siècle*. It would seem that the morals of competition
have become stronger than they were in the previous *fin de
siècle*, and that the morals of Christianity – as he understood
them – are weaker than ever. Perhaps the postmodernist claims
that humanity is witnessing the end of history and the end of
Enlightenment narratives constitute more than hyperbole.
However, like Durkheim but unlike the Marxists, Veblen does
not seek to supplant barbaric habits with socially engineered
derivatives of Christian self-abnegation. Rather, he sought to
offset barbaric egoism with what he considered archaic self-
abnegation.

Veblen locates the origins of Christianity in the late Roman period, those of competitive morals to the principle of Natural Rights that dates from the eighteenth century. According to Veblen, a form of the Christian principle to love thy neighbor as thyself "seems, in its elements at least, to be a culturally atavistic trait, belonging to the ancient, not to say primordial, peaceable culture of the lower savagery" (ibid.: 215). Here we touch on Veblen's subscription to Bachofen's ([1861] 1967) myth, such that "throughout all the vicissitudes of cultural change, the golden rule of the peaceable savage has never lost the respect of occidental mankind, and its hold on men's convictions is, perhaps, stronger now than at any earlier period of the modern time" (Veblen [1910] 1943: 215). Durkheim, too, held the seemingly contradictory position that altruism preceded egoism in human development while at the same time he felt that "primitive" forms of solidarity are inferior when compared to the greater social solidarity in "advanced" societies.

One way to resolve this apparent contradiction in Veblen and Durkheim is to suggest that ideal (but not vulgar) Christianity offers a distilled, purified version of the self-less, altruistic tendency that is essential to the sustained and vigorous existence of all societies. In Veblen's words, "these two codes of conduct, Christian morals and business principles, are the institutional by-products of two different cultural situations" (ibid.: 214) that are peculiar to the West even if they are built upon the *homo duplex* formula that is universal.

Veblen argues that egoism was appropriate to eighteenth-century craftsmanship because it was restrained by small, personal, primary groups and by the Christian notion of "fair play." But "times have changed since the eighteenth century, when this system of pecuniary egoism reached its mature development," Veblen writes (ibid.: 213). He elaborates that

> The excellence and sufficiency of an enlightened pecuniary egoism are no longer a matter of course and of common-sense to the mind of this generation, which has experienced the current era of machine industry, credit, delegated corporation management, and distant markets.
>
> (Ibid.: 214)

Moreover, "the ancient Christian principle of humility, renunciation, abnegation, or non-resistance has been virtually eliminated from the moral scheme of moral Christendom," Veblen wrote (ibid.: 216).

In his conclusion, Veblen observes that both Christian and competitive habits of thought "are in process of disintegration" (ibid.: 218). He predicted that humankind would realize that pecuniary self-interest is no longer appropriate as the major driving force behind culture in a complex, modern society. For reasons he never explained, Veblen ends his essay with the claim that while competitive morals will disintegrate, "the Christian principle of brotherhood should logically continue to gain ground at the expense of the pecuniary morals of competitive business" (ibid.: 218). Apparently, and again like Durkheim, Veblen sought a precarious balance between egoism and altruism in which altruism might hold the upper hand. Yet no commentator on postmodern culture has uncovered any semblance of the alleged victory of Christian self-abnegation over pecuniary self-interest, although many suggest the contrary, from Lasch (1979) to Bellah *et al.* (1985). In fact, postmodern philosophers tend to ignore Christian morals, as if these were part of the oppressive narratives they purport to rebel against, or perhaps because they still subscribe to the positivistic fact–value distinction.

Veblen's focus on peaceable habits that might offset barbaric habits of the fight is central to his *Theory of the Leisure Class*, but has been the aspect most neglected by contemporary analysts:

> Among these archaic traits that are to be regarded as survivals from the peaceable cultural phase, are that instinct of race solidarity which we call conscience, including the sense of truthfulness and equity, and the instinct of workmanship, in its naive, non-invidious expression.
>
> ([1899] 1967: 221)

Veblen never advocated the systemic inculcation of these peaceable habits, and like Durkheim, criticized Marx and his disciples for their utopian visions. More in line with the doctrine of pessimistic humanism that we have traced from Schopenhauer to Horkheimer, Veblen felt that "where life is largely a struggle between individuals within the group, the possession of the ancient peaceable traits in a marked degree would hamper an individual in the struggle for life" (ibid.: 223). A colloquial summary of Veblen in this regard might be that nice guys finish last. A more high-brow version might be Nietzsche's conclusion that virtue is not even its own reward. Veblen elaborates on his pessimistic appraisal:

> Under any known phase of culture, other or later than the presumptive initial phase here spoken of, the gifts of good-nature, equity, and indiscriminate sympathy do not appreciably further the life of the individual . . . The individual fares better under the regime of competition in proportion as he has less of these gifts. Freedom from scruple, from sympathy, honesty and regard for life, may, within fairly wide limits, be said to further the success of the individual in the pecuniary culture. The highly successful men of all times have commonly been of this type . . . it is only within narrow limits, and then only in a Pickwickian sense, that honesty is the best policy.
>
> (Ibid.: 223)

Veblen does not mince words: the peaceable type of person with a sense of goodwill toward fellow humans is regarded in highly competitive, Western societies as "good-for-nothing" (ibid.: 224). On the other hand, "the competitive individual can best achieve his ends if he combines the barbarian's energy, initiative, self-seeking and disingenuousness with the savage's lack of loyalty or clannishness" (ibid.: 226). The peaceable traits that are absolutely essential to the preservation of the family and society "are disserviceable to the individual" (ibid.: 228) whereas the predatory habits that help the modern barbarian compete simultaneously destroy the very fabric of society:

> The ideal pecuniary man is like the ideal delinquent in his unscrupulous conversion of goods and persons to his own ends, and in a callous disregard of the feelings and wishes of others and of the remoter effects of his actions; but he is unlike him in possessing a keener sense of status.
>
> (Ibid.: 237)[3]

Clearly, like Durkheim and Freud, Veblen is aware of a dialectical relationship between the egoistic and peaceable habits that he ascribes to human nature. One ideal type cannot exist without the other. Veblen's formulation elaborates on the Platonic myth that seems to inform the works of many of his *fin de siècle* contemporaries. Baudrillard is completely oblivious to this Platonic myth and this aspect of Veblen's thought.

CONCLUSIONS

Plato and Aristotle summarized the problem of human virtue as follows: The sorts of knowledge that constitute virtue are not the same sorts of knowledge one gains through a study of the sciences. Consequently, virtue cannot be taught. Rather, virtue is a matter of character that is developed through habitual actions. One becomes virtuous through habitual virtuous actions, and barbaric through habitual barbaric actions. They posed a problem for Western culture that is yet to be resolved: If virtue cannot be taught, and barbarism cannot be eliminated, then how is the good society possible?

The Enlightenment stands out as a period of Western history in which humankind became so arrogant that its finest philosophers thought they could escape the confines of habits and culture. They thought that Nature could be tamed, and virtue could be taught. In Durkheim's critical words,

> The *esprit simpliste* of the seventeenth century applied at first only to the physical world. People at that time did not speculate on the social and moral order, which was considered too sacred to be subjected to the profanation of lay thought – in other words, to science. With the eighteenth century that reservation went by the board. Science dared much more . . . it attacked social problems . . . It therefore brought to the study of the new problems it attacked, i.e., the study of the social world, the same naive simplicity that was the inspiration of the previous century in the study of the material world.
>
> ([1925] 1961: 259)

The previous *fin de siècle* rebelled at this simplistic rationalism, the Cartesian "attempt to reduce knowledge of the world to universal mathematics" (ibid.: 262). The sociologies of Veblen, Durkheim, Freud, Weber, and Simmel constituted part of that rebellion. However, their efforts were obfuscated by another attempt to resuscitate the Enlightenment project at the beginning of the twentieth century. Durkheim's characterization of the eighteenth century applies equally well to the twentieth century efforts by Parsons and the modernists:

> When the philosophers of the eighteenth century applied Cartesian principles to social phenomena they imagined that

the new science could be conceived and constructed at a single stroke, by way of definitions and deductions, with no need to resort to observation – in other words, to history.

([1925] 1961: 262)

The non-cultural, ahistorical, and deductive social systems model promulgated by Parsons eclipsed the only sociological remnants of the spirit of the previous *fin de siècle*, namely, Sorokin and the critical theorists. Overall, sociology revived Descartes and Comte, and tried to emulate the mathematical and natural sciences. Communism could be regarded as one of its grandest experiments in social engineering, and it failed (Bauman 1992: 222), but others come to mind readily: President Lyndon Johnson's war on poverty, desegregation and school bussing in the United States, the deinstitutionalization of the mentally ill, and the ongoing American wars on crime, drugs, and other social problems.

In the present *fin de siècle*, all these efforts at social engineering have failed or are in serious trouble. Especially in its heyday in the 1960s, sociology promised much more than it could ever deliver. And these promises were based on Cartesian assumptions and neo-Kantian methods: sociologists began to talk to each other almost exclusively in terms of numbers and mathematical formulas, correlations, and path diagrams. The idea of progress was hardly questioned. What passed for theory might still be described in Durkheim's words as a rationalism so facile that it bordered on mysticism: "Simplicism, therefore, is an act of faith in abstract reasoning" (ibid.: 261). From Parsons to Habermas and Giddens, leading social theorists made reasoning a central issue in the last half of the twentieth century, while they ignored almost completely the central concerns of the *fin de siècle* founders of sociology: habits, feelings, culture, the unconscious, and the non-rational.

As the twentieth century and the millennium draw to a close, sociology has lost what little stature it once possessed. The American public in particular, along with other Westerners in general, are showing symptoms of the cynicism and malaise that characterized the previous *fin de siècle*. Then as now, crime, recession, corruption, scandal, and in general, the institutionalization of what Veblen termed predatory habits of the barbarian, have overshadowed the Enlightenment faith in progress.

Postmodernism emerged as a peculiarly Western cultural movement in the present *fin de siècle*. It caters to apocalyptic themes that allege the end of culture, modernity, history, pedagogy, and a number of other phenomena, including the end of sociology. The thrust of our argument has been that despite its vocabulary of protest, postmodernism does not constitute a genuine rebellion against the simplified rationalism of the Enlightenment. Baudrillard's work, in particular, remains trapped in a neo-Kantian world of mere fictions and a Cartesian simplicity – a world devoid of culture, history, habits, the unconscious, and all other concepts that point to complexities that defy the simplistic, mathematical elegance with which society is approached.

We turned to Veblen, Durkheim, Freud, and Simmel in the context of Schopenhauer – who gave the previous turn of the century its signature – in order to point to the beginnings of a genuinely postmodern critical theory. Our aim was not to systematize yet another modern theory that can be falsified, nor to revive Horkheimer and Adorno. Rather, the aim was to uncover the lost trajectory of the rebellion that sociologists in the previous *fin de siècle* began, but never had a chance to complete.

The central insight of this lost trajectory is the horrifying idea that enlightenment cannot contain the forces of barbarism – that the will is stronger than rationality. If that is true, then all utopian schemes and efforts at social engineering are suspect. Modernity cannot tame Nature once and for all. Rather, human societies and culture are a part of Nature. If anything like a cosmopolitan humanity is to emerge, one that is mindful of the planet and of the human rights of all its citizens, it must learn to balance its barbaric tendencies with peaceable habits that have been ignored for too long. Veblen and his colleagues offered no blueprint for this balancing act, no utopian promises, and neither do we. If we can convince the reader to take Veblen and his contemporaries seriously, we will have achieved our aims. We pose a problem that is worthy of serious study, but do not offer a solution.

However, we shall conclude with a forceful disavowal of the temptation to engage in another round of social engineering and oversimplified rationalism. This skepticism toward excessive rationalism sets Freud, Durkheim, Veblen, and their contemporaries – along with this author – apart from some of the most popular social movements of the twentieth century. For example, Marx apparently holds many affinities with the doctrine of Saint-Simon and his belief that through successive "critical" and "organic" epochs, humankind would finally reach an "organic" epoch in which brotherhood and love will reign, and egoism will be eradicated. Because Marx felt that he grasped this secret historical plan, he concluded arrogantly that he could hasten the end of history. Such a goal is a complete impossibility for Schopenhauer, Freud, Veblen, Durkheim, and the other intellectuals whose thought we have been following. A social program based on their views would rather attempt to manage and channel creatively the dualistic aspect of the will to life, its destructive as well as constructive qualities. We deliberately and self-consciously choose not to be any more specific than that.

Notes

1 How to comprehend barbarism in the midst of enlightenment

1 This cultural context for apprehending Veblen includes the works of Kant, Hegel, Darwin, Freud, Spencer, Bellamy, Marx, Peirce, and Kropotkin, among others. See Diggins (1979), Dugger (1979, 1984), Dugger and Lopreato (1981), Dyer (1986b), Edgell and Tilman (1989), Eff (1989), Kennedy (1987), Leathers (1986, 1989), Machalek (1979), Mirowski (1987), Posnock (1987), Riesman (1953), Ryan (1982), Schneider (1948, 1971), Stanfield (1989), Suto (1979), Tilman (1985), and Waller (1988), among others. In Meštrović (1992), I pursue only one strand in this interesting sea of affinities, between Henry Adams and Veblen. For more on this connection, see Harpham (1976), Lears (1983), Moreland (1989), and Partenheimer (1988).

2 See Grignon (1976), Jay (1988), Kanter and Mirvis (1989), Kennedy (1990), Lutz (1990), Meštrović (1991), Neveu (1990), Oliver (1989), Roche (1988), Schorske (1980), Schwartz (1990), Showalter (1990), Sonn (1989), Stokes (1989), Teich and Porter (1990), and Eugen Weber (1987), among others.

3 Riesman goes on to note that Veblen also criticized Germany and Japan for barbarism. This is an interesting contradiction in Veblen's thought, but it would take us too far astray to pursue it here.

4 This term was coined by Robert N. Bellah (1967), who drew upon the works of Tocqueville and Durkheim for inspiration.

5 One should note also that in "The Psychopathology of Everyday Life", Sigmund Freud held that "superstition derives from suppressed hostile and cruel impulses" ([1901] 1965: 260).

6 In *The Freudian Psychology and Veblen's Social Theory* (1948), Louis Schneider argues convincingly that Veblen holds many affinities with Freud's psychoanalysis.

7 Veblen adds on ibid.: 142 that "the case of the fast horse is much like that of the dog" because "he is on the whole expensive, or wasteful or useless – for industrial purpose." And, "beyond this,

the race horse proper has also a similarly non-industrial but honorific use as a gambling instrument" (ibid.: 143). One has only to think of the famous Kentucky Derby, a host of smaller derbies, and the multi-billion dollar horse-gambling industry to find contemporary illustrations. See also Synnott (1987).

8 According to Veblen, "It is on this basis that the printers of to-day are returning to 'old-style,' and other more or less obsolete styles of type which are less legible and give a cruder appearance to the page than the 'modern'" (1917: 163).

9 See, for example, the references to Veblen by Christopher Lasch (1977, 1979, 1986, 1991).

10 See Ingram (1986, 1988), Kennedy (1987), Partenheimer (1988), Posnock (1987), Waller (1988).

11 See, for example, James ([1890] 1950, [1896] 1931).

12 See also Jung (1961, 1966, 1973). On Jung's relevance to sociology, see Greenwood (1990), Meštrović (1992), and Staude (1976).

13 This is in line with Veblen's observation that the "infirmly delicate, translucent, and hazardously slender" standard of beauty for the female suggests a woman who is not fit for useful work, hence prestigious ([1899] 1967: 112). See also Glassner (1989, 1990) and Turner (1984, 1990).

14 Tocqueville also wrote with regard to the black population in America that "if oppressed, they may bring an action at law, but they will find none but whites among their judges" ([1845] 1945: 373). Judges in America are still overwhelmingly white. On page 370 he made this ominous prediction: "These two races [black and white] are fastened to each other without intermingling; and they are alike unable to separate entirely or to combine. The most formidable of all the ills that threaten the future of the Union arises from the presence of a black population upon its territory."

15 Veblen writes:

> The conditions under which men lived in the most primitive stages of associated life that can properly be called human, seem to have been of a peaceful kind; and the character – the temperament and spiritual attitude – of men under these early conditions of environment and institutions seems to have been of a peaceful and unaggressive, not to say an indolent, cast. For the immediate purpose this peaceable cultural stage may be taken to mark the initial phase of social development.
>
> ([1899] 1967: 219)

On p. 221, he adds: "Among these archaic traits that are to be regarded as survivals from the peaceable cultural phase, are that instinct of race solidarity which we call conscience, including the sense of truthfulness and equity, and the instinct of workmanship, in its naive, non-invidious expression."

16 See Burston (1986), Cantarella (1982), Engels ([1884] 1972), Fluehr (1987), Greisman (1981), Hermand 1984, Kramer et al. (1985), Mitzman (1977), and Riesman (1953) among many other sources.

17 See the controversy that surrounds Raymond Gastil's 1967 hypothesis that there exists a Southern "subculture of violence."

18 Despite my critical tone toward Elias, I note that some theorists find affinities between his thought and that of Adorno. See Bogner (1987), Ingram (1986, 1988), Lepenies (1978), Sica (1984).

19 I am using "sacred" here in Durkheim's sense, from *The Elementary Forms of the Religious Life* ([1912] 1965).

20 Baudrillard writes similarly about American perceptions of the Vietnam war:

> Left brittle by the Vietnam War, which was as unintelligible to them as the irruption of little green men in a cartoon strip – and which, incidentally, they dealt with as though it were a cartoon, as something remote from them, a television war, with no understanding of the world's condemnation of their action and only able to see their enemy, since they are the achieved utopia of goodness, as the achieved utopia of Evil, Communism – they have taken refuge in the tranquility of the easy life, in a triumphal illusionism.

> (1986: 108)

21 See also the critique of Elias by Christopher Lasch (1985).

2 Methodological and empirical issues in perceiving modern barbarism

1 Durkheim ([1912] 1965) echoes this idea by arguing that science stems from religion, and more importantly, that the difference between science and religion is one of degree, not fundamental.

2 See Riesman (1956, 1980a, 1980b, 1981), Riesman and Grant (1978), Riesman, Gusfield, and Gamson (1970), Riesman and Jencks (1968).

3 See the *Chronicle of Higher Education*, 6 May 1992: A1.

4 In this paragraph I am elaborating on the examples used by Earl Babbie in his article entitled "Sociology: An Idea Whose Time Has Come" published in the American Sociological Association's newsletter, *Footnotes*, May 1992: 3.

5 On the back cover of Veblen's *The Theory of the Leisure Class*, C. Wright Mills is quoted: "Thorstein Veblen is the best critic of America that America has produced." For more on the affinities between Veblen and Mills, see Jaksic (1979). Obviously, Mills concludes along the trajectories already established by Veblen. For a recent account of scientific waste and uselessness in collaboration with corporate and governmental deregulation, see the interview with Ralph Nader in *Playboy*, June 1992: 53–72.

6 He refers to "the genuine excess of corporal punishment, the orgy of violence that historians describe in the schools of the fourteenth, fifteenth, and sixteenth centuries, when, according to Montaigne, one could hear 'only the cries, both of the beaten children and of

the teachers drunk with rage'" (Durkheim [1925] 1961: 192).

7 It is important to note that Durkheim did not hold the Renaissance in high regard. Instead, he refers to the "moral crisis" of the Renaissance ([1938] 1977: 225), and describes it as a period in which aspirations tended toward "l'infini," marked by intemperance and immorality, and "un fléchissement général du sentiment moral" (1938: 218–43 passim). He concludes: "Le XVIe siècle est donc une époque de crise pédagogique et morale" (1938: 260). But the problem posed by the Renaissance has not yet been solved in our postmodern era, namely, how should one pursue humanism and freedom in education without succumbing to egoism ([1938] 1977: 228)?

8 Durkheim adds: "He overflows in violence, quite like the tyrant whom nothing can resist. This violence is a game with him, a spectacle in which he indulges himself, a way of demonstrating that superiority he sees in himself" ([1925] 1961: 193). It is interesting in this regard that in the chronicles of his travels through America, Baudrillard (1986) never mentions a popular tourist attraction, the Battle of Little Big Horn, in which General George Custer failed in his bid to exterminate the Native Americans. This and the many other direct as well as indirect allusions to genocide in America's Wild West failed to impress Baudrillard. Yet they suggest that postmodern culture consists of more than rootless fictions: genocide is a firmly rooted, barbaric reality that modernists have not eliminated, notwithstanding dreams for an end to history.

9 Elsewhere in this work, Durkheim writes: "To-day we are beginning to realize that law, morals and even scientific thought itself were born of religion, were for a long time confounded with it, and have remained penetrated with its spirit" ([1912] 1965: 87). "The explanations of contemporary science are surer of being objective because they are more methodical and because they rest on more carefully controlled observations, but they do not differ in nature from those which satisfy primitive thought" (ibid.: 270). "In reality, then, there are no religions which are false. All are true in their own fashion; all answer, in different ways, to the given conditions of human existence" (ibid.: 15). In a fascinating criticism of Comte's positivism, Durkheim writes:

> So the idea of force is of religious origin. It is from religion that it has been borrowed first by philosophy, then by the sciences. This has already been foreseen by Comte and this is why he made metaphysics the heir of "theology." But he concluded from this that the idea of force is destined to disappear from science; for, owing to its mystic origins, he refused it all objective value. But we are going to show that, on the contrary, religious forces are real, however imperfect the symbols may be, by the aid of which they are thought of. From this it will follow that the same is true of the concept of force in general.
>
> (Ibid.: 234)

As for the hard and fast distinction between religion and science that is the staple of modernist thought, Durkheim writes: "There is no religion that is not a cosmology at the same time that it is a speculation upon divine things. If philosophy and the sciences were born of religion, it is because religion began by taking the place of the sciences and philosophy" (ibid.: 21). Elsewhere he adds, "thus, between the logic of religious thought and that of scientific thought there is no abyss" (ibid.: 271). As for Kant's famous categories, Durkheim writes: "We have established the fact that the fundamental categories of thought, and consequently of science, are of religious origin. It may be said that nearly all the great social institutions have been born in religion" (ibid.: 466). Thus, "scientific thought is only a more perfect form of religious thought" (ibid.: 477).

To anyone who really reads *The Elementary Forms of the Religious Life*, there can be little doubt that it is an anti-modernist manifesto, and opposes a cultural view of science against Comte, Kant, and other high priests of the Enlightenment. Yet it continues to be misread as an empirical treatise on the aborigines. For an extended critique of Durkheim's interpreters, see Meštrović (1988).

10 Among them, Bell (1976, 1985), Bellah (1981, 1986), Bloom (1987), Caporale and Grumelli (1971), Harvey (1985, 1989), Kanter and Mirvis (1989).

11 Gellner opposes René Descartes's efforts to escape culture completely with Durkheim's insistence that culture is the ground and referent for all knowledge. Contrast with La Capra's summary of Durkheim's thought as a "Cartesianized and socialized neo-Kantianism" (1972: 8). I am more inclined to agree with Hirst that "in Durkheim's epistemology there is little immediate trace of the Kantian division of the forms of knowledge which has bedeviled the social sciences" (1975: 2).

3 Barbarism and the idea of progess

1 See also Bauman (1978, 1985, 1987).

2 See Estrada (1980), Freedman and Lazarus (1988), Held (1978), Hoffman (1984), Jay (1984, 1988), Kellner (1990), Korthals (1985), Rosenthal (1978), Siebert (1979), Staude (1976), and Whitebook (1988a, 1988b).

3 See Atwell (1990), Cartwright (1984, 1987, 1988a, 1988b), Fox (1980), Gellner (1992), Hamlyn (1980), Hübscher (1989), Janaway (1989), Luft (1988), Magee (1983), and Safranski (1990).

4 See also Fromm (1947, 1950, 1955, 1959, 1963, 1964), as well as Fromm and Maccoby (1970). Fromm's influence on David Riesman (1950) should also be noted.

5 In a letter dated 4 September 1991, Professor David Cartwright, President of the North American Schopenhauer Society, writes: "I am aware of four articles by Horkheimer concerning Schopen-

hauer. All were originally published in the *Schopenhauer Jahrbuch*. They are: 'Schopenhauer und die Gesellschaft,' (1955); 'Pessimismus heute,' (1971); 'Bemerkungen zu Schopenhauer im Verhältnis zu Wissenschaft und Religion,' (1972); and 'Die Aktualität Schopenhauers,' (1961). As far as I know, only the last one was translated – 'Schopenhauer Today.' Horkheimer also wrote a newspaper article on Schopenhauer, 'Die Zeitgemässheit Schopenhauers,' Neue Zürcher Zeitung, 21 March 1971."

6 Martin Jay claims that Adorno was instructed in Kant by Kracauer, "whereas Horkheimer's fascination with Arthur Schopenhauer and G.W.F. Hegel meant that he was drawn away from the phenomenal world to the allegedly more essential realities beneath, which he then interpreted in increasingly Marxist terms" (1988: 85). On Adorno, Martin Jay writes:

> Adorno began to practise a kind of immanent critique of ideology that was clearly indebted to the Hegelian reading of Marx contained in many of their works. Here too there was a bond with Horkheimer, whose philosophical inclinations, despite a certain sympathy for Schopenhauer, ran in the same direction.
> (1984: 29)

For more on Kracauer, see also David Frisby's (1986) analysis.

7 See especially Gupta (1980), although numerous other authors are also aware of the connection between Freud and Schopenhauer, from Ellenberger (1970) to Jones (1981).

8 Although it would take us too far astray to delve further into the connection between Jung and Durkheim *vis-à-vis* Schopenhauer's philosophy, it is noteworthy. See especially Susan Greenwood's (1990) discussion of this connection. Jung's explanation for how barbarism can exist within the heart of modernity follows the same *fin de siècle* logic that found its way into Veblen and Durkheim. Jung advocated the harmonization of the Persona and Shadow, of heart and mind, of the rational consciousness with the collective unconscious. One-sidedness in either direction can result in an explosion of seemingly inexplicable violence. See, for example, Jung's discussion of Nazism in his *Collected Works*, vol. 10.

9 This is a crucial distinction, because pity and charity can mimic genuine compassion, and can lend prestige (from Veblen) to the person who likes to make a show of his or her good heart. Cartwright's (1984) excellent discussion of the German concepts used by Kant, Schopenhauer, and Nietzsche in this discourse leads one to rethink Nietzsche's famous attack on compassion.

10 It is important to appreciate Durkheim's own criticisms of Kant in this regard, as when he wrote: "Vainly Kant has tried to deduce from his categorical imperative that group of duties, surely badly defined, but universally recognized, called the duties of charity. His method of argument is reduced to a game of concepts" ([1893] 1933: 418). Because Durkheim was a cultural theorist, he noticed that "what Kant's system does not explain, however, is the

origin of this sort of contradiction which is realized in man"
([1912] 1965: 445). Especially in *Moral Education*, Durkheim
criticizes Kant on Schopenhauerian grounds:

> With some people, it is the sensitivity to the rule, a disposition
> for discipline that predominates. They do their duty as they see
> it, completely and without hesitation, simply because it is their
> duty and without any particular appeal to their hearts. These are
> men of substantial intellect and strong will – Kant is an ideal
> example – but among whom the emotional faculties are much
> less developed than those of the intellect.
>
> ([1925] 1961: 99–100

11 Durkheim is keenly aware that neo-Kantians exhibit "coldness,
severity, rigidity" and that they lack the capacity for joyful giving or
self-sacrifice ([1925] 1961: 100). Durkheim criticizes Kant's a
priorism:

> Kant was obliged to admit that the will . . . does not depend on the
> laws of nature. He was obliged to create a reality apart from the
> world, on which the world exerts no influence, and which, re-
> acting on itself, remains independent of the action of external
> forces. It does not seem profitable just now to discuss this meta-
> physical conception, which can only mislead us in our thinking.
>
> (Ibid.: 112)

This is another important distinction between the neo-Kantian trajectory followed by the positivists and the postmodernists, versus
Schopenhauer's aims. Schopenhauer wrote ([1818] 1969b: 596):

> According to my view, the basis of criminal law should be the
> principle that it is not the person, but only the deed that is
> punished, so that it may not recur. The criminal is merely the
> subject in which the deed is punished . . . [but] according to
> Kant's explanation, amounting to a *jus talionis*, it is not the deed
> but the person who is punished. The penitentiary system also
> tries to punish not so much the deed as the person, so that he
> may change for the better. In this way it sets aside the real aim of
> punishment, determent from the deed, in order to achieve the
> very problematical aim of improvement . . . Moreover, however
> large may be the share that brutality and ignorance, in con-
> junction with external distress, have in many crimes, we must not
> regard them as the principal cause of these, since innumerable
> persons living under the same hard conditions and in entirely
> similar circumstances do not commit any crimes.

Compare Schopenhauer's view of punishment with Durkheim's in
Division of Labor ([1893] 1933) and *Moral Education* ([1925] 1961).
Durkheim understands punishment to be nothing more than an
expression of society's moral disapproval, not a program of reform,
and he is against brutal punishment for that reason. Compare also
with Jack Katz's argument in *Seductions of Crime* (1988)

12 Baudrillard writes:

> The very possibility of the Eternal Return is becoming precarious: that marvellous perspective presupposes that things unfold in a necessary, predestined order, the sense of which lies beyond them. There is nothing like that today; things merely follow on in a flabby order that leads nowhere. Today's Eternal Return is that of the infinitely small, the fractal, the obsessive repetition of things on a microscopic and inhuman scale. It is not the exaltation of a will, nor the sovereign affirmation of an event, nor its consecration by an immutable sign, such as Nietzsche sought, but the viral recurrence of microprocesses.
>
> (1986: 72)

One could argue that both Schopenhauer and Nietzsche were merely refracting Solomon's message in Ecclesiastes, that there is nothing new under the sun.

4   Finding a ground for discourse

1 Because this claim is not obvious to many modernists, let me cite a number of studies that trace Schopenhauer's influence on a host of important artists, philosophers, and other intellectuals: Richard P. Adams, "Wallace Stevens and Schopenhauer's *The World as Will and Idea*," *Tulane Studies in English*, vol. 20, 1972, pp. 135–68; William W. Bonney, "Eastern Logic Under My Western Eyes: Conrad, Schopenhauer, and the Orient," *Conradiana*, vol. 10, 1978, pp. 225–52; William R. Brashear, "O'Neill's Schopenhauer Interlude," *Criticism*, vol. 6, 1964, pp. 256–65; Rose M. Burwell, "Schopenhauer, Hardy, and Lawrence: Toward a New Understanding of *Sons and Lovers*," Western Humanities Review, vol. 28, 1973, pp. 105–17; Olive L. Fite, "Billy Budd, Claggart, and Schopenhauer," *Nineteenth-Century Fiction*, vol. 23, 1969, pp. 336–43; Eleanor H. Green, "Schopenhauer and D.H. Lawrence on Sex and Love," *The D.H. Lawrence Review*, vol. 8, 1975, pp. 329–45; C. Jansohn, "On the Influence of Schopenhauer on D.H. Lawrence," *Arcadia*, vol. 21, 1986, pp. 263–75; M. Kelly, "Thomas Hardy's Reading in Schopenhauer," *Colby Library Quarterly*, vol. 18, 1982, pp. 183–98; J.M. Kertzer, "T.S. Eliot and the Problem of Will," *Modern Language Quarterly*, vol. 45, 1984, pp. 373–94; E.A. McCobb, "Daniel Deronda as Will and Representation: George Eliot and Schopenhauer," *Modern Language Review*, vol. 80, 1985, pp. 533–49; Ruth Nevo, "Yeats and Schopenhauer," *Yeats Annual*, vol. 3, 1985, pp. 15–32; Vincent Pecora, "Heart of Darkness and the Phenomenology of Voice," *English Literary History*, vol. 52, 1985, pp. 993–1015; W. Scheick, *Schopenhauerian Compassion, Fictional Structure, and the Reader: The Example of Hardy and Conrad*, Tucson: University of Arizona Press, 1987; among many other sources.

2 For discussions of how the concept of internalization has been

used and misused in social science, see Benjamin (1977, 1978), Bogner (1987), Sica (1984), Staude (1976).

3 I disagree with Bloom's conservative world-view, but I do share his estimation of Talcott Parsons: "Compare the character and concerns of Talcott Parsons with those of Max Weber and you have the measure of the distance between the Continent and us. In Parsons you see the routinization of Weber" (1987: 151).

4 Here one is reminded of Douglas Kellner's (1989b) observation that Baudrillard begins his career as a liberal Marxist but ends up as a conservative reactionary.

5 I agree with Yash Nandan:

> But Durkheim, Mauss, Simiand, and other sociologists were not in the least interested in Kantian neo-criticism or Hegelian neo-spiritualism – or, for that matter, in any philosophic mechanism that neglected an empirically verifiable experience of reality and the *sui generis* existence of facts. Speculating on and understanding reality through *a priori* method is not what the logic of science deals with.
>
> (1977: 27)

See also Nandan (1970).

6 For these and other reasons, Bauman (1992) calls for the establishment of a genuinely postmodern sociology. But he does not spell out why such a sociology would not suffer from the same impotence and fragmentation that one finds in the rest of postmodern discourse.

7 See Baillot (1927), Cartwright (1984, 1987), Durant (1961), Ellenberger (1970), Goodwin (1967), Hamlyn (1980), Janik and Toulmin (1973), Lalande ([1926] 1980), Levy (1904), Magee (1983), Meštrović (1988, 1991, 1992), Simmel ([1907] 1986), among others.

8 See Horkheimer (1980), Hübscher (1989), Luft (1988), Magee (1983), Mann (1939), and Safranski (1990), among others.

9 For example, Charles Gehlke notes:

> Durkheim has admitted as true the resemblance between his social representations and the Platonic ideas. 'Face to face with this system of ideas, the individual mind is in the same situation as the *nous* [soul] of Plato, before the world of ideas. It (the individual mind) is compelled to absorb them (*se les assimiler*), for it needs them in order to be able to have communion with its fellows; but the absorption is always imperfect.' And he notes a difference between his 'social representation' and the 'idea' of Plato. 'The ideas of Plato are self-sufficient. They have no need of matter in order to exist; they cannot mingle with matter without undergoing a kind of degradation. On the contrary, society has need of individuals in order to exist'.
>
> ([1915] 1968: 87).

10 Horkheimer's *Eclipse of Reason* (1947) tends to be neglected relative to his other works. In this important work, he interprets the Platonic high regard for rationality as integrated and in touch with its opposite, the irrational.

11 Discussed in Meštrović (1988: 15–18).

12 However, Erich Fromm (1962) attempts just such a synthesis of Marx and Freud. For criticisms of Fromm, see especially C.G. Schoenfeld (1962, 1966, 1984).

13 See Estrada (1988), Hohendahl (1985), Korthals (1985), Torpey (1986).

14 Similarly, Diggins (1977) argues that Veblen construed the origins of private property as emanating, not from alienated labor, but from the cultural heritage that can be traced back to nomads, hunters, and warriors.

15 For a contrary view, see La Capra (1972). I disagree with La Capra's argument that Durkheim's program was neo-Kantian for the obvious reason that Durkheim rejected completely the *a priori* basis for knowledge. For Durkheim, culture is the ultimate basis for knowledge.

16 I am aware that Giddens repudiates Parsons. However, Ian Craib (1992), Bryant and Jary (1991) and other analysts of Giddens are probably right to point to Giddens as extending Parsons's hyper-abstract systems theory devoid of culture which he renames structuration theory.

17 With the notable exception of Pitirim Sorokin (1948, 1957), of course.

18 One of Durkheim's teachers, Charles Renouvier (1892), was among the first French philosophers to write on Schopenhauer (a fact that Lukes does not even mention). Théodule Ribot (1874, 1896, 1899), another one of Durkheim's teachers, also wrote extensively on Schopenhauer.

19 Consider also the following secondary analyses of this far-reaching Schopenhauerian influence: Clark (1975), Crawford (1984), Durant (1981), Greenwood (1990), Levi and Amado (1975), Manschreck (1976), Menand and Schwartz (1982), Mudragei (1979), Simmel ([1921] 1971).

20 For a small portion of this vast secondary literature, see Bell (1981), Harpham (1976), Kennedy (1990), Lears (1983), Meštrović (1992), Partenheimer (1988).

21 From personal correspondence in March of 1991.

22 As explained to me by Durkheim's grandson, Etienne Halphen. See the exact account in Meštrović (1988).

23 I am referring to the use of psychiatrists to predict "dangerousness" with regard to the commitment of mental patients even though the psychiatric profession admits that it is not qualified to make this distinction.

5   Choosing philosophical trajectories regarding barbarism

1 According to Tocqueville ([1845] 1945: 219), "in America society seems to live from hand to mouth, like an army in the field" with regard to history, because "no one cares for what occurred before his time." He adds that "if the United States were ever invaded by barbarians, it would be necessary to have recourse to the history of other nations in order to learn anything of the people who now inhabit them." What a perfect setting for the circulation of fictive forms, decentering, and hyper-reality discussed by postmodernists!

2 Here I shall note only in passing that Schopenhauer ([1818] 1969b: 440) was critical of history conceived as the mere chronicle of events and the life-stories of individuals. History must have an intent, a will, that works beneath the events. Hegel ([1899] 1965) and Nietzsche ([1874] 1983) agree in part. However, Schopenhauer felt that history's intent is hidden and leads ultimately to chaos. In this regard, he differs profoundly from Hegel and other nineteenth-century philosophers. For a fuller discussion, see Luft (1988). See also Durkheim's (1908) similar critique of Seignobos and the historians who are concerned only with events, even though he felt that history and sociology overlap regarding the study of social facts.

3 See also Baudrillard (1991).

4 It would be wrong to dismiss cannibalism from the list of modern barbaric acts. The discovery in July 1991 in Ohio that Jeffrey Dahmer killed, dismembered, and ate parts of seventeen individuals makes one take notice of Schopenhauer's comments on cannibalism as the most primal act of evil. A year later, a psychopath was brought to trial in Russia for cannibalizing over fifty bodies. Moreover, we are not talking about events, but about collective representations. The film *Body Parts* opened during the same week that Dahmer's crimes were reported, and there exist many similar films (such as *Eating Raoul*). A week later, the *Wall Street Journal* was running full-page advertisements with the caption that those who are slow to make aggressive moves in business become "lunch meat" – and it featured a butcher knife embedded in a wooden cutting board. The phrases, "You're dead meat," "They'll make mince meat out of you," "They'll serve you for lunch" are very common, habitual phrases in the present *fin de siècle*. Finally, it is interesting that many of the families of Dahmer's victims filed lawsuits to make sure that they would get a share of the millions of dollars in profit that they believe a film based on Dahmer will make. All sorts of discussions have ensued from Dahmer's grisly crime, from racism to making a profit, but few have addressed the issue of cannibalism in 1991, modern America.

5 It would take us too far astray to pursue the meaning of the doctrine of original sin from a sociological perspective for the thinkers we are discussing, but its importance must be underscored. See Horkheimer's (1972b: 119) fascinating allusions to the

role of women in the family in relation to the symbolism of Eve and the Virgin Mary and Bachofen's theory of matriarchy. In this regard, see also Henry Adams's ([1901] 1983) fascinating essay, "The Dynamo and the Virgin" and his conclusion that Protestants abandoned the New Testament and the Virgin in order to go back to the beginning, and renew the quarrel with Eve. Siebert's (1979: 25) remark is also important to pursue: "In relation to the Judeo-Christian teaching of the original sin, Horkheimer is not only a disciple of Schopenhauer, but also of the latter's opponent – Hegel. According to Horkheimer, in relation to the problem of evil, Hegel was closer to Schopenhauer than the latter knew."

6 Psychoanalysts are well aware that for Freud, the healthy person must be able to love. In this regard, see the penetrating essays by C.G. Schoenfeld (1968, 1974).

7 For example, this is the basis for Bloom's (1987) unfair dismissal of Freud's relevance to our time.

8 It is easy to apply Horkheimer's remarks regarding Nietzsche's cruelty to Baudrillard's (1986) equally cruel remarks concerning the poor and the "fourth world," all of whom "must exit."

9 Even though this is a well-kept secret with regard to Durkheim; see Mike Gane's (1981) and (1984) discussions. See also Wells (1928, 1935, 1939).

6 Deconstructing the problem of social order

1 Durkheim writes: "There is the ontological explanation for which Plato gave the formula. Man is double because two worlds meet in him: that of non-intelligent and amoral matter, on the one hand, and that of ideas, the spirit, and the good, on the other" ([1914] 1973: 157).

2 Durkheim writes:

> Kant more than anyone else has insisted on this contrast between reason and sensitivity, between rational activity and sensory activity. But even if this classification is perfectly legitimate, it offers no solution to the problem that occupies us here; for the important thing to determine from our consideration of the fact that we have aptitudes for living both a personal and an impersonal life, is not what name it is proper to give to these contrary aptitudes, but how it is that in spite of their opposition, they exist in a single and identical being. How is it that we can participate concurrently in these two existences? How is it that we are made up of two halves that appear to belong to two different beings? Merely to give a name to each being does nothing toward answering the fundamental question.
>
> ([1914] 1973: 158)

Durkheim's non-Kantian reply is that the rational part of the human person is social and cultural, while the sensory part is bodily and private. And his reference to the two halves seems to be an allusion to Plato's parable in *The Symposium*.

3 Durkheim writes:

> There are in each of us, as we have said, two consciences: one which is common to our group in its entirety, which, consequently, is not ourself, but society living and acting within us; the other, on the contrary, represents that in us which is personal and distinct, that which makes us an individual.
>
> ([1893] 1933: 29)

He adds: "There are, here, two contrary forces, one centripetal, the other centrifugal, which cannot flourish at the same time" (ibid.: 130).

4 On ibid.: 224 he writes: "By the very requirements of man's nature, consciousness is simultaneously oriented in those two directions conventionally opposed to each other – the inward and the outward; it cannot be self-contained, and it cannot be entirely outside of itself."

5 Durkheim proposes that there are two beings in the human person: "An individual being which has its foundation in the organism and the circle of whose activities is therefore strictly limited, and a social being which represents the highest reality in the intellectual and moral order that we can know by observation – I mean society" ([1912] 1965: 29).

6 For example, Durkheim's writings are peppered with jabs at Descartes's "oversimplified" rationalism, as in *Moral Education*:

> It is something we might call oversimplified rationalism. This state of mind is characterized by the fundamental tendency to consider as real in this world only that which is perfectly simple and so poor and denuded in qualities and properties that reason can grasp it at a glance and conceive of it in a luminous representation, analogous to that which we have in grasping mathematical matters.
>
> ([1925] 1961: 250)

See also Gellner (1992).

7 Derek Humphrey's "self-help" book on how to achieve suicide efficiently, entitled *Final Exit*, achieved best-seller status in 1991. The fact that modern heirs to the Enlightenment would flock to a book that cites precise dosages to achieve an efficient suicide illustrates the pessimistic message in Durkheim's *Suicide* – suicide is a disease that afflicts decadent, aging individuals and cultures. Moreover, the title of Humphrey's book reminds one of Baudrillard's (1986) focus on the "must exit" sign as a key referent in the sea of postmodernist, circulating fictions.

8 But that is not clear to Jacobs, who writes:

> It should be clear from the above [definition] that Durkheim's initial emphasis in deriving his definition of suicide was based

upon psychological considerations, i.e. intentionality. Equally clear is the way in which he completely ignored this basic construction in the remainder of his book. At no point does he seek to establish the intentionality of any of the persons comprising his official rates.

(1980: 5)

9 For example, in "Classifications of Suicidal Phenomena," Edwin S. Shneidman (1972: 11) claims that Freud was narrow-minded to conceptualize "self-destruction as hostility directed toward the introjected love object" because this does not explain the suicidal person's other emotions toward the love object, like dependency, anguish, hopelessness, perturbation, and shame. According to Shneidman, Freud should have seen that humans commit suicide not only out of hate but also from shame, guilt, fear, loyalty and a variety of other reasons. Shneidman's critique misses the point that the "will" encompasses these other emotions, and that the unintegrated, unleashed will in general is the root of murder, suicide, and other forms of aggression.

7 Moving beyond hermeneutics

1 Even when it appears that they are taken at face value, that is not really true. The so-called value-free, hard scientist is still working off a neo-Protestant, Western European cultural legacy that can be traced back to Descartes, Kant, and other specific collective legacies (see Gellner 1992).

2 Simon claims that:

> With an examination of Homer, the tragedians, Plato, and Hippocrates I explore the nature and origins of the two fundamental polarities in psychiatry today: the intrapsychic versus the social model of the origins and treatment of mental disturbance, and the medical versus the psychological model.
>
> (1978: 10)

This is a commendable claim that undercuts the positivistic version of the origins of psychiatry. However, it seems that Simon ventures into more intellectually hazardous territory, as when he writes:

> It will become quickly apparent that I not only explore the precursors of psychoanalysis in ancient Greece but also use psychoanalysis as a tool in historical exploration. Despite the risk of methodological confusion, I have found psychoanalysis most helpful in clarifying the questions raised by thinkers in antiquity as well as their proposed solutions.
>
> (Ibid.: 12)

3 For example, I agree with Magee (1983: 260) that in some ways, Hegel laid the cultural groundwork for sociology more than Schopenhauer, with his "rampant individualism and his militant

misanthropy." See also Knapp (1985) on Hegel's influence upon Durkheim. However, I agree also with Georg Simmel ([1907] 1986) that because Schopenhauer's pessimism gave the previous *fin de siècle* its signature, he contributed indirectly to the establishment of sociology by providing a philosophical ground for challenging Hegel's extreme optimism. Sociology probably would not have been established had everything worked well with the modernist project. In any event, these are intricate matters susceptible to many opinions, and I certainly do not want to appear dogmatic about the choices that I do pursue. All of them are open to criticism.

4 "Equated" is too strong a word for me, although definite similarities exist.

5 Thus, Laplanche and Pontalis observe that instinct is "a concept which in Freud's view bridges the gap between the somatic and the mental" (1973: 364). They continue:

> On the somatic side, the instinct has its source in organic phenomena generating tension from which the subject is unable to escape; but at the same time, by virtue of its aim and of the objects to which it becomes attached, the instinct undergoes a "vicissitude" (Triebschicksal) that is essentially psychical in nature.
>
> (Ibid.: 364)

Indeed, in "Instincts and their Vicissitudes," Freud writes that an instinct may be defined as "the psychical representative of the stimuli originating from within the organism and reaching the mind" ([1915b] 1974: 122). In Schopenhauer's vocabulary, Freud seems to be claiming that the instinct is the objectification of the will. Furthermore, the English word "instinct" is used to translate two different German words, *Instinkt* and *Trieb*, and:

> The Freudian conception of *Trieb* – a pressure that is relatively indeterminate both as regards the behavior it induces and as regards the satisfying object – differs quite clearly from theories of instinct whether in their traditional form or in the revised version proposed by modern researchers (the concepts of behavior patterns, innate trigger-mechanisms, specific stimuli-signals, etc.).
>
> (Laplanche and Pontalis 1973: 214; emphasis added)

The indeterminacy of Freud's *Trieb* might be a reflection of Schopenhauer's will, a vague but all-powerful pressure that operates without a conscious aim or end. This is an extremely important observation, as it delineates Freud's thought from biology, which seems to treat instinct as a goal-patterned phenomenon.

6 Kalberg (1987) offers one of the best discussions of this problem.

7 See especially Veblen's ([1915] 1964) discussion in this regard.

8 See especially Schopenhauer's influential chapter entitled, "The Metaphysics of Sexual Love," [1818] 1969b: 531–60).

8   Reconstructing *homo duplex*

1   This is a passage that Schopenhauer quotes approvingly from Plato as well ([1818] 1969b: 463).

2   Compare Durkheim's position especially with vol. 2 of Schopenhauer's *The World as Will and Representation* in which he refers to the "double existence" we all lead relative to the will and idea ([1818] 1969b: 371). It is almost as if Durkheim plagiarized portions of Schopenhauer's argument.

3   See also Simmel's [1907] 1986 explicit elaboration of Schopenhauer's thesis in this regard.

4   For an extended discussion of the role of compassion in Durkheim's sociology, see Meštrović (1991: 108–35).

5   Because of space constraints, our interpretation bypasses the objections raised by Jung, Fromm, Rank and other disciples of Freud on the grounds that he neglected the authority of the mother. For one such discussion among many, see Schoenfeld (1962).

9   Civilized barbarism: the nature of psychic wounds

1   Consider, for example, Selye's opening line in *Stress Without Distress*: "Almost four decades of laboratory research on the physiological mechanisms of adaptation to the stress of life have convinced me that the basic principles of defense on the cellular level are largely applicable also to people and even to entire societies of man" (1974: 1). But despite the adulation accorded him, no progress has been made with regard to Selye's excursions into sociology, nor his proposal that the antidote to stress lies in the social philosophy of altruistic egoism, argued in the closing chapters of *The Stress of Life*.

2   Hirst's (1975) analysis of the similarities between Claude Bernard ([1867] 1957) and Emile Durkheim ([1893] 1933) with regard to organic equilibria does not inform stress research. Selye's (1978) call to study society as a cybernetic system, which is but an echo of similar musings by Claude Bernard into the study of "life," has been distorted into the Parsonian version of cybernetics as a dehumanized social system, not the natural cybernetics of "life" which can be traced ultimately back to Schopenhauer and Plato.

3   Freud writes:

> We must perceive that the Nirvana principle, belonging as it does to the death instinct, has undergone a modification in living organisms through which it has become the pleasure principle . . . The Nirvana principle expresses the trend of the death instinct; the pleasure principle represents the demands of the libido; and the modification of the latter principle, the reality principle, represents the influence of the external world.
>
> ([1924] 1974: 161)

At least in this passage, wearing away is a process in the service of the death instinct; it is another link between Freud's earliest writings and his later writings; and it is related to cultural problems and the great dualisms that are his recurrent theme.

4　Again, it is not the case that what is repressed is strictly a biological urge or phenomenon. All sorts of things are repressed, and they behave more like metaphysical entities than actual instincts. Laplanche and Pontalis hint at this: "Strictly speaking, repression is an operation whereby the subject attempts to repel, or to confine to the unconscious, representations (thoughts, images, memories) which are bound to an instinct" (1973: 390). But again, these instincts are not biological instincts.

5　Especially Erich Fromm (1962) and Max Horkheimer (1947).

6　Obviously, Veblen ([1899] 1967) would agree with Durkheim that leisure in general and art in particular are "useless" (by his definition) to society as a whole, and therefore barbaric habits.

7　It does not seem far-fetched to make the connection that Durkheim treats society more like the Saviour of the New Testament than the stern God of the Old Testament who demands complete obedience, and who is refracted in Parsonian functionalism.

8　As Durkheim put the matter in *Professional Ethics and Civic Morals*: "It is not possible for a social function to exist without moral discipline. Otherwise, nothing remains but individual appetites, and since they are by nature boundless and insatiable, if there is nothing to control them they will not be able to control themselves" ([1950] 1983: 10). It is important to note that Durkheim believes that appetites belong to the realm of the "will," and that humans will not control themselves of their own accord. In that regard, he shares Freud's conception of the individual as the enemy of civilization, and of secondary processes as having their origin outside the individual.

10　Barbarism and human agency

1　This linkage between Durkheim and Freud is discussed in detail in Meštrović (1988).

2　On ibid.: 45, Durkheim writes:

Suicides do not form, as might be thought, a wholly distinct group, an isolated class of monstrous phenomena, unrelated to other forms of conduct, but rather are related to them by a continuous series of intermediate cases. They are merely the exaggerated form of common practices.

3　Though they may also be prolongations of collective representations, which is entirely different.

11   Conclusions

1   This is also clear when one considers the works by the most vocal socialist in Durkheim's group, Celestin Bouglé (1896, [1908] 1971, 1909, 1918, 1930).
2   For an excellent discussion of the affinities between Marx and Durkheim, see Pearce (1989).
3   Veblen adds on p. 241: "But the economic man, whose only interest is the self-regarding one and whose only human trait is prudence, is useless for the purposes of modern industry." This is because modern industry requires the peaceable traits, including the "instinct for workmanship," that is paradoxically devalued in competitive cultures.

References

Adams, H. (1983) *The Education of Henry Adams*. New York: Viking.
Adorno, T. W. (1991) *The Culture Industry*. London: Routledge.
Alexander, J. C. (1982) *The Antinomies of Classical Thought: Marx and Durkheim. Theoretical Logic in Sociology*, Vol. 2. Berkeley: University of California Press.
—— (1988) *Durkheimian Sociology: Cultural Studies*. Cambridge: Cambridge University Press.
Alford, C. F. (1987) "Habermas, Post-Freudian Psychoanalysis, and the End of the Individual," *Theory, Culture and Society* 4(1): 3–29.
Alpert, H. (1937) "France's First University Course in Sociology," *American Sociological Review* 2: 311–17.
—— (1951) "Reviews of *Suicide: A Study in Sociology* by E. Durkheim, and *The Rules of Sociological Method* by E. Durkheim," *American Sociological Review* 10: 565–7.
—— (1961) *Emile Durkheim and His Sociology*. New York: Russell & Russell.
—— (1973) "Review of *Emile Durkheim: His Life and Work* by Steven Lukes," *Contemporary Sociology* 12: 198–200.
Alvarez, A. (1970) *The Savage God*. New York: Bantam.
Atwell, J. E. (1990) *Schopenhauer: The Human Character*. Philadelphia: Temple University Press.
Bachofen, J. J. ([1861] 1967) *Myth, Religion, and Mother Right*. Princeton: Princeton University Press.
Bailey, R. B. (1958) *Sociology Faces Pessimism: A Study of European Sociological Thought Amidst a Fading Optimism*. The Hague: Martinus Nijhoff.
Baillot, A. (1927) *Influence de la philosophie de Schopenhauer en France (1860–1900)*. Paris: J. Vrin.
Baudrillard, J. (1981) *Critique of the Political Economy of the Sign*, translated by C. Levin. St. Louis, MO: Telos Press.
—— (1986) *America*. London: Verso.
—— (1988) *Selected Writings*. Stanford: Stanford University Press.
—— (1990) *Seduction*. New York: St Martin's Press.
—— (1991) "The Reality Gulf," *The Guardian*.

Bauman, Z. (1978) *Hermeneutics and Social Science.* New York: Columbia University Press.
—— (1985) "On the Origins of Civilization: A Historical Note," *Theory, Culture and Society* 2(3): 7–14.
—— (1987) *Legislators and Interpreters: On Modernity, Post-Modernity, and Intellectuals.* Ithaca, NY: Cornell University Press.
—— (1989) *Modernity and the Holocaust.* Ithaca, NY: Cornell University Press.
—— (1990) "Assimilation and Enlightenment," *Society* 27: 71–81.
—— (1991) *Modernity and Ambivalence.* Ithaca, NY: Cornell University Press.
—— (1992) *Intimations of Postmodernity.* London: Routledge.
Bell, D. (1976) *The Cultural Contradictions of Capitalism.* New York: Basic Books.
—— (1977) *The Coming of Post-Industrial Society: A Venture in Social Forecasting.* New York: Basic Books.
—— (1981) "First Love and Early Sorrows," *Partisan Review* 48(4): 532–51.
—— (1985) "The Revolt Against Modernity," *Public Interest* 81: 42–63.
—— (1987) "The World and the United States in 2013," *Daedalus* 116(3): 1–31.
—— (1988) *The End of Ideology.* Cambridge: Harvard University Press.
Bellah, R. N. (1959) "Durkheim and History," *American Sociological Review* 24: 447–61.
—— (1967) "Civil Religion in America," *Daedalus* 96: 1–21.
—— (1970) *Beyond Belief.* New York: Harper & Row.
—— (1973) *Emile Durkheim on Morality and Society.* Chicago: University of Chicago Press.
—— (1981) "Democratic Culture or Authoritarian Capitalism?" *Society* 18(6): 41–50.
—— (1985) "Creating a New Framework for New Realities: Social Science as Public Philosophy," *Change* 17(2): 35–9.
—— (1986) "Are Americans Still Citizens?" *Tocqueville Review* 7: 89–96.
Bellah, R. N., Madsen, R., Swidler, A., Sullivan, W. M. and Tipton, S. M. (1985) *Habits of the Heart.* Berkeley: University of California Press.
Bellamy, E. ([1888] 1951) *Looking Backward, 2000–1887.* New York: Random House.
Benjamin, J. (1977) "The End of Internalization: Adorno's Social Psychology," *Telos* 32: 42–64.
—— (1978) "Authority and the Family Revisited: Or, A World Without Fathers?" *New German Critique* 13: 35–57.
Benjamin, W. (1968) "The Work of Art in the Age of Mechanical Reproduction." Pp. 219–66 in *Illuminations,* edited by Hannah Arendt. New York: Harcourt, Brace & World.
—— (1973) *Charles Baudelaire: A Lyric Poet in the Era of High Capitalism,* translated by H. Zohn. London: NLB Press.

Bergson, H. ([1932] 1954) *The Two Sources of Morality and Religion*, translated by R. A. Audra and C. Brereton. Garden City, NJ: Doubleday.

Bernard, C. ([1865] 1957) *An Introduction to the Study of Experimental Medicine*. New York: Dover.

—— (1974) *Lectures on the Phenomena of Life Common to Animals and Plants*. Springfield, IL: Charles Thomas.

Bibring, E. (1936) "The Development and Problems of the Theory of the Instincts," *Imago* 22: 147–59.

Bleicher, J. (1980) *Contemporary Hermeneutics: Hermeneutics as Method, Philosophy, and Critique*. London: Routledge & Kegan Paul.

Bloom, A. (1987) *The Closing of the American Mind*. New York: Simon & Schuster.

Bocock, R. J. (1979) "The Symbolism of the Father – A Freudian Sociological Analysis," *British Journal of Sociology* 30: 205–17.

Bogner, A. (1987) "Elias and the Frankfurt School," *Theory, Culture and Society* 4(2–3): 287–316.

Boorse, C. (1977) "Health as a Theoretical Concept," *Philosophy of Science* 44: 542–73.

Bottomore, T. (1984) *The Frankfurt School*. London: Tavistock.

Bouglé, C. (1896) *Les Sciences Sociales en Allemagne*. Paris: Alcan.

—— ([1908] 1971) *Essays on the Caste System*. Cambridge: Cambridge University Press.

—— (1909) "Darwinism and Sociology." Pp. 465–76 in *Darwin and Modern Science*, edited by A. C. Seward. Cambridge: Cambridge University Press.

—— (1918) *Chez les Prophètes Socialistes*. Paris: Alcan.

—— (1926) *The Evolution of Values*, translated by Helen Sellars. New York: Henry Holt & Co.

—— (1930) "The Present Tendency of the Social Sciences in France." Pp. 64–83 in *The New Social Science*, edited by Leonard D. White. Chicago: University of Chicago Press.

—— (1938) *The French Conception of "Culture Générale" and its Influences upon Instruction*. New York: Columbia University Press.

Breuer, J. and Freud, S. ([1893–1895] 1974) *Studies on Hysteria*. Vol. 2 in *The Standard Edition of the Complete Psychological Works of Sigmund Freud*, edited by J. Strachey. London: Hogarth.

—— (1909) *Studien Uber Hysterie*. Leipzig: Franz Deuticke.

Bryant, G. G. and Jary, D. (1991) *Giddens' Theory of Structuration: A Critical Appreciation*. London: Routledge.

Brzezinski, Z. (1989) *The Grand Failure: The Birth and Death of Communism in the Twentieth Century*. New York: Scribner's Sons.

Burston, D. (1986) "Myth, Religion and Mother Right: Bachofen's Influence on Psychoanalytic Theory," *Contemporary Psychoanalysis* 22(4): 666–87.

Camic, C. (1986) "The Matter of Habit," *American Journal of Sociology* 91: 1039–87.

Camus, A. (1955) *The Myth of Sisyphus and Other Essays*. New York: Random House.

Cannon, W. (1963) *The Wisdom of the Body.* New York: Norton.

Cantarella, E. (1982) "J. J. Bachofen Between History and the Sociology of Law," *Sociologia del Diritto* 9(3): 111–36.

Caporale, R. and ·Grumelli, A. (1971) *The Culture of Unbelief.* Berkeley: Universitiy of California Press.

Carlisle, R. B. (1988) *Saint-Simonianism and the Doctrine of Hope.* Baltimore: Johns Hopkins University Press.

Cartwright, D. (1984) "Kant, Schopenhauer, and Nietzsche on the Morality of Pity," *Journal of the History of Ideas* 45 (1): 83–98.

—— (1987) "Kant's View of the Moral Significance of Kindhearted Emotions and the Moral Insignificance of Kant's View," *Journal of Value Inquiry* 21: 291–304.

—— (1988a) "Schopenhauer's Compassion and Nietzsche's Pity," *Schopenhauer Jahrbuch* 69: 557–67.

—— (1988b) "Schopenhauer's Axiological Analysis of Character," *Revue International de Philosophie* 42: 18–36.

—— (1989) "Schopenhauer as Moral Philosopher – Towards the Actuality of his Ethics," Paper presented at the bicentennial of Schopenhauer's birth.

Clark, P. (1975) "Suicide, Société et Sociologie: De Durkheim à Balzac," *Nineteenth-Century French Studies* 3: 200–12.

Comte, A. (1974) *The Positive Philosophy.* New York: Columbia University.

Copleston, F. (1980) "Schopenhauer and Nietzsche." Pp. 215–25 in *Schopenhauer: His Philosophical Achievement,* edited by M. Fox. Totowa, NJ: Barnes & Noble.

Craib, I. (1992) *Anthony Giddens.* London: Routledge.

Crawford, R. (1984) "The Savage and the City in the Work of T. S. Eliot." Unpublished doctoral dissertation, Oxford University.

Deploige, S. ([1911] 1938) *The Conflict Between Ethics and Sociology,* translated by Charles C. Miltner. London: B. Herder Book Co.

Deutsch, K. W. (1963) *The Nerves of Government: Models of Political Communication and Control.* New York: Free Press.

Diggins, J. P. (1977) "Animism and the Origins of Alienation: The Anthropological Perspective of Thorstein Veblen," *History and Theory* 16(2): 113–26.

—— (1979) "Veblen, Weber and the Spirit of Capitalism," *Critica Sociologica* 49 (March): 7–12.

Dohrenwend, B. P. (1959) "Egoism, Altruism, Anomie, and Fatalism: A Conceptual Analysis of Durkheim's Types," *American Sociological Review* 24: 466–73.

Dohrenwend, B. P. and Dohrenwend B. S. (1974) *Stressful Life Events: Their Nature and Effects.* New York: Wiley.

Douglas, J. (1967) *The Social Meanings of Suicide.* Princeton: Princeton University Press.

—— (1969) "The Absurd in Suicide," Pp. 111–119 in *On the Nature of Suicide,* edited by E. S. Shneidman. San Francisco: Jossey-Bass.

Dugger, W. M. (1979) "The Origins of Thorstein Veblen's Thought," *Sociological Quarterly* 60(3): 424–31.

—— (1984) "Veblen and Kropotkin on Human Evolution," *Journal of Economic Issues* 18: 971–85.

Dugger, W. M. and Lopreato, J. (1981) "Sociobiology for Social Scientists," *Social Science Quarterly* 62(2): 221–33.

Durant, W. (1981) *The Story of Philosophy*. New York: Simon & Schuster.

Durkheim, E. ([1887] 1976a) "La Science positive de la morale en Allemagne." Pp. 267–343 in *Textes*, edited by V. Karady, vol. 1. Paris: Editions de Minuit.

—— ([1887] 1976b) "L'Avenir de la religion." Pp. 149–65 in *Textes*, edited by V. Karady, Vol. 2. Paris: Les Editions de Minuit.

—— ([1887] 1976c) "La Philosophie dans les Universités Allemandes." Pp. 437–86 in *Textes*, edited by V. Karady, Vol. 3. Paris: Les Editions de Minuit.

—— ([1892] 1965) *Montesquieu and Rousseau: Forerunners of Sociology*. Ann Arbor: University of Michigan Press.

—— ([1893] 1967) *De la Division du Travail Social*. Paris: Presses Universitaires de France.

—— ([1893] 1933) *The Division of Labor in Society*, translated by George Simpson. New York: Free Press.

—— (1895) *Les Règles de la Méthode Sociologique*. Paris: Alcan.

—— ([1895] 1938) *The Rules of Sociological Method*, translated by S. Soloway and J. H. Mueller. New York: Free Press.

—— ([1895] 1982) "The Rules of Sociological Method." Pp. 31–163 in *Durkheim: The Rules of Sociological Method and Selected Texts on Sociology and Its Method*, edited by S. Lukes. New York: Free Press.

—— ([1897] 1951) *Suicide: A Study in Sociology*, translated by John A. Spaulding and George Simpson. New York: Free Press.

—— ([1897] 1983) *Le Suicide: Etude de sociologie*. Paris: Presses Universitaries de France.

—— ([1897] 1963) *Incest: The Nature and Origin of the Taboo*, translated by E. Sagarin. New York: Stuart Lyle.

—— ([1900] 1973) "Sociology in France in the Nineteenth Century." Pp. 3–22 in *Emile Durkheim on Morality and Society*, edited by R. Bellah. Chicago: University of Chicago Press.

—— (1908) "Remarks in l'Inconnu et l'Inconscient en Histoire," *Bulletin de la Société Française de Philosophie* 8: 217–47.

—— ([1912] 1965) *The Elementary Forms of the Religious Life*, translated by J. Swain. New York: Free Press.

—— ([1914] 1973) "The Dualism of Human Nature and Its Social Conditions." Pp. 149–66 in *Emile Durkheim on Morality and Society*, edited by R. Bellah. Chicago: University of Chicago Press.

—— ([1920] 1978) "Introduction to Morality." Pp. 191–202 in *Emile Durkheim on Institutional Analysis*, edited by M. Traugott. Chicago: University of Chicago Press.

—— ([1924] 1974) *Sociology and Philosophy*, translated by D. F. Pocock. New York: Free Press.

—— ([1925] 1961) *Moral Education*, translated by Everett K. Wilson and Herman Schnurer. Glencoe, IL: Free Press.

—— ([1928] 1958) *Socialism and Saint-Simon*, translated by Charlotte Sattler. Yellow Springs, OH: Antioch Press.

—— ([1938] 1977) *The Evolution of Educational Thought*, translated by Peter Collins. London: Routledge & Kegan Paul.

—— ([1950] 1983) *Professional Ethics and Civic Morals*, translated by Cornelia Brookfield. Westport, CT: Greenwood Press.

Dyer, A. W. (1986a) "Veblen on Scientific Creativity: The Influence of Charles S. Peirce," *Journal of Economic Issues* 20(1): 21–41.

—— (1986b) "Semiotics, Economic Development and the Deconstruction of Economic Man," *Journal of Economic Issues* 20(2): 541–9.

Edgell, S. and Tilman, R. (1989) "The Intellectual Antecedents of Thorstein Veblen: A Reappraisal," *Journal of Economic Issues* 23(4): 103–26.

Eff, E. A. (1989) "History of Thought as Ceremonial Genealogy: The Neglected Influence of Herbert Spencer on Thorstein Veblen," *Journal of Economic Issues* 23: 689–716.

Ehrman, J. (1970) *Structuralism*. New York: Anchor.

Eissler, K. R. (1978) *Sigmund Freud: His Life in Pictures and Words*. New York: Harcourt, Brace, & Jovanovich.

Elias, N. (1982) *The Civilizing Process*. Oxford: Basil Blackwell.

Ellenberger, H. (1970) *The Discovery of the Unconscious*. New York: Basic Books.

Elster, J. (1984) "The Contradictions of Modern Societies," *Government and Opposition* 19(3): 304–11.

Engels, F. ([1884] 1972) *The Origin of the Family, Private Property and the State*. London: Lawrence & Wishart.

Estrada, J. (1988) "Max Horkheimer's Critiques of Marxism," *Estudios Filosoficos* 37: 545–62.

Featherstone, M. (1988) "In Pursuit of the Postmodern," *Theory, Culture and Society* 5(2–3): 195–216.

Fisher, S. and Greenberg, R. P. (1977) *The Scientific Credibility of Freud's Theories and Therapy*. New York: Basic Books.

Flew, A. (1985) *Thinking About Social Thinking: The Philosophy of the Social Sciences*. New York: Basic Blackwell.

Fluehr, L. (1987) "Marxism and the Matriarchate: One Hundred Years After the Origin of the Family, Private Property and the State," *Critique of Anthropology* 7(1): 5–14.

Foucault, M. (1965) *Madness and Civilization: A History of Insanity in the Age of Reason*, translated by R. Howard. New York: Random House.

Fox, M. (1980) *Schopenhauer: His Philosophical Achievement*. Totowa, NJ: Barnes & Noble.

Frazer, J. ([1890] 1981) *The Golden Bough*. New York: Avenel.

Freedman, A. M. and Kaplan, H. I. (1967) *Comprehensive Textbook of Psychiatry*. Baltimore: Williams & Williams.

Freedman, C. and Lazarus, N. (1988) "The Mandarin Marxism of Theodor Adorno," *Rethinking Marxism* 1(4): 85–111.

Freud, S. ([1886] 1974) "Observations of a Severe Case of Hemi-

Anaesthesia in a Hysterical Male." Pp. 23–43 in *The Standard Edition of the Complete Psychological Works of Sigmund Freud*, vol. 1, edited by J. Strachey. London: Hogarth.

—— ([1887–1902] 1974) "The Project for a Scientific Psychology." Pp. 281–392 in *The Standard Edition of the Complete Psychological Works of Sigmund Freud*, vol. 1, edited by J. Strachey. London: Hogarth.

—— ([1888] 1974) "Preface to the Translation of Bernheim's *Suggestion*." Pp. 71–85 in *The Standard Edition of the Complete Psychological Works of Sigmund Freud*, vol. 1, edited by J. Strachey. London: Hogarth.

—— ([1893a] 1974) "Sketches for the Preliminary Communication of 1893." Pp. 147–54 in *The Standard Edition of the Complete Psychological Works of Sigmund Freud*, vol. 3, edited by J. Strachey. London: Hogarth.

—— ([1893b] 1974) "On the Psychical Mechanism of Hysterical Phenomena: Preliminary Communication of 1893." Pp. 1–19 in *The Standard Edition of the Complete Psychological Works of Sigmund Freud*, vol. 2, edited by J. Strachey. London: Hogarth.

—— ([1893c] 1974) "On The Psychical Mechanism of Hysterical Phenomena: A Lecture." Pp. 25–40 in *The Standard Edition of the Complete Psychological Works of Sigmund Freud*, vol. 3, edited by J. Strachey. London: Hogarth.

—— ([1893d] 1974) "Some Points for a Comparative Study of Organic and Hysterical Motor Paralyses." Pp. 155–72 in *The Standard Edition of the Complete Psychological Works of Sigmund Freud*, vol. 1, edited by J. Strachey. London: Hogarth.

—— ([1895] 1974) "Extracts from the Fliess Papers." Pp. 173–280 in *The Standard Edition of the Complete Psychological Works of Sigmund Freud*, vol. 1, edited by J. Strachey. London: Hogarth.

—— ([1896a) 1974) "Heredity and the Aetiology of the Neuroses." Pp. 141–56 in *The Standard Edition of the Complete Psychological Works of Sigmund Freud*, vol. 3, edited by J. Strachey. London: Hogarth.

—— ([1896b] 1974) "Further Remarks on the Neuro-Psychoses of Defence." Pp. 157–86 in *The Standard Edition of the Complete Psychological Works of Sigmund Freud*, vol. 3, edited by J. Strachey. London: Hogarth.

—— ([1896c] 1974) "The Aetiology of Hysteria." Pp. 187–222 in *The Standard Edition of the Complete Psychological Works of Sigmund Freud*, vol. 3, edited by J. Strachey. London: Hogarth.

—— ([1900] 1965) *The Interpretation of Dreams*, translated by J. Strachey. New York: Avon.

—— ([1901] 1965) "The Psychopathology of Everyday Life," in *The Standard Edition of the Complete Psychological Works of Sigmund Freud*, vol. 6, edited by J. Strachey. London: Hogarth.

—— ([1905a] 1974) "Three Essays on the Theory of Sexuality." Pp. 125–243 in *The Standard Edition of the Complete Psychological Works of Sigmund Freud*, vol. 7, edited by J. Strachey. London: Hogarth.

—— ([1905b]] 1974) "Fragment of an Analysis of a Case of

Hysteria." Pp. 3–122 in *The Standard Edition of the Complete Psychological Works of Sigmund Freud*, vol. 7, edited by J. Strachey. London: Hogarth.

—— ([1905c] 1974) "Jokes and Their Relation to the Unconscious," in *The Standard Edition of the Complete Psychological Works of Sigmund Freud*, vol. 8, edited by J. Strachey. London: Hogarth.

—— ([1907a] 1974) "Obsessive Acts and Religious Practices." Pp. 117–28 in *The Standard Edition of the Complete Psychological Works of Sigmund Freud*, vol. 9, edited by J. Strachey. London: Hogarth.

—— ([1907a] 1974) "Delusions and Dreams in Jensen's *Gradiva*." Pp. 1–96 in *The Standard Edition of the Complete Psychological Works of Sigmund Freud*, vol. 9, edited by J. Strachey. London: Hogarth.

—— ([1908] 1974) "Character and Anal Eroticism." Pp. 169–76 in *The Standard Edition of the Complete Psychological Works of Sigmund Freud*, vol. 9, edited by J. Strachey. London: Hogarth.

—— ([1909a] 1974) "Notes Upon a Case of Obsessional Neurosis." Pp. 153–8 in *The Standard Edition of the Complete Psychological Works of Sigmund Freud*, vol. 10, edited by J. Strachey. London: Hogarth.

—— ([1909b] 1974) "Analysis of a Phobia in a Five-Year-Old Boy." Pp. 3–148 in *The Standard Edition of the Complete Psychological Works of Sigmund Freud*, vol. 10, edited by J. Strachey. London: Hogarth.

—— ([1910a] 1974) "Five Lectures on Psycho-Analysis." Pp. 3–58 in *The Standard Edition of the Complete Psychological Works of Sigmund Freud*, vol. 11, edited by J. Strachey. London: Hogarth.

—— ([1910b] 1974) "Contributions to a Discussion on Suicide." Pp. 231–2 in *The Standard Edition of the Complete Psychological Works of Sigmund Freud*, vol. 11, edited by J. Strachey. London: Hogarth.

—— ([1912] 1950) *Totem and Taboo*. New York: Norton.

—— ([1914a] 1974) "On Narcissism: An Introduction." Pp. 69–104 in *The Standard Edition of the Complete Psychological Works of Sigmund Freud*, vol. 14, edited by J. Strachey. London: Hogarth.

—— ([1914b] 1974) "Remembering, Repeating and Working-Through." Pp. 147–56 in *The Standard Edition of the Complete Psychological Works of Sigmund Freud*, vol. 12, edited by J. Strachey. London: Hogarth.

—— ([1915a] 1958) "Thoughts for the Times on War and Death." Pp. 206–35 in *Sigmund Freud on Creativity and the Unconscious*. New York: Harper & Row.

—— ([1915b] 1974) "Instincts and Their Vicissitudes." Pp. 83–122 in *Freud: Character and Culture*, edited by P. Rieff. New York: Collier Books.

—— ([1915c] 1974) "Mourning and Melancholia." Pp. 239–58 in *The Standard Edition of the Complete Psychological Works of Sigmund Freud*, vol. 14, edited by J. Strachey. London: Hogarth.

—— ([1916] 1966) *Introductory Lectures on Psychoanalysis*. New York: Norton.

—— ([1918] 1974) "From the History of an Infantile Neurosis." Pp. 3–122 in *The Standard Edition of the Complete Psychological Works of Sigmund Freud*, vol. 17, edited by J. Strachey. London: Hogarth.

—— ([1919] 1974) "Preface to Reik's *Ritual.*" Pp. 259–66 in *The Standard Edition of the Complete Psychological Works of Sigmund Freud*, vol. 17, edited by J. Strachey. London: Hogarth.

—— ([1920] 1974) "The Psychogenesis of a Case of Homosexuality in a Woman." Pp. 145–72 in *The Standard Edition of the Complete Psychological Works of Sigmund Freud*, vol. 18, edited by J. Strachey. London: Hogarth.

—— ([1920] 1961) *Beyond the Pleasure Principle.* New York: Norton.

—— ([1921] 1961) *Group Psychology and the Analysis of the Ego.* New York: Norton.

—— ([1922] 1974) "Dreams and Telepathy." Pp. 197–220 in *The Standard Edition of the Complete Psychological Works of Sigmund Freud*, vol. 18, edited by J. Strachey. London: Hogarth.

—— ([1923a] 1974) "The Ego and the Id." Pp. 1–59 in *The Standard Edition of the Complete Psychological Works of Sigmund Freud*, vol. 19, edited by J. Strachey. London: Hogarth.

—— ([1923b] 1974) "A Seventeenth Century Demonological Neurosis." Pp. 69–108 in *The Standard Edition of the Complete Psychological Works of Sigmund Freud*, vol. 19, edited by J. Strachey. London: Hogarth.

—— ([1924] 1974) "The Economic Problem of Masochism." Pp. 157–73 in *The Standard Edition of the Complete Psychological Works of Sigmund Freud*, vol. 19, edited by J. Strachey. London: Hogarth.

—— ([1925] 1959) *An Autobiographical Study.* New York: Norton.

—— ([1925] 1974) "The Resistances to Psycho-Analysis." Pp. 213–22 in *The Standard Edition of the Complete Psychological Works of Sigmund Freud*, vol. 20, edited by J. Strachey. London: Hogarth.

—— ([1926] 1959) *Inhibitions, Symptoms and Anxiety.* New York: Norton.

—— ([1926] 1974) "The Question of Lay Analysis." Pp. 179–250 in *The Standard Edition of the Complete Psychological Works of Sigmund Freud*, vol. 20, edited by J. Strachey. London: Hogarth.

—— ([1927] 1955) *The Future of an Illusion.* New York: Norton.

—— ([1930] 1961) *Civilization and Its Discontents.* New York: Norton.

—— ([1932] 1963) "Why War?" Pp. 134–47 in *Sigmund Freud on Character and Culture*, edited by P. Rieff. New York: Collier.

—— ([1933] 1965) *New Introductory Lectures on Psychoanalysis.* New York: Norton.

—— ([1938] 1969) *An Outline of Psycho-Analysis.* New York: Norton.

—— ([1939] 1974) "Moses and Monotheism." Pp. 1–138 in *The Standard Edition of the Complete Psychological Works of Sigmund Freud*, vol. 23, edited by J. Strachey. London: Hogarth.

—— ([1941] 1974) "Psycho-Analysis and Telepathy." Pp. 175–94 in *The Standard Edition of the Complete Psychological Works of Sigmund Freud*, vol. 18, edited by J. Strachey. London: Hogarth.

Frisby, D. (1984) *Georg Simmel.* London: Tavistock.

—— (1986) *Fragments of Modernity: Theories of Modernity in the Work of Simmel, Kracauer and Benjamin.* Cambridge: MIT Press.

Fromm, E. (1947) *Man for Himself.* New York: Rinehart.

—— (1950) *Psychoanalysis and Religion*. New Haven: Yale University Press.

—— (1955) *The Sane Society*. Greenwich: Fawcett.

—— (1956) *The Art of Loving*. New York: Simon & Schuster.

—— (1959) *Sigmund Freud's Mission*. New York: Harper.

—— (1962) *Beyond the Chains of Illusion*. New York: Simon & Schuster.

—— (1963) *The Dogma of Christ and Other Essays on Religion, Psychology and Culture*. New York: Holt, Rinehart, & Winston.

—— (1964) *The Heart of Man: Its Genius for Good and Evil*. New York: Harper.

Fromm, E. and Maccoby, M. (1970) *Social Character in a Mexican Village: A Sociopsychoanalytic Study*. Englewood Cliffs: Prentice-Hall.

Fukuyama, F. (1992) *The End of History and the Last Man*. New York: Free Press.

Gane, M. (1981) "Institutional Socialism and the Sociological Critique of Communism," *Economy and Society* 10(3): 301–30.

—— (1984) "Durkheim: The Sacred Language," *Economy and Society* 12(1): 1–47.

—— (1991) *Baudrillard: Critical and Fatal Theory*. London: Routledge.

Gastil, R. (1967) "Homicide and a Regional Culture of Violence," *American Sociological Review* 36 (June): 412–27.

Gellner, E. (1992) *Reason and Culture*. London: Basil Blackwell.

Ghelke, C. E. ([1915] 1968) *Emile Durkheim's Contribution to Sociological Theory*. New York: Columbia University Press.

Gibbs, J. P. and Martin, W. T. (1958) "A Theory of Status Integration and Its Relationship to Suicide," *American Sociological Review* 23: 140–7.

—— (1964) *Status Integration and Suicide: A Sociological Study*. Eugene, OR: University of Oregon Press.

Giddens, A. (1970) "Durkheim as a Review Critic," *Sociological Review* 18: 171–96.

—— (1971) "The Individual in the Writings of Emile Durkheim," *European Journal of Sociology* 12: 210–28.

—— (1976a) "Classical Social Theory and the Origins of Modern Sociology," *American Journal of Sociology* 81(4): 703–29.

—— (1976b) *New Rules of Sociological Method*. New York: Basic Books.

—— (1986) *Durkheim on Politics and the State*. London: Polity Press.

—— (1987) *Social Theory and Modern Sociology*. Stanford: Stanford University Press.

—— (1990) *The Consequences of Modernity*. Stanford: Stanford University Press.

Glassner, B. (1988) *Bodies*. New York: Putnam.

—— (1989) "Fitness and the Postmodern Self," *Journal of Health and Social Behavior* 30(2): 190–7.

—— (1990) "Fit for Postmodern Selfhood." Pp. 214–43 in *Symbolic Interaction and Cultural Studies*, edited by H. S. Becker and M. M. McCall. Chicago: University of Chicago Press.

Gold, M. (1958) "Suicide, Homicide, and the Socialization of Aggression," *American Journal of Sociology* 63: 651–70.

Goodwin, P. (1967) "Schopenhauer." Pp. 325–32 in *The Encyclopedia of Philosophy*, vol. 7, edited by P. Edwards. New York: Macmillan.

Gouldner, A. (1958) "Introduction." Pp. v–xxviii in *Socialism and Saint-Simon*, by Emile Durkheim. Yellow Springs, OH: Antioch Press.

—— (1965) *Enter Plato: Classical Greece and the Origins of Social Theory*. New York: Basic Books.

—— (1970) *The Coming Crisis of Western Sociology*. New York: Basic Books.

Greenwood, S. (1990) "Emile Durkheim and C. G. Jung: Structuring a Transpersonal Sociology of Religion," *Journal for the Scientific Study of Religion* 29: 482–95.

Greisman, H. (1981) "Matriarchate as Utopia, Myth, and Social Theory," *Sociology* 15(3): 321–36.

Grignon, C. (1976) "Tristes topiques," *Actes de la recherche en sciences sociales* 1(February): 32–42.

Grunwald, H. (1992) "The Year 2000," *Time* 139 (13): 73–6.

Guala, C. (1973) "The Use and the Significance of the Concept of Totality in the Work and Thinking of Marcel Mauss," *Sociologia* 7(1): 5–42.

Gupta, R. K. (1980) "Freud and Schopenhauer." Pp. 226–35 in *Schopenhauer: His Philosophical Achievement*, edited by M. Fox. Totowa, NJ: Barnes & Noble.

Guyau, J. ([1885] 1907) *Esquisse d'une Morale Sans Obligation ni Sanction*. Paris: Alcan.

—— ([1887] 1909) *L'Irréligion de l'Avenir*. Paris: Alcan.

Habermas, J. (1970) *Toward a Rational Society*. Boston: Beacon.

—— (1979) *Communication and the Evolution of Society*. Boston: Beacon.

—— (1981) "Modernity Versus Postmodernity," *New German Critique* 22: 3–14.

—— (1984) *The Theory of Communicative Action*. Boston: Beacon.

—— (1987) *The Philosophical Discourse of Modernity*. Cambridge: MIT Press.

Halbwachs, M. ([1912] 1974) *La Classe Ouvrière et les Niveaux*. London: Gordon & Breach.

—— (1918) "La Doctrine d'Emile Durkheim," *Revue Philosophique* 85: 353–411.

—— (1925) "Les Origines Puritaines du Capitalisme," *Revue d'Histoire et de Philosophie Religieuses*. 5: 132–57.

—— ([1930] 1978) *The Causes of Suicide*. London: Routledge & Kegan Paul.

—— (1939) "Individual Conscience and Collective Mind," *American Journal of Sociology* 44: 812–22.

—— ([1950] 1980) *The Collective Memory*. New York: Harper & Row.

Hall, J. A. (1988) *Liberalism: Politics, Ideology, and the Market*. Chapel Hill: University of North Carolina.

Hall, R. T. (1987) *Emile Durkheim: Ethics and the Sociology of Morals*. New York: Greenwood Press.

Hamlyn, D. (1980) *Schopenhauer*. London: Routledge & Kegan Paul.

Harpham, G. (1976) "Time Running Out: The Edwardian Sense of Cultural Degeneration," *Clio* 5(3): 282–301.

Harvey, D. (1985) *Consciousness and the Urban Experience*. Baltimore: Johns Hopkins University Press.

—— (1989) *The Condition of Postmodernity*. London: Basil Blackwell.

Hegel, G. W. F. ([1899] 1965) *The Philosophy of History*. New York: Dover.

Held, D. (1978) "Adorno," *New Society* 43(7): 185–7.

Hendin, H. (1964) *Suicide and Scandinavia: A Psycho-Analytic Study of Culture and Character*. New York: Grune & Stratton.

Henry, A. F. and Short, J. F. (1954) *Suicide and Homicide: Some Economic, Sociological, and Psychological Aspects of Aggression*. New York: Free Press.

Hermand, J. (1984) "All Power to the Women: Fascist Concepts of Matriarchy," *Argument* 26: 53–4.

Hirst, P. Q. (1975) *Durkheim, Bernard and Epistemology*. London: Routledge & Kegan Paul.

Hoffman, L. E. (1984) "Psychoanalytic Interpretations of Political Movements, 1900–1950," *Psychohistory Review* 13(1): 16–29.

Hohendahl, P. (1985) "The Dialectic of Enlightenment Revisited: Habermas's Critique of the Frankfurt School," *New German Critique* 35: 3–26.

Horkheimer, M. (1947) *The Eclipse of Reason*. New York: Oxford University Press.

—— (1955) "Schopenhauer und die Gesellschaft," *Schopenhauer Jahrbuch* 36: 49–57.

—— (1971a) "Pessimismus Heute," *Schopenhauer Jahrbuch* 52: 1–8.

—— (1971b) "Die Zeitgemässheit Schopenhauers," *Neue Zürcher Zeitung* 21 March: 1.

—— (1972a) "Bemerkungen zu Schopenhauer im Verhältnis zu Wissenschaft und Religion," *Schopenhauer Jahrbuch* 53: 71–9.

—— (1972b) *Critical Theory: Selected Essays*. New York: Herder & Herder.

—— (1973) "The Authoritarian State," *Telos* 15 (Spring): 3–20.

—— (1974) *Critique of Instrumental Reason*. New York: Seabury Press.

—— (1978) *Dawn and Decline*. New York: Seabury Press.

—— (1980) "Schopenhauer Today." Pp. 20–36 in *Schopenhauer: His Philosophical Achievement*, edited by M. Fox. Totowa, NJ: Barnes & Noble.

—— (1986) "Materialism and Morality," *Telos* 69: 85–118.

Horkheimer, M. and Adorno, T. (1972) *Dialectic of Enlightenment*. New York: Continuum Press.

Hübscher, A. (1989) *The Philosophy of Schopenhauer in Its Intellectual Context: Thinker Against the Tide*, translated by J. T. Baer and D. E. Cartwright. Lewiston, NY: Edwin Mellen Press.

Hynes, E. (1975) "Suicide and Homo Duplex," *Sociological Quarterly* 16(1): 87–104.

Ingram, D. (1986) "Foucault and the Frankfurt School: A Discourse on Nietzsche, Power, and Knowledge," *Praxis International* 6(3): 311–27.

—— (1988) "The Postmodern Kantianism of Arendt and Lyotard," *Review of Metaphysics* 42(1): 51–77.

Izzo, A. (1980) "Durkheim and Socialism," *Critica Sociologica*. 55: 19–26.

Jacobs, J. (1980) *Adolescent Suicide*. New York: Wiley.

Jaksic, B. (1979) "A Contribution to C. Wright Mills's Intellectual Biography," *Socioloski Pregled* 13(3–4): 7–23.

James, W. ([1890] 1950) *The Principles of Psychology*. New York: Dover.

—— ([1896] 1931) *The Will to Believe, and Other Essays in Popular Philosophy*. New York: Longmans.

Janaway, C. (1989) *Self and World in Schopenhauer's Philosophy*. New York: Oxford.

Janik, A. and Toulmin, S. (1973) *Wittgenstein's Vienna*. New York: Simon & Schuster.

Jay, M. (1982) "Positive and Negative Totalities: Implicit Tensions in Critical Theory's Vision of Interdisciplinary Research," *Thesis Eleven* 3: 72–87.

—— (1984) *Adorno*. Cambridge: Harvard University Press.

—— (1988) *Fin de Siècle Socialism and Other Essays*. London: Routledge.

Johnson, B. D. (1965) "Durkheim's One Type of Suicide," *American Sociological Review* 30: 875–86.

Jones, E. (1981) *The Life and Work of Sigmund Freud*. Vols. 1–3. New York: Basic Books.

Jung, C. G. (1959) *Four Archetypes*. Princeton: Princeton University Press.

—— (1961) *Memories, Dreams, Reflections*. New York: Pantheon.

—— (1966) *The Spirit in Man, Art, and Literature*. Princeton: Princeton University Press.

—— (1973) *Man and His Symbols*. New York: Dell.

Kaern, M., Phillips, B. S. and Cohen, R. S. (1990) *Georg Simmel and Contemporary Sociology*. Boston: Kluwer.

Kalberg, S. (1987) "The Origin and Expansion of *Kulturpessimismus*: The Relationship Between Public and Private Spheres in Early Twentieth Century Germany," *Sociological Theory* 5: 150–65.

Kant, I. ([1788] 1956) *Critique of Practical Reason*. Indianapolis: Bobbs-Merrill.

—— (1963) *On History*. Indianapolis: Bobbs-Merrill.

Kanter, D. L. and Mirvis, P. H. (1989) *The Cynical Americans*. San Francisco: Josey-Bass.

Käsler, D. (1988) *Max Weber*. Chicago: University of Chicago Press.

Katz, J. (1988) *The Seductions of Crime*. New York: Basic Books.

Kellner, D. (1988) "Postmodernism as Social Theory," *Theory, Culture, and Society* 5(2–3): 239–70.

—— (1989a) "Boundaries and Borderlines: Reflections on Jean Baudrillard and Critical Theory," *Current Perspectives in Social Theory* 9: 5–22.

—— (1989b) *Jean Baudrillard: From Marxism to Postmodernism and Beyond.* Stanford: Stanford University Press.

—— (1990) "Critical Theory and the Crisis of Social Theory," *Sociological Perspectives* 33 (1): 11–33.

Kennedy, G. (1987) "Fin de Siècle Classicism: Henry Adams and Thorstein Veblen, Lew Wallace and W. D. Howells," *Classical and Modern Literature* 8(1): 15–21.

Kennedy, P. (1990) "Fin de Siècle America," *New York Review of Books* 37 (11): 31–40.

Kierkegaard, S. (1954) *Fear and Trembling and the Sickness Unto Death,* translated by W. Lowrie. Princeton: Princeton University Press.

Knapp, P. (1985) "The Question of Hegelian Influence Upon Durkheim's Thought," *Sociological Inquiry* 55: 1–15.

Kohlberg, L. (1981) *Essays in Moral Development.* San Francisco, CA: Harper & Row.

Kojeve, A. (1969) *Introduction to the Reasoning of Hegel.* New York: Basic Books.

Korthals, M. (1985) "The Critical Theory of the Early Horkheimer," *Zeitschrift für Soziologie* 14(4): 315–29.

Kramer, F. W., Jell, B. and Werts, D. (1985) "Empathy-Reflections on the History of Ethnology in Pre-fascist Germany: Herder, Creuzer, Bastian, Bachofen, and Frobenius," *Dialectical Anthropology* 9: 337–47.

Kroker, A. and Cook, D. (1986) *The Postmodern Scene: Excremental Culture and Hyper-Aesthetics.* New York: St Martin's.

Kurzweil, E. (1990) *The Freudians: A Comparative Perspective.* New Haven: Yale University Press.

La Capra, D. (1972) *Emile Durkheim: Sociologist and Philosopher.* Ithaca: Cornell University Press.

Lalande, A. ([1926] 1980) *Vocabulaire Technique et Critique de la Philosophie.* Paris: Presses Universitaires de France.

—— (1960) "Allocution." Pp. 20–3 in *Centenaire de la Naissance d'Emile Durkheim.* Paris: Annales de l'Université de Paris.

Laplanche, J. (1976) *Life and Death in Psychoanalysis,* translated by J. Mehlman. Baltimore: Johns Hopkins University Press.

Laplanche, J. and Pontalis, J. B. (1973) *The Language of Psychoanalysis.* New York: Norton.

Lasch, C. (1977) *Haven in a Heartless World.* New York: Basic Books.

—— (1979) *The Culture of Narcissism.* New York: Norton.

—— (1985) "Historical Sociology and the Myth of Maturity: Norbert Elias's 'Very Simple Formula,'" *Theory and Society* 14(5): 705–20.

—— (1986) "The Communitarian Critique of Liberalism," *Soundings* 69(1–2): 60–76.

—— (1991) *The One and Only Heaven.* New York: Norton.

Lears, T. J. (1983) "In Defense of Henry Adams," *The Wilson Quarterly* 7: 82–93.

Leathers, C. G. (1986) "Bellamy and Veblen's Christian Morals," *Journal of Economic Issues* 20: 107–19.

—— (1989) "Thorstein Veblen's Theories of Governmental Failure," *American Journal of Economics and Sociology* 48(3): 293–306.

Lepenies, W. (1978) "Norbert Elias: An Outsider Full of Unprejudiced Insight," *New German Critique* 15: 57–64.

Levi, V. and Amado, E. (1975) "Sin and Salvation in the Ontology of D. H. Lawrence," *Human Context* 7(2): 264–92.

Lévy, A. (1904) *Stirner et Nietzsche*. Paris: Société Nouvelle.

Luft, E. (1988) *Schopenhauer: New Essays in Honor of his 200th Birthday.* Lewiston, NY: Mellen.

Lukacs, G. (1980) *The Destruction of Reason,* translated by Peter Palmer. Atlantic Highlands: Humanities Press.

Lukes, S. (1985) *Emile Durkheim: His Life and Work.* Stanford, CA: Stanford University Press.

Lutz, T. (1990) *American Nervousness, 1903: An Anecdotal History.* Ithaca: Cornell University Press.

Lyotard, J. (1984) *The Postmodern Condition.* Minneapolis: University of Minnesota Press.

Machalek, R. (1979) "Thorstein Veblen, Louis Schneider and the Ironic Imagination," *Social Science Quarterly* 60(3): 460–4.

Magee, B. (1983) *The Philosophy of Schopenhauer.* New York: Oxford University Press.

Mann, T. (1939) *The Living Thoughts of Schopenhauer.* New York: Longmans, Green, and Co.

Manschreck, C. (1976) "Nihilism in the Twentieth Century: A View From Here," *Church History* 45: 85–96.

Marcus, S. (1984) *Freud and the Culture of Psychoanalysis: Studies in the Transition From Victorian Humanism to Modernity.* Boston: Allen & Unwin.

Marcuse, H. (1962) *Eros and Civilization: A Philosophical Inquiry into Freud.* New York: Random House.

Margolis, J. (1976) "The Concept of Disease," *The Journal of Medicine and Philosophy* 1: 238–54.

Maris, R. W. (1969) *Social Forces in Urban Suicide.* Homewood, IL: Dorsey Press.

Marks, S. R. (1972) "Durkheim's Theory of Anomie," *American Journal of Sociology* 80: 329–63.

Marx, K. ([1858] 1977) *Capital.* Vol. 1. New York: Random House.

—— (1983) *The Portable Karl Marx,* edited by E. Kamenka. New York: Penguin.

Masaryk, T. ([1881] 1970) *Suicide and the Meaning of Civilization.* Chicago: University of Chicago Press.

Mauss, M. ([1950] 1979) *Sociology and Psychology.* London: Routledge & Kegan Paul.

Mayes, S. G. (1980) "Sociological Thought in Emile Durkheim and George Fitzhugh," *British Journal of Sociology* 31: 78–94.

Menand, L. and Schwartz, S. (1982) "T. S. Eliot on Durkheim: A New Attribution," *Modern Philology* 79: 309–15.

Menninger, K. (1966) *Man Against Himself.* New York: Harcourt, Brace, Jovanovich.

Merton, R. K. (1957) *Social Theory and Social Structure*. New York: Free Press.

Meštrović, S. G. (1988) *Emile Durkheim and the Reformation of Sociology*. Totowa, NJ: Rowman & Littlefield.

—— (1991) *The Coming Fin de Siècle: An Application of Durkheim's Sociology to Modernity and Postmodernism*. London: Routledge.

—— (1992) *Durkheim and Postmodern Culture*. Hawthorne, NY: Aldine de Gruyter.

Meštrović, S. G. and Glassner, B. (1983) "A Durkheimian Hypothesis on Stress," *Social Science and Medicine* 17: 1315–27.

Meštrović, S. G., Goreta, M. and Letica, S. (1993) *The Road From Paradise*. Lexington, KY: University Press of Kentucky.

Mill, J. S. (1968) *Auguste Comte and Positivism*. Ann Arbor, MI: University of Michigan Press.

Mills, C. W. (1959) *The Sociological Imagination*. New York: Oxford University Press.

Mirowski, P. (1987) "The Philosophical Bases of Institutionalist Economics," *Journal of Economic Issues* 21: 1001–37.

Mischel, T. (1974) *Understanding Other Persons*. London: Basil Blackwell.

Mitzman, A. (1977) "Anarchism, Expressionism and Psychoanalysis," *New German Critique* 10: 77–104.

Mizruchi, E. (1983) *Regulating Society*. Chicago: University of Chicago Press.

Molitierno, A. (1989) "Georg Simmel's Cultural Narcissism: A Non-ideological Approach," *Midwest Quarterly* 30(3): 308–23.

Moreland, K. (1989) "Henry Adams, the Medieval Lady, and the 'New Woman'." *Clio* 18: 291–305.

Mudragei, S. (1979) "The Problem of Man in the Irrationalist Teachings of Søren Kierkegaard," *Voprosy Filosofii* 33: 76–86.

Murphy, J. W. (1989) *Postmodern Social Analysis and Criticism*. New York: Greenwood.

Nandan, Y. (1970) *Emile Durkheim: Contributions to L'Année Sociologique*. New York: Free Press.

—— (1977) *The Durkheimian School: A Systematic and Comprehensive Bibliography*. Westport, CT: Greenwood Press.

Neveu, E. (1990) "Sociostyles: Une *Fin de Siècle* Sans Classes," *Sociologie du Travail* 32(2): 137–51.

Nietzsche, F. ([1874] 1965) *Schopenhauer as Educator*. South Bend, IN: Gateway.

—— ([1874] 1983) *Untimely Meditations*. Cambridge: Cambridge University Press.

—— ([1901] 1968) *The Will to Power*. New York: Random House.

—— (1968) *The Portable Nietzsche*, translated by W. Kaufmann. New York: Viking Library.

Nisbet, R. A. (1966) *The Sociological Tradition*. New York: Basic Books.

—— (1974) *The Sociology of Emile Durkheim*. New York: Oxford University Press.

—— (1976) *Sociology as an Art Form*. New York: Oxford University Press.

O'Keefe, D. L. (1982) *Stolen Lightning: A Social Theory of Magic*. New York: Random House.

Oliver, D. W. (1989) *Education, Modernity, and Fractured Meaning: Toward a Process Theory of Teaching and Learning*. Albany, NY: SUNY Press.

Park, R. E. and Burgess, W. E. (1921) *Introduction to the Science of Sociology*. Chicago: University of Chicago Press.

Parsons, T. (1937) *The Structure of Social Action*. Glencoe, IL: Free Press.

—— (1948) "The Position of Sociological Theory," *American Sociological Review* 13: 156–64.

—— (1962) "Psychoanalysis and the Social Structure." Pp. 46–62 in *Psychoanalysis and Social Science*, edited by H. Ruitenbeek. New York: Dutton.

—— (1971) "Belief, Unbelief, and Disbelief." Pp. 207–46 in *The Culture of Unbelief*, edited by R. Caporale and A. Grumelli. Berkeley: University of California Press.

Partenheimer, D. (1988) "The Education of Henry Adams in German Philosophy," *Journal of the History of Ideas* 49: 339–45.

Pearce, F. (1989) *The Radical Durkheim*. London: Unwin Hyman.

Pearlin, L. (1981) "The Stress Process," *Journal of Health and Social Behavior* 22: 337–56.

Piaget, J. (1926) *The Language and Thought of the Child*. London: Routledge.

—— ([1932] 1965) *The Moral Judgment of the Child*. New York: Free Press.

—— (1970) *Structuralism*. New York: Basic Books.

Pickering, W. S.F. (1984) *Durkheim's Sociology of Religion: Themes and Theories*. London: Routledge & Kegan Paul.

Plato (1968) *The Dialogues*, translated by B. Jowett. Oxford: Clarendon Press.

Pope, W. (1973) "Classic on Classic: Parsons's Interpretation of Durkheim," *American Sociological Review* 38(4): 399–415.

Popper, K. R. ([1934] 1961) *The Logic of Scientific Discovery*. New York: Science Editions.

Posnock, R. (1987) "Henry James, Veblen and Adorno: The Crisis of the Modern Self," *Journal of American Studies* 21(1): 31–54.

Powell, E. H. (1958) "Occupation, Status, and Suicide: Toward a Redefinition of Anomie," *American Sociological Review* 23: 131–9.

Ranulf, S. (1939) "Scholarly Forerunners of Fascism," *Ethics* 50: 16–34.

Renouvier, C. (1892) "Schopenhauer et la métaphysique du pessimisme," *L'Année Philosophique* 3: 1–61.

Restivo, S. (1991) *The Sociological World-view*. London: Basil Blackwell.

Riba, T. (1985) "Romanticism and Nationalism in Economics," *International Journal of Social Economics* 12: 52–68.

Ribot, T. (1874) *La Philosophie de Schopenhauer*. Paris: Librairie Gerner Bailliere.

—— (1896) *The Psychology of Attention*. Chicago: Open Court.

—— (1899) *German Psychology of Today*, translated by James M. Baldwin. New York: Charles Scribner's Sons.

Ricœur, P. (1970) *Freud and Philosophy: An Essay on Interpretation.* New Haven: Yale University Press.
—— (1979) *Major Trends in Philosophy.* New York: Holmes Meier.
Riesman, D. (1950) *The Lonely Crowd.* New Haven: Yale University Press.
—— (1953) *Thorstein Veblen: A Critical Interpretation.* New York: Charles Scribner's Sons.
—— (1954) *Individualism Reconsidered and Other Essays.* Glencoe, IL: Free Press.
—— (1956) *Constraint and Variety in American Education.* Lincoln: University of Nebraska Press.
—— (1964) *Abundance For What?* Garden City, NY: Doubleday.
—— (1976) "Liberation and Stalemate," *Massachusetts Review* 17(4): 767–76.
—— (1977) "Prospects for Human Rights," *Society* 15(1): 28–33.
—— (1980a) "Egocentrism," *Character* 1(5): 3–9.
—— (1980b) *On Higher Education: The Academic Enterprise in an Era of Rising Student Consumerism.* San Francisco: Jossey-Bass.
—— (1981) "The Dream of Abundance Reconsidered," *Public Opinion Quarterly* 45(3): 285–302.
Riesman, D. and Grant, G. (1978) *The Perpetual Dream: Reform and Experiment in the American College.* Chicago: University of Chicago Press.
Riesman, D., Gusfield, J. and Gamson, Z. (1970) *Academic Values and Mass Education.* Garden City, NY: Doubleday.
Riesman, D. and Jencks, C. (1968) *The Academic Revolution.* Garden City, NY: Doubleday.
Riesman, D. and Riesman, E. T. (1967) *Conversations in Japan: Modernization, Politics, and Culture.* Chicago: University of Chicago Press.
Roazen, P. (1968) *Freud: Political and Social Thought.* New York: Random House.
Roche, S. (1988) "Insecurity, the Feeling of Insecurity and Social Reconstruction: Comparable Ends to Two Centuries," *International Review of Community Development* 19 (Spring): 11–20.
Rojek, C. (1990) "Baudrillard and Leisure," *Leisure Studies* 9(1): 7–20.
Rosenau, P. (1992) *Postmodernism and the Social Sciences.* Princeton: Princeton University Press.
Rosenthal, A. S. (1978) "A Utopian Vision of the Frankfurt School," *Humanity-Society* 2(2): 90–103.
Ryan, B. E. (1982) "Thorstein Veblen: A New Perspective," *Mid-American Review of Sociology* 7(2): 29–47.
Safranski, R. (1990) *Schopenhauer and the Wild Years of Philosophy.* Cambridge: Harvard University Press.
Saint-Simon, H. ([1828] 1972) *The Doctrine of Saint-Simon*, translated by G. Iggers. New York: Schocken Books.
Schleiermacher, F. (1977) *Hermeneutics.* Missoula, MO: Scholars Press.

Schneider, L. (1948) *The Freudian Psychology and Veblen's Social Theory.* Morningside Heights, NY: King's Crown Press.
—— (1971) "Dialectic in Sociology," *American Sociological Review* 36: 667–78.
Schoenfeld, C. G. (1962) "God the Father – and Mother: Study and Extension of Freud's Conception of God as an Exalted Father," *The American Imago* 19(3): 213–34.
—— (1966) "Erich Fromm's Attacks Upon the Oedipus Complex – A Brief Critique," *Journal of Nervous and Mental Disease* 141(5): 580–5.
—— (1968) "Psychoanalytic Guideposts for the Good Society," *The Psychoanalytic Review* (Spring): 91–114.
—— (1974) "International Law, Nationalism, and the Sense of Self: A Psychoanalytic Inquiry," *Journal of Psychiatry and Law* (Fall) 303–17.
—— (1984) *Psychoanalysis Applied to the Law.* Port Washington, NY: Associated Faculty Press.
Schoenfeld, E. (1987) "Militant Religion." Pp. 125–37 in *Religious Society,* edited by W. Swatos. Westport, CT: Greenwood Press.
—— (1989) "Justice: An Illusive Concept in Christianity," *Review of Religious Research* 30: 236–45.
Schopenhauer, A. ([1813] 1899) *On the Fourfold Root of the Principle of Sufficient Reason and On the Will in Nature.* London: G. Bell & Sons.
—— ([1818] 1969a) *The World as Will and Representation,* translated by E. F. J. Payne. Vol. 1. New York: Dover.
—— ([1818] 1969b) *The World as Will and Representation,* translated by E. F. J. Payne. Vol. 2. New York: Dover.
—— ([1841] 1965) *On the Basis of Morality.* Indianapolis: Bobbs-Merrill.
—— (1970) *Essays and Aphorisms.* London: Penguin.
—— (1985) *Early Manuscripts (1804–1818).* Oxford: Berg.
Schorske, C. (1980) *Fin de Siècle Vienna: Politics and Culture.* New York: Alfred A. Knopf.
Schwartz, H. (1990) *Century's End: A Cultural History of the Fin de Siècle.* New York: Doubleday.
Scott, B. A. (1986) "The Decline of Literacy and Liberal Learning," *Journal of Education* 168(1): 105–16.
Selye, H. (1974) *Stress Without Distress.* Philadelphia: Lippincott.
Shneidman, E. S. (1969) *On the Nature of Suicide.* San Francisco: Josey-Bass.
—— (1972) "Classifications of Suicidal Phenomena." Pp. 10–43 in *Self-Destructive Behavior,* edited by B. Q. Hafen. Minneapolis: Burgess.
Showalter, Elaine (1990) *Sexual Anarchy: Gender and Culture at the Fin de Siècle.* New York: Viking.
—— (1978) *The Stress of Life.* New York: McGraw-Hill.
Sica, A. (1984) "The Unique Sociology of Norbert Elias," *Mid-American Review of Sociology* 9(1): 49–78.
—— (1988) *Weber, Irrationality, and Social Order.* Berkeley: University of California Press.

Siebert, R. J. (1979) *Horkheimer's Critical Sociology of Religion: The Relative and the Transcendent.* Lanham, MD: University Press of America.

Simmel, G. (1902) "Tendencies in German Life and Thought Since 1870," *International Monthly* 5: 93–111.

—— ([1907] 1986) *Schopenhauer and Nietzsche.* Amherst: University of Massachusetts Press.

—— ([1921] 1971) "Eros, Platonic and Modern." Pp. 235–48 in *On Individuality and Its Social Forms,* edited by D. Levine. Chicago: University of Chicago Press.

—— (1971) *On Individuality and Its Social Forms.* Chicago: University of Chicago Press.

Simon, B. (1978) *Mind and Madness in Ancient Greece: The Classical Roots of Modern Psychiatry.* Ithaca: Cornell University Press.

Sloterdijk, P. (1987) *Critique of Cynical Reason,* translated by Michael Eldred. Minneapolis: University of Minnesota Press.

Smart, B. (1992) *Modern Conditions, Postmodern Controversies.* London: Routledge.

Sonn, R. D. (1989) *Anarchism and Cultural Politics in Fin de Siècle France.* Lincoln: University of Nebraska Press.

Sorokin, P. (1943) *The Crisis of Our Age.* New York: E. P. Dutton.

—— (1944) *Russia and the United States.* New York: E. P. Dutton.

—— (1947) *The Ways and Power of Love.* New York: American Book Company.

—— (1948) *The Reconstruction of Humanity.* Boston: Beacon Press.

—— (1957) *Social and Cultural Dynamics.* New York: American Book Company.

—— (1959) *Social and Cultural Mobility.* Glencoe, IL: Free Press.

—— (1963) *A Long Journey: The Autobiography of Pitirim A. Sorokin.* New Haven, CT: College and University Press.

Spengler, O. ([1926] 1961) *The Decline of the West. Vol. 1. Form and Actuality,* translated by Charles F. Atkinson. New York: Alfred A. Knopf.

—— ([1928] 1961) *The Decline of the West. Vol. 2. Perspectives on World-History,* translated by Charles F. Atkinson. New York: Alfred A. Knopf.

Stanfield, J. R. (1989) "Veblenian and Neo-Marxian Perspectives on the Cultural Crisis of Late Capitalism," *Journal of Economic Issues* 23(3): 717–34.

Staude, J. R. (1976) "From Depth Psychology to Depth Sociology: Freud, Jung, and Levi-Strauss," *Theory and Society* 3 (3): 303–38.

Steinmetz, S. K. and Straus, M. A. (1974) *Violence in the Family.* New York: Harper & Row.

Stevens, A. (1983) *Archetypes.* New York: Quill.

—— (1989) *The Roots of War.* New York: Paragon.

Stokes, John. (1989) *In the Nineties.* Chicago: University of Chicago Press.

Sulloway, F. J. (1979) *Freud, Biologist of the Mind: Beyond the Psychoanalytic Legend.* Cambridge: Harvard University Press.

Suto, M. (1979) "Some Neglected Aspects of Veblen's Social Thought," *Social Science Quarterly* 60(3): 439–53.
Synnott, A. (1987) "Lions, Tigers and Cows: Zoological Sociology and Anthropology," *Society* 11(2): 9–12.
Teich, M. and Porter, R. (1990) *Fin de Siècle and Its Legacy.* Cambridge: Cambridge University Press.
Tertulian, N. and Parent, D. J. (1985) "Lukacs, Adorno and German Classical Philosophy," *Telos* 63: 79–96.
Tilman, R. (1985) "The Utopian Vision of Edward Bellamy and Thorstein Veblen," *Journal of Economic Issues* 19(4): 879–98.
Tocqueville, A. ([1845] 1945) *Democracy in America*. Vol. 1. New York: Vintage.
Tomasic, D. (1948) *Personality and Culture in Eastern European Politics.* New York: George W. Stewart, Publisher.
—— (1953) *The Impact of Russian Culture on Soviet Communism*. Glencoe, IL: Free Press.
Tönnies, F. ([1887] 1963) *Community and Society*, translated by C. Loomis. New York: Harper & Row.
—— ([1921] 1974) *Karl Marx: His Life and Teachings*, translated by C. Loomis and I. Paulus. Lansing: Michigan State University Press.
—— (1961) *Custom: An Essay on Social Codes*. New York: Free Press.
Torpey, A. (1986) "Ethics and Critical Theory: From Horkheimer to Habermas," *Telos* 69: 68–84.
Trigg, R. (1985) *Understanding Social Science*. New York: Basil Blackwell.
Turner, B. (1984) *The Body and Society*. London: Basil Blackwell.
—— (1985) "Review of *The Civilizing Process* by N. Elias," *Theory, Culture and Society* 2(3): 158–61.
—— (1990) *Theories of Modernity and Postmodernity*. London: Sage.
Veblen, T. ([1899] 1967) *The Theory of the Leisure Class*. New York: Penguin Books.
—— ([1910] 1943) "Christian Morals and the Competitive System." Pp. 200–28 in *Essays in Our Changing Order*, edited by L. Ardzrooni. New York: Viking.
—— ([1915] 1964) *Imperial Germany and the Industrial Revolution*. New York: Sentry Press.
—— (1917) *An Inquiry Into the Nature of Peace and the Terms of its Perpetuation*. New York: Macmillan.
—— ([1919] 1961) *The Place of Science in Modern Civilization*. New York: Russell & Russell.
—— (1943) *Essays in Our Changing Order*. New York: Viking.
—— (1948) *The Portable Veblen*, edited by Max Lerner. New York: Viking.
—— (1973) *Essays, Reviews, and Reports*. New York: Sentry Press.
Vitz, Paul C. (1988) *Sigmund Freud's Christian Unconscious*. New York: Guilford Press.
Waller, W. T. (1988) "The Concept of Habit in Economic Analysis," *Journal of Economic Issues* 22: 113–26.
Wallwork, E. (1972) *Durkheim: Morality and Milieu*. Cambridge: Harvard University Press.

Waugaman, R. (1973) "The Intellectual Relationship Beween Nietzsche and Freud," *Psychiatry* 36(4): 458–67.

Weber, E. (1987) *France, Fin de Siècle*. Cambridge: Harvard University Press.

Weber, M. ([1904] 1958) *The Protestant Ethic and the Spirit of Capitalism*, translated by T. Parsons. New York: Charles Scribner's Sons.

Weinstein, F. and Platt, G. (1973) *Psychoanalytic Sociology*. Baltimore: Johns Hopkins University Press.

Wells, H. G. (1906) *The Future in America: A Search After Realities*. New York: Harper & Brothers.

—— (1928) *The Way the World is Going*. London: Benn.

—— (1935) *The New America: The New World*. London: Cresset.

—— (1939) *The Fate of Man*. New York: Longmans.

West, D. J. (1967) *Murder Followed by Suicide*. Cambridge: Harvard University Press.

Whimster, S. and Lash, S. (1987) *Max Weber, Rationality, and Modernity*. Boston: Allen & Unwin.

Whitebook, J. (1988a) "Reconciling the Irreconcilable? Utopianism After Habermas," *Praxis International* 8(1): 73–90.

—— (1988b) "Perversion and Utopia: A Study in Psychoanalysis and Social Theory," *Psychoanalysis and Contemporary Thought* 11(3): 415–46.

Wilson, E. (1978) *On Human Nature*. Cambridge: Harvard University Press.

Wrong, D. (1961) "The Oversocialized Conception of Man in Modern Sociology," *American Sociological Review* 26: 183–93.

Wulf, E. J. (1987) "The Semiophoric Body," *Societies* 15: 21–3.

Wundt, W. ([1886] 1902) *Ethics: An Investigation of the Facts and Laws of the Moral Life*. New York: Macmillan.

Zilboorg, G. (1939) "Sociology and the Psychoanalytic Method," *American Journal of Sociology* 31: 341–55.

Name index

Adams, Henry 21, 72, 81, 94
Adorno, Theodor xi, 18, 52–7,
  64, 70, 77, 79, 83–6, 91,
  106–7, 110–12, 155, 213, 278
Alvarez, A. 150–1
Aristotle 13

Bachofen, Johann J. 21, 85, 273
Baudrillard, Jean x, xii, xiv, 1–5,
  13–14, 16–18, 20–1, 26, 52,
  61–2, 65, 68–72, 74–7, 81,
  83, 85, 89, 91, 100–9,
  110–12, 114–16, 141–2, 152,
  188–9, 193, 201, 208, 275,
  278
Bauman, Zygmunt xiii, 51–2, 55,
  60, 90, 136
Bell, Daniel 77
Bellah, Robert N. x, xvii, 16, 18,
  155, 252, 261
Bergson, Henri 85, 94
Bernard, Claude 196–7
Bloom, Allan xvii, 71–3, 74,
  77–8, 96, 102–3, 125, 153,
  155, 236, 238, 261
Burgess, Everett 35, 49–51
Bush, Barbara 5
Bush, George 9, 20, 111, 117

Camus, Albert 152
Cannon, Walter 191, 195, 220
Comte, Auguste 49–51, 85,
  93–4, 251, 268, 277

Descartes, René 36, 49–50,

94–9, 122, 248, 277
Dohrenwend, Bruce P. 134–5,
  192
Douglas, Jack D. 37, 150, 153,
  242–3, 270
Durkheim, Emile x, xi, xiv–xvii,
  13–22, 28, 30, 37, 40–51,
  57, 62, 64–5, 69–71,
  74–9, 82–9, 91–9, 114–35,
  142–53, 158–77, 180–1, 186,
  189–98, 201–3, 206–22,
  225–30, 235–7, 240–3, 244–53,
  255–7, 261–79

Einstein, Albert 90
Elias, Norbert 24–6, 40,
  104–15, 126, 187–8, 212,
  238
Ellenberger, Henri 77, 79, 94–6,
  123, 131, 155, 158, 173
Engels, Friedrich 21

Freud, Sigmund xi, xiv–xvii, 4,
  13–14, 19–21, 42, 47, 53–7,
  65, 68–9, 72, 74–7, 80, 82,
  84–9, 91, 94–9, 108, 115–26,
  130–1, 134–8, 141–3,
  148–50, 153–5, 158–68,
  173–5, 186, 188, 190–9,
  204–37, 238–58, 260–4,
  268–71, 275–9
Fromm, Erich 55, 77, 115
Fukuyama, Francis 21,
  30, 38–9, 50, 54, 56, 61,
  72

Subject index